MW01114598

Rockville
PORTRAIT OF A CITY

Eileen S. McGuckian

Printed in the United States of America

05 04 03 02 2 3 4 5

Library of Congress Catalog Card Number: 2001096761

ISBN: 1-57736-235-7

Cover design by Gary Bozeman.

Front cover photo of Glenview Mansion by Rob Orndorff, courtesy of City of Rockville.

Back cover photos, clockwise from top right: photo by Richard Miller; postcard in Charles Brewer collection; Charles Brewer collection; Charles Brewer collection; courtesy of Warren G. Crutchfield; courtesy of the Montgomery County Historical Society.

Author photo by Dean Evangelista. All cover photos except Glenview Mansion courtesy of Peerless Rockville.

238 Seaboard Lane Franklin, Tennessee 37067
800-321-5692
www.providencepubcorp.com

Contents

FOREWORD

What is it about Rockville that makes it such a special place? It is not its size, its climate, or its location just outside of Washington, D.C., although these factors are all certainly appealing. Instead, it is a vast array of intangibles, known by those of us who live and work here as the "Rockville State of Mind." It is the sense of pride that we have in our city's vibrant neighborhoods, our diverse population, our excellent services, numerous parks, and many cultural offerings. Perhaps even more important, it is our sense of place, created by the city's long, varied, and interesting history.

Rockville is not your traditional bedroom suburb. Its history dates back to America's earliest days. One of the documents that led up to the Revolutionary War, the *Hungerford Resolves*, was signed in Rockville. The city has served as the government seat of Montgomery County since 1776. Rockville endured the Civil War, and several stops on the Underground Railroad can be found within the city limits. Noted author F. Scott Fitzgerald spent his summers here, while World War II brought significant new growth. Slowly but surely, Rockville became the bustling, modern place it is today.

With such a rich and exciting history, it seems only appropriate to capture it all in a book. Surprisingly, while some accounts of portions of Rockville's history do exist, a comprehensive look at the many events and people who shaped our city had never been written. With that in mind, the Mayor and Council agreed that it would be a fitting millennium project to endorse and fund such an effort.

As has often been said, it is difficult to move successfully into the future if you don't understand the past. We wanted to preserve the past, both in words and in pictures. The result is now in your hands. It is our hope that our residents, their children, friends, and visitors will read and treasure *Rockville: Portrait of a City*.

Rose G. Krasnow, Mayor

Robert E. Dorsey, Councilmember

Anne M. Robbins, Councilmember

Glennon J. Harrison, Councilmember

Robert J. Wright, Councilmember

Preface and Acknowledgments

I inherited my interest in American history from my Dad. I enjoyed reading it, visiting it, and teaching it, but I never quite understood it until I explored the history in my own backyard. Curious about the places I saw in Rockville every day, I attempted some research and loved the dust of nineteenth century primary sources. In the early 1970s, when West Montgomery Avenue was planned for widening and the B&O Station was scheduled for demolition, my longtime interest developed into a passion for preserving the visible evidence of our past.

Rescuing historic buildings kept me busy for many years. Research required for each preservation project and for historic district designation piqued further inquiry into dusty records. Rockville, as representative of American communities and unique unto itself, did not lack in subject matter for research and for preservation. Buildings remained important as artifacts, as places to experience local history, and as community landmarks.

Two local history efforts in the 1980s helped me to look beyond buildings when uncovering an area's past. "Rockville: Identity in Change," a humanities project, interviewed Rockville residents from all walks of life and combined the stories with historic photographs into a fascinating presentation. Documenting Haiti, Rockville's oldest black neighborhood, on Martin's Lane pointed out multifaceted ways to approach local history. This documentary showed me that families, property, public policy, and traditions melded with architecture to become a cultural landscape, of which the past was an integral part. Rockville's identity derived from its people, neighborhoods, experiences, tribulations, successes, and, yes, its buildings.

Over the years, Peerless Rockville published booklets and guides to various aspects of Rockville history. I wrote a column about historic Rockville for the *Rockville Gazette* for many years. The public enjoyed and used them, but still asked for a comprehensive history of our city. As time went on, it became increasingly important to write this book. I have enjoyed it immensely and learned more than I could have imagined about myself as well as about my backyard.

Rockville, Maryland, has been some ten thousand years in the making. The evidence may be found along our waterways, on brick sidewalks and bike paths, in religious sanctuaries and political landmarks, in modest homes and mansions, and in cemeteries and historic districts. The drama of life and events formed Rockville's identity: wayfaring Indians and colonists, slaves clearing fields to plant tobacco, hot political debates in local taverns, stagecoaches and Confederate cavalry kicking up dust on the Rockville Pike, long-skirted ladies greeting evening trains, the bustle of biannual court sessions, clanging trolleys, sputtering automobiles, low-flying planes, church bells ringing in the end of World War II, clearing farms for housing developments, small shops yielding to strip malls and office towers, high-tech industry, ball fields and recreation programs, multilane roads and metro trains, Asian grocery stores, and city festivals.

As people lived, worked, and played in Rockville, they left their mark. Individuals who arrived after World War II broke new ground no less than those newly freed in the 1860s or new to America in the 1980s. Each generation and perspective added complexity to the town's social, economic, religious, and physical makeup. Each new group held a secure place in the continuum of Rockville history, although each may have believed the city's history began when they arrived. In a way it did—each group brought its own perspective on the past and on the changes it initiated.

By the time the Maryland General Assembly designated the town as "Rockville" in 1801, the tiny colonial settlement had already fixed its future course. Transportation connections to and from the seat of Montgomery County government were in place. Agricultural and wooded lands yielded to town streets and building lots. Newcomers appreciated the location in the beautiful Piedmont frontier as they bought into the young town's future. The small town evolved as it experienced the major developments and trends of the nineteenth and twentieth centuries and became the center of one of the richest jurisdictions in America.

This history is intended to provide an anchor for Rockville's past within the context of Montgomery County, Maryland, and the United States. Topics addressed by previous scholars have been noted in the bibliography or notes. Local lore about such subjects as the location of Charles Hungerford's colonial tavern and Rockville's role in the Civil War provided openings to resolve long-running disputes. I sincerely hope this book and the materials generated will inspire further inquiry into Rockville's history, for I believe that understanding our past permits us to define the present and strengthen the future.

Throughout the book, I use terms and spellings of the times. Early chroniclers (who were rarely consistent) referred to George Town, Court House, and Twin-Brook where today we compound those and most other names. People called Rockville a *town* from its humble beginnings, through incorporation in 1860, until about 1950. Since then, *city* has been used by elected officials, newspapers, and, finally, its residents. In the hierarchy of municipalities in America, Rockville is a small city.

My debts from this venture are multitudinous. I am equally beholden to the Board of Directors of Peerless Rockville Historic Preservation, Ltd. and to the Mayor and Council of Rockville. Peerless Rockville permitted me an extended leave of absence to undertake this work and unlimited access to the organization's extensive collections, plus talented staff who found room on their already full plates to meet high expectations while I was gone. Mayor Rose Krasnow and the city council embraced this project when the Rockville Millennium Committee proposed it, and the rest is history. In addition to the city, *Rockville: Portrait of a City* gained financial support from the Maryland Commission for Celebration 2000 making this publication possible.

At every turn, I received encouragement in this project. Current and former Rockville residents shared photographs, memories, and family stories to enliven and personalize the official documents I found. Geneaologists pulled out charts and research; scholars and buffs offered assistance. Neighborhood, business, and institutional representatives brought papers, photos, and scrapbooks. People enthusiastically answered my questions, formally on tape or through telephone or mail. I cherish the new contacts made this year as well as those of long standing, but must confess my softness for personal descriptions of small-town Rockville. I am grateful to the late Frederick Gutheim, my mentor in historic preservation, who appreciated the value of local history before this volume was a gleam in my eye.

Local institutions and experts could not have been more generous. My sincere appreciation goes to Montgomery County Historical Society librarians Patricia Abelard Andersen and Jane Chinn Sween and to Madeleine Tolmach at the Montgomery County Archives for their knowledge and many kindnesses. For the early period of Rockville's history, I am grateful to archeologist James D. Sorensen and naturalist John Baines, to Eleanor M. V. Cook for unsurpassed ability to ferret out information in eighteenth and early nineteenth century records, to Dottie Brault and Higgins Cemetery researchers, and to Florence Howard for sharing her work on land patents. Charles Jacobs, Montgomery County's authority on the Civil War, answered all of my queries and more, complemented by the research of David Hill. Tony Cohen drew upon nineteenth and twentieth century documents to provide hard-to-reach data. I thank Frank Tosh, Carolyn Bryant, and Steve Murfin for sharing information on trolleys, bands, and recreation and sports, respectively. I enjoyed running conversations with Alex and Jayne Greene, Steve Cromwell, and Ed Duffy once I entered the twentieth century. Contact with people, living and dead, who make Rockville history, who research and write about it, who care about it, and who preserve it was the icing on my literary cake.

Logistics and city resources played no small part in this venture. Glenview Mansion is a magical place to read, reflect, and write. Lew Dronenburg and his staff extended many kindnesses to me, as did Glenview's historian and docents. Roald Schrack set up my work space and maintained computer support without visibly wincing. City of Rockville staff were all so helpful that I hesitate to name individuals who located materials, answered questions, and smoothed my path. We often learned together. I admire the creativity of Pedro Flores and Nancy Zombolas. One city staffer I must identify is Christine Heckhaus, who skillfully undertook roles of taskmaster, timekeeper, inquirer, interpreter, and foil for this project.

I am grateful to Judy and Chris Christensen, Eugene Becker, Howard Gillette Jr., John Moser, Don Boebel, Jane Chinn Sween, Helen Heneghan, Burt Hall, David Cahoon, James Marrinan, and Christine Heckhaus for reading chapter drafts and suggesting how to improve them. Special thanks go to Charles Burroughs for his thoughtful cartography, to Professor Gillette for his challenges, and to photographer Dean Evangelista for his keen eye.

I now understand why authors reserve final words for their families. During the writing my mother sacrificed her bridge games, and my first grandchild burst into my rarefied world. My sweet daughters cheered me on. But to my husband, Philip L. Cantelon, by day a professional historian with a flowing pen, fell the chores of cooking dinner, representing me at social events, groaning over first drafts, and encouraging me when I flagged. I can never thank them enough.

Eileen S. McGuckian

Eileen S. McGuckian

Chapter One

SETTING THE STAGE

Prehistory–1755

"Munday, April the 14th—
We Marched to larance Owings
or Owings Oardianary,
a Single House,
it being 18 miles
and very dirty."

As the April day wore on, the soldiers grew tired. Muscle pain increased with each mile as the grade became more pronounced. Muskets and packs seemed heavier, and wool uniforms reeked of sweat. Horses and oxen kicked dust onto the scarlet-coated British regulars and the blue-coated Virginia recruits.

The Rock Creek Main Road or Great Road, as it was variously known, was twenty feet wide, thanks to the Maryland Assembly, which fifty years before set the standard for main thoroughfares. The troops and wagons dodged large branches and the deep ruts left by last season's travelers. Occasionally they passed cleared fields where they could see the first signs of spring tobacco seedlings. But mostly, on either side of the road were miles and miles of endless forest.

It was April 14, 1755, and Major General Edward Braddock was on a mission. The Crown had ordered him to press British claims to America's western frontier. England's coastal settlements and control of commerce in the Ohio Valley were threatened by the growing presence of French traders. In an attempt to define their territory, the French had built four frontier forts, the easternmost of which was Fort Duquesne at the forks of the Ohio River. Braddock's orders were to destroy this fort.

Braddock set up his headquarters at Williamsburg, Virginia, then moved to Alexandria to plan the campaign. He met with colonial governors from Virginia, Maryland, and Massachusetts, and acquired a young aide-de-camp named George Washington, who had recently lost a military confrontation with the French. Braddock packed up Conestoga wagons, artillery, and a herd of livestock, divided his army into two groups, and began his northward march. He planned to pick up colonial recruits along the way to reach full strength. One regiment, led by Sir Peter Halkett and accompanied by George Washington, marched up the Virginia side of the Potomac River.

Braddock and the smaller regiment—two thousand men—took the Maryland route. They crossed the Potomac and stopped near newly established George Town on the night of April 13. Early the next morning, they broke camp, heading north on the crude road over the rolling hills. In those times, towns were few and far apart, and places took their names from a prominent feature—an inn or tavern, a mill, a stream, or a farm—something easily recognizable and usually on a known trail.

That April evening, Braddock reached his objective—the place known as Owen's Ordinary—after twelve weary hours. Troops tended to horses, cooks started fires, and others set up tents on the high ground. Nearby, oriented to the road, were a few crude buildings in what today is Rockville's town center. Not long before, Lawrence Owen had opened a small inn, or ordinary, where a traveler could rest, freshen his horse, buy food and drink, and then move on. One of Braddock's men wrote in his log: "Munday, April the 14th—We Marched to larance Owings or Owings Oardianary, a Single House, it being 18 miles and very dirty."[1]

The next day Braddock's expedition pressed on. The army marched another fifteen miles to Dowden's Ordinary in present-day Clarksburg, encountering a ferocious storm of thunder, lightning, and rain which changed to snow. Braddock continued on the main road to the new German settlement of Frederick Town, where he connected with Halkett's regiment before continuing.

Troubles increased as the troops pushed farther into the frontier of colonial Maryland and Pennsylvania. West of Fort Cumberland the road dwindled to a narrow path, and Braddock's army yielded to colonial engineers who cut a new twelve-foot right-of-way for the advancing army. On July 9, having marched two hundred miles to within sight of Fort Duquesne, they were surprised by French regulars, French Canadian militia, and Indian warriors. Braddock's troops were handily defeated, and Braddock was fatally wounded.[2]

Braddock was too preoccupied to consider the significance of his April 14 rest stop at Owen's Ordinary. He may not have known that the road he traveled had been carved by Indians thousands of years before. And he could never have imagined how his campground would change in the 250 years that followed.[3]

GEOGRAPHIC SETTING

Rockville's history begins with the land. It is difficult to imagine what General Braddock saw in 1755, but he was better poised to appreciate Rockville's original attractions than today's traveler in an automobile. The undulating hills, thick forests, and stream valleys crossed by Braddock's troops are veiled 250 years later by brick, mortar, steel, glass, and concrete. Still, Rockville's past is present, even as new history is being made.

Rockville is located in the Piedmont region, midway between the tidewater lands of the Chesapeake and the mountains of western Maryland. Geologically, the center of Rockville perches on a southeast point of Parr's Ridge at an elevation of about 450 feet. Within present-day city limits are both upland and lowland Piedmont areas. The rolling hills of the upland are mostly to the north; lowland areas fall off to waterways toward the south.

Each of Rockville's three creeks, or branches as they are called in the southern United States, is fed by smaller streams that weave through narrow valleys and strengthen the larger waterways as they wend southward to the Potomac River. Rock Creek, on the east side of town, empties into the Potomac at Georgetown. The drop and water volume of the stream's fall gave rise to numerous water-powered mills. Cabin John Creek flows southwest from the town center. Watts Branch picks up strength in Rockville, then flows west of today's interstate and south to the Potomac.

These streams and the surrounding woodlands furnished fresh water and attracted abundant food supplies for the Indians who were Rockville's first inhabitants. Good quality soil of clay loam, well timbered with yellow and white poplar, hickory, and black and white oak, provided good lands on which European colonists later settled. It did not take future generations long to find minerals such as gneiss granite, quartz, soapstone, mica, slate, and even gold.

The elevated ridges furnished natural transportation routes that did not wash out in the rains. Along these natural ridges the Indians traveled, camping at rock shelters and leaving tantalizing clues for today's archaeologists.

PREHISTORIC INHABITANTS

Archaeologists and historians have long speculated about Indians in the area. Why did they arrive, and when? Who were they, how did they live, and what caused them to leave? Chance findings of Indian artifacts have sparked research and excavations over more than a century, revealing some answers and inspiring successive generations to reassess. More information exists than one may expect, yet many questions remain.[4]

Earliest to appear were hunters following big game herds. Toward the end of the last Ice Age—perhaps fifteen thousand years ago—the mastodon and mammoth roamed large expanses of open grassland south of the glaciers. Herd hunters moved long distances to maintain their source of food. As temperatures slowly rose, the ice sheets retreated from their southern edge just above Maryland, water filled in the furrows to form the Chesapeake Bay, the rivers, and the many Piedmont streams, and thick forests of pine and spruce overtook the grasslands.[5]

THE GREAT ROAD

Braddock's road, the main road, the Great Road, Rock Creek road, Sinequa Trail, the rolling road, the road from Frederick to George Town, the road west, the Rockville Pike, Route 240, and Route 355 all refer to Montgomery County's most-traveled route, the Rockville Pike.

Indians defined the original path ten thousand years ago. Groups of Piscataways, Senecas, and Susquehannocks followed game, set up seasonal camps, and marked an inland north-south route along this Piedmont ridge. By the 1690s, European settlers had displaced the Indians and appropriated the old road known as the Sinequa Trail.

Travelers and planters in the area of present-day Rockville relied on the colonial route. They appreciated the Maryland Assembly's attempts to keep the roadway cleared of obstructions, notched for directions, and free of standing water. As early as the 1740s, local planters shipped hogsheads of cured tobacco down the *rolling road* to the port of George Town. Pioneers heading to western Maryland, the Ohio territory, and beyond traveled the Great Road.

The roadway proved even more valuable during the nineteenth century. In the national road-building era, the Maryland General Assembly incorporated the Washington Turnpike Company. Improvements to the Rockville Pike depended upon revenue from tolls charged for stagecoaches, herded cattle and sheep, and horses, but repairs were always inadequate to the need. In the 1860s, the pike saw heavy use by Union and Confederate troops, as well as multiple skirmishes between the two.

After the Civil War, the pike had to compete with other modes of transportation. The B&O Railroad and the trolley served farmers, local businesses, commuters, fairgoers, and travelers more efficiently than the deteriorated road. However, the automobile's popularity for business, residential, and leisure-time use focused early twentieth century attention on the Great Road. Auto-related attractions arrived at the pike, as well as paving, buses, and traffic signals.

By the mid-twentieth century, the Great Road teemed with new residential and commercial areas. Soon additional lanes, a Rockville bypass, a parallel interstate highway, and a subway augmented the capacity of the north-south route. As the pace increased through the last decades of the century, the old rolling road transformed into the economically successful destination known as the Golden Mile.

By perhaps 8000 B.C., in what archaeologists term the Archaic period, these early inhabitants had adapted to the Potomac region's developing environment by staking out prescribed territories. Indian groups made seasonal rounds at hunting, trapping, fishing, and quarrying camps.

As climatic conditions stabilized, populations traveled less. They added nuts, seeds, wild grains, fish, and shellfish to their diets. They developed stone tools for woodworking and stone mortars and bowls for cooking. These Archaic hunters and gatherers left clues for archaeologists and historians, including samples of raw and finished materials traded with other groups.[6]

Significant change occurred in the Woodland period, a time beginning in the first millennium B.C. The seminomadic lifestyle of these early residents gave way to small but year-round agricultural villages. Native plants such as sunflower and marsh elder were domesticated along with varieties of maize (corn) and squash acquired by trade. Stone gave way to ceramic pots and hunting spears to bows and arrows. Men focused on hunting, and women on cultivating crops. Soapstone quarries, such as those near Olney and Ednor, provided the steatite for useful objects.

During the 1930s investigations of the Shepard site along the Potomac River, archaeologists termed this subculture the Montgomery Complex. At Shepard and subsequent excavations, archaeologists found projectile points, fishhooks, and needles shaped from bone. They unearthed remains that indicate a varied protein diet, including deer, beaver, fox, bobcat, elk, bear, turtle, fish, clams, snails, turkey, and duck.

Starting around A.D. 1200, Montgomery Indians found themselves competing for river and forest resources with other groups who moved across the Potomac from Virginia and down from New York and Pennsylvania. The Susquehannocks frequently came into Maryland, claiming hunting grounds both west and east of the Chesapeake Bay. When stockades around the villages did not protect the Montgomery groups from the newcomers, they abandoned their agricultural settlements. In the next three hundred years these displacements occurred in rapid succession. The Montgomery people moved toward southern Maryland, forming part of the Piscataway Confederacy described by Captain John Smith and other early European explorers.

Interpretation of Indian culture in Montgomery County is still in its infancy. As little is known about these Indians, they are usually grouped linguistically. Thus, we refer to the Sinequas (Senecas) and the Susquehannocks, two of the five Iroquois nations, as Iroquoian speakers. The name Seneca continues in local use, as do other Indian names.

Within present-day city limits, six prehistoric sites have been documented.[7] Triangular points have been dated to the Archaic or Woodland period. Until more information is available, studies on other Piedmont Indian sites must suffice.[8]

Courtesy of Judy French

Projectile points found in Rockville. Left, a Brewerton-like point from the Late Archaic period (c. 2000 B.C.). Right, a Madison-like point from the Late Woodland period (A.D. 900–1300). Both points were fashioned from chert, a fine-grained non-local cryptocrystalline mineral suited to chipping for points or working for tools.

CONTACT, PATHS, AND ROADS

In the brief contact period of the 1690s between colonists and Indians, the area was a buffer zone between Indian cultures. European traders met the peaceful Piscataways who sought protection from the hostile Susquehannocks and Senecas. Early settlers formed a volunteer cavalry known as the Potomac Rangers, which attempted to control Indian activity from their garrison at the mouth of Rock Creek. By 1700, under increasing pressure, Indians left Montgomery County to the colonists who began to clear hunting and foraging grounds in order to plant tobacco.

Discernible today are the routes Indians traversed for thousands of years. These well-worn paths were quickly appropriated by the settlers. The Monocacy path, a north-south route from the Susquehanna River valley into Montgomery County, is today the Darnestown Road (Maryland Route 28). River Road connected low-lying points. Trails along Parr's Ridge took travelers across northern areas. Current State Route 355, from above Frederick, across Seneca Creek, south through Rockville, and down through the valley of Rock Creek to the Potomac, was a long-established north-south route known as the Sinequa Trail.[9]

Numerous references to Indian paths, fords over creeks, and old roads may be found in the surveys made for land patents. Improvements made for colonial travelers can be imagined through the Maryland Assembly's 1704 dictum that all public and main roads be cleared and grubbed, fit for traveling, and twenty feet wide. Notches on roadside trees signaled destinations such as chapels, courthouses, and other roads.[10]

By the 1740s, the inland north-south Indian path through the Piedmont had been transformed into a primitive road for planters hauling hogsheads filled with cured tobacco leaves to the budding settlement at the mouth of Rock Creek.

SETTLING MARYLAND'S PIEDMONT—LAND PATENTS AND INDENTURES

Settlement of the Rockville area followed a feudal pattern of land distribution set in place by Lord Baltimore in 1632. Land, cheap and abundant in a new continent, was not only the primary form of wealth in the proprietary colony, but was also the main vehicle of investment and speculation.

In 1632, King Charles I of England cut off a liberal slice from northern Virginia for a new colony. He granted Maryland to Cecil Calvert, the second Lord Baltimore, whose father had repeatedly attempted to found a settlement in America. Generations of the Calvert family adroitly managed their territory through political and military authority. As lord proprietor, Baltimore granted Maryland colonists enjoyment of all the rights of Englishmen and allowed them to meet in a general assembly of freemen. From 1632 until the American Revolution, the Calverts and their successor governors distributed land, appointed public officials, established ports and market towns, and sent colonial products back to England.

From the first settlement at Saint Mary's, Lord Baltimore intended that Maryland be a profitable venture. Rather than selling the land outright, he distributed his vast holdings in order to generate continuing income for himself as well as to attract settlers to the growing colony. Calvert granted parcels to men in sizes proportional to the number of settlers they brought to Maryland.

The Calvert scheme was well thought out. A transplanted Englishman would obtain a warrant from the proprietor's agent. The settler would have a piece of land surveyed and then apply to the Land Office for a patent to prove his valid ownership. The tract was then his to sell or to will to his descendants. The Calverts maintained a steady stream of income through quit rents, semiannual payments usually paid by settlers in tobacco. Often years would pass between the survey and the patent, possibly because no rent was due until the patent was filed. Land reverted to the proprietor if the settler did not pay the quit rent, committed suicide, was sentenced to death for treason or a felony, or died without male descendants.[11]

The patent holder was not likely to live on or even clear his parcel of land. He offered indentures (contracts binding one party into the service of another for a specific period of time) to men who could afford to relocate in America only by pledging to work as a servant for a number of years. At the end of the specified time, the indentured servant would own the land. This proved to be a successful way to attract skilled and unskilled workers to the new colony, and Maryland enjoyed huge population increases in the mid-seventeenth century. Thus, most settlers were tenants on property owned by absentee speculators who years before had obtained substantial tracts and warranted their holdings through Maryland's proprietary government.[12]

In 1683, Lord Baltimore, recognizing that he no longer needed to attract settlers with free land, began to require caution money for warrants. Through the proprietor's agent, an individual would purchase land. At one point this cost one hundred pounds of tobacco for fifty acres; by 1776 the price had risen to five pounds sterling per one hundred acres.

By the third quarter of the seventeenth century, Maryland colonists had moved beyond the coastal plain of the Tidewater. They reached the banks of Rock Creek in the 1680s and began to clear the woods of the Piedmont region above the fall line. By the time Lord Baltimore issued the first land patent in what became Montgomery County in 1688, plantation tracts were considerably smaller than earlier grants. Soon, without the threat of Indians, speculators opened the lower Piedmont for settlement.[13]

In the early eighteenth century, Arthur Nelson obtained the first land patents in the Rockville area, which was then still part of Prince George's County. Nelson, seeking to invest in land, surveyed and patented tracts of land totaling 3,162 acres between 1717 and 1735. He named his tracts Valentine's Garden (his wife's name was Valentine), Valentine's Garden Enlarged (adding acreage in 1722), The Exchange, The New Exchange (then resurveyed both tracts as Exchange and New Exchange Enlarged for 1,620 total acres in 1721), Bowling Green, and Cuckold's Delight. Within thirty years, the first tiny buildings in what is now the center of Rockville were

FOLLOWING PAGES: Colonial land patents in the Rockville area issued by the Lords Baltimore, superimposed on a year-2000 map of Rockville.

Early Land Patents in the Rockville Area

Tract Name	Acres	Patentee	Patent Date	Approximate Location
Adamsons Choice	100	John B. Adamson	1729	Hungerford, Dogwood Park
Addition, The	576	Philip Lee	1720	Spring Lake Park, Twinbrook Metro
Advantage, Resurvey on	151	Robert Owen	1765	Woodley Gardens, West End
All We Can Get	58	Zachariah Gatton	1768	Fallsmead, Wootton High School
Allisons Discontent	127.75	John Allison	1788	North Farm
Allisons Park	620	John Allison	1715	Falls Orchard, Potomac Woods,
Despair (part of Allisons Park)	522	Joseph Wilson	1764	Orchard Ridge
Ashley	1398.75	Anna Orme, etc.	1801	Lincoln Park, Croydon Park, Southlawn
Back Land	260	Edward Willett	1747	Horizon Hill
Baniston	100	N. Wickham Sr. and Jr.	1732	Glenora, Glen Hills
Black Oak Thickett, Resurvey	720	Ninian Magruder	1734	Fortune Terrace
Bowling Green	128	Arthur Nelson	1722	Lincoln Park, Stonestreet Avenue
Burgundy	632	Ignatius Diggs	1770	Maryvale, Janeta, Burgundy, Croydon Park, Rockwood
Conclusion, The	500	James Holmard	1724	I-270 Industrial Park, King Farm
Conjuror Detected (part of Token of Love)	294.75	Lawrence O'Neale	1796	Rockville Pike (Twinbrook area)
Constant Friendship	300	Jas. Holmard, etc.	1722	Woodmont, Token of Love
Coup De Main, The	9.25	Michael Litten	1799	Veirs Mill Road, upper Rockcrest
Cuckolds Delight	164	Arthur Nelson	1727	Fallsmead
Discontent	617	Chas. and Wm. Beall	1736	Woodley Gardens, Woodley Woods, Rockville Estates,
Discontent, Resurvey on west part of	169	Benjamin West	1764	Watts Branch Meadows, Rockshire
Easy Come By (resurveyed as Burgundy)	300	William Pottinger	1725	(See Burgundy)
Exchange, The and New Exchange Enlarged (resurvey plus vacant land added)	1620	Arthur Nelson	1735	Town Center, Rose Hill, Falls Road, New Mark, Markwood,
Exchange and New Exchange Enlarged, Resurvey on part of	955	James Dick	1764	Monument, Tower Oaks, Seven Locks, Saddlebrooke, Orchard Ridge
Fishers Neglect, The	39.5	Zach. Gatton	1768	Horizon Hill
Haymonds Additon	50	John Haymond	1734	Rockville Pk, Richard Montg. High School,
Haymonds Addition, Resurvey	300	John Haymond	1743	St. Mary's Church, Hungerford
Hobson's Choice	408	William Williams Sr.	1758	King Farm
I Am Content	18	John Allison	1771	North Farm, Woodmont Country Club
I Will Not Yet I Will	121.75	Barton Harris	1769	Montrose and I-270
Joseph & James, The	535	J. West and Holmard	1722	Danac Technological Park
Josephs Good Will	150	Charles Walker	1722	Cambridge Heights
Locust Thickett	100	John Walford	1732	Southlawn
Resurvey on Locust Thickett	267	William Dent	1768	
Long Discovered	5.25	Jesse Leach	1819	Rockville Pike
Lost Hammer, The	104	Nicholas Baker	1753	Twinbrook
Marthas Delight, Resurvey on	136	Sam'l Beall Jr.	1764	Burgundy Estates, Redgate
Meadow Hall, Resurvey on	118	Jas. Beall of J.	1771	Twinbrook
Mill Land	214	Edward Dawson and Jr.	1724	Glenview, Rockville High School
Millys Dislike	553	William Baker	1775	Rock Creek
Needwood	1000	John Cook	1780	Rock Creek
Resurvey part of Needwood	410.5	William Dent	1765	
Oatry (Autra)	405	Caleb Litton	1722	Pike, Rockcrest, Broadwood, Twinbrook
Partnership	200	Henry Massey	1728	
Partnership (unpatented)	420.5	W. O'Neale, etc.	Surveyed 1784	(See Wheel of Fortune)
Pines, The	479	J. West and Holmard	1723	Rockshire
Prevention (part of which later became Philadelphia)	1182	Wm. Beall, etc.	1732	Twinbrook, Spring Lake Park
Race Ground, The	30.5	Lawrence O'Neale	1763	Roxboro
Rock Spring	20	Richard Allison	1762	Glenview, Burgundy Estates
Rock Spring, Resurvey on	85	Elisha Allison	1795	
Saint Mary	67	Caleb Litton	1727	Veirs Mill Road, Broadwood
Saint Mary, Resurvey on	290	Thos. Allison	1759	Rockville Pike, Silver Rock
Stubb Hill	100	William Collier	1741	North Farm, Woodmont Country Club

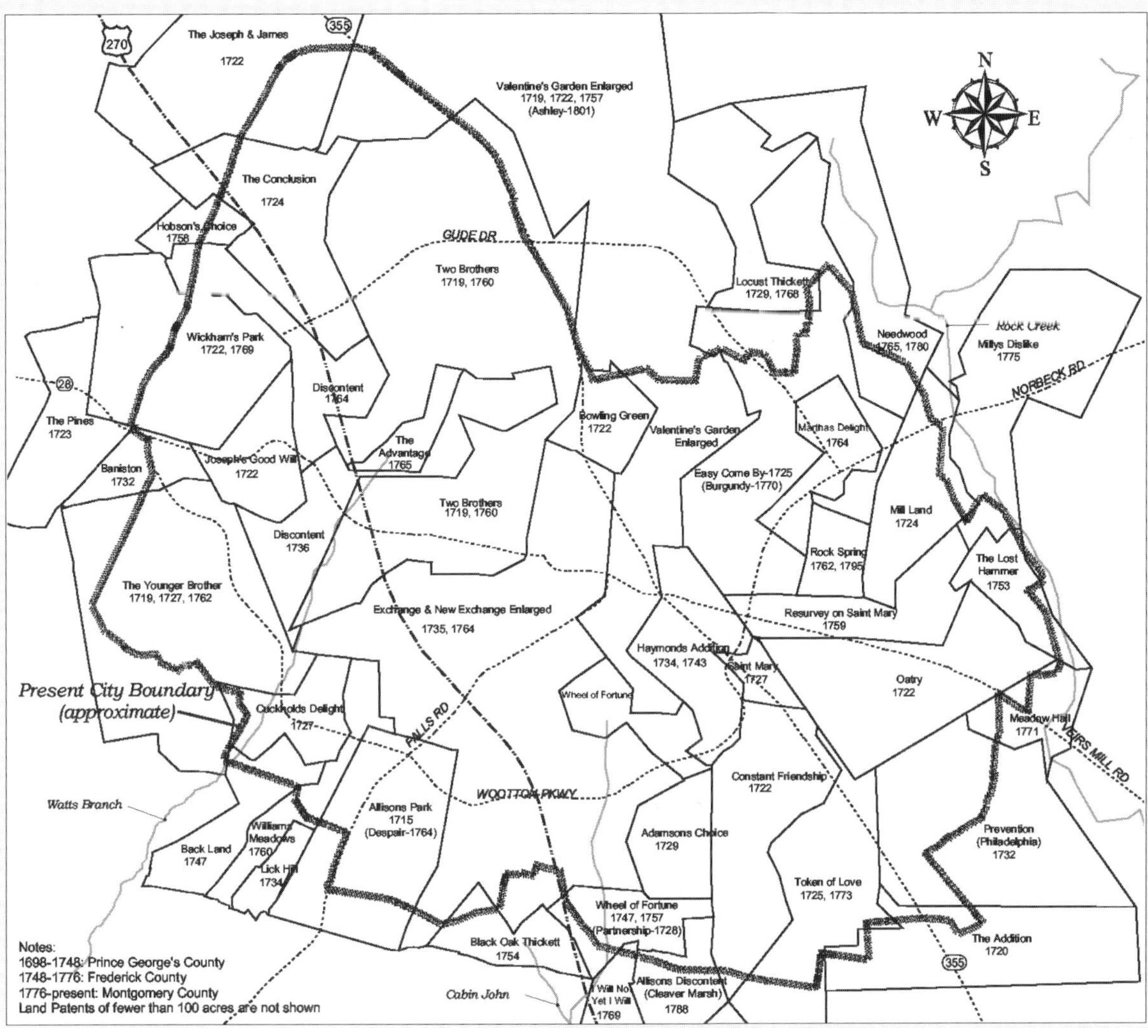

Land patent research and delineation by Florence Howard; interpretation by Eileen McGuckian; cartography by C. A. Burroughs; GIS by Pedro Flores

Token of Love, The	394	J. Holmard, etc.	1725	Montrose
Token of Love, Addition to	326.5	Lawrence O'Neale	1773	
Two Brothers, The	1200	Jas. Holmead, etc.	1719	West End, Woodley Gardens, Montgomery College, King Farm
Two Brothers, Addition to	25	Samuel West	1760	
Valentines Garden	300	Arthur Nelson	1719	Northeast of Town Center,
Valentines Garden Enlarged	950	Arthur Nelson	1722	Hungerford Drive, B&O Station, Lincoln Park, Croydon Park, Southlawn, England's Addition
Valentines Garden Enlarged, Resurvey on	2085	Henry Wright Crabb	1757	
Walkers First Survey	9	Ralph Holt	1770	Woodmont Country Club
Walkers Second Survey	10.75	Lawrence O'Neale	1771	
Whats Left	20	Birch Chesshire	1763	Woodmont Country Club
Wheel of Fortune	100	William O'Neale	1747	North Farm, Wheel of Fortune,
Wheel of Fortune, Resurvey on (same as Partnership)	320	William O'Neale	1757	Hungerford-Stoneridge, Lynfield
Wickham's Park	400	N. Wickham	1722	Thomas Farm/Fallsgrove, Glenora
Wickham's Park, Resurvey on	434	James Perry	1769	
Williams Meadows	150	William Fee	1760	Fallsmead
Younger Brother, The	600	William Offutt	1719	Rockshire, Glenora Hills, Lakewood, Glen Hills, Falls Road
Younger Brother, Resurvey on	370	Joseph West	1727	
Younger Brother, Resurvey on	1020	Joseph West	1762	

built on Valentine's Garden Enlarged and Exchange and New Exchange Enlarged.

Other early patents on land now included within city boundaries are: Mill Land, surveyed for Edward Dawson in 1724 (214 acres, including the land on which Glenview Mansion now sits); Oatry (or Autra), for Caleb Litton (405 acres near the Pike); I Will Not Yet I Will, for Barton Harris (121 acres near Montrose and I-270); The Lost Hammer (104 acres for Nicholas Baker in Twinbrook area); The Two Brothers (1,200 acres on Watts Branch for James Holmead in 1717); The Younger Brother (out Falls Road for William Offutt, 600 acres later enlarged in 1717); Haymond's Addition, surveyed for John Haymond in 1743 (300 acres around Richard Montgomery High School); and The Conclusion (the King Farm area).[14]

Many survey descriptions used white oaks or rocks as reference points. Because of creeks and topography, lines were often irregular. Most surveys were imprecise, so tracts often overlapped. Spaces between tracts were later consolidated into nearby grants.[15] We know little about the men (and a few women) who patented the early tracts, except that most were of English or Scottish descent, wealthy and often influential tobacco merchants and merchant-planters. Resident taxables (free white males, male servants, male and female slaves sixteen years old and older) of Potomack Hundred in 1733 included a number of patentees,[16] although more often than not they would sell acreage directly to colonists rather than clear land themselves.

Rockville's location was determined by topography and experience.

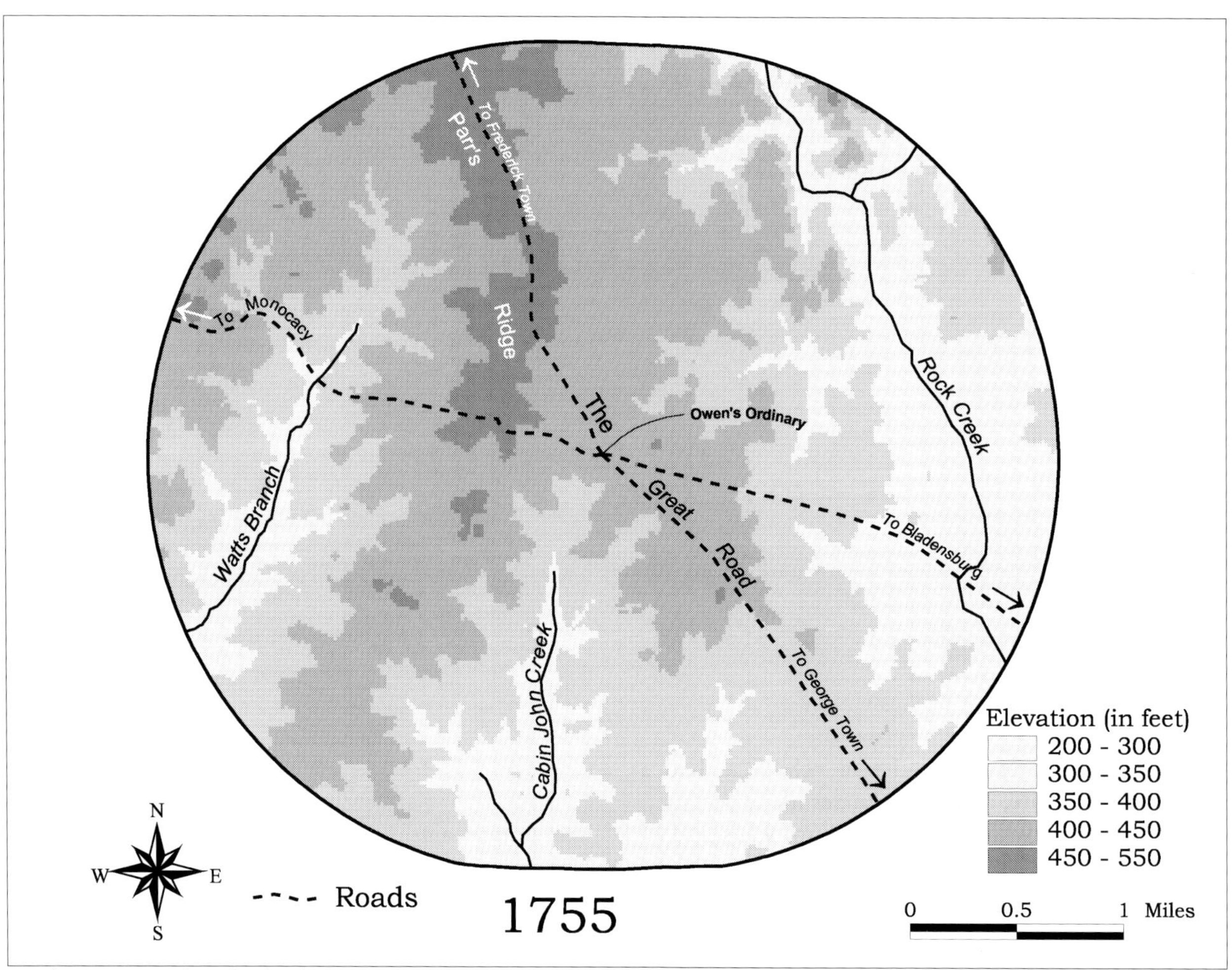

Map by C. A. Burroughs and Pedro Flores

WHY IS ROCKVILLE HERE?

Rockville's appeal through centuries of human occupation is location, location, location. Geography has combined with healthfulness, beauty, and convenience to maintain this enduring attraction.

Prehistoric travelers cut paths on the high ground of Parr's Ridge, which begins in northern Montgomery County and divides several times before reaching the Potomac River at Great Falls. Rockville's perch atop a divide furnished a destination long before a town was envisioned. The gently graded trails were equally suited to the European newcomers of the early 1700s. In a climate with thirty-nine inches of annual rainfall, high ground ensured a usable path year-round. And what a fine location for a stop over, where the north-south path from the Susquehanna River valley to Rock Creek crossed the east-west trail from the Anacostia to the Potomac.

As early as 1624, explorers extolled the healthful climate and pleasant habitat of the rolling hills beyond the Potomac River marshlands. The view from high ground to rolling terrain with lush forests and meadows was picturesque. Early descriptions frequently mentioned plentiful supplies of fresh water and food.

To superiority of climate add convenience, which became more pronounced as colonists settled in. Rockville was located midway between the mountains and the Tidewater. Three good-sized waterways and numerous feeder streams provided water power to industry. The soil was fertile for agriculture, and there was plenty of timber and a rich variety of minerals. It was just a few miles from the Potomac River. And, most important of all in those early days, Rockville was situated on the main road used by residents, travelers, and those doing business in the important towns of Frederick and George Town. Later, selection of the village as Montgomery County's seat of government, continuation of the transportation connections in all directions, and independent status reinforced its strong position.

EARLY EIGHTEENTH CENTURY COLONIAL ACTIVITY

Maryland grew quickly. The colony's mild climate, abundance of natural resources, steady governance by the Lords Baltimore, religious tolerance, and profitability of tobacco all encouraged stability and progress. Settlers moved outward from the lower Potomac and Chesapeake Bay. Prince George's County was formed in 1695, and in 1722 land west of Rock Creek was designated as a new civil district known as Potomack Hundred.

From the tiny settlement at Saint Mary's, Maryland grew to forty-three thousand people by 1710. By that time, men and women born in America comprised a majority of the population. People were healthier, married earlier, had more children, had a lower mortality rate, and had a longer life expectancy. This was true of white indentured Europeans and of Africans imported as slaves. Although slavery existed in Maryland from the earliest times, planters at first relied more on indentured servants. After the Maryland Assembly passed a *black code* in 1664 declaring all blacks servants for life, slave traders targeted the colony. As Maryland's settled areas expanded, slaves were increasingly concentrated in large holdings and accounted for higher percentages of the total population.[17]

Maryland colonists of the early 1700s lived in an orderly world that favored wealthy white males. Fathers lived long enough to acquire property which they left to their sons, consolidating wealth in interrelated families. Less fortunate families who had limited opportunities relocated to the frontier. There they felled trees, opened up new lands for tobacco, and experimented with diversified crops such as wheat and corn. Some began industries such as iron furnaces, grain mills, and small crafts.

Towns were needed for tobacco inspection and export points, for shipping and shipbuilding, and as centers for small merchants and newly arriving immigrants, and they thrived in the early eighteenth century. The new capital Annapolis, seat of colonial government since 1694, became an urban center of culture and crafts, claiming a newspaper by 1727. On the fall line, Baltimore opened in 1730 as a port for wheat and tobacco. In 1745, Daniel Dulaney laid out Frederick Town for German settlers in the Piedmont. Five years later, it was the largest settlement in Maryland, with a population of one thousand. This boom triggered separation of the western part of Prince George's County into new Frederick County in 1748. In 1751, at the convergence of Rock Creek with the Potomac River, George Town was laid out.[18]

Courtesy of Library of Congress, Prints and Photographs Division

Hogsheads filled with cured tobacco were hauled down crude "rolling roads" to the ports of George Town and Bladensburg.

TOBACCO PRODUCTION

From the start, tobacco was Maryland's most important crop. The *sotte weed* was the source of most wealth, serving as currency and affecting every aspect of colonial life. Maryland soil produced a stronger-scented, bulkier leaf than either the type grown by Indians or that planted by colonists in Virginia.

Growing tobacco was a tedious business involving multiple steps over eight months, with lots of room for failure. Tobacco was always a gamble, for the value of harvested crops was influenced by supply and demand, government taxes, wars, and the charges imposed by those who handled the crop along the way. A prosperous period for tobacco encouraged settlement of the Piedmont lands from the 1720s through the 1770s. Planters gradually improved agricultural practices so that during this period they could expect to produce fifteen hundred to two thousand pounds of tobacco each season.[19]

Partners in this economy were the agents for firms that regularly purchased tobacco grown in the colonies for resale in Europe. Piedmont planters dealt with Scottish merchants who were willing to take their crop, which was of lower grade than Tidewater tobacco. Retail stores in George Town provided spring credit to planters against summer crops and sold imported goods. Many merchants also speculated in land.[20]

Planters devised a method of transporting their crop to market. Following the harvest, after thoroughly drying the tobacco, they packed the leaves into large wooden barrels called hogsheads. A sapling was then attached to each end of the hogshead, forming a pair of shafts and axle. With the help of oxen or horses, planters walked alongside the hogshead and rolled it on a *rolling road* to the nearest port. By midcentury, Marylanders packed one thousand pounds of cured tobacco leaves into one hogshead.[21] In 1747, the Assembly established a system of inspecting and grading tobacco. To process crops grown in the Piedmont, warehouses were built at the new ports of George Town on the Potomac and Bladensburg on the Anacostia River.

RELIGION

The Calverts were Roman Catholics, but from the start, the colony accommodated other Christians also. The Maryland Toleration Act of 1649 introduced this dramatic concept to the new world and invited migration. This balance worked for forty years, until William and Mary ascended the English throne, encouraged Maryland Protestants to peacefully overthrow Lord Baltimore, and sent the first royal governor to take his place.

The Crown also undertook the task of organizing the Church of England in Maryland. In 1692, the Assembly voted to establish the Church of England as the official faith in the royal colony. Justices divided Maryland's counties into thirty parishes and imposed an annual tax on each freeholder, regardless of religious persuasion, to build churches and support the few clergy sent to the colony. They provided for elected vestrymen with considerable religious and civil responsibilities. Although in 1715 the Crown restored proprietary rights to the fourth Lord Baltimore, the powers of the Anglican Church held until the outbreak of the Revolutionary War and inspired the first religious building in Rockville.[22]

The growth of the church followed the population. By 1726 there were sufficient settlers to create Prince George's Parish, which contained all of western Maryland. This included what became Montgomery, Frederick, Washington, Alleghany, Garrett, and part of Carroll Counties, plus the District of Columbia. In 1738, Thomas Williams conveyed two acres to the vestry, which soon built a chapel of ease of log and frame. Every three weeks Rev. George Murdock came from Prince George's County to preach at the tiny chapel, which was located near Rock Creek on land now part of Rockville Cemetery on Baltimore Road.

As the area population grew, the parish size decreased and the little chapel was enlarged. Prominent local men, such as Lawrence Owen, served on the vestry. By the 1740s, Rev. Murdock preached at the chapel every Sunday, at times returning to conduct burial rites in the surrounding cemetery. In this ancient churchyard is located the oldest gravestone in Rockville, that of John Harding, who died in 1752. The Anglican chapel was used until it was replaced by a brick building and consecrated at a lengthy service as Christ Episcopal Church in 1808. Seventy-two years later, the old churchyard was incorporated into the grounds of Rockville Cemetery.[23]

Photograph by Dean Evangelista

John Harding's stone, in what is now Rockville Cemetery, is the oldest known gravestone in Rockville. Harding, born in 1683, died in 1752.

It took nearly ten thousand years for people to generate the beginnings of the community that Rockville residents treasure today. But once commenced, the pace of history picked up quickly.

Chapter Two

BECOMING ROCKVILLE 1755–1803

"And be it enacted,
That the said lots. . .
shall be and are hereby erected
into a town,
to be called and known
by the name of Rockville."

Early on, travelers knew the small settlement that was to become Rockville by a variety of names: Owen's Ordinary, Hungerford's Tavern, Daley's Tavern, Montgomery Court House, Williamsburgh. By 1750, it was situated on the northwestern frontier of the Maryland colony. Descendants of the original English and Scottish settlers had pushed north into the Piedmont, east beyond the Chesapeake Bay, and west to the mouth of the Monocacy River at its juncture with the Potomac. In 1748, the Maryland Assembly created a new Frederick County to govern the western lands.

For this new jurisdiction, Frederick Town—laid out in 1745—became the county seat. At the mouth of Rock Creek, the assembly established the port of George Town in 1751. In between these two fast-growing settlements were forests dotted with cleared fields and a dusty route which had been marked by local Indians centuries before. The road was known as the Rock Creek Main Road, the Great Road or, among local planters, simply the rolling road. Along this highway, near the junction of other crude thoroughfares which led east and west, Lawrence Owen kept a tavern to serve up food, spirits, lodging, and entertainment. Travelers began to refer to the crossroads as Owen's Ordinary.

It was on this route that Major General Edward Braddock marched in the spring of 1755, in the conflict colonists called the French and Indian War. Although seven years later the Treaty of Paris virtually eliminated the French presence in North America, Braddock's ill-fated expedition revealed to observant colonials the weakness of the British Army in America. And the roadway from George Town through Frederick Town to Fort Duquesne became the major route for generations of pioneers seeking the western frontier of America.

In 1763, peace returned to North America, and colonists resumed their westward movement. From 1765 to 1775, the population of Frederick County rose by 54 percent.[1] The booming Potomac River port of George Town continued to add commercial and professional wealth to the Piedmont. Encouraged by attractive immigration policies, economic stability, and markets accessed by crude roads, men and women began to clear land on which to plant tobacco, set up services for travelers, and erect simple dwellings for their families. Those who owned land along these roads in the inland frontier believed their future was bright.

By the 1760s, the tiny crossroads settlement that would become Rockville was a way station to the flourishing ports of Baltimore, George Town, and Bladensburg and to the Piedmont metropolis of Frederick Town. Lawrence Owen had closed his establishment, but travelers on the main road could stop in the vicinity at Thomas Davis's inn or Charles Hungerford's tavern to freshen a horse, take food and drink, and perhaps stay the night before continuing on. Local residents accustomed to gathering at Hungerford's for entertainment, news, and business referred to the village by that name.[2] And it was at Charles Hungerford's tavern that patriots of lower Frederick County met to discuss their growing dissatisfaction with British treatment of the American colonies.

THE AMERICAN REVOLUTION

Like most dramatic events, the Declaration of Independence did not occur without warning. Maryland's colonial government in the 1760s attempted to balance interests on the east and west shores of the Chesapeake, to continue attracting artisans to Baltimore and Frederick Town while recognizing the increasing indebtedness of inland planters, and to keep non-Anglicans from resenting taxes paid to support the established church. It was during this decade that a new, young generation of leaders emerged who were ready to change the way Maryland did business and to test the delicate balance between royal control and colonial self-government.[3]

At first, England detected no change. The government of George III was trying to settle problems in the west, to raise funds in America for its defense, and to enforce conduct of all colonial trade through the mother country. Settlers saw it differently. Beginning with the imposition of the Stamp Act in 1765, the first direct tax imposed by Parliament on Americans, colonists throughout the East Coast organized local *committees of correspondence* to protest British imposition of duties on colonial activities. Although Parliament repealed the Stamp Act the following year, it followed with the Townshend Acts, which permitted the levy of duties on English manufactures (such as tea) entering America.

When American protesters dumped English tea into Boston harbor in December 1773, Parliament responded with a series of "Intolerable Acts," which included blockading the port until the tea was paid for. Local committees passed the word that "the town of Boston is now suffering for the common cause of America" and, sixteen months later, that shots had been fired at Concord and Lexington. Between the end of May and early July 1774, men in every Maryland county met to pass resolutions not to trade with Great Britain until the Boston port act was repealed.

On June 11, 1774, residents of lower Frederick County met in the large room at Charles Hungerford's tavern. Dr. Thomas Sprigg Wootton and Capt. Henry Griffith, representatives to the Maryland Assembly, chaired the group. Although most were seeking to

THE HUNGERFORD RESOLVES: 1774

In response to the British blockade of Boston harbor, patriots of lower Frederick County met at Charles Hungerford's tavern on June 11, 1774. They expressed support for the Boston protesters by passing and publishing five bold resolutions, and selected ten men to represent their sentiments at an upcoming meeting in Annapolis. The Hungerford Resolves were Rockville's contribution to the events that led to the Declaration of Independence two years later and to the American Revolution.

"*Resolved,* unanimously, That it is the opinion of this meeting that the Town of Boston is now suffering in the Common Cause of America.

Resolved, unanimously, That every legal and constitutional measure ought to be used by all America for procuring a repeal of the Act of Parliament for blocking up the Harbour of Boston.

Resolved, unanimously, That it is the opinion of this meeting that the most effectual means for the securing of American Freedom will be to break off all Commerce with Great Britain and the West Indies until the said act be repealed and the right of taxation given upon permanent principles.

Resolved, unanimously, That Mr. Henry Griffith, Dr. Thomas Sprigg Wootton, Nathan Magruder, Evan Thomas, Richard Brooke, Richard Thomas, Zadok Magruder, Dr. William Baker, Thomas Cramphin, Jr., and Allen Bowie be a committee to attend the general committee at Annapolis, and that any six of them shall have the power to receive and communicate intelligence to and from their neighboring committees.

Resolved, unanimously, That a copy of these our sentiments be immediately transmitted to Annapolis, and inserted in the *Maryland Gazette.*

At Hungerford's Tavern,
11th June, 1774
Signed per Order,
Archibald Orme, Clerk"[4]

preserve current liberties, not to establish independence from England, they united in a spirit of resistance to express support for the protesters in Boston. Archibald Orme, planter and surveyor, kept track of the resolutions as each was adopted.[5]

The pace quickened, and Marylanders continued to flaunt their principles. The resolves appeared in the June 17, 1774, edition of the *Maryland Gazette*, published in Annapolis. The Maryland Convention opened in the capital city five days later. Delegates agreed to halt all imports from Great Britain and to refuse to export tobacco if Virginia and North Carolina would agree. Women such as Madeline Sheffey "resolved to drink no more tea for years to come."[6] Men intercepted tea bound for George Town and cheered the *Peggy Stewart* tea party in Annapolis harbor. Lower Frederick County delegates attended the first Continental Congress in Philadelphia and voted at the second Maryland Convention to establish a militia.

Through the events of 1775 and early 1776, resistance changed to rebellion. Maryland had few hot-headed rebels, and until the end most considered themselves loyal subjects of the British king. Most delegates to the conventions and the Continental Congress were moderates, wealthy men of political standing who had a stake in maintaining the status quo. Again, citizens met at Hungerford's tavern to elect delegates from lower Frederick County.

Maryland's decision did not come easily. Colonists rejected not only British rule, but also 140 years of proprietary history. They discarded the crown government's practices of favoritism, fees, and selecting officials while inciting a groundswell of popular participation. At the same time, colonists concerned for the breakdown of law and order returned to long-respected leaders to represent them at the various forums. On June 28 and July 3, 1776, the Maryland Convention voted for independence. A new nation was born the following day, an event surely toasted at Hungerford's tavern.

Marylanders had little time to rejoice, for not only was there a war to be won, but also a new governing order to be established. Men twenty-one years of age who owned fifty or more acres of land or property valued at least forty pounds sterling voted at Hungerford's in August to select representatives to another convention which would form a new state government. The result was the Maryland Constitution of 1776. This document established voting qualifications, provided for four delegates from each county, and specified state and county officials such as judges, clerks, surveyors, and justices of the peace. Dr. Thomas Sprigg Wootton, who lived near Watts Branch, was elected the first Speaker of the Maryland House of Delegates when it convened in February 1777.[7]

In the fight for independence, Maryland issued a quota of 156 men to be recruited from Montgomery County. Most served in the Seventh Regiment of the Maryland Continental (standing) Army, while others joined the militia to defend home territory and to be available as needed. Militia units used able-bodied short-term volunteers, sixteen to fifty years of age, who provided their own guns and munitions. During the eight-year conflict, almost 10 percent of Maryland's entire population served in George Washington's army, including the seven regiments who formed the famous Maryland Line and perhaps five thousand militiamen.[8]

Charles Brewer collection, courtesy of Peerless Rockville

On June 11, 1774, local patriots met at Charles Hungerford's tavern on Washington Street, the main road, to protest British actions against the colonists. The resolves adopted that day began a path which led to the American Revolution.

Early in the war all male citizens, especially those voting and doing business in the state, were required by the Maryland Assembly to sign the Oath of Fidelity and Support. Two Rockville signers of the oath, John Summers and Thomas Linstid, were later buried in the tiny graveyard in the middle of Twinbrook.[9]

In August 1777, James Higgins, a forty-three-year-old Rockville area farmer with a wife and ten children, enrolled as a private in the Fifth Company of the Lower Battalion of the Montgomery County Militia. Higgins took the Oath of Allegiance to the Maryland Assembly in January 1778, and rejoined the militia in July of 1780. Higgins may have joined fellow Marylanders in the Flying Camp, a special reserve unit prepared to move into action on short notice, or fought with the Maryland Line in southern campaigns later in the war. When peace came, Higgins returned to farm his land in the area today considered south Rockville. He, his wife, and generations of descendants were buried in a tiny family cemetery which is located near Twinbrook Parkway.[10]

No battles were fought on Maryland soil, but the little crossroads village and its neighbors contributed to the war effort in addition to providing soldiers. George Town, with a population of 433 in 1776, became the collection and distribution center for military supplies, clothing and blankets, horses, and storage of wheat, flour, grain, hay, forage, salt beef and pork, and other food for soldiers and horses. The war added to the commercial and political power of George Town, preparing it for eventual incorporation into the new national capital.

Patriots everywhere applauded the return of peace in 1783. On April 13, the jubilant colonists celebrated at the tiny courthouse with an elegant dinner, a Hessian band playing marches and gavottes, a ball, and thirteen formal toasts. The fighting was over, but the war years had set in motion major changes in trade, views on slavery, and the lives of the small farmers, which would influence future developments in the area.[11]

ROCKVILLE SELECTED SEAT OF NEW MONTGOMERY COUNTY

Early in the war, an event of major import to the future of Rockville occurred. On September 6, 1776, the delegates to the Maryland Constitutional Convention passed, by a small majority, a bill introduced by Dr. Thomas Sprigg Wootton. Effective October 1, the largest and most populous county in Maryland was divided into three smaller government units. The central section remained Frederick, the northern section became Washington County, and the southern section was named Montgomery County. The two new counties honored America's first heroes. General Richard Montgomery, a British officer until he settled in New York, was thirty-eight years old when he fell while attacking the city of Quebec on December 31, 1775. He never set foot in most of the eighteen counties named for him in a spate of revolutionary passion.

The question which immediately arose was where to locate the new local government. No settlement rivaled George Town in size or importance, but its location at the southern edge of the new county rendered it unacceptable. Colonists were accustomed to greeting friends and casting ballots at Hungerford's tavern, a place with no extraordinary natural assets but situated on a well-traveled road roughly equidistant between Frederick Town and George Town. It was logical for voters of the new county to designate the crossroads village as the seat of local government.[12]

Anchoring county government in the tiny settlement surrounding Hungerford's tavern was the most

THOMAS SPRIGG WOOTTON

Dr. Thomas Sprigg Wootton made the successful motion in 1776 to divide Frederick County into three separate counties, one of them being Montgomery. For such an important person—delegate from Frederick County to the Lower House of the Colonial Assembly, patriot who served on committees that ultimately proposed independence from England and, in the new state of Maryland, delegate to the 1776 Maryland Constitutional Convention, Judge of the Orphans Court, Justice of the Peace, and member of the House of Delegates—we know very little about his personal life.

Dr. Wootton was born about 1740 and died in 1789. He moved to Frederick County before 1769, and in 1771 he became a vestryman of Prince George's Parish at Rockville. He owned land on Watts Branch near the high school named for him, his house sited on the hill on the west side of Wootton's Mill Park (now part of the Watts Branch Meadows neighborhood). Dr. Wootton likely was buried in the little family cemetery nearby, which was last noted in the 1940s. He owned other property in George Town and near Needwood Park, and in his will he requested that his slaves remain in families.[13]

important decision in Rockville's history. The selection as county seat, with assurance that a courthouse, jail, and polling place must be located there, stimulated entrepreneurs of all persuasions. Places of lodging, of eating and drinking, offices for attorneys and surveyors, and businesses which catered to traveler, visitor, and resident alike must be opened. Buildings, privies, stables, services, and workers were needed. From the fall of 1776 onward, the village now addressed as Montgomery Court House grew immensely in importance.

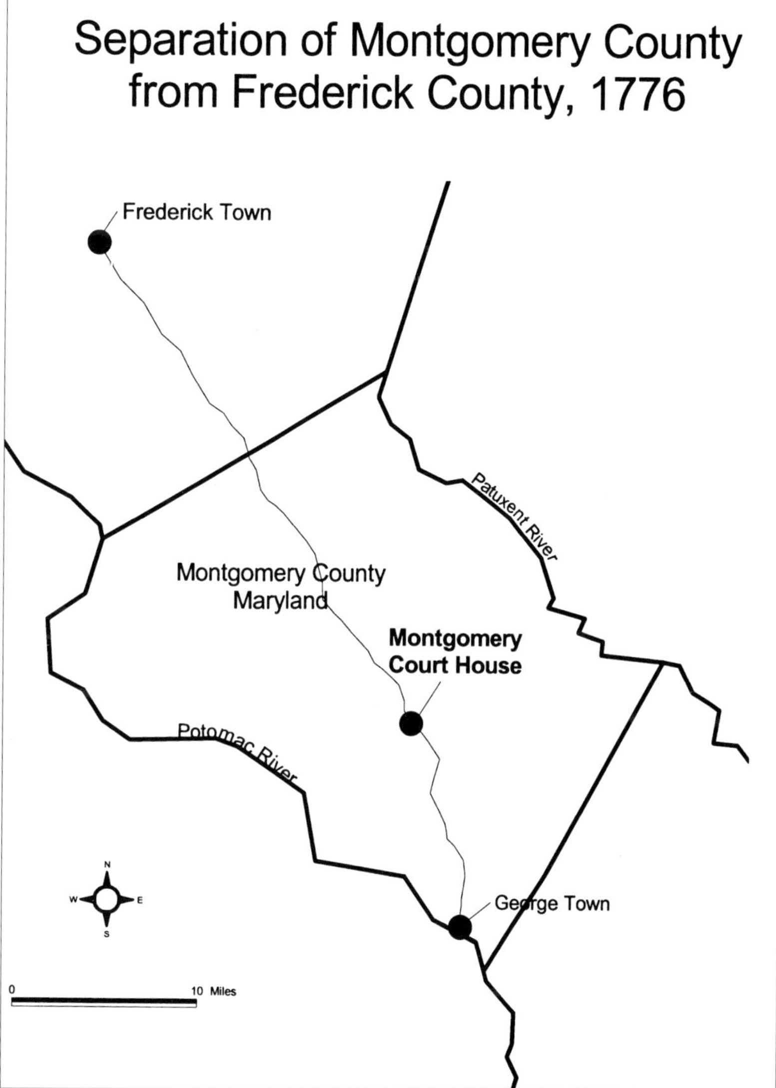

Map by Pedro Flores, GIS manager, City of Rockville

In 1776, the Maryland Assembly split Frederick County into three parts. The southernmost section became Montgomery County, with its seat of government at present-day Rockville.

THE COURTHOUSE AND COURTHOUSE SQUARE

The first court sessions opened at the tavern in May of 1777. By then, Leonard Davis had taken over the business. The new county commissioners were authorized to buy land, but meanwhile they needed a convenient place to hold court, store official papers, and keep prisoners until buildings were erected. They paid Davis twenty-four hundred pounds of tobacco "for finding a House to hold the Courts in & prison for the reception of Prisoners." Circuit Court Clerk Brooke Beall was allowed "to remove the Clerk's office to the house where Clerk resides in George Town until a proper place shall be provided."[14] To fund the land purchase and salaries for justices, the sheriff, and jurors, the assembly set taxes based upon the value of real estate and personal property.

County records indicate that Leonard Davis's tavern was used as the courthouse from May 1777 through March 1779. The justices then paid Thomas Owen Williams to renovate an existing building for use as the courthouse and arranged for it to be rent free for three years. In 1783, Williams paid taxes on property which included "1 framed Court House, 3 dwelling houses, 4 old out houses. 100 acres cleared."[15]

Court met in session four times a year, in May, July, August, and November. Early proceedings record that the Court heard cases of felony and indecent behavior, ordered road construction, protected apprentices and orphans, and issued licenses for taverners.

In 1784 and 1785, the General Assembly authorized assessments to pay for a new courthouse. County Surveyor Archibald Orme measured out the lot, jurors determined the value of land taken from six property owners, and Court House Square was formed. It was a notch taken from the east side of the plan of Williamsburgh, almost square in shape—twenty-three perches by twenty perches, for a total of two and seven-eigths acres. (A perch is a linear measure of five and one-half yards or sixteen and one-half feet.) In this square, about 1788, was constructed Montgomery County's new brick courthouse. Little is known about it, but maintenance records indicate that it was a two-story brick building. It must have been small, for in 1810 a separate building was built on the square to house the clerk and his records.

Before a jail was constructed, the commissioners paid local property owners to supply fit places to keep prisoners and to provide stocks, whipping posts, and a pillory. In 1786, Sheriff William Robertson built a house at the corner of Washington and Jefferson Streets to use as his home, office, and *gaol*. This proved insufficient, so the sheriff directed constables to keep prisoners in irons in their houses until a new jail could be erected. Finally, the General Assembly authorized the county to build a jail, which was completed in 1801.

The courthouse lot retained its shape until the 1820s. Through road changes, urban renewal, and late twentieth century revitalization efforts, this prominent public space in the center of Rockville kept the name "Court House Square."

WILLIAMSBURGH—ROCKVILLE'S FIRST SUBDIVISION

One family that cast its future in the new county seat was named Williams. By the 1740s, William and Barbara Williams resided in Prince George's (Episcopal) Parish. In 1766, William Williams purchased Young Man's Delight, a two-hundred-acre tract of land, which was part of Exchange and New Exchange Enlarged that Arthur Nelson had patented thirty years earlier. Following William's death in 1767, and Barbara's in 1791, their seven children divided up land and slaves. Third son William Prather Williams inherited property on Captain John Branch of the Potomac River as well as Young Man's Delight in 1784 after he paid his three brothers their portion of the value of the latter.

In 1784, William Prather Williams enlisted Archibald Orme to survey part of Young Man's Delight into "lotts with streets fit, convenient and suitable for a town." Several buildings were already there, including the framed courthouse, three dwelling houses, four old outhouses, and the Hungerford-Davis tavern. Williams sold Lot 5, on the east side of what we know today as South Washington between Jefferson and Vinson Streets, to Allen Bowie, Thomas Cramphin, and Richard Wootton for fifteen pounds sterling in March of that year. It was on the south side of the "main road" whereon the men "hath now built a store house."[16] Soon other one-half and three-eighths acre lots sold.

The sale of a lot to William McGrath for fifteen pounds current money on January 21, 1788, marked the first mention of the Town of Williamsburgh. Thereafter, in almost all of the transactions conveying lots to new owners between 1788 and 1800, the deed carried that name. A deed to Upton Beall in January 1803 referred to "Williamsburgh or Montgomery Court House" as the locale.[17]

THE TOWN IN 1800

At the turn of the nineteenth century, because George Town had been ceded to the new District of Columbia, the area now called Rockville was the largest settlement in Montgomery County. It was known interchangeably as Williamsburgh or Montgomery Court House. As county seat, it was an important place, but it was small. Perhaps 150 people lived in town. There were about thirty-eight buildings around the crossroads, half of them houses. Most were built of wood and several of crude logs, although a few brick homes fronted on the main road. The other buildings were stores, offices, and shops. The town boasted a saddlery, blacksmith's shop, and even a post office. Several taverns, such as George Stevens's Sign of the Blue Ball, offered beds, a stable, provisions, and liquor. There also was a prize house, where tobacco grown by local planters was packed into casks, and a warehouse, where the casks were stored before shipment to port inspection stations.[18]

Owing its success to the confluence of roads, the town was the hub from which six dirt roads radiated. Two led to tobacco shipping points; what is now the Rockville Pike was the road to George Town, and a combination of current Veirs Mill Road and University Boulevard provided access to Bladensburg. Roads to Great Falls and to the Mouth of the Monocacy (later named Darnestown Road) took travelers westward, and by heading east beyond Sandy Spring one could eventually reach the fastest-growing city in America—Baltimore—and its port.

Most people traveled by horse, since few were wealthy enough to own wheeled carriages or coaches. Oxen pulled carts, wagons, and hogsheads of tobacco. The stage stopped in Montgomery Court House every Tuesday and Friday on its route between George Town and Frederick.

One traveler, George Washington, wrote in his diary:

> On Thursday, June 30, 1791: The business which brought me to George Town being finished, . . . I set off this morning a little after 4 Oclock in the prosecution of my journey toward Philadelphia; and being desirous of seeing the nature of the Country North of George Town, . . . and along the upper road, I resolved to pass through Frederick Town in Maryland. . . . Breakfasted in a small village called Williamsburgh in which stand the Ct. House of Montgomerie County, 14 M from George Town. . . . Dined at one Peters's Tavern 20 miles further and arrived at Frederick town about Sundown the whole distance 43 miles.[19]

Having been set in motion by the earliest land patentees, new landowners and tenant farmers continued to alter the landscape around the crossroads.

EIGHTEENTH CENTURY TAVERNS IN ROCKVILLE

Colonial inns—also known as taverns or ordinaries—provided much more than food and lodging. All levels of society gathered to share local gossip and political news, to play cards or billiards, and to conduct business. Often settlements were known by the name of the local establishment. Government issued licenses to proprietors and closely regulated tavern location, accommodations and drinks offered, prices, and personal conduct.

In the 1750s, Lawrence Owen operated an ordinary along the main road between George Town and Frederick Town, at the colonial crossroads that became Rockville. General Braddock encamped there in 1755. Two decades later, at a nearby location, Charles Hungerford rented a small building for his tavern. It faced South Washington Street, then part of the main road, and was one and one-half stories high, of logs covered with boards. Here in 1774, patriots issued five resolves as the first local protest against the British crown.

At the time the county seat was selected, Leonard Davis held a license for "that noted and well frequented TAVERN at Montgomery Court-House, known by the name of HUNGERFORD's Tavern." Davis described it as being "26 by 20 feet, two rooms, and a very convenient bar-room, on the lower floor . . . a kitchen adjoining the dwelling house, 20 feet by 16. One other dwelling house about 15 or 20 steps from the former, 20 by 22 feet, three good well-furnished rooms on the lower floor, with an exceeding good fireplace, very convenient for the reception of travellers. . . ."[20] As Davis maintained the six furnished bedsteads required by law for an ordinary in a county seat, the commissioners turned to him for the first court-house and jail, until suitable structures could be built. Davis sold the tavern to his father-in-law, Joseph Willson,[21] who continued the business until his death in 1791. By that time Montgomery Court House boasted three or four other taverns.

Lot 19, location of the Hungerford-Davis-Willson tavern, later was the subject of a complicated equity suit. In 1847 Susan Russell, Willson's granddaughter, purchased the property at tax sale.[22] Although tradition maintained the house as the revered colonial tavern, the Janet Montgomery Chapter of the Daughters of the American Revolution could not authenticate this so it declined to purchase the dilapidated house.[23] In 1912, the Baptist Church razed it to make way for a new church and parsonage.

Archeological excavations conducted on Lot 19 in 1973 and 1987 located mostly fragments of pottery, clay pipes, and wine bottles mixed with building rubble and soil in the old foundation.[24] The work was complicated by new construction on Lot 19 and by dramatic changes in the level of South Washington Street. Perhaps a future generation will further investigate this important eighteenth century site.

They felled large and small trees and cleared more and more land on which to plant tobacco. A man on horseback could ride from farm to farm on dirt roads or through the woods.[25] Although the pace of development had slowed, parcels of land were still available to be surveyed and patented. Anna Orme, one of a very few female patentees, surveyed 1,398.75 acres (including the Lincoln Park area) as Ashley in 1786 and obtained a patent in 1801. Elisha Allison resurveyed Rock Spring in 1793, while Jesse Leach did not receive a patent to Long Discovered until 1819, rather late in the settlement period.

In a quarter of a century, county government had made its impression on the village. A courthouse and jail, offices and residences of public officials, accommodations for jurors and litigants, and other services had arisen. So had industry, previously prohibited when America's role was to provide raw materials for Britain. Two water-powered grist- (grain) and sawmills operated by 1800, currently identified only by the road names "Muncaster Mill" and "Horner's Mill."

Pride in the new nation and optimism for the new county seat's future ran high. There was room to grow—the Williams brothers offered forty-eight town lots for newcomers to purchase and build upon. Honoré Martin, who immigrated from France in the 1780s, bought fourteen lots in Williamsburgh. He built a mansion house and store, granary, lumber shop, stable, tobacco and prize house. He touted the town as "situated in a beautiful and healthy part of the country. . . . the most public place in the county, as there are four public roads intersects in view thereof—and make no doubt but in a few years it will be perhaps the most public inland town on the continent, as all, or a major part, of the back trade by land must come directly through said town, on its

Dennis Griffith map of Maryland, 1794.

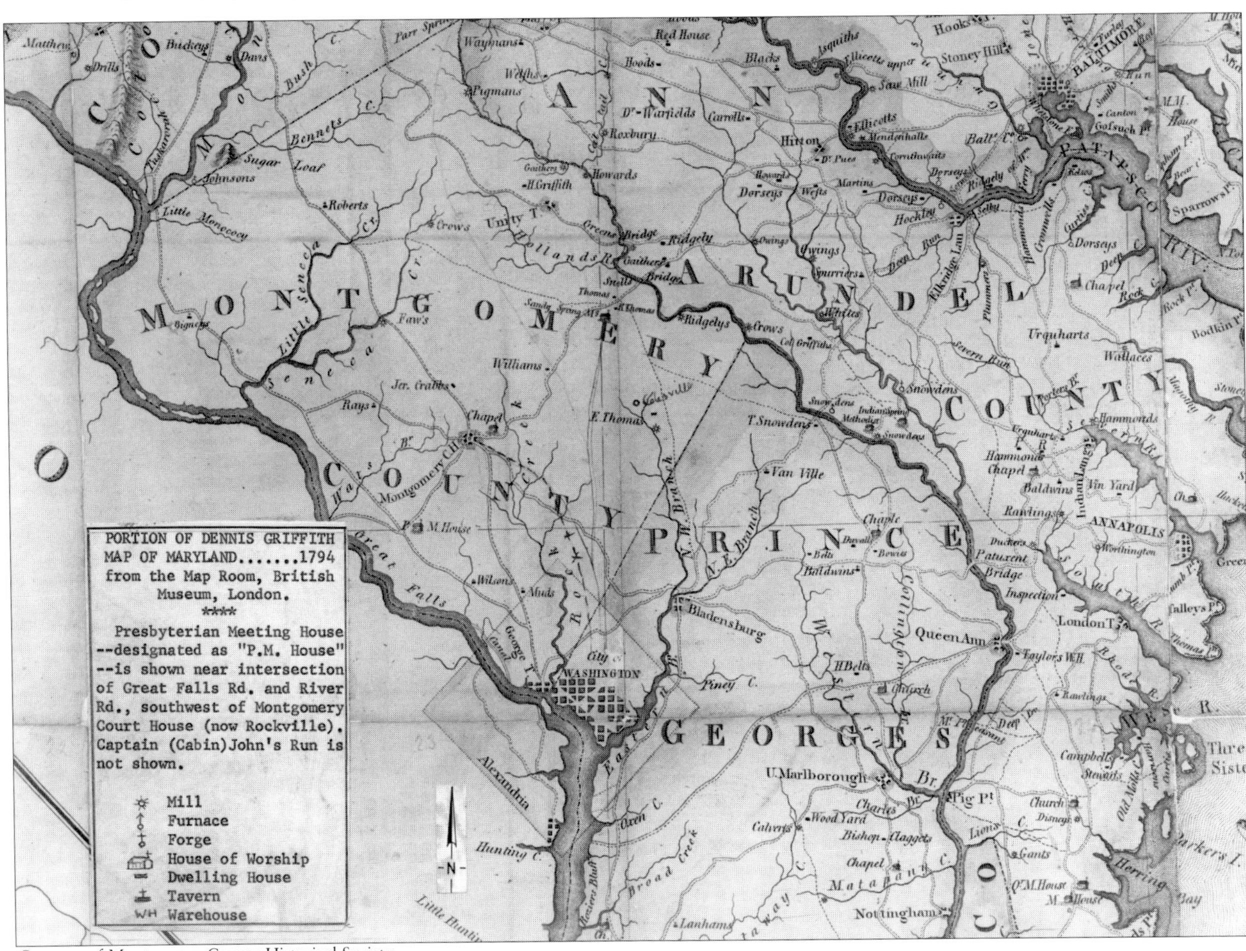

Courtesy of Montgomery County Historical Society

way down to the above-mentioned metropolis, which renders it the most valuable stand, I may say in America, for a store."[26]

Montgomery Countians still looked to George Town for commerce and connections to the greater world. The flourishing town owed its rise to the opening of new tobacco lands in the Piedmont, and the frontier gravitated to the cosmopolitan port for news, supplies, and schools, as well as to ship crops. In 1800, Montgomery citizens could take heart not only in the success of George Town, but also in the promise of the national government's eminent move into the new federal city.

The population of the entire county in 1800 totaled 15,058, of whom 8,508 were white and 6,550 black.[27] Nearly all of the whites were of western European descent, primarily second-generation English, German, and Scottish. Ninety-six percent of blacks were slaves, considered essential for the tobacco-based economy. Slaveowners in Montgomery Court House averaged four to six slaves per household. In 1800, an eleven-year-old girl cost forty pounds current money, the going rate for two unimproved lots in Williamsburgh. Slaves in Maryland legally had been slaves for life since 1664, as differentiated from indentured servants and apprentices whose bondage was defined in years. But as masters freed slaves through their wills and the numbers of free blacks in Maryland increased, their rights declined. Free, adult black and white males with sufficient property could vote for Jefferson or Adams for president in 1800. Two years later the General Assembly rescinded the voting rights of free blacks.[28]

Legal circumstances and wealth determined the lives of all persons, black and white. Wealth was concentrated in a few who lived in brick houses and who could vote, afford slaves, and send their children to school. In Montgomery Court House or on small nearby farms, people lived in family groups in tiny homes with a loft upstairs. They could usually read, but owned few clothes or pieces of furniture. In town, farmers lived among store keepers, tobacco traders, tavernkeepers, and public officials. Most men held multiple jobs. By 1800, the county operated an Alms House near the town, insisting that all able-bodied poor people labor for room and board.

Women's work was never done. Like the pioneer captured in the *Madonna of the Trail* statue, they balanced rifle and children. Partners in the small family farm, they ran home-based businesses, made clothing for the extended family, and practiced the arts of herbal healing and midwifery. They directed the domestic sphere, feeding and supervising apprentices, indentured servants, and slaves. Frequent pregnancies made them subject to maladies more so than their husbands and children. Legally women were the daughters and wives of citizens, inheriting and bringing a dowry but unable to hold land in their own names or to control inherited property until 1859. As a practice, wives were taken aside and asked under oath if they were signing deeds without coercion.[30]

Rockville's Oldest Remaining Building

The oldest building still standing in Rockville is 5 North Adams Street. Philip Jenkins bought Lot 76 in 1792, and by the following year constructed a house which he rented to Benjamin Jones for fourteen pounds a year. Today this one-room-up-and-down wood structure is the section of the house closest to the street. When Jenkins moved to Kentucky in 1824, he sold it to John Braddock, whose daughter married John Miller. The Millers enlarged the house in the 1860s and again in the 1880s, adding the Victorian siding, gable, detailing, verandah, and space for Mrs. Miller's millinery shop. The McFarland family lived there for fifty years, and in 1974 the house was renovated for the office use it has today.[29]

Photograph by Dean Evangelista

5 North Adams Street is Rockville's oldest remaining building.

All children worked, except for the very wealthy. The apprenticeship system bound boys to masters for a specified number of years and provided the benefits of learning a skill which would enhance their future earnings. Masters fed and clothed their apprentices and often provided some education. Most apprentices were eleven- to fifteen-year-old boys, free blacks as well as whites. Girls learned sewing, cooking, and other housekeeping skills. Saddler Enoch Busson and merchant Honoré Martin, both of Montgomery Court House, took in apprentices.[31]

Photograph by Dean Evangelista

Boundary stone of Rockville, at the new town's southeast boundary. "BR" stands for "beginning of Rockville."

After the Revolution, the Anglican Church ceased to be the established church in Maryland. Episcopalians continued to worship at the small chapel of ease, but this change opened the way for other religions. By 1800, Montgomery Court House could claim Methodist, Presbyterian, and Roman Catholic adherents.

WILLIAMSBURGH BECOMES ROCKVILLE

A county seat with so much promise deserved a distinctive name. By 1788 William Williams referred to the plan of town lots laid out by county surveyor Archibald Orme as Williamsburgh. As time went on, however, purchasers (called proprietors) of these lots were increasingly uncomfortable because Orme's plat was not officially recorded in the Montgomery County Land Records.

This discomfort evolved into a "petition of sundry inhabitants of Montgomery county" to the Maryland General Assembly which, in its 1801 session, passed an act to survey, mark, bound, and "erect into a town" the Williams land adjacent to the courthouse. The legislation noted that "there being no record of the same, the titles of the proprietors thereof are precarious and uncertain."[32]

The Assembly appointed five commissioners to plot out exact lines "most agreeably to their original location, according to the best evidence that can be obtained." They could hire a surveyor, summon witnesses to testify about the boundaries, and observe the proprietors as they installed boundary stones. Costs of the surveyor and commissioners, each at two dollars per day, were to be borne by the proprietors. The act further stated that the lots "shall be and are hereby erected into a town, to be called and known by the name of Rockville" and that the levy court shall appoint a constable for this town.[33]

Apparently the original commissioners found this difficult, for in the following year the General Assembly passed a supplemental act which appointed three other men to perform those duties. The problems are suggested in the 1802 wording: Including a time schedule, marking improved lots (those with buildings) only where they border those unimproved, permitting the commissioners to appoint "proper persons" to collect expenses from each proprietor, and allowing the collectors a percentage of the funds collected.[34]

Recognizing that all was "precarious and uncertain" until titles were confirmed and a plan recorded, no lots were sold between May 1800 and January 1803. The commissioners met at the courthouse on March 10 to appoint William Smith as surveyor. They hired chain carriers, pole carriers, and an axman, and employed "David Howe and a negro man of Adam Robb and proceded to plant the Boundarys of Rockville."[35] Smith completed his work on May 9. Signed by Commissioners Thomas Orme and Richard West, the plan explanation noted that "Rockville was surveyed, marked and bounded (agreeably to the Original Location thereof.)"[36] With a written description of each of the eighty-five lots and street names updated to include the first three American presidents, the clerk copied the certificate into the Land Records of Montgomery County on July 16, 1803.

Thus did Williamsburgh become Rockville. Who coined the name, and to what does it refer? Thomas Anderson Esq. stated in an address delivered at the Centennial Celebration of Montgomery County held in 1876 that, "It was at first contemplated to call the town Wattsville, but Watt's Branch being regarded as too insignificant a stream, it was finally concluded to honor its more pretentious neighbor, Rock Creek, and hence its name, Rockville."[37] Not knowing where Mr. Anderson obtained his information, it is hard to comment. Regardless, the name "Montgomery Court House" continued to appear on maps and in documents through the 1820s.

There's more to this story. When surveyor Archibald Orme died in 1812, the county commissioners ordered his 1787 plat of the courthouse lot recorded in the Land Records. Perhaps Orme's unrecorded plan of Williamsburgh was also found in his desk, but by that time it had been superceded by the 1803 plan of Rockville. The hand-colored 1803 plan hangs in a place of honor at City Hall, after being anonymously donated to the city in 1987.

In 1958, a paving crew clearing the corner of Vinson Street and Perry Street/Maryland Avenue kicked up a large stone. On it, "B.R." is faint but legible, marking the southeastern corner of Lot 1 of Rockville. B.R. stands for "Beginning of Rockville" in the 1803 survey. In 1961 the Mayor and Council of Rockville returned the stone to its historic location at Maryland Avenue and Vinson Street and dedicated a bronze plaque explaining its significance. A second, smaller stone is located at the northwest end of Lot 17.[38]

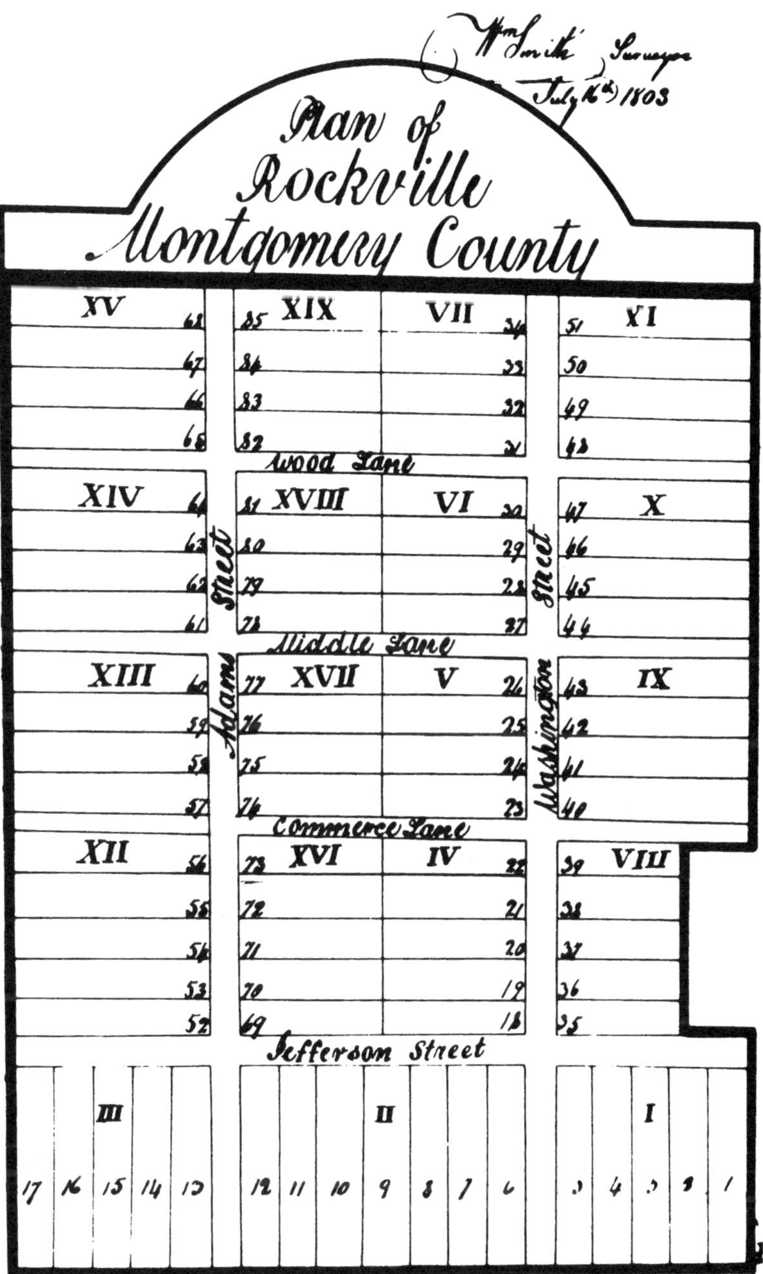

Plan of Rockville, 1803.

The 1803 plan marked identification of Rockville as a singular place. It was the county seat and was recognized as a town, although incorporation would not occur for another six decades. Naming a public official for Rockville—a constable, who would assist the county sheriff with judicial and peacekeeping duties—suggests the status which the Maryland Assembly assigned to the crossroads village.

Chapter Three

Rural Crossroads to Incorporated Community 1803–1860

"Montgomery court house, established by an act of assembly, under the title of Rockville, is situated about 14 miles north west of Washington city, on the great road leading from thence to Fredericktown. It contains about 40 dwellings, some of which are tolerably well built of brick. The public buildings are a brick court-house and jail, without either taste or elegance."[1]

The half century before the Civil War solidified Rockville as a community, although the issue of slavery cast a dark shadow. By the turn of the nineteenth century, the seeds of Rockville's future were sown: county seat, a grid street pattern, developing economy, and promise for growth. Residents of this small agricultural village, in improving social institutions, industry, transportation, and communication, regarded Frederick, George Town, Baltimore, and Annapolis as models. On the eve of war, although the presence of county government remained a powerful factor, Rockville took control of its future in a quiet but dramatic manner.

POLITICS AND WAR IN ROCKVILLE

Rockville politics in the early 1800s were more local than national. Three decades of national union could not easily replace 170 years of looking to the Maryland Assembly for legal authority and political leadership.

Rockville men assumed political leadership roles. General Jeremiah Crabb, whose land extended from what is now Derwood into the center of the county seat, served in the state House of Delegates and then the U.S. Congress as a Federalist. Dr. Thomas Sprigg Wootton, Lawrence O'Neale, Richard Wootton, and Brice Selby all were elected to the Maryland General Assembly. Richard West served as a county commissioner, and Honoré Martin was a leader in the national Democratic-Republican party.[2]

Alexander Contee Hanson Jr. founded the *Federal Republican* newspaper in 1808. From his editor's desk in Baltimore, the brash young attorney blasted policies that would push a European power into war with an unprepared America. His arrogance earned him enemies and an indictment for libel.

Hoping to further his political career, in 1811 Hanson bought a house in Rockville on Jefferson Street. Hanson was in Rockville in June 1812 when a mob, angry at his condemnation of President James Madison for declaring war, broke into the Baltimore shop to smash the presses. Hanson wrote from Rockville that he would continue to oppose Mr. Madison's war through his newspaper.

The day the *Federal Republican* reappeared in Baltimore, July 27, 1812, a furious mob again destroyed the presses. Taken by police into protective custody, Hanson and his friends were clubbed, stabbed, and tarred and feathered by the mob. Hanson became a political hero, winning election in 1813 in the Third Congressional District which included Rockville, all of Montgomery, and part of Frederick County. In 1818, Hanson sold his Rockville home and relocated to Anne Arundel County.[3]

Once Maryland was invaded by the British in 1814, Americans closed ranks. The young United States had declared war on Great Britain in June of 1812 after Congress determined that England had impressed more American sailors and more egregiously violated neutral shipping rights than France. The war started slowly, but after Napoleon's defeat in March 1814, British attention turned to the United States.

The following month, four thousand troops under Major Gen. Robert Ross arrived at the Chesapeake Bay to find a relatively defenseless population. British warships attacked towns from Norfolk to Havre de Grace, looting, pillaging, raping, and burning. In August, the invaders moved up the Patuxent and Potomac Rivers. Marylanders hastily assembled under young, inexperienced Brigadier Gen. William Henry Winder but had no idea of whether the British were heading for Baltimore, Annapolis, or Washington.

After the armies engaged in Bladensburg at noon on August 24, the larger American force retreated six miles into Washington. One of the few American officers to distinguish himself in this battle was Maj. George Peter, a George Town resident who later represented Montgomery County in Congress and whose descendants became prominent Rockville citizens. Word of what became known as the Bladensburg Races did not take long to reach the Federal city, and most families, including President and Mrs. Madison, fled with their possessions or prepared for a siege.

Hours later, the British entered Washington. They made the most of their twenty-four hours of occupation, torching the Capitol, White House, and Treasury buildings in retaliation for the American plundering of public buildings in York, Upper Canada. From different refuges, President Madison, George Town attorney Francis Scott Key, and General Winder watched in shock as fire and smoke lit the sky for miles around. Mercifully, a violent thunderstorm helped contain the conflagration. The following evening, under cover of darkness, the British pulled out. General Ross retraced his route to the Patuxent, where he reboarded the ships and headed for the next target, Baltimore.[4]

Courtesy of The Maryland Historical Society, Baltimore, Maryland

"The Conspiracy Against Baltimore, or The War Dance at Montgomery Court House," (1812) engraving shows Alexander Contee Hanson in the center as a horned devil leaning toward the seated musician.

General Winder abandoned Washington on August 25. He retreated to Tennally Town, then turned west and arrived at Montgomery Court House[5] via Great Falls Road. Supplies he had anticipated were nowhere to be found, so as the troops camped near the courthouse, they searched for food nearby. They likely admired the brick mansion house under construction for Upton Beall, and may have stolen his lumber to stoke their campfires.

The government also left town. President Madison and his cabinet had agreed to reconvene in Frederick if Washington fell, each to get there as best he could. President and Mrs. Madison met at Wiley's Tavern in Great Falls, Virginia, after which the president crossed the river into Maryland.

Winder and his men left Montgomery Court House about noon on Friday, August 26. They marched out Baltimore Road and up the turnpike to Brookeville, then past Sandy Spring to camp at Snell's Bridge en route to Ellicott City and Baltimore. About 6:00 P.M. the same day, President Madison and his party—trying to connect with Winder—arrived at the county seat. Madison followed Winder, arriving at Caleb Bentley's house in Brookeville at nightfall. The following day, Madison returned to a still-smoldering

RIGHT: Map of the Chesapeake Campaign of 1814.

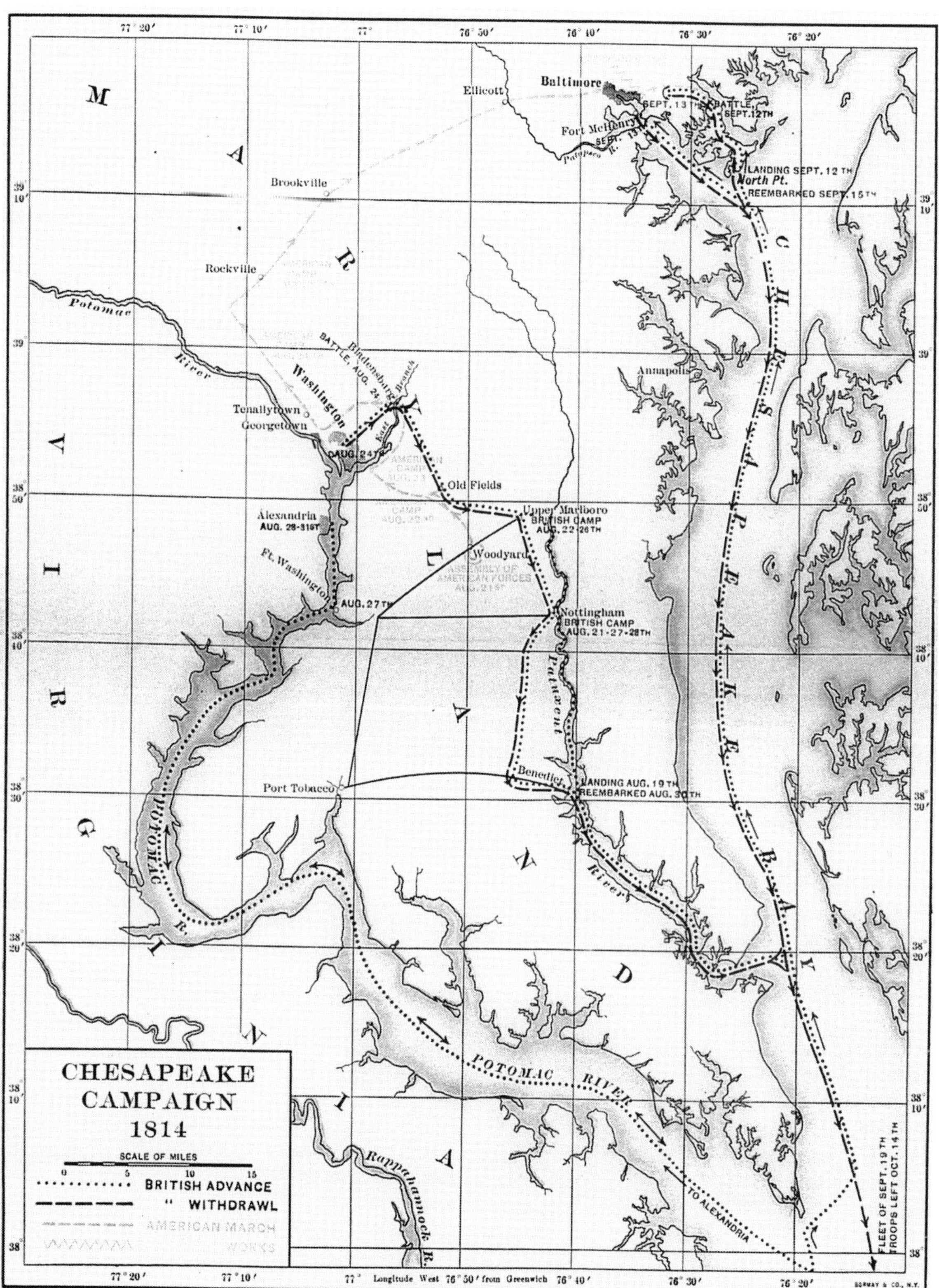

From Kendric J. Babcock, *The Rise of American Nationality* (New York: Harper and Brothers, 1906)

THE BEALLS AND THEIR MANSION HOUSE

The Beall (pronounced *Bell*) family figured prominently in antebellum Montgomery County. Beall was an officer in the county militia and a Federalist elector for the Maryland Senate in 1801. Matilda

Photograph by Dean Evangelista

The Beall-Dawson House, built 1812–15, is now owned by the City of Rockville and is home to the Montgomery County Historical Society.

Brooke Beall, a wealthy George Town merchant and landowner, was the first clerk of the court. When he died in 1795, his son Upton succeeded him and served as clerk until his death in 1827. Both men lived in George Town, owned a mill and plantation called Beallmont on the Potomac River, and traveled frequently to Montgomery Court House. As clerks, they received fees for recording deeds, keeping court minutes, issuing marriage licenses, and maintaining court dockets.

In 1796, Upton Beall married Matilda Price, daughter of a wealthy Frederick resident. Soon they took up residence at Montgomery Court House, likely on Washington Street. Beall died in 1806, followed six months later by their young son, Edmund. Upton remained in Rockville and in 1810 married Jane Robb, twenty-three years his junior. Jane was the daughter of Adam Robb, a Scotsman who moved to Montgomery Court House in the 1790s and opened several taverns.

The brick mansion house on Lots 57 and 58 was completed in 1815. Eventually, the Bealls owned sixty-seven and one-half acres extending from North Adams Street through the woods to Forest Avenue and from the Darnestown Road through fields to Martin's Lane. In addition to the mansion house, the property contained three slave dwellings, a dairy, carriage house, ice house, stable, and windmill. The family relied upon slave labor in George Town, in the country, and at their Rockville dwelling.

Upton Beall was active in the life of the county seat. He served as a director of the Washington Turnpike Company and on the board of the Rockville Academy, and with others attempted to start a bank in Rockville. An Episcopal warden and vestryman, he purchased pew one in the new church. Even so, the Bealls continued their association with George Town's social life for most household purchases and for their children's schooling.

Jane and Upton Beall had five children, of whom three daughters outlived their parents. When Upton died in 1827 at age fifty-six, he was the sixth largest landowner in the county. Jane died in 1849, and the mansion house passed to the three unmarried daughters. One of them, Margaret Johns Beall, became the sole owner in 1870 and lived in the house until 1901.

Margaret willed the property to the three daughters of her cousin Amelia Somervell who, with her husband John L. Dawson and eight children, lived at the house. Their heirs sold the Beall-Dawson to Mr. and Mrs. Edwin Davis. In 1965, the City of Rockville purchased the property. Today, the Beall-Dawson House is a museum complex owned by the city and operated by the Montgomery County Historical Society.[6]

Descendants of Beall slaves—from the Wood, Ross, Smith, and other families—still live in Rockville, as do Beall and Dawson descendants.

Washington. He acted quickly to regroup his cabinet, halt the looting, find a new place to live, and determine where the British would strike next.

The action shifted to Baltimore, already America's third-largest city. On September 13, English rockets bombarded Fort McHenry, which inspired Francis Scott Key to pen "The Star Spangled Banner" as Americans claimed their first victory of the war.

Two Baltimore defenders hailed from the Rockville area. George Graff had recently dissolved a business in Frederick, Maryland, and was farming three miles north of the village when war broke out. He provided his own uniform and rifle, and purchased a cannon for the Maryland Militia Seventh Artillery, in which he served as lieutenant. Graff's body servant, Shadrach Nugent, interviewed almost seventy years later, claimed he kept his master's canteen filled with whiskey during the battle. The son of a convict Irishwoman and a servant from Guinea, Nugent earned his free papers at the Battle of Baltimore and lived to the end of the century. Graff's property today is part of the King Farm development.[7]

Five months after the march through Montgomery Court House, the United States and Great Britain signed the Treaty of Ghent to end the war.[8]

DEVELOPMENT OF THE RURAL COMMUNITY—TRANSPORTATION

By 1814, America was ready to stretch. The federal government moved its 131 employees from Philadelphia to Washington, the country doubled in size by purchasing Louisiana and, in terms of settlement patterns, Rockville briefly occupied the center of population of the United States. In this period, Maryland and other eastern states planned to build roads, canals, and railroads which would connect inland agricultural lands and new domestic industries to expanding markets on the Chesapeake Bay and in the west.

Maryland's prospects depended upon developing an adequate transportation system, but Montgomery County farmers split between the competing economic interests of Potomac River canal boosters and rail promoters who looked to Baltimore and the bay. Planned years before, the C&O Canal and the B&O Railroad both began construction in earnest in 1828. By the time Montgomery County's part of the canal opened in 1833, railroad track had been laid from Baltimore to Frederick and almost reached the Potomac at Point of Rocks. Canal construction was hampered by labor shortages and cholera epidemics which struck down hundreds of laborers. Tradition says that Irish canal workers who perished in the epidemics of the 1830s were buried in mass graves at Saint Mary's Church in Rockville.[9]

Miles away from the planned canal and railroad routes, Rockville residents viewed improved roads as key to their economic success. Local merchants and farmers asked the General Assembly to authorize a corporation which would maintain the busiest road in the area, for the appointed, unpaid overseers proved to be inadequate caretakers of public highways.

In 1805, the Maryland Assembly chartered the Washington Turnpike Company, the first in Montgomery County. Originally, the plan was to improve the existing roadway from the District of Columbia line, through Rockville and Clarksburg, to the main square in Frederick. This would be financed by shares of capital stock for twenty dollars each, with George Town, Washington City, Frederick, Elizabeth-town (Hagerstown), and Rockville each responsible for raising subscriptions.

The twenty foot wide roadway, soon known as the Rockville Pike, was completed by the mid-1820s. The company erected guideposts and milestones to inform travelers of distances from the District to toll gates, other turnpikes, and destination towns. As proposed by Scotsman John McAdam, engineers prepared the roadbed with deep foundations, then laid courses of rock starting large at the base and growing smaller for surface layers. Gravel and dust topped the surface, which was rolled until it bound together. A center crown shed water into drainage ditches on either side of the road.[10] Although the *macadam* system

TOLL RATES ON THE ROCKVILLE PIKE, 1820

Per score (a score is twenty) of sheep or hogs—12 1/2¢
Per score of cattle—25¢
For every horse and his rider, or led horse—6 1/4¢
For a chariot, coach, or stage with two horses and four wheels—25¢
For a carriage with four horses—37 1/2¢

permitted the use of fewer, less skilled workers, construction still proceeded slowly and cost nearly ten thousand dollars per mile.[11]

The turnpike company depended upon user revenue to keep the road in repair. Travelers paid tolls at gates in Tenallytown, Bethesda, and the Willson farm (now Georgetown Prep). The Maryland legislature set the rates.

With the turnpike in place, Rockville was now poised to take advantage of its location. At Court House Square, the Pike linked roads leading to the Potomac River, Baltimore, Frederick, and Washington. The General Assembly chartered other connections which became the Columbia, Brookeville, and Colesville Pikes. Some proposed routes for connections to the National Road, a federally funded project, came through or near Rockville,[12] but a Congressional act for a Rockville-to-Frederick Pike was vetoed in 1830 by President Andrew Jackson, who had traveled that route to his inauguration the year before. Jackson's opposition to federal government involvement in internal improvement projects had much to do with the shift of Rockville voters—whose economic growth depended upon links with larger markets—to the Whig party for the next two decades.[13]

TOP: Letter mailed from Montgomery Court House in 1810. BOTTOM: Letter postmarked Rockville, Md., dated 1833.

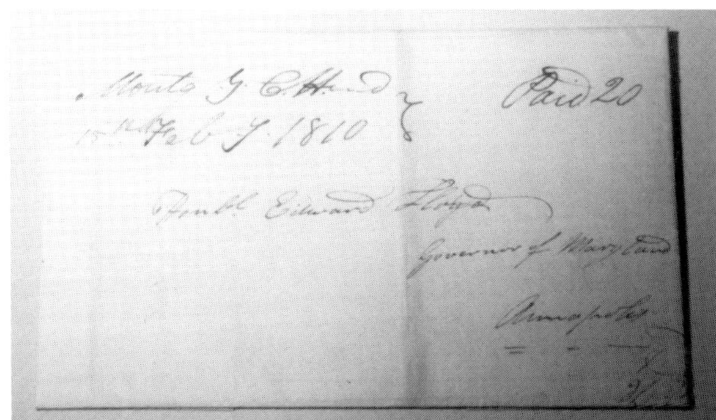

Montg. C. House
15th Feb. 1810
Paid 20
Honble Edward Lloyd
Governor of Maryland
Annapolis

Courtesy of Gordon Baker

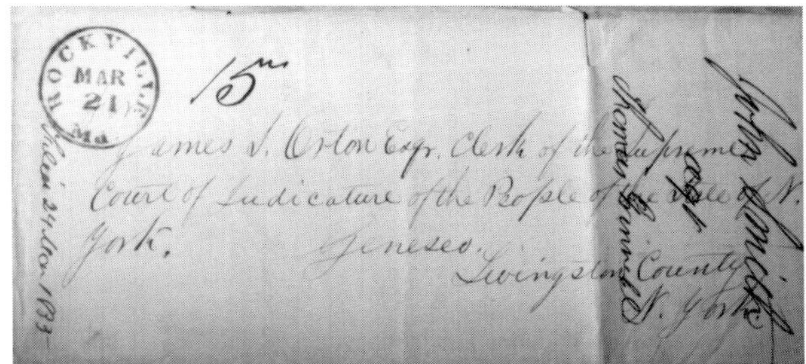

ROCKVILLE MAR 21 Md
15
James S. Orton Esqr. Clerk of the Supreme
Court of Judicature of the People of the State of N.
York,
Geneseo,
Livingston County
N. York

Courtesy of Judith Christensen

The Rockville Pike, although poorly maintained and often barely passable, was a major thoroughfare. Mules and horses pulled wagons carrying farm products to market in Washington, sparking entrepreneurs to open travel-related businesses such as taverns, general stores, and blacksmith and wheelwright shops between the open fields and woodlots. Presidents Andrew Jackson and James Polk, as well as the Marquis de Lafayette, were some of the notables known to have stopped at Pike inns. Fugitive slaves paralleled the Pike en route to Underground Railroad havens in the county and to freedom in the North.

The turnpike company constantly attempted to improve service. Horse and foot travelers between George Town and Frederick in the 1820s shared the road twice weekly with a two-horse stage, which cost three dollars. By 1838, a passenger stage went daily; for four dollars, a passenger could ride from George Town to Frederick, then link to Hagerstown, Pittsburgh, or Wheeling. By then, the loop between Bethesda and Montrose, present-day Old Georgetown Road, had been bypassed with a straighter route.[14] Still, the three-dollar cost and crowded three-hour ride were so prohibitive for James Anderson of Rockville in the 1850s that he lived in a boardinghouse near his Washington job at the U.S. Post Office.

The Washington Turnpike Company remained solvent through most of the nineteenth century but, in the end, it could not stimulate Rockville's antebellum economy. It fought constant wash-outs and could not raise funds to install planks in the deep wheel ruts in 1852.[15] Public financing of the canal and the railroad westward from Baltimore provided an edge that road-connected towns did not match until the mid-twentieth century. Without such a boost, Rockville's growth slowed to a trickle. The village had to be content as county seat and a stop leading to the National Road until the B&O trains arrived decades later.

COMMUNICATING WITH THE WORLD—POSTAL SERVICE AND NEWSPAPERS

In 1794, the federal post office introduced service to Montgomery Court House and designated the route between Frederick and George Town a post road.

Within a decade, the mail stage, also carrying newspapers, packages, and paying passengers, left Washington City three times a week at 2:00 A.M., arriving for breakfast at Mr. Campbell's in Rockville, and then on to Frederick hours later. It reversed the ride the following morning.[16]

Rockville residents paid postage when they picked up their mail from the postmaster, a political appointee who was usually a local merchant. Rockville's first postmaster, Thomas Perry Willson, operated from 101 North Adams Street until 1813. Other postmasters in the antebellum period included miller Samuel Veirs, printer Matthew Fields, and slave trader Charles Price. Local newspapers regularly published a list of residents for whom mail was waiting. The town's post office moved from one location to another until a permanent building opened in 1939.

Rockville readers demanded more local coverage than George Town or Frederick newspapers provided. Beginning in 1807 with the *Maryland Register and Montgomery Advertiser*, Rockville had a local weekly paper. The *Centinel of Freedom*, *True American and Farmer's Register*, *The Maryland Journal and True American*, *Farmer's Friend*, *Montgomery County Advocate*, and other papers appeared briefly, then folded. It was not until 1855, when Matthew Fields began to print the *Montgomery County Sentinel*, that Rockville could count on a local paper with a promising future.[17]

Charles Brewer collection, courtesy of Peerless Rockville

The Rockville Academy, where many of Montgomery County's leaders received their education. This 1880s photograph shows the original building, which faced Jefferson Street.

EDUCATION

Schooling was a luxury in rural areas such as Montgomery County. A few children had private tutors or attended schools in Frederick or George Town. Most parents taught skills necessary for life on the family farm, in the house or shop, or by hiring out to a local artisan.

As the county's population increased and communities gained stability, demand grew for educational opportunities. The private Rockville Academy, initially funded by an 1805 lottery and chartered in 1810, catered to the sons of well-to-do farmers, merchants, and professionals. In 1812, the Rockville Academy, one of about one hundred private secondary schools in the nation, opened in a two-story brick building in the west end of town.

Early principals and teachers were religious leaders who earned the academy a reputation for a solid classical education. The curriculum included surveying, navigation, geography, English grammar, Latin, Greek, French and German, reading, writing, mathematics, history, elocution, rhetoric, anatomy and physiology, bookkeeping, and mental, natural, and moral philosophy.[18]

The community nurtured the Academy's program, from which a majority of its public-spirited professionals graduated. School enrollment varied from thirty to eighty boys, many boarding with teachers or other residents. The General Assembly appropriated eight hundred dollars annually from 1811 through 1916 to educate indigent students free of charge. Annual commencement exercises brought large audiences to hear speeches, listen to music, and to see who received academic medals.

Young women of monied families could obtain a basic or ornamental education in Rockville. Academy trustees permitted a female teacher one room, recognizing that admitting female scholars helped to keep the institution afloat. Other female schools set up by women with qualifications endorsed by a male teacher opened in private homes, stores, or hotels in Rockville. Ads in local newspapers described the "branches of a substantial and polite female education"—fancy needlework, music, painting, leaf and flower preservation and framing, writing, and a foreign language.

In 1848, Misses Walley and Dugan established the Rockville Female Seminary, giving lessons in the three Rs, English, and French, but promising that "Latin, Algebra, and Geometry would be taught by a master when required."[19] Soon they moved from a small house to a large brick building on the corner of Washington Street and Commerce Lane. In 1874 the founders' new school, supported by the pastor of Saint Mary's, opened in larger quarters on Montgomery Avenue at Bridge Street under the name Saint Mary's Institute.[20]

It is likely that Rockville children—white and black—attended public primary schools before the Civil War. Surely, a populace of two hundred or three hundred would have erected a schoolhouse, and as early as 1839 the General Assembly permitted free primary schools if taxpayers agreed. Rockville residents such as Samuel Veirs encouraged primary education; he was treasurer of the Maryland Free School fund in the 1840s. When the General Assembly formally established the Maryland public school system in 1860, Rockville families were ready.

RELIGIOUS INSTITUTIONS

The period between the Revolution and the Civil War brought new people, denominations, and church buildings to the village. On the eve of the Civil War, the 365 residents of Rockville boasted six meeting houses, or churches, within as many blocks.

Antebellum Rockvillians could worship in Episcopal, Catholic, Methodist, Baptist, Christian, or Presbyterian congregations. Black and white members attended the same services, although slaves and free blacks were usually relegated to the balcony or outside. With the exception of the Episcopalians, fledgling groups met in private homes until twenty or thirty members purchased land for a church building.

Rural Rockville hosted traveling preachers one or two Sundays a month. Each denomination delineated routes convenient for its membership. The preachers stayed wherever they could, as few parsonages existed in Montgomery County before 1860. They also might turn to teaching, for the Rockville Academy courted educated men to fill positions.

Moncure Daniel Conway described his work for the Methodist Episcopal Church in 1851: "Rockville Circuit was flourishing and arduous. . . . the junior (unmarried) minister . . . was supposed to live on horseback, with his wardrobe and library in his saddlebags. . . . I could rarely stay anywhere more than a day, as there were about ten appointments to be filled each week, and these meeting-houses were distant from each other five, ten, fifteen miles. . . . It was an agricultural region, in which crime and even vices were rare. . . . The county was divided up between denominations friendly to each other and hospitable to me. . . ."[21]

Saint Mary's Roman Catholic Church, the oldest extant church building in Rockville, initially was part of a large parish. When Father James Redmond paid three hundred dollars for four acres of land near the top of the

Saint Mary's Catholic Church as it appeared in 1896.

Courtesy of Saint Mary's

Rockville Pike, his congregations included Rock Creek, Rockville, Barnesville, Seneca Creek, and Hollin's River. Eighty people attended the first mass at Saint Mary's on December 14, 1817, and they began burying their dead in the adjacent cemetery two years later.

As the number of Catholics in the area increased, additional churches organized and improvements were made to the Rockville chapel. Saint Mary's welcomed free blacks, slaves, and Irish immigrants. Energetic pastors and members erected a new steeple, built a rectory and purchased a buggy for the traveling priest, installed an organ, balcony, and Stations of the Cross, and began the fund-raising tradition of a strawberry festival before the start of the Civil War.[22]

The Episcopal Church prospered in Rockville after the American Revolution despite losing its status as Maryland's established church. Adherents replaced the old chapel of ease with a brick building at the same site near Rock Creek in 1808 but, appreciating the potential in Rockville, accepted a gift of town lots and moved into a new church on Washington Street in 1822. Perhaps due to dissension within the church over slavery or to the availability of other denominations, membership at Christ Church dipped to a low of thirty-nine by the eve of the Civil War.

Rockville Baptists formed Bethel Church in 1821, when fifteen members withdrew from the more conservative congregation on the north side of Seneca Creek. Two years later they purchased land on Jefferson Street at the western limits of Rockville, built a brick church, and established a cemetery that may be visited today. The first pastor was Joseph H. Jones, whose house still stands at 106 North Adams Street. In 1860, the Baptist congregation numbered sixty-six.

Largely due to the efforts of Francis Asbury and Robert Strawbridge, by 1773 nearly half of the 1,160 Methodists in America lived in Maryland. Rockville shared a traveling preacher with communities in Montgomery County and beyond. Trustees of the Rockville Methodist Episcopal Church bought land on Wood Lane in 1835 and soon built a church that became the center of a separate Rockville circuit. For the preacher's family, in 1852 the circuit built a parsonage in the county seat. Most of Rockville's black residents belonged to the Methodist church, where they took active though subservient roles as local preachers, exhorters (who assisted the minister), and class leaders.[23]

Local Presbyterians organized in 1822, when Rev. John Mines arrived from Leesburg, Virginia, to serve

Charles Brewer collection, courtesy of Peerless Rockville

Rockville Presbyterian Church on Court Street. This church replaced a frame building which burned in 1873.

congregations in Rockville, Darcy's Store (now Bethesda), and Captain John (Potomac). He married Elizabeth Wootton Beall, and they lived west of Rockville at Rose Hill. Reverend Mines also served as principal and then as a trustee of the Rockville Academy. In 1832, the Rockville congregation built a church at the corner of Jefferson and Adams Streets, and in 1858, they moved to a new meeting house on Court Street near the courthouse. When this building was destroyed by fire in 1873, the congregation built a brick church in its place.[24]

The Disciples of Christ, or Rockville Christian Church, organized in 1820, but met in private homes until the arrival of William McClenahan in 1835. A native of Ireland, McClenahan became head of the English Department at the Rockville Academy. His small brick home still stands on Falls Road. In 1858, church members purchased the former Presbyterian meeting house at Jefferson and Adams Street.[25]

In the period 1803 to 1860, five new faith institutions opened doors in Rockville. From the government-supported religion of the eighteenth century, the community had matured to a diverse selection of Christian denominations. Religion and education provided stability to the village.

An event the night of November 12, 1833, caused the generally religious populace to believe the end was near. A local man wrote that he was suddenly awakened by "fearful balls of fire [shooting] madly towards the earth. . . ." Entering a Rockville hotel barroom the following morning, he saw "lawyers, physicians, ministers, farmers, wagoners, sportsmen in the chase and at the card-table, all repenting of their sins, confessing to one another, taking and denying positions, and covering up tracks." For years afterward, residents recounted events of the great meteor shower with awe, and slaves commonly calculated their ages from "the night the stars fell."[26]

PEOPLE AND POLITICS

The population of Montgomery County grew slowly in the antebellum decades. In 1800, the total county numbered 15,058, 43 percent of whom were black. In 1860, the population was 18,322, nearly 70 percent of whom were white. Continued settlement augmented by Irish newcomers working on the C&O Canal produced increases in population, while the decreases resulted from poor agricultural practices and economic recessions. Rockville numbers surged to about 365 from 150 in 1800.[27]

More Marylanders lived on farms than in towns, and Rockville's economy was largely local. Farmers grew what vegetables they needed, with a small surplus for

THOSE MARTIN MEN

Three gentlemen by the surname of Martin figured prominently in the early history of Rockville. Honoré Martin, white merchant, judge, and slaveholder, enthusiastically supported progress in the town. Samuel Martin Sr., a free black man and landowner, and his son Samuel Martin Jr., who founded Haiti, Rockville's oldest black community, exemplify the changes occurring in the black population during the nineteenth century.

Honoré Martin emigrated from France to Frederick County soon after the American Revolution. He quickly linked his success with that of Montgomery Court House. Beginning in the 1780s, Martin purchased fourteen lots in the new town and proceeded to build a granary, lumber shop, tobacco and prize house, and storehouse. He lived on Washington Street.

Honoré Martin believed in Rockville. He was an incorporator of the Washington Turnpike Company in 1805. As Episcopalians and Rockville-boosters, Martin and his wife Sarah helped relocate the congregation into a new church in town in 1822.

Honoré Martin used slaves and apprentices in his business ventures. He was a leader in the Democratic-Republican party. Martin served as judge of the Orphans' Court from 1803 to 1812 and as chief judge from 1819 until 1828. When he died in 1828 at the age of seventy, he left a substantial amount of land and personal property.[28]

Purchasing a spade for sixty cents at Honoré Martin's estate sale was a free black man named Samuel Martin. For a brief period the two Martins had jointly owned Lot 32, which faced Washington Street just north of Wood Lane. Little is known about Samuel Martin, but at his death in 1837, he left "a log dwelling house 40' by 16' and a paled [fenced] garden in good order" on Lot 32. The inventory of his estate also listed livestock, furniture, and bushels of cabbage, potatoes, and other vegetables.[29]

Martin's second wife Hellen willed the property to Dr. Horatio Clagett of Washington County in return for "support and clothing" of her daughter Mahala, who was then Clagett's slave.[30] Eventually, through the courts, Lot 32 became the property of Samuel Martin Jr.

Samuel Martin Jr. was born a slave in Rockville in 1800. By 1842 a free man, in addition to the house on Washington Street, he owned eight and one-half acres north of town. The way from Frederick Road to his farmhouse became known as Martin's Lane. Martin also owned a small number of slaves, who may have been his wife and children, and kept five head of cattle.

market. Nearly every farm kept a small flock of sheep, a few dairy cows, and hogs for family use and for sale to local butchers. Farmers hauled grain to a nearby mill to process flour and cornmeal and sent excess bushels to Washington or Baltimore for sale. A few farmers shipped butter to city markets.[31]

Maryland's early rejection of property qualifications generated interest, and political parties courted Rockville leaders. The Peter family of Georgetown, Darnestown, and Rockville dominated the Democratic party from 1815. In the 1830s, Rockville attorney Richard Johns Bowie helped organize the Whig party, which ruled the General Assembly through the 1850s. By the Civil War, Montgomery County politics centered in Rockville, the jurisdiction's county seat and largest settlement, home to lawyers, public officials, and prominent merchants.[32]

Photograph by Dean Evangelista

The log section of 22 Martin's Lane was constructed by slave carpenter Alfred Ross for his family before 1860. It is still owned by his descendants.

SLAVERY IN ROCKVILLE

The agricultural economy of Maryland, a southern state, depended upon a sizable black labor force. Even nonslaveowners felt obliged to protect the institution for reasons of racial solidarity as well as economics. But slavery strained Maryland's traditional middle temperament. In addition to national North-South dissension, the state divided internally along settlement lines. Rockville and western Montgomery County felt closer to southern Maryland's slaveholding tradition than to northern Maryland's free labor, overwhelmingly white population.[33]

On the issue of slavery, Rockville residents and institutions were in step with their region. While there were exceptions, most Rockville planters and merchants who could afford slaves owned them. They purchased labor for work and at home. When Rockville slave trader Charles Price advertised "Negroes Wanted" and that he was "just below the Catholic Church in Rockville"[34] in a proslavery newspaper published by the county sheriff, local citizens accepted these situations. While some individuals did not own slaves on principle, they were in the minority in Montgomery County.

Temperament and ownership patterns affected the lives of Rockville slaves. Although slaves comprised about 30 percent of the population just prior to the Civil War, local owners maintained a pattern of holding small numbers of slaves.[35] State law protected them from abuse and severe physical punishment and required masters to provide adequate food, clothing, shelter, and rest. However, treatment varied greatly from household to household, and laws were not well enforced. Slave and master developed a close association as they worked side by side to plant, harvest, cook, and sew. In addition to farm and domestic work, slaves might be hired out for odd jobs or to small manufacturers. As generations of slaves stayed with the same white families, stable domestic arrangements existed, but members of one slave family frequently belonged to different owners. Native blacks were less likely to be sold South away from their families, and many were permitted to earn money on their own time.

Experiences of Rockville slaves demonstrate slavery's ongoing moral and economic issues. State law and the nearness of free territory worked to keep the worst features of slavery in check, as owners were concerned about their public image and anxious about uprisings, which would deprive them of their property.

Alfred Ross was a slave owned by the Beall family, who lived in a large brick house on Commerce Lane in Rockville. Rooms for household slaves and domestic servants at the Beall-Dawson House likely were above the kitchen wing, but other Beall slaves lived in quarters elsewhere on the acreage. An 1827 inventory at Upton Beall's death listed twenty-five slaves. When his daughter Jane was assessed for twenty-two slaves in

1853, one was twenty-three-year-old Alfred, a carpenter who maintained a life-long relationship with the Beall family.

The dwelling built by Alfred Ross, the man on Jane Beall's list, and his wife Jane still stands in Rockville today. The distance of the log house from the Beall mansion, close to the farmstead of free blacks, suggests the trust that existed between one Rockville mistress and slave. The property on Martin's Lane is still owned by descendants of Alfred and Jane Ross.[36]

Josiah Henson's experience in Rockville became known through the famous novel *Uncle Tom's Cabin*, adapted from Henson's memoirs by Harriet Beecher Stowe. Henson was born in Charles County, Maryland in 1789. Five years later, he watched his brothers and sisters auctioned off. His mother was purchased by Isaac Riley, a farmer and blacksmith who lived on the Rockville-George Town road. According to Henson, his mother begged Riley to buy her youngest son, but Riley brutally kicked her away.

Henson was bought by Adam Robb, a Rockville taverner, who held him with about forty other slaves. Robb soon arranged to send the ill five year old to Isaac Riley in return for horse-shoeing if he lived, no payment required if he died. Josiah regained his health and lived on Riley's plantation for nearly thirty years. Henson later described Isaac Riley as coarse and vulgar, unprincipled, and cruel to his slaves.

In 1825, Riley sent Henson and twenty-one other slaves to his brother Amos Riley in Kentucky. Henson saved money to purchase his freedom by preaching but, when he returned to Rockville, Riley would not honor the papers. A few years later Henson escaped to Ontario, Canada with his wife and two children. There he became a leader in the fugitive slave colony, publishing his memoirs in order to raise funds to support the venture.

The Life of Josiah Henson, Formerly a Slave, published in 1849, caught the eye of Harriet Beecher Stowe, who later explained that her 1852 novel, *Uncle Tom's Cabin*, was heavily based upon Henson's experiences. The novel produced so much sympathy for American slaves that President Abraham Lincoln later greeted Mrs. Stowe as "the little woman who wrote the book that made this big war." Josiah Henson, the sickly Rockville slave, died in Canada at the age of ninety-four in 1883. The log kitchen where Henson slept the night he returned from Kentucky still stands, now attached to a modern dwelling on the old Riley plantation.[37]

Courtesy of Montgomery County Historical Society

Josiah Henson, slave, preacher, and fugitive abolitionist, lived near Montgomery Court House where he learned of the Underground Railroad. Henson's autobiography portrayed the hardship of slave life in early Rockville, a story upon which Harriet Beecher Stowe based her character Uncle Tom in her famous novel.

FREEDOM'S MANY FACES

Rockville residents debated slavery and abolition as vigorously as their counterparts elsewhere in America. Most obeyed Maryland's laws which permitted slavery and discouraged escape. Some Rockville slaveholders manumitted slaves in their lifetimes, as did John H. Higgins at the demand of his wife Sophia. Upton Beall and other owners freed slaves through their wills. A few, such as Richard Johns Bowie of Glenview, tried to interest free blacks in a colony in Liberia through the Maryland Colonization Society. However, these efforts met with minimal results.[38]

Maryland's free black population increased steadily in number between 1803 and 1860. While most lived in cities such as Baltimore, in 1860 they comprised only 8 percent of rural Montgomery County's population. They lived throughout the town of Rockville. James Jones, a slave who obtained his freedom in 1815, purchased lots on Adams Street two years later and subdivided them. By the 1830s, Samuel Martin Jr. had established a farmstead on the Frederick Road, where the road into his property is still known as Martin's Lane. The home of Nathan Martin, a blacksmith, was on Washington Street near Wood Lane. Ann Wilson, a free black woman who likely was married to a slave, lived on Falls Road across from Rose Hill.

Many slaves opted for escaping to freedom. However, this pursuit was dangerous. Reward notices for slaves who disappeared from Montgomery Court House appeared in local newspapers before 1800. Whites, slaves, and free blacks who helped runaways were treated harshly. Others watched for runaways in hopes of collecting reward money.

By the 1830s Maryland, as the northernmost slaveholding state, was well established on the Underground Railroad. This network of antislavery activists and sympathizers who helped slaves escape to freedom had its southern terminus in Washington, D.C., which had a substantial free black population. The first destination was the Mason-Dixon line, then Philadelphia, New York, and Boston, with Canada the northern end. Loosely organized and often spontaneous, the railroad's operation required secrecy. Caution was vital, for missteps led to imprisonment, punishment, being sold South, and constraints on later escape attempts.

Slaves followed the Potomac River, Rock Creek, or roads such as the Rockville Pike through Montgomery County. In Washington, abolitionist Jacob Bigelow, from his Washington Gas Light Company office, secretly connected local runaways with safe-houses in the District, Montgomery County, upper Maryland, and into the free state of Pennsylvania. In 1856 he helped Ned Brannum, a Rockville slave, escape on a ship carrying coal from Georgetown through the Chesapeake Bay and on to Philadelphia. Brannum's owner, Henry Harding, offered a reward of two hundred dollars for his return. In the *Sentinel*, editor Fields warned that, as other Rockville slaves disappeared around that same time, there may have been a conspiracy among them.[39]

Five children of free blacks Paul and Milly Edmonson of Norbeck were slaves. In 1848, they escaped aboard the *Pearl*, a ship headed from Washington to New Jersey. After the plot was discovered, the Edmonson children were sent to slave markets in New Orleans, freed only with funds raised by New York abolitionists, Methodist ministers, and such notables as Rev. Henry Ward Beecher and singer Jenny Lind.[40]

One of the most dramatic and best documented escapes was that of Ann Maria Weems, who lived in the Rockville home of slave trader Charles M. Price. After unsuccessful attempts to purchase the young girl, Jacob Bigelow, the Washington conductor, arranged for her escape. In league with William Still, an Underground Railroad stationmaster, he sent her north

$500 REWARD.

RAN away on Sunday night, the 23d instant, before 12 o'clock, from the subscriber, residing in Rockville, Montgomery county, Md., my NEGRO GIRL "Ann Maria Weems," about 15 years of age; a bright mullatto; some small freckles on her face; slender person, thick suit of hair, inclined to be sandy. Her parents are free, and reside in Washington, D. C. It is evident she was taken away by some one in a carriage, probably by a white man, by whom she may be carried beyond the limits of the State of Maryland.

I will give the above reward for her apprehension and detention so that I get her again.

sep 29—3t CHAS. M. PRICE.

Courtesy of Montgomery County Historical Society

Reward notice from the Sentinel*, December 8, 1855. Frequent descriptions of runaways were printed in Rockville's newspapers, indicating the degree of discontent that Maryland's slaves felt about their condition.*

disguised as a coachman named Joe Wright until she reached Philadelphia. While Price offered a five hundred dollar reward for her return, the girl continued through New York to relatives in Canada.[41]

The experiences of other runaways were not so positive. Rewards for informers, white or black, were sizable. The *Sentinel* reported arrests of fugitives and warned of escapes. After 1850, the Fugitive Slave Law required the return of runaways to their owners. In his memoirs, fugitive slave John Thompson wrote of men and dogs searching for him and a companion as they traversed Rockville woods and fields. In 1845, a group of forty armed runaways from Charles County were pursued on the road toward Frederick and captured. The runaways were arrested and thrown into the jail in Rockville.

FARMING, INDUSTRY, AND BUSINESS

Throughout the nineteenth century and into the early twentieth, most residents of the Rockville area described their occupations as farming. Farm fields, pasture, and woodlots surrounded the small town.

The nature of agriculture changed dramatically between 1803 and 1860. Although planters had gradually improved tobacco production through the late eighteenth and early nineteenth centuries, they recognized that farming practices took their toll on the land. As the crop yield diminished with loss of nutrients in the soil, farmers abandoned their worn-out fields and moved westward to cut new trees and plant new land. By 1840, Montgomery County was known as the "Sahara of Maryland." Lands on either side of the Rockville Pike were, in one observer's words, "a succession of uninclosed [*sic*] old fields."[42]

County farmers fought to maintain their livelihood by diversifying. Near Rockville, they planted wheat, corn, rye, and other grains. Led by Quakers in Sandy Spring, local farmers experimented with crop rotation, deep plowing, improved agricultural machinery, and the use of guano or bird droppings as fertilizer. One innovator was Rockville farmer Beverly R. Codwise, who in 1867 patented a lever-type of wagon brake.[43] By the eve of the Civil War, although land values remained low, Montgomery County's agricultural economy had improved.

Courtesy of Menare Foundation Archives

Ann Maria Weems escaped from Rockville on the Underground Railroad in 1855, one of an estimated one hundred thousand slaves who fled bondage 1830–1865.

Farmers also expanded their markets. Baltimore, with its huge population and road access, replaced Bladensburg as a market for Rockville products. Despite its distance from Rockville, the C&O Canal, which opened in 1832, offered another means for farmers to send produce westward or down to George Town, which maintained its status in the growing interregional economy.

Discussions about farm improvements led to organized agricultural efforts. In 1846, Rockville farmers, including Richard Johns Bowie of Glenview farm, helped to establish the Montgomery County Agricultural Society. Two years later, Court House Square overflowed with displays of agricultural implements at the first county fair. The register of wills opened his office for exhibits of household manufactures, and the county clerk's place teemed with fruits and vegetables. Women competed for cash prizes in the categories of homespun fabrics, fancy handwork, pickles, preserves, butter, cheese, and honey. Men exhibited livestock on the grounds of the Beall-Dawson House. Richard Johns Bowie spoke to society members.[44]

In a few years the fair moved to Samuel T. Stonestreet's woodlot adjacent to Saint Mary's Church. The annual fairs became week-long gatherings to showcase innovation, compete, and socialize. The property on the Rockville Pike was used until 1932, after which much of the land became Richard Montgomery High School.[45]

Richard Johns Bowie managed one of Rockville's most productive farms. Soon after marrying Catharine Williams of Hagerstown in 1833, he began to acquire land on the road to Baltimore, about two miles east of Rockville. By 1860, the Bowies owned a comfortable farmhouse that they named Glenview, numerous outbuildings, and 508 acres of land, 368 of which were cultivated. The land, worked by twenty-one slaves and valued at a little over seventeen dollars per acre, produced corn, wheat, potatoes, hay, and rye. Livestock at Glenview included cows, horses, oxen, sheep, pigs, and donkeys.[46]

The shift to grain production from tobacco provided ample grist for new Rockville industry. In the antebellum period, four mills operated on Rockville area waterways. Muncaster, Veirs, and Needwood (later called Horner) Mills on Rock Creek and Wootton's Mill on Watts Branch were small, seasonal, family-run operations grinding wheat and sawing logs for local farmers. In the days before packaged, mass-marketed flour and cornmeal or machine-cut lumber, these water-powered local mills provided vital services to Rockville residents and businesses.

Other small industries appeared on Rockville farms prior to the Civil War. European grape vines usually succumbed to American insects and disease, but a few produced local wine. The Catawba grape, which may have come to Rockville by way of Clarksburg and New Market, grew in the Rockville area at Zadok Magruder's in Redland and Mrs. Lewis Beall's Rose Hill farm on Falls Road.[47] Jane Beall earned extra income at the Beall-Dawson House from the sale of homemade wine and butter. In another

NINETEENTH CENTURY MILLS IN THE ROCKVILLE AREA

For nearly two hundred years, small industry on the banks of Rockville waterways served area residents and businesses. Enterprising millers harnessed the power of Piedmont streams with huge wheels and millstones which could grind, crush, saw, and cut. Grains were converted into flour and meal for home use and for market. Mills were important to the commercial life of Rockville and as places for farmers to exchange news and discuss current problems. Local patrons respected millers as hard and honest workers.

Two early mills took advantage of the water power on Rock Creek. Muncaster Mill northwest of Rockville, one of the longest operating of Montgomery County's mills, dated from 1763. Millers Joseph Elgar, then George Robertson, Otho, Edwin and William Muncaster, George Gingle, and William Gloyd, served Rockville farmers until 1925. Needwood Mill, which opened nearby in the 1760s, was operated in the nineteenth century by John and Frank Horner. The millrace and stone foundation of the grist- and sawmill may still be seen near Avery Road.

Courtesy of Historical Society of Washington, D.C.

Wootton's Mill as it appeared in the early twentieth century. At one time Rockville waterways supported several water-powered mills, an obsolete industry by the mid-1920s.

On Watts Branch west of Rockville, a mill on property owned by the Woottons was functioning by about 1820. An overshot wheel, where the weight of water conducted through the race to the top of the wheel caused it to turn, powered the grist- and sawmill. After the death of her husband, Dr. Turner Wootton, in 1855, Olivia Wootton leased the mill and the miller's house to Benjamin F. Sparrow. Although the mill no longer exists, the log miller's house is still perched above the creek.

In 1838, Samuel C. Veirs purchased several hundred acres of land about three miles south of Rockville along Rock Creek. He built a house on high ground which he named Meadow Hall. Its terraced gardens are still visible in the woods below Meadow Hall Drive. Veirs's grist- and sawmill business, Rock Creek Mills, drew customers from Rockville and Mitchell's Crossroads (later named Wheaton), through the route that became known as Veirs Mill Road.

venture, Rockville farmers joined the short-lived silk craze that swept Maryland in the late 1830s, but costly mulberry trees and silkworms never supported a profitable industry. In the 1850s, James and Mary Anderson tried growing sugar cane that soon perished in an uncooperative climate.[48]

As the population of Montgomery County grew, so did the demand for goods and services in the county seat. Taverns remained popular for visitors and town residents, as did hotels serving food, liquors, and *segars*. Merchants frequently opened new stores, offering specific wares or selling everything from food to agricultural implements to clothing, but most of them did not survive long. Small manufacturing operations such as Jesse Leach's saddlery of the 1820s gave way in later years to ready-made items available from middlemen who sold their wares through shops in Rockville.[49]

By the 1830s, Rockville residents could patronize a wide range of establishments offering a variety of items. Rockville had several tailors and a boot and shoemaker. Dry goods manufactured in Baltimore were sold by local merchants. William E. Pumphrey, a carpenter who began building houses in Rockville in the 1830s, added coffin-making and undertaking services in the mid 1850s. Still, those who desired special items or could afford to shop in Washington City did so.

Lawyers, county officials, and clerks valued proximity to Court House Square. Hotel proprietors, restaurateurs, and taverners opened offices and rooms for litigants, jurors, and visitors, particularly during court sessions. Peter Leapley advertised that persons stopping at the Washington Hotel "may rely upon their horses being well attended to."[50] In 1850, the town, population about four hundred, claimed six hotels, six resident physicians, seven attorneys, eight dealers in dry goods and groceries, and even a baker. By 1860, a stone cutter had set up shop in Rockville.[51]

Despite these advances, antebellum Rockville largely retained its hinterland village atmosphere. In 1813, the General Assembly passed a bill to "prevent geese and Swine from going at large in the Town of Rockville." It encouraged free white persons to impound any geese or swine wandering around the town and to bring them to public sale, where half the proceeds would go to the captor and the other half to the owner.[52]

THE COUNTY PRESENCE

Joseph Scott's 1807 account of a "brick courthouse and jail, without either taste or elegance" described Court House Square early in the nineteenth century. The courthouse was busy, particularly during semiannual court sessions. Since 1792 the clerk had been required to hold office hours at the courthouse every day except Sunday from 9:00 A.M. until sunset. He maintained lists of attorneys admitted to the Montgomery County bar, who in the first third of the nineteenth century included Roger Brooke Taney, Francis Scott Key, Zadok Magruder, and Richard Johns Bowie.[53]

As Montgomery County grew, so did the need for government space. In 1810, with the county population nearly 18,000, the commissioners augmented the little courthouse with a separate building for the clerk and his records. In 1840, a new courthouse opened on the public square. Originally a two-story brick structure with one-story wings, it was sufficiently sized to contain all local services. In 1872, the county raised the wings to the height of the main building.

The Montgomery County Commissioners continually improved Court House Square, installing an iron fence around the square and permitting Nicholas Offutt to erect hay and cattle scales in the public triangle north of the courthouse. They paid Henry Lyday ten dollars a year to keep horses and cows outside of the fence and to prevent visitors from hitching their horses to it.[54]

The county jail, built in 1801 near Court House Square, also saw considerable activity. In addition to the jailer, the building held persons convicted of horse stealing, running away from slavery, and the felony and misdemeanor crimes with which we are familiar today. Whipping was common, as was imprisonment for nonpayment of debts. In the years before the Civil War, crimes such as assisting a runaway, allowing free blacks and slaves to congregate, or selling a free black as a slave merited punishment. However, the most common crimes of the 1850s involved liquor (sales on the Sabbath, without a license, or to a slave) and assault and battery.[55]

The county commissioners purchased 50 acres in 1789 to care for its neediest citizens. Trustees of the poor supervised an almshouse with an adjacent work house for "vagrants, beggars, vagabonds and offenders as may be committed."[56] More land was added in 1825, 1876, 1882, and 1902, for a total of one 147.75 acres. Today this property, which straddles highway I-270, contains the Detention Center and Tower Oaks development.

The almshouse, also known as the Poor Farm, at any given time held ten to fifty people. Most were aged, blind, crippled, insane, or deaf and dumb. White and black inmates had separate quarters. An overseer or keeper lived on the farm with his family, as did laborers and servants. A doctor, usually from Rockville, was always on call. For those with no alternative, a *potter's field* in the woods served as the burial ground.

THE TOWN EXPANDS

By the time the surveyor completed Rockville's plan in 1803, the young nation had elected three presidents. What first in Williamsburgh had been called the Main Road, First and Second Streets, and West and First Lanes, were renamed Jefferson, Washington, and Adams Streets and Commerce, Middle, and Wood Lanes. Adding a government building in the new central square caused through traffic to be redirected from Jefferson Street into Court House Square. Within a few years, people called the main road leading southeast from the courthouse the "Turnpike Road."

In 1805, Elizabeth Crabb, widow of Congressman Jeremiah Crabb, petitioned to enlarge the town boundaries. The General Assembly appointed three commissioners to survey eight acres east of Court House Square, and the First Addition to Rockville was recorded in the Land Records twenty years later. It included sixteen lots and new streets named Madison

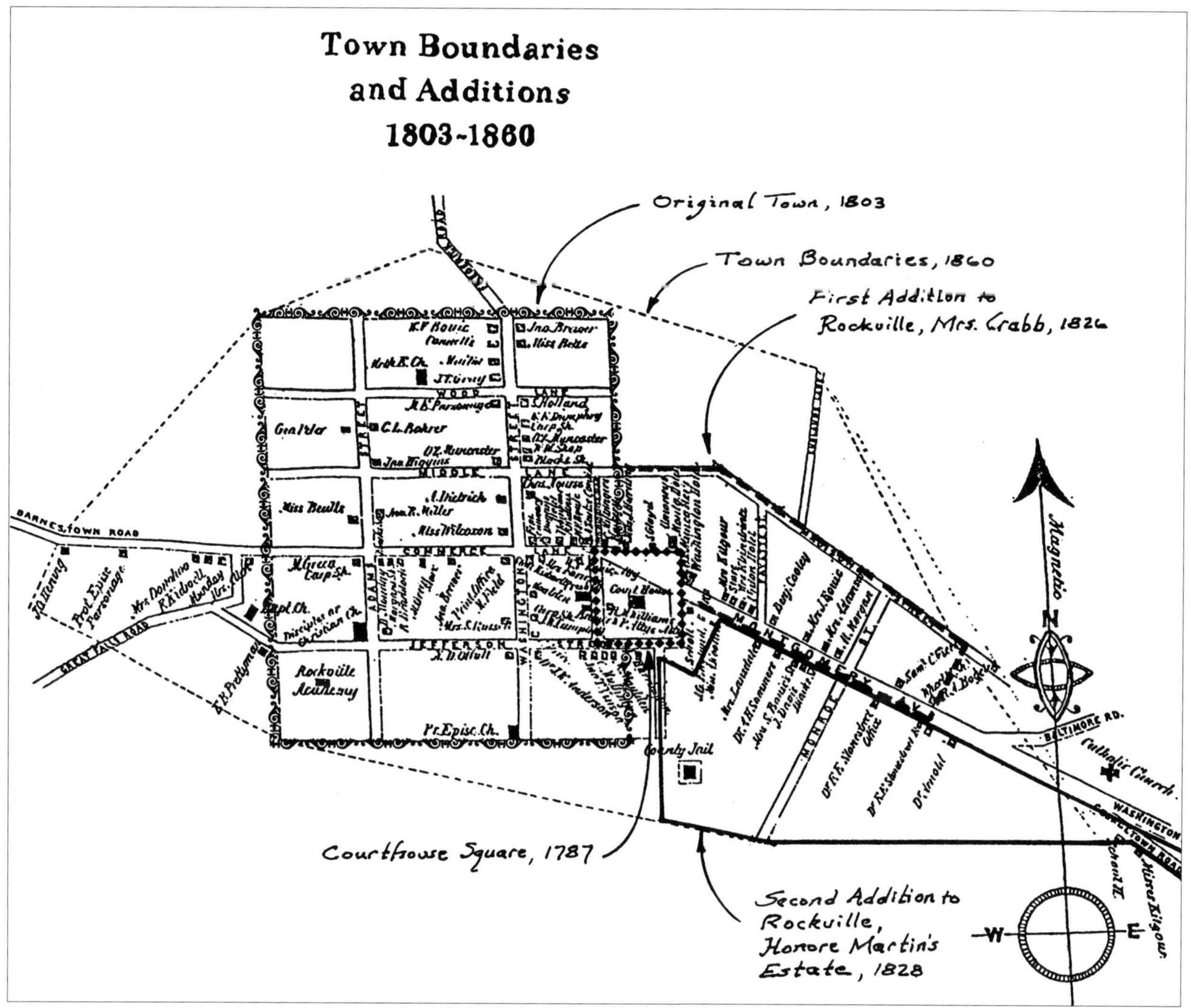

Notations by C. A. Burroughs on Plan of Rockville, Martenet and Bond's "Map of Montgomery County, Maryland," 1865

Map of Rockville about the time of incorporation, showing the original town, with additions.

and Monroe. Another street and also a Rockville hotel honored the Marquis de Lafayette, the young Frenchman who captivated Americans during the War for Independence and again during his triumphal return tour in 1824–25.[57]

With this addition to the town, the diagonal main street, recently called the Turnpike Road, took on the grand name of Montgomery Avenue. On the north side of the courthouse, the triangle formed by cutting the diagonal became a public park. The center of Rockville maintained that configuration until urban renewal in the 1960s.

The next addition to Rockville soon followed. Part of Honoré Martin's land on the south side of Montgomery Avenue, just east of Court House Square, was subdivided after his death into one-half and one-acre lots. Lots 86 through 102 in Mrs. Crabb's addition and Lots 1 through 18 of Martin land went up for sale.[58]

Between 1803 and 1860, many Rockville lots filled in with buildings, although speculators held others. The original town became more dense, and the number of improved properties more than doubled to about ninety by 1860. Prosperous men such as Upton Beall, John Braddock, and Samuel T. Stonestreet built their homes of brick, described in the tax records as *mansion houses*.

Latrobe sketchbook VI-14. Courtesy of The Maryland Historical Society, Baltimore, Maryland

Watercolor by Washington architect Benjamin Latrobe entitled "Out of Robb's Window, Montgomery Court House," 1811.

Even as it continued to grow, Rockville remained a modest commercial center surrounded by farmland. A walk of eight blocks would take a person from one end of town to another. Dwellings mingled on streets and lanes with blacksmith shops, offices, taverns, tinsmiths, grocers, and an assortment of stores. Streets were dusty in dry weather, muddy when it rained. There were no sidewalks, street lights, or storm drains. Animals wandered the streets, compounding the odors from backyard privies and manure piles.

Black and white owners and tenants lived evenly throughout the village, and on small farms nearby. Most laborers and slaves resided in the same household with their employers. A few free black families lived on Washington Street and in the poorly drained area on Middle Lane behind the main street.

INCORPORATION

Although it had evolved from a crossroads in the 1750s to a thriving center of local government and commerce, Rockville in 1860 was merely the largest settlement in Montgomery County, Maryland. Residents referred to it as a village.

From 1776, Rockville was ruled by the state legislature in Annapolis and the county commissioners. The town plat, a lottery for a fire engine and schoolhouse, impoundment of at-large animals, and a bailiff all required authorization from the General Assembly. State government provided for court-appointed trustees to improve town streets and to survey new lots. The configuration of county districts, redrawn several times in the nineteenth century, affected Rockville's influence in state and local issues and elections. By mid-century, residents began to dream of something more.

On Saturday evening, January 28, 1860, Rockville citizens met at the courthouse to "take into consideration the propriety of petitioning the legislature of Maryland for an act of incorporation for the village of Rockville."[59] Those assembled unanimously favored the idea and appointed a committee of three attorneys—John Brewer, John Vinson, and William Veirs Bouic—to prepare the legislation and report at a meeting the following week.

The *Sentinel* noted the result in its March 16, 1860, edition:

> INCORPORATED—An act to incorporate the town of Rockville, as adopted by our citizens, passed both branches of the Legislature the last night of the session, and is now a law. The first Monday of May next is, we believe, the day fixed by the act for the election of three Town Commissioners and a Police officer—SAMUEL C. VEIRS and LAWRENCE LYDDANE, Esqs., are appointed judges to hold the first election. We hope soon to have our streets graded and otherwise improved, and our sidewalks nicely paved, which must greatly enhance the value of our town property. Let us all unite as a unit in these much needed improvements.

Such a momentous event received no more press, except to remind voters of the election. On March 19, 1860, Mary Anderson wrote to her husband James, who worked in Washington: "Mr. England was here yesterday. He says Dr. Harding and Duvall [local representatives in the General Assembly] were received in any thing but a flattering manner on their return

THE INCORPORATION OF ROCKVILLE

Passed Maryland General Assembly: March 10, 1860:

> Whereas, it is represented to the General Assembly, That it would greatly contribute to the advantage and improvement of the village of Rockville, in Montgomery county, if the same should be placed under the care and regulation of certain commissioners, to be elected by the citizens thereof, and vested with sufficient powers to forward and effect the purposes intended; therefore. . . . Be it enacted by the General Assembly of Maryland, That the inhabitants of the town of Rockville in Montgomery county, are a body corporate by the name of the commissioners for Rockville, and by that name may have perpetual succession, sue and be sued, and have and use a common seal.[60]

from Annapolis. There is great dissatisfaction about incorporating the town of Rockville and other matters to which I did not pay much attention."[61]

Regardless, the incorporation of Rockville proved to be a vital determinant of its history, second only to selection as county seat. The 1860 Act put in place the framework of Rockville government and its relationship to Montgomery County. The town limits were described. Inhabitants would elect three commissioners to serve for one year without pay, the person receiving the most votes acting as president. Town employees were specified: a clerk to keep minutes, a supervisor of the streets, and an elected bailiff to collect taxes and keep the peace. The Act stated that the commissioners may pass ordinances "as they may deem beneficial to the town" but not be contrary to state law. The town could assess real and personal property and levy taxes, but could not outspend its income. Lastly, and with far-reaching consequences, public buildings and other county property in Rockville were not subject to taxation. However, Montgomery commissioners were to appropriate funds for the improvement of Rockville streets.[62]

Rockville was the first town in Montgomery County to incorporate. When both it and Rising Sun in Cecil County became municipal corporations in 1860, they joined forty-five other Maryland settlements of all sizes in taking control of their future character and growth. The new charter made direct decision making and accountability for the most local of concerns possible.

At the start of incorporation, Rockville's governing body had few of the powers it would later possess. In 1860, the commissioners could only enforce whatever local ordinances the General Assembly specifically passed for Rockville. For example, Rockville's commissioners had no power to annex land nor to review and approve land use. Any changes required authorization by the state, a process that would continue until amendment of the Maryland constitution in 1954.

The seeds for a thriving community, present in 1803, began sprouting over the next half century. On the eve of the American Civil War, Rockville had in place handsome residential and commercial buildings, churches and schools, a post office, adequate communications and transportation for the time, the beginnings of self-government, a solid business base and a small amount of industry, and the assurance of a continued county judicial and administrative presence. All of these characteristics signaled economic stability and strengthened Rockville's opportunities for success as an urban center in a rural jurisdiction adjacent to the nation's capital.

Chapter Four

WAR AND RECONCILIATION 1860–1873

"I broke through the charging columns with the pistol balls flying, rushed through the back way to the Church. . . . I remember nothing but the thick rank and clanking of sabres, yells and furious charges. They were pouring in at every lane and road from the Falls."

Dora Higgins

On July 20, 1861, the sound of cannonfire startled Charles Abert at Homewood, his farm on the road from Rockville to Norbeck, now Manor Country Club. Abert, a Washington attorney and staunch Union man who attended many local political meetings with his friend, Judge Richard Johns Bowie of Glenview, and whose three brothers were officers in the U.S. Army, later learned that the noise came from across the river in Manassas, at the first Battle of Bull Run.[1] That day the first Rockville soldier perished in the war. He was Levin Hoskinson, a nineteen-year-old apprentice printer at the *Montgomery County Sentinel*, who served the Confederate cause in the Seventh Virginia Infantry.[2]

Rockville residents made painful choices in the early 1860s—a time of divisiveness, coexistence, and adjustment. They chose sides for philosophical, practical, political, economic, and family reasons. With blue and gray troops constantly moving through the county, the town could not escape the conflict. Rockville's role in the Civil War, while of limited national importance, greatly affected the lives of its citizens. Strong leadership from Rockville residents on both Confederate and Union sides, the town's relatively large population and its status as county seat, and Rockville's strategic location in a slaveholding border state close to Washington made it a flashpoint of action and debate.

ROCKVILLE IN THE CIVIL WAR

In 1860 and 1861, as Americans debated whether or not to remain in the Union, Rockville residents were keenly aware that they lived in a state where slaveholding was a zealously protected right. Although Rockville residents fought in Northern and Southern armies and the town's noncombatants supported both sides, majority sentiment was clearly for the Confederate cause. Matthew Fields, editor of Rockville's weekly newspaper, was twice arrested for his anti-Union writings. Whenever rebel armies came to Rockville, they fully expected a welcome from the local populace.

Union strategists viewed Rockville—the largest settlement and the legal, political, economic, and geographic center of Montgomery County—as vital to Northern interests. It was close to Washington, D.C. and to crossings of the Potomac River through which Confederate forces could attack. Maryland had to be kept in the fold, for the Federal capital could not afford to be surrounded by enemy territory. Rockville's location on the major road between Washington and the West was of strategic import for troop movements and territorial control. The town saw frequent skirmishes and occupation, as local residents contributed men, supplies, horses, food, and moral support to both South and North.

The conflict left Rockville depleted of livestock, in mourning for lost sons, and resolved to make the best of a changed economic, social, and political situation. The upheaval caused by the Civil War and its aftermath influenced Rockville for decades. Those who experienced the war passed its memories on to their children.[3]

CHOOSING SIDES

America's centuries-old debate over slavery reached a climax in the presidential election of November 1860. From a field of four candidates, Rockville (and Maryland) split the overwhelming majority of its votes in favor of Southern Democrat John Breckinridge and John Bell of the Constitutional Union Party. The nation, however, selected Republican Abraham Lincoln, and set into motion a series of rapid-fire events as the election results came in. Starting with South Carolina in December 1860, states south of the Mason-Dixon line began to secede from the Union.

Political leaders of Montgomery County met at the courthouse on January 1, 1861 "to confer with each other upon the perilous condition of the country, and to adopt such measures as the exigencies of the times, in their wisdom, may demand." Two prominent Rockville attorneys with contrary opinions, Democrat John Brewer and Unionist John T. Vinson, attempted to navigate the debate, and pro-Union Richard Johns Bowie called for calm and patience. Resolutions were proposed along party lines, and attendees suggested committees which would formulate other resolutions. The assembled, who voted 133 to 131 that Maryland should make every attempt to remain in the Union, agreed that the federal government must continue to protect the institution and practice of slaveholding.[4]

The Confederate States of America (CSA) organized in February, and on March 4, Abraham Lincoln was inaugurated president of the United States. On April 12, the rebels fired on Fort Sumter in Charleston harbor. Three days later, Lincoln called for seventy-five thousand volunteers and declared the ports of all seceded states under blockade. Maryland entered the fray on April 19, when local citizens attacked Federal troops as they changed trains in Baltimore. Union troops occupied the city for the remainder of the war.

On April 22, Governor Thomas Hicks called a special session of the Maryland General Assembly in Frederick. Despite the 1860 legislature's resolution to cast Maryland's lot with the South if the Union were dissolved, Hicks attempted to juggle pressures, rumors, and the highly charged atmosphere. Marylanders in and out of public office debated secession, but no consensus existed. In the end, Hicks's support of the Union and Lincoln's suspension of the writ of habeas corpus, a bold measure that enabled the military to arrest anyone in the General Assembly suspected of disloyalty and hold them indefinitely, kept Maryland firmly with the North.[5]

Lincoln also acted quickly to hold the Union position in Maryland and to protect the city of Washington. Federal troops moved into Baltimore, Annapolis, Cumberland, Havre de Grace, and points along the railroad. By June 1861 they occupied Rockville in a military action known as the Rockville Expedition. One of the first actions of Union soldiers was to disarm the Rockville Riflemen, a militia unit formed in December 1859 and captained by pro-South State's Attorney William Veirs Bouic.

From June 10 to July 7, troops under the command of Col. Charles P. Stone raided homes and shops of suspected "secesh" Rockville residents, seizing weapons and arresting outspoken anti-Unionists. Stone then moved to Darnestown, Seneca, and Poolesville after leaving detachments in Rockville to guard routes into Washington. By that time, approximately thirty-eight thousand Union infantry, artillery, and cavalry were stationed in Montgomery County.[6]

By the end of June 1861, the field at the top of the Rockville Pike near Saint Mary's Church had become a camping ground for Union troops assigned to the area or passing through. The nearby fairgrounds were strewn with tents, livestock, campfires, and New Englanders who had never traveled so far South.

Union soldiers wrote home about Rockville. "The regiment . . . encamped upon the Montgomery County Fairgrounds, a most delightful place which they christened 'Camp Lincoln'. The first impression produced upon the people of Rockville seemed to be one of fear and consternation. . . . the prevailing sentiment of the people were secesh. But a single Union flag was to be seen in Rockville and that was displayed in the private yard of Rev. L. S. Russell, rector of the Episcopal Church . . ." Despite the prevailing Southern sentiment, a New Yorker noted that the people of Rockville "showed many courtesies to the members of the regiment during the brief encampment." Another soldier described Rockville as "by far the prettiest village these blue clad wanderers had seen since passing through New Jersey."[7]

Not all of the descriptions were flattering, however. A reporter for the *Philadelphia Inquirer* wrote:

> The main route from Washington up passes through Rockville, a small and dilapidated looking town of four or five hundred inhabitants. . . . Rockville contains, besides some four "hotels", the ruins of a jail, a newspaper office (alas! the poor printer), a couple of lawyers' offices, courthouse and a prominent looking brick house, in which our informant said there resided "three old maids, who wouldn't marry the best man who ever lived, if he offered hisself to 'em."
>
> It is unnecessary to describe this venerable town. It does not differ from the generality of small villages in the interior of Maryland, being made up of the usual number of "setters" on the tavern stoops, decrepid colored persons, and an air of monotony that is painful to one who has been accustomed to the din of city life. . . .[8]

Courtesy of Mary Dawson Gray

Mollie Dawson, who lived at the family farm on the Rockville Pike, was nine years old when her father was captured by Confederate cavalryman Jeb Stuart in 1863.

The courthouse hosted numerous meetings in 1861. As most Montgomery County citizens favored the South, the predominant subject was dissolving Maryland's ties with the Union. *The New York Times* described a meeting on September 7 where secessionists elected delegates to a convention in Baltimore. Rockville attorneys William Veirs Bouic and George Peter, editor Matthew Fields, wheelwright Melchisdec Green, and Ben Cooley, the mail contractor, attended, as did "rampant Secessionist" John W. Jones, a Rockville merchant whose building housed the telegraph office. The *Times* wrote of secessionists "armed with revolvers and knives, striking terror to the hearts of the quiet Union men."[9]

A few days later, Union soldiers arrested attorneys Bouic and Brewer in their Rockville homes on the charge of "having attended a disloyal meeting" and carried them under guard to Gen. Nathaniel Banks near Darnestown.[10] After their imprisonment for three weeks in Washington without a hearing, U.S. Postmaster General Montgomery Blair obtained their release.

Cousins and staunch Unionists Richard Johns Bowie and Allen Bowie Davis started a local newspaper in late 1861. Although open only a year, the *National Union* rivaled the *Sentinel*'s vigorous support of the Southern cause. When publication ceased, Matthew Fields suggested that the "nondescript offspring of the Abolition part of this county" went out of business for "want of proper pabulum."[11]

THE REALITY OF WAR

Rockville boys found it easy to follow their allegiances. Although Marylanders were not subject to the Southern draft, many slipped across the Potomac River to join the Confederate army. Union recruitment became more complex by mid-1862, when volunteer enlistments began to lag. From then through the end of the war, President Lincoln and Congress issued numerous conscription calls, and a Federal draft office opened in Rockville to register all men aged twenty to forty-five. The profile of an average soldier on both sides was a farmer's son under the age of twenty-one.

Lawrence Dawson, a farmer and attorney who provided one of Lincoln's fifty votes in Montgomery County in 1860, and John H. Higgins, a merchant, were appointed Union enrollment officers for Rockville. Like Richard M. Williams, who provided clerical assistance, and John DeSellum, who drew names from a box, those associated with the Federal draft were "ostracized from society."[12] A draftee could join a fighting unit, pay a three hundred dollar commutation fee to be excused from this particular draft, or obtain a substitute to serve in his stead. Lawyers advertised that for a fee they could locate substitutes, and the *Sentinel* as well as the *Baltimore Sun* published names of draftees and the substitutes who enabled them to evade service.

Other exemptions from Federal military service were also possible. Dr. Edward E. Stonestreet, who had opened his office at the corner of Montgomery Avenue and Monroe Street in 1853, exempted 233 men for medical reasons in October 1862. Stonestreet received four dollars per day as examining surgeon for Montgomery County. His exemption diagnoses included

RICHARD JOHNS BOWIE

Richard Johns Bowie (1807–1881) was one of the most respected public figures in nineteenth century Rockville. His interests, involvement, and leadership in major issues and events from the 1830s to 1881 provide insight into those problematic and difficult times.

Born to a large and well-to-do family, by the end of the 1830s, Bowie had married Catharine Williams and established a large farmstead, which they named Glenview, located two miles east of Rockville. By then he had passed the bar and had been elected to the Maryland General Assembly. Bowie was an enlightened farmer who practiced improved agriculture and helped organize the Montgomery County Agricultural Society in the 1840s. A devoted churchman, he served on the vestry of Christ Episcopal Church for most of his life. He helped establish and took leadership roles in local institutions, such as the Rockville Library Association, Rockville Riflemen, Rockville Academy, and the Benevolent Aid Society.

Courtesy of Montgomery County Historical Society

This 1870s photograph of Judge Bowie was the basis for an 1881 engraving and the portrait that hangs at Glenview Mansion, Bowie's home.

In politics Bowie was a Whig, serving under that banner in the state legislature, as state's attorney, and in the U.S. Congress. His friend Henry Clay received Bowie's support for compromise between Northern and Southern interests. Bowie lost a bid for governor of Maryland in 1853. After the demise of the Whigs in the late 1850s, Bowie moved to the Constitutional Union party. Bowie was not opposed to slavery, and at one time owned twenty-one slaves. He appreciated this national dilemma, in the 1830s attempting with the Maryland Colonization Society to settle free blacks in Africa.

Bowie vigorously opposed Maryland's secession, despite offence taken by many of his neighbors. In 1860 and 1861, he spoke eloquently at numerous Rockville gatherings for patience and preservation of the Union. With his cousin, Bowie started a short-lived pro-Union newspaper, the *National Union*, to counter the *Sentinel*. Glenview was the scene of encampments by troops of both armies, and Bowie several times used his stature to protect property of Rockville citizens on both sides. He emerged from the mid-1860s as a staunch Republican.

Bowie's leadership, legal background, and political affiliation landed him an appointment to the Court of Appeals in 1861. He presided over Maryland's highest court during the troublesome days of war and reconstruction. As a judge, he stayed aloof from local issues, but his sentiments were well known. With other Union sympathizers, Judge Bowie was arrested by Jeb Stuart's rebel cavalry and taken prisoner in June 1863, prior to the Battle of Gettysburg.

One of Judge Bowie's final civic actions was to incorporate the Rockville Cemetery Association. He served as the first president and donated five acres of land for the community burying ground. When he died in 1881 at the age of seventy-three, Bowie was buried at the cemetery adjacent to Glenview. In tribute to Judge Bowie, the courthouse was draped in black and public activities were postponed. Catharine Bowie remained at the farm until her death in 1891.[13]

rupture (hernia), lung disease, deafness, rheumatism, mental derangement, spinal disease, and hemorrhoids.[14]

Possibly the first from Rockville to enlist in the Union army was George Patterson, a free black man. In August 1862, soon after President Lincoln signed a bill emancipating slaves of District of Columbia residents, Patterson joined the teamsters of the Eleventh New York Cavalry. He was followed by three Rockville slaves, who probably enrolled in late 1863 or early 1864 when Maryland offered bounties for black soldiers. James Barber, owned by Olivia Wootton, enlisted in the army. When Reuben Hill, a slave of Samuel Stonestreet, and William Preston, owned by Chandler Keys, were drafted, these men and their owners were compensated by the federal government. Preston served in the Twenty-eighth Regiment of U.S. Colored Troops.[15]

Many local rebels joined the First Maryland Cavalry, CSA, formed by Ridgely Brown, or rode with Elijah Veirs White in the Thirty-fifth Battalion of Virginia Cavalry.[16] Edward Wootton and James Anderson enlisted in White's unit. James's father, James Wallace Anderson, lost his job at the post office in Washington for refusing to sign the loyalty oath presented to him in May 1861. Young James, a teacher and surveyor before the war, became captain of Company D of the Thirty-fifth Virginia Cavalry. He was captured twice during the war and was held prisoner in Baltimore, Washington, Ohio, Delaware, and South Carolina.[17]

The experience of Lawrence Dawson and his family indicates the pain of those times. Dawson, fifty-four years old in 1861, practiced law in Rockville and operated a large farm on the Rockville Pike just south of the Union camp at the fairgrounds. His brothers from Dawsonville fought for the Confederacy, his wife Mary Elizabeth (Kiger) was a strong Unionist although most of her Virginia family supported the South, and the Dawsons kept three slaves to work the farm. Confederate cavalrymen singled out Lawrence Dawson for capture when they arrived in June 1863.

Lawrence and Mary Dawson's daughter Mollie, nine years old at the start of the war, later described how her mother nursed wounded and ill soldiers from both sides, and how one sent her a coffee pot still cherished by the family. Mollie recalled the Union soldiers hidden in the pine woods on the farm and the Confederates who tied their horses to the persimmon tree and demanded dinner. After her father's capture by rebels in 1863, the child was jeered by her pro-South schoolmates and was forever terrified of men in gray uniforms.[18]

The federal government nervously operated in Rockville among a populace largely sympathetic to the South. Citizens who discouraged volunteer enlistments, aided the enemy, or engaged in any other disloyal practice against the United States were subject to arrest and imprisonment. To secure control, the U.S. War Department stationed military units in Rockville throughout the war and in 1862 assigned a special provost marshal for Montgomery County.

Mortimer Moulden, a thirty-five-year-old clerk who lived on Jefferson Street near the courthouse, became Provost Marshal. His job was to root out fraud and disloyalty against the government and to discourage desertion. Moulden zealously guarded Federal interests, reporting disloyal citizens who displayed signal lights, disclosed Union cavalry movements, or aided rebel marauders. From Rockville, Moulden wrote, "Is the Government aware that a letter could be thrown across the river at the Falls by wrapping it around a stone, thus giving the rebels a chance to learn our movements? And there are plenty of rebel sympathizers to do it."[19]

Courtesy of Montgomery County Historical Society

Ambrotype of Captain James Anderson, Company D, Thirty-fifth Battalion, Virginia Cavalry, Confederate States of America.

Matthew Fields, the feisty pro-South editor and publisher, keenly felt the government's attempts at control. He learned the printing trade with Jesse Leach, publisher of the *Maryland Journal and True American*, and briefly partnered with John Braddock Jr. In 1850, Fields married Rebecca Beckwith and was appointed postmaster of Rockville. The following year, he was elected sheriff of Montgomery County. Fields introduced the first issue of the *Montgomery County*

Sentinel on August 11, 1855. Each Friday, the *Sentinel* rolled off a hand-operated press located in a log building adjacent to the Fields's white frame house at the corner of Washington Street and Commerce Lane (now West Montgomery Avenue).

But politics—local and national—were Matthew Fields's passion. A former Whig who feared Know-Nothings (an anti-immigrant and anti-Catholic political party) and hated Black Republicans (Northern abolitionists), Fields left no reader doubting his support of Southern Democrat John C. Breckinridge in 1860. After Lincoln's election he editorialized that "God placed Maryland in the South."[20]

Charles Brewer collection, courtesy of Peerless Rockville

This earliest photograph of Montgomery County Courthouse was taken about 1870. During the Civil War, the courthouse served as a meeting place and hospital.

Once fighting began, Fields wrote about Federal heavy-handedness. The *Sentinel* reported misconduct of Federal troops and arrests of Rockville citizens who were considered disloyal. Three of his printing staff joined the Virginia Cavalry. In 1862, armed with evidence from Rockville Unionists, authorities charged the editor with disloyalty and on October 4 confined him at Old Capitol Prison in Washington. There he remained for seven weeks without a trial, until he signed an oath not to bear arms against the U.S. Government nor aid or comfort its enemies. Again with no formal charge lodged against him, in April of 1864 Fields was arrested and taken to Old Capitol Prison, where he remained for two months until Rebecca Fields's appeal to a Maryland congressman effected his release.[21]

General George McClellan's Army of the Potomac headquartered in Rockville in the month before the Battle of Antietam. McClellan stayed the night of September 7, 1862 at the house of the pro-Union Beall sisters in Rockville, then spent several days encamped near the intersection of Great Falls and Seven Locks Roads. Thousands of Federal troops sprawled on the Carter farm west of Rockville and pitched tents at Glenview on the Baltimore Road.[22]

Before McClellan moved west toward Antietam, the courthouse in Rockville became a Union hospital holding about 325 patients. A Union army surgeon had previously assessed Rockville's position: "The houses are few and of poor quality, affording limited accommodations for the sick and wounded. . . . and as the roads are now nearly impassable from the deep mud, it will be impracticable to transport the sick either to Frederick or to Washington without much suffering." Nevertheless, during the 1862 Maryland campaign, Federal forces assigned a surgeon and a nurse to supervise the field hospital and to obtain from local families items the army could not provide.[23]

After the bloody battle at Antietam Creek on September 17, 1862, which killed 4,000 Americans and injured 18,000 more, the entire countryside was called upon to assist wounded from both armies. Horse-drawn ambulances delivered casualties to Rockville. One observer wrote that "the extensive grounds of the court house were soon occupied by the soldiers who had fallen out from the commands and many sick soldiers were already in the rooms of the court house lying upon the bare floor. . . . I was dispatched with the army wagon to the farm houses to get a load of straw and later for a couple of sheep to be slaughtered for soup. . . ." This member of the U.S. Christian Commission (which cared for the spiritual needs of Union soldiers) also held an impromptu religious meeting under the trees in front of the courthouse.[24]

JEB STUART'S VISIT TO ROCKVILLE

Sophia Dorothy "Dora" Barnard Higgins was born in Georgetown of British parents. Family tradition is that she was generally regarded in Rockville as an "overly-educated, blue stock woman, pro-Union and anti-slavery."[25] Dora insisted that her husband, John H. Higgins, free his slaves and move into Rockville. During the Civil War, Mr. Higgins was an outspoken Unionist, town commissioner, and Union enrollment officer for the draft.

"Rockville, June 29, 1863
My dear Mother:

After breakfast [on Sunday, June 28], I was getting the children ready for Sabbath School. . . . I heard a terrific yell. . . . Dora screamed, 'Rebels, Ma!' I thought it impossible. The next moment I saw a whole column with the Rebel Flag charging furiously. . . . I broke through the charging columns with the pistol balls flying, rushed through the back way to the Church just in time to warn Mr. Higgins, Mr. Bowie, Mr. Dawson and Williams to stay in the Vestry room, for they, the Secessionists, were vowing vengeance on them. . . . I remember nothing but the thick rank and clanking of sabres, yells and furious charges. They were pouring in at every lane and road from the Falls."

Mrs. Higgins stood in front of her Commerce Lane store for six hours, resisting Rebel entreaties to open up or to pay for items in Confederate script. She hid a horse in the garden. "George Peter, Messrs. Miller, White and Brown [pro-Southerners] pleaded that Union men should not be molested. Had it not been for their endeavors, every Union man would have been taken and every store laid open." They took Judge Bowie, John Higgins, and Lawrence Dawson from the church and marched them out under guard. "In solemn procession, we moved up the street as far as the square, when the Captain said, 'Ladies, you can go no farther.'" Although "the Secessionists gathered around Mrs. Bowie and myself declaring they had nothing to do with it," Dora replied that she knew some local person had furnished Gen. Stuart a written list of names of Union men.

The three vestrymen were taken to Brookeville, perhaps on foot, as the Rebels had no horses to spare. The captives slowed Stuart's move toward General Lee's army in Pennsylvania, so were released to return to Rockville. Eblen, a seventeen-year-old Union soldier whom Dora had rescued, along with Mr. Bailey the postmaster and Mr. Moulden the Provost were taken into Carroll County. The two Federal officials refused to leave Eblen and carried him several miles on their backs, because they had seen several disabled prisoners shot along the march. "In all they marched nearly 70 miles."

"With love to all, I am
Your affectionate daughter,
Dora B. Higgins."[26]

The presence of so many soldiers created problems in Rockville. Union troops frequently plundered nearby farms for fresh eggs, chickens, pigs, and milk. In September 1862, Unionists Judge Bowie, James Henning, and John England asked Gen. Nathaniel Banks to protect Rockville and its vicinity from further annoyance and loss. Banks replied that although it was not practicable to station a provost guard permanently at Rockville, cavalry would be sent out to pick up military stragglers on Rockville roads and farms.[27]

JEB STUART COMES TO TOWN

The tense but relative quiet in Rockville ended abruptly on Sunday, June 28, 1863. Elated by an early May victory in Chancellorsville, Virginia, Confederate Gen. Robert E. Lee invaded Northern territory the following month. As the bulk of Lee's army moved through western Maryland toward Pennsylvania, 8,000 cavalrymen under Gen. J. E. B. "Jeb" Stuart crossed the Potomac near Seneca on the night of June 27. In this adventurous detour around the Union army, one Confederate brigade approached Rockville via the Darnestown Road. The other two arrived on Falls Road, engaging Union pickets and small garrisons along the way.

Stuart's reception in Rockville on June 28 was boisterous. Southern sympathizers—whose families would later claim Stuart kissed their babies, doffed a plumed hat to them, or shook their hands—cheered the dashing hero. Unionists scrambled to find hiding places in town and to protect their stores, families, and livestock. Students at the girls' seminary near the courthouse fluttered handkerchiefs and ran out to greet the boys in gray. One Southern soldier described "a spectacle which was truly pleasing. . . . It was Sunday, and the beautiful girls in their fresh gaily coloured dresses, low necks, bare arms, and wildernesses of braids and curls, were . . . burning with enthusiasm to welcome the Southerner. . . . The whole facade of the building was a tulip-bed of . . . joy and welcome!"[28]

The Confederates used the day in Rockville to their advantage. They cut the telegraph lines and took horses and supplies from area farms. Some dined at friendly homes. The *New York Tribune* reported that "Stuart commanded the Rebels in person, and was introduced to several of the Rebel sympathizers in Rockville. The Rebels took every horse within four miles of Rockville, whether the owner was Unionist or traitor."[29] A detail of the Ninth Virginia Cavalry rode down the Rockville Pike pursuing a four-mile-long Union wagon train, capturing some 170 wagons and hundreds of mules. The Confederates charged down the pike for six miles, breaking and burning wagons, enjoying Northern bacon and whiskey, taking prisoners, and emptying the Quartermaster's store of forty thousand dollars in soldiers' wages.

Stuart apparently knew who the pro-Union residents were, and where some might be, for he located the Episcopal Church on Washington Street where Northern-sympathizing vestrymen had taken refuge. Hours later, the Confederates left Rockville with shopkeeper John Higgins, Judge Richard Johns Bowie, commissioner of the draft Lawrence Dawson, Mortimer Moulden, the Provost Marshal, and postmaster Thomas Bailey in tow. They went as far as Brookeville but, perhaps uneasy about the health of their prestigious captives, paroled most of them there. The remainder were released late Monday night, after which Dora Higgins, John's wife, sat down to write her mother a detailed description of recent events. "There were three brigades of Rebels in all, about 8,000," Dora wrote. "I broke down once only, through the day and that was when the children knew that their father was a prisoner. . . . [The Rebels] behaved better than I expected; never entered the house. They had feasted on Uncle Abe's army rations."[30]

Oldest photograph of Rockville's main thoroughfare, dated 1864–72 by the hay scale in the public triangle. The courthouse is out of the picture, to the right.

Charles Brewer collection, courtesy of Peerless Rockville

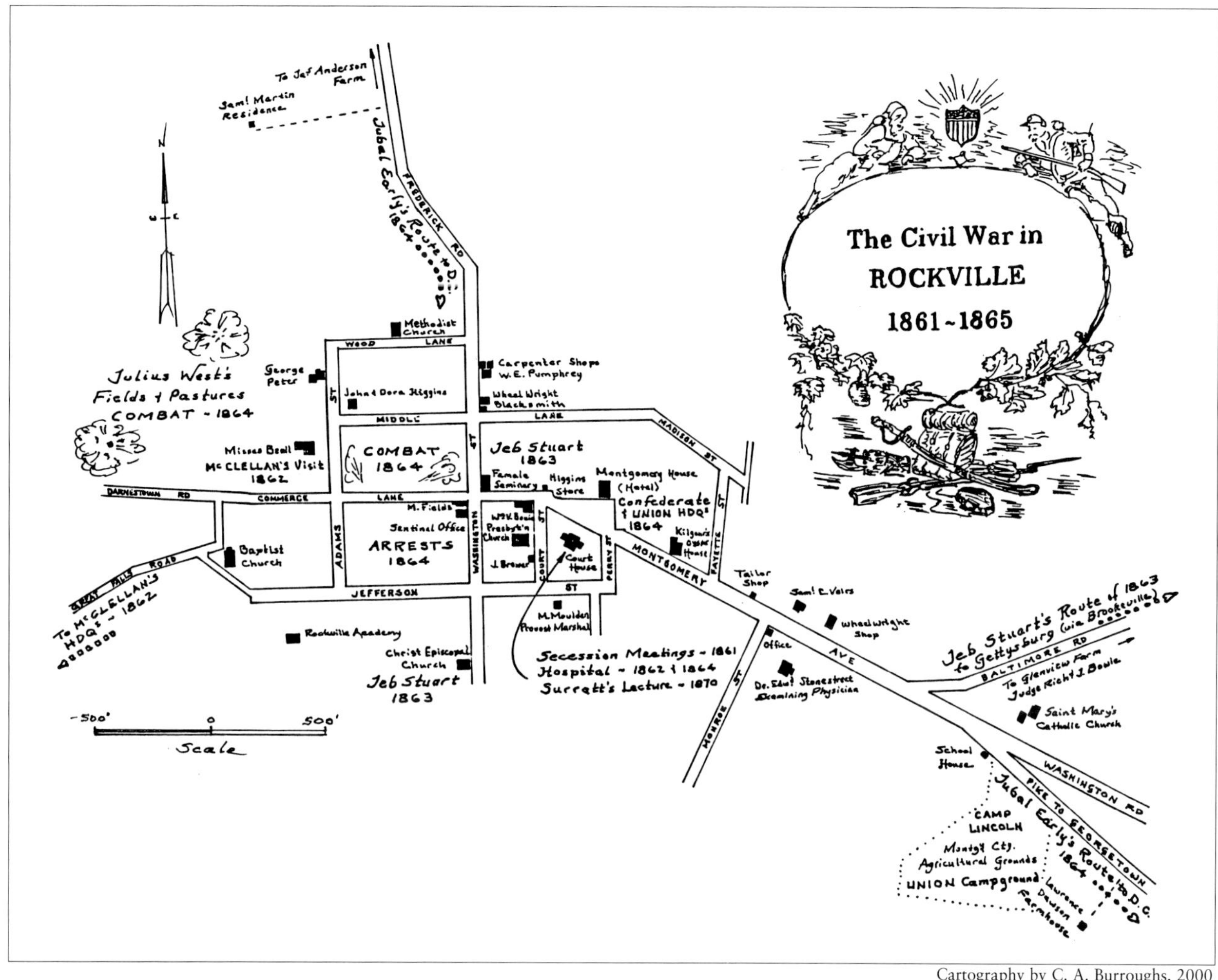

Cartography by C. A. Burroughs, 2000

Events in Rockville during the Civil War, with locations of homes and businesses of major players.

When Jeb Stuart met up with General Lee and the Army of Northern Virginia on the evening of July 2, two of three days of the Battle of Gettysburg were already over. Had Stuart's cavalry not spent two days flirting with young ladies and rounding up wagons and Unionists in Rockville, perhaps the outcome of the battle would have been different.

FIGHTING IN ROCKVILLE

A year later, the Rebels returned. In July 1864, the Confederates made their only attack on Washington of the war. On July 9, Confederate Gen. Jubal Early defeated a Union force along the Monocacy River in Frederick County and continued south on the main road to Washington, D.C. Most of the Federal army was engaged in heavy fighting around Richmond and Petersburg, so Washington was then held by a ragged collection of convalescents, government clerks, home guards, draftees, militia, and stragglers.

In a race to the capital city, Early sent Gen. John McCausland's cavalry down the Frederick Road. A hastily assembled Union force under the command of Maj. William Fry met McCausland two miles north of Rockville, at a hill near present-day Gude Drive. Major Fry, trying to buy time for Washington, formed up in two lines, one a mile above Rockville, the other on Commerce Lane. Using information from a Southern sympathizer, the Confederates charged the small Union force, breaking both lines, and a spirited battle ensued while Fry's unit reformed

Courtesy of Frances Robey Barnes

Montgomery House Hotel, on Commerce Lane, hosted blue- and gray-clad soldiers throughout the war.

at a hill near present-day Edmonston Drive for a last stand. When McCausland added artillery to his attack, the Federals melted into the woods farther south on the Pike.

McCausland ate dinner at the Montgomery House Hotel across from the courthouse, while his men camped on the fairgrounds. Just after dawn the next morning, July 11, Early arrived in Rockville with eight thousand infantry, forty pieces of artillery, and two cavalry brigades. A reporter noted that "the streets were blockaded with passing infantry, artillery and wagon trains. Nearly every regiment was headed by a band of music, which, generally, as they marched through the town, discoursed fine music." Depending upon their loyalties, the locals cheered the soldiers or kept out of sight.[31]

Leaving guards at Rockville, Early sent McCausland down the Pike to Fort Reno in Tennallytown (now Tenleytown) while he led a larger group past Sam Veirs's mill and on toward Washington. After testing the capital's defenses at Fort Stevens, taking a shot at President Lincoln, losing more than two thousand men, and assessing Union reinforcements, Early fell back into Maryland on July 12.

By Wednesday morning, July 13, General Early and his generals were back at the Montgomery House in Rockville. Depressed over his failed plans, he contented himself with having "scared Abe Lincoln like hell."[32] He sat for an hour on the long piazza of the hotel studying his map. As the morning grew warm, Early mounted up and rode west with his men. The Confederates set up a defensive line along Watts Branch a mile out of town on the Darnestown Road, then headed across the river and home without a victory in Washington.

Union Col. Charles Lowell watched from high ground near Saint Mary's, then moved his eight hundred cavalrymen through Rockville behind the Confederates. He watched the superior rebel force withdraw, sat down at the Montgomery House to write a report to Washington, and sent a small force to monitor the rebel movements. But Early, annoyed that the Federals had retaken Rockville, ordered Gen. Bradley Johnson and his all-Maryland cavalry to drive them back. As some of Lowell's men prepared to charge, Johnson attacked and drove the Union forces eastward through Julius West's pastures and back into the center of Rockville.

For two hours Rockville's streets, yards, alleys, gardens, and buildings were the scene of hot, close, confused combat. General Johnson wrote that the "dust was so thick"[33] that men could not see the houses in front of them. In the fighting Union Pvt. James Hill, from California, was wounded near the grounds of the Beall sisters' house, taken in by them, and nursed back to health.

Lowell dropped his pen when he heard the sounds of battle on Commerce Lane. He positioned his men on rooftops, behind trees, and along the triangle in front of the courthouse. When the Rebels rushed down the hill, the Yankees fired short-range volleys at them. Hours later, the outnumbered Union troops fell back to Saint Mary's, then to what is now Woodmont Country Club on the Rockville Pike. Johnson moved back into Rockville, leaving about thirty men to hold the town while he withdrew toward the Potomac.

Both sides suffered casualties, exhaustion, deaths, and captures. Ambulances from Washington picked up perhaps a hundred men around the town and brought them to the courthouse. There they stayed for a day or two before being transferred to hospitals in Washington.[34]

Somewhere in these three confusing days, the Confederates "carried off and destroyed" the records of the newly incorporated town of Rockville. Perhaps the theft occurred when General Early briefly occupied the clerk's office in the courthouse as reported by the *Baltimore Sun* on July 19, 1864. More likely, it was the result of an unofficial side action, perhaps by Rebels, perhaps not. As a consequence, the General Assembly passed, in 1867, special legislation guaranteeing the validity of the acts of the town commissioners.[35]

Rockville's location on the main road, which figured in several of the war's major campaigns, again involved the village in the final month of conflict. On April 15, 1865, the morning after John Wilkes Booth shot President Lincoln, one of Booth's accomplices, George Atzerodt, boarded the Rockville mail stage in Georgetown. At Tennallytown he avoided Union pickets by catching a wagon ride with a farmer to the Gaither farm in Derwood. He walked the final seven miles to the home of his cousin Hartman Richter in Germantown. There he was arrested and returned to Washington, where he was tried and hanged on July 7.

EMANCIPATION AND RECONSTRUCTION

Slaves in the border state of Maryland gained their freedom through a variety of opportunities between 1862 and 1864. In 1862, the U.S. Congress freed slaves who lived or worked in Washington, D.C., qualifying slaveholders for compensation of the loss of human property if they owned land or slaves in Washington. The Beall sisters of Rockville manumitted seventeen slaves under this policy in 1862. Later that year, both Congress and President Lincoln proclaimed free the slaves of owners disloyal to the United States. Heartened, Maryland slaves more frequently slipped to freedom in the capital city.

Another route to freedom for black men was enlistment in the Union army. The use of black soldiers, authorized by mid-1862 although unpopular in middle-ground Maryland, was unavoidable by the following year. The War Department's General Orders No. 329, which established regulations for recruiting free blacks and slaves in the border states, eventually resulted in nearly nine thousand Maryland blacks serving in six U.S. regiments. Depending upon rules and attitudes at the time of their enlistments, Rockville slaves Reuben Hill, James Barber, and William Preston and their owners may have been promised freedom and/or money for their military service.

By 1864, with an uncertain military and political climate, the authority of Maryland slaveholders had totally collapsed. All willing slaves, physically fit or not, were mustered in an attempt at full recruitment. The state authorized additional bounties for enlisting slaves of agreeable masters. On the political front, Unionists, former Whigs, Republicans, and others ready for statewide emancipation joined to elect a majority to the General Assembly. On October 3, 1863, Postmaster General Montgomery Blair spoke in Rockville to defend President

Lincoln's policy of peaceful reunion of the country in opposition to extremists who would not accept the South as equals again. With the blessing of Governor Augustus W. Bradford, Unconditional Union delegates assembled in April 1864 to rewrite the state constitution. Soldiers voting in the field in October 1864 ensured passage of the document, although 73 percent of Montgomery County voters did not approve. It outlawed slavery in Maryland, effective November 1 of that year, and disenfranchised Southern sympathizers by requiring a strict loyalty oath. For a brief time, Reconstruction reigned in the state of Maryland.[36]

Three years later, the pendulum swung back. A new General Assembly, a new governor, and a populace with a 250-year history of slavery convened to write a new Maryland constitution in 1867. Pro-Southern Democrats retained many elements of the old order and reenfranchised former Rebels. A legacy of the new constitution was a census of slaves and owners, as of November 1, 1864, made in the unfulfilled hope that the federal government might compensate slaveholders in gratitude for Maryland's loyalty to the Union. Two powerful former antagonists, William Veirs Bouic and Montgomery Blair, laid aside past differences to keep former secessionists on the Maryland voting rolls.

Newly freed blacks looked to the federal government for protection from physical attacks, legal abuse, and the reinstatement of prewar relationships. The Bureau of Refugees, Freedmen, and Abandoned Lands, popularly known as the Freedmen's Bureau, opened in Maryland in September 1865. Captain, later Colonel, R. G. Rutherford supervised Montgomery County's program from an office in Rockville. He adjudicated claims for collection of wages, taking some to trial in circuit court. He met with blacks interested in building school houses, attempted to connect freedmen with prospective employers, kept lists of black property owners, and intervened for parents whose hired-out children were not returned when promised. It is clear from the records that labor was much in demand in the postwar period, and that many verbal understandings turned into disagreements.

Three Rockville cases demonstrate the scope of the Freedmen's Bureau. When Mrs. Richard Johns Bowie found it difficult to fill the jobs of former slaves at Glenview, she wrote Captain Rutherford to request that he deliver a letter for her. Mrs. Bowie sought a "middle aged woman who would desire a good home—with liberal wages—A Cook, Washer & Ironer, of good character, coming well recommended—Many wish to hire in the Country—who do not like the City."[37] In 1866, Daniel Brogdon and

ROCKVILLE SLAVES GAIN THEIR FREEDOM

Rockville slaveholders, with their options changing frequently, held onto their human property well into the war. After April 1862, when Congress freed slaves in Washington, D.C., some Rockville slaveholders who owned property or employed their slaves in the city qualified for compensation. The Beall sisters, who lived on Commerce Lane, received $9,400 for seventeen slaves who were valued on the basis of age, occupation, and physical condition. Thereafter, and particularly following President Lincoln's Emancipation Proclamation, Rockville slaves could more easily attain freedom in the capital city.

Another manumission route was through service in the Union army. Reuben Hill, James Barber, and William Preston may or may not have received the consent of their owners to enlist. After October 1863, the U.S. War Department encouraged recruitment of black troops in the border states. This policy targeted free black men and, at first, provided compensation for consenting owners. Later on, recruiters signed slaves without their masters' permission and with the promise of freedom. In early 1864, the Maryland legislature sweetened the pot with additional bounties for black soldiers. Reuben Hill's receipt of fifty dollars when he was drafted may indicate compensation for his owner, Samuel Stonestreet, and perhaps a promise of freedom and cash if he survived the war.

The remainder of Rockville's slaves obtained freedom by running away to the Union army or, toward the end of the war, through state law. Maryland's wartime constitution, narrowly adopted with the help of soldier ballots in 1864, freed all slaves in the state on November first of that year.

Solomon Williams, through the Freedmen's Bureau, accused J. Mortimer Kilgour of having left Rockville in 1861 to enter the rebel army, taking with him funds they had collected and entrusted to him in 1858 toward purchasing a church. The Bureau also represented freedman Hillary Powell, who was severely caned by Dr. A. H. Sommers for an impertinent reply. Rutherford obtained a cash settlement from Kilgour but could not convince a Maryland jury to indict the Rockville doctor.[38]

THE AFTERMATH OF WAR

In addition to two rebel invasions within thirteen months, Rockville's war experience was a series of small incidents of valor, near-misses, poignant encounters, making do, cruelty, and compassion. Citizens took in wounded, exhausted, and hungry soldiers, and slipped food to prisoners being herded through town. They tolerated big city correspondents and opposing hometown papers. The conflict disrupted many Rockville lives and fortunes.

War-weary Rockville residents welcomed the end of four years of divisiveness and tension. Whether they chose sides from sentiment, practicality, or ideology, every family had been touched by the lengthy conflict. No household was immune to the anxiety and reality of house searches, high prices, curfews, and nighttime alarms. Foraging troops of both camps took food, horses, and livestock as spoils of war, sharply hurting local farmers. Villagers and nearby farmers were terrified of injury or capture, of losing lives and property, and of being informed on by neighbors.

In Rockville, opposing loyalties coexisted before, during, and after the war. They continued each of the multiple times the small town changed hands. Although Unionists pointed out Rebels to be imprisoned without trial, and Southrons handed Jeb Stuart a list of Union men, Rockvillians of both persuasions used their good offices on behalf of accused, arrested, or mistreated friends. Lifelong neighbors did not require unanimity in order to respect each other or to mourn their sons.

As the town returned to the harmony of daily life, concrete signs of reconciliation—necessitated by the alteration of economic and social conditions through all levels of Rockville society—appeared. Residents resumed the important work of raising children, earning a living, and improving the community. They continued prewar friendships and business relationships, repaired the physical damage, and replaced lost crops and livestock. Citizens united to advance education, physical improvements, town governance, and other community concerns. Recent adversaries such as Richard Johns Bowie and William Veirs Bouic, who had worked together before the war to form the Montgomery County Agricultural Society, after the war united to establish the Rockville Library Association and the Rockville Cemetery Association. Following a turbulent decade in which a generation lost its youth, one-third of the population forged a new identity as it gained freedom, and a legacy of reverence for the lost cause was established. The citizens of Rockville prepared to move on.

Rockville property owners filed a number of claims against damage caused by Federal troops. The Montgomery County Agricultural Society estimated a cost of nearly $8,300 to rebuild fences, lay out a new race track, repair fields, and reverse four years of use by Union troops. James Anderson, Margaret Beall, and Charles Maddox also filed claims, supported by former Unionist friends and neighbors who confirmed the claimant's loyalty as well as damages incurred.[39]

The crowd which filled the courtroom on the evening of December 6, 1870, demonstrated Rockville's continuing fascination with the war. John H. Surratt, son of the woman hanged for the assassination of Abraham Lincoln, told his version of the plot and its execution to a captive audience. The *Washington Star* reported "the village deserted of everything save horses and empty vehicles of all kinds" to hear him, but later scolded Surratt for not having attempted to exonerate his mother. John Surratt's trial for complicity in 1867 resulted in a hung jury, after which he taught for a time at the old Montrose School (demolished in 1909) on the Rockville Pike. His Rockville lecture was one of several presented to raise funds to support himself.[40]

Soldier survivors, particularly Confederates, were revered war heroes for the remainder of their lives. Four principals of the Rockville Academy were ex-Rebels. Two, Cooke Luckett and William Pinckney Mason, had been injured while serving the Confederate cause. According to local lore, former Navy Lieutenant Mason, wounded aboard an ironclad boat in early 1865, would rub his leg on damp days and declare "Damn that Yankee!"[41] Locals who frequented the wall in front of the courthouse heard the tales of Elgar Tschiffely, a Southern cavalryman and the last Montgomery County survivor, who died in 1930 at the age of eighty-eight.

Returning veterans formed organizations to maintain connections with their extraordinary experience. The Grand Army of the Republic, formed by Union veterans in 1866, established two posts in Maryland. Although Rockville's Independence Post No. 67 and O. A. Horner Post No. 70 participated in encampments and reunions, no monument to Union soldiers was erected in Montgomery County. Southern veterans formed the Ridgely Brown Camp of the United Confederate Veterans in 1892, and contributed to the Silver Spring monument erected two years later for Southerners killed at the Battle of Fort Stevens in 1864. The first goal of the United Daughters of the Confederacy, which formed a chapter in Rockville in 1911, was to erect a monument to Montgomery County soldiers who had fought for the South. The bronze statue was dedicated on June 3, 1913.

COMMUNITY BUILDING

Town Government

Dissension and war did not deter Rockvillians from learning how to govern a town. Official town proceedings for the first five years must be surmised from surviving town records. Available for May 1860–March 1865 are election results, assessment lists, oaths of election judges, and oaths of elected town officials not to aid or encourage those in rebellion against the United States. On May 7, 1860, two months after General Assembly authorization, fifty-two free white men cast ballots for town commissioners for the first time. Elected to one-year terms were three commissioners and a bailiff. Receiving the highest number of votes to become president of the commissioners was James W. Campbell, who lived and operated a carpentry shop on Washington Street near the courthouse. William Veirs Bouic, State's Attorney and farmer, aged forty-four, and John H. Higgins, merchant, aged forty-five, also were elected commissioners. To collect taxes and keep the peace, voters chose James McNahaney as bailiff.[42]

The new commissioners set out immediately to address local issues of most concern to Rockville residents. The greatest needs, according to the editor of the *Sentinel*, were public improvements such as street

ROCKVILLE'S CONFEDERATE MONUMENT

On June 3, 1913, a large group, including fifty to seventy-five Confederate veterans, gathered on the public triangle in front of the Red Brick Court House to unveil a life-size bronze statue. Members of the United Confederate Veterans and the United Daughters of the Confederacy had raised thirty-six hundred dollars to erect the monument in Rockville. Atop an eight-foot granite pedestal stood a six-foot cavalryman with arms folded, facing south. Spencer C. Jones, Master of Ceremonies, Commander of the Ridgley Brown Camp, had served in the First Maryland Cavalry for the entire war, then established a law practice in Rockville in 1868. Tradition says that Jones's head was the model for this statue.

The inscription on the monument reads "To our heroes of Montgomery Co. Maryland—That we through life may not forget to love the thin gray line—erected A.D. 1913." Fifty years after the Battle of Gettysburg, veterans and their families saluted American, Confederate, and Maryland flags and sang both "Dixie" and "the Star Spangled Banner" in the lengthy ceremony that symbolized nationalism and reunification.[43]

Charles Brewer collection, courtesy of Peerless Rockville

Monument to Confederate veterans from Montgomery County, erected 1913 in the triangular public park across from the courthouse.

paving and repair. The commissioners also had to develop a list of taxable property and taxpayers and to authorize the bailiff to collect the money for town activities. They appointed Mordecai Morgan as clerk.

The second election, in May 1861, brought William Veirs Bouic to the presidency of the commissioners for his first of five terms. By this time he was actively involved in secessionist activities in Rockville. He served with Matthew Fields, the forty-seven-year-old editor of the pro-Southern *Sentinel* and outspoken Unionist Higgins. John R. Miller, a bricklayer, received most votes for chief bailiff, and stonecutter Anthony Dettrich was appointed as underbailiff by the commissioners. Also elected as commissioners in these early years were wheelwright Melchisdec Green and George Peter, a lawyer.

Courtesy of Montgomery County Historical Society

Rockville merchant John H. Higgins, Unionist, town commissioner and president, was captured by Jeb Stuart in 1863.

Rockville's commissioners took up the spirit of improvement in the newly incorporated town and revealed how seriously they took their responsibilities. In the first decade, they codified practices and procedures. They met an average of five times a year at a convenient location, usually Bouic's law office, John Higgins's store, the courthouse, or the *Sentinel* office. Not until the 1870s did the officials begin meeting regularly, once a month. Almost all votes were unanimous. The fiscal year began June 1 and ended May 30. The commissioners paid the chief bailiff sixty dollars annually and the clerk twenty dollars, later twenty-five dollars.

Business conducted at the April 1, 1865, meeting suggests the work of the commissioners. In addition to adopting the assessment list, approving a levy of twelve cents per each one hundred dollar assessment, requesting a plat of the town, and preparing for the upcoming election, much time was spent in ordering payments to local officials for materials or work done.

Corporation ordinances posted for Rockville on June 12, 1866, framed a picture of town life. Major issues were animal control, health, keeping the peace, and protection of public streets and places. No horse, hog, shoat, goose, or goat was allowed to run loose in the streets or public places of the town. Dogs could run at large, but their owners had to obtain an annual license for one dollar. The bailiff could kill any animal at large having a contagious or incurable disease. Fines would be levied against persons who "disturb the public peace and quiet of the Town by discharging any firearms in the streets or public places of the town or by drunken or riotous conduct noises whooping profane swearing or vulgar language. Fast driving or riding throwing stones."[44] Citizens were prohibited from driving a wagon or buggy or riding an animal upon any sidewalk in Rockville, hitching an animal on the pavements, obstructing the streets, allowing a horse to run at large, or allowing dead carcasses to remain in the streets. Lastly, no person could obstruct the sidewalks, hitch horses to the courthouse fence, or injure the courthouse building, fence gates, or trees of Court House Square. Offenders were fined from one dollar to ten dollars and committed to jail until they paid.

Controlling citizens and animals, assessing and collecting taxes, and authorizing payment of bills were vital, but maintaining streets was most important of all. At each meeting the town commissioners authorized public funds to repair streets, dig ditches to channel water, install curbing stone, construct bridges and stepping blocks, and plank and pave sidewalks. In 1867, they ordered a survey of town streets and lanes, thereafter requiring the installation of sidewalks, four feet on each side of a lane and six feet for a street. Four years later, the board installed the first eight street lamps and posts, purchased lamp oil, chimneys, matches, and a step ladder. They paid Edward Wood $1.50 to $2 per month to light the oil lamps each evening.[45]

Public Schools

A slave state that spent large sums on internal improvements, Maryland viewed education somewhere between Northern interest in public schooling and Southern regard for private academies. On the eve of the Civil War, it had no statewide public school system.

The breakthrough came in 1860, when the General Assembly authorized Montgomery County to provide tax-supported education for white children. Despite ongoing public debate about cost, the Board of School Commissioners proceeded to hire teachers, operate thirty schools that first year from available buildings, and develop a primary school curriculum. County efforts were reinforced by the 1864 Maryland constitution and establishment of the State Normal School (teachers' college) the following year. One of the few reforms of 1864 not reversed by the new 1867 constitution was the public school system.

On March 1, 1861, the *Sentinel* reported that "A new school house is being built near the Fair Grounds. . . . It is twenty feet front, by twenty-four. . . . When completed, it will supply a want much needed." Ten years later the school board authorized $114.54 for an addition, as teacher Sophie P. Hungerford had more than sixty pupils. This was the first two-room school in the county.

Early public schools considered the reality of rural families. Attendance was not compulsory, and the term did not compete with planting and harvest times. The school commissioners calculated teacher salaries according to the number of pupils and their days of attendance. About three-fourths of the teachers and three-fifths of the students were male. Pupils over nineteen years old could attend school "upon any terms they might make with the teachers thereof."[46]

As the county seat, Rockville's role in the new school system was central. Rarely did the school board, which met at the courthouse, not include Rockville men. In-service training for county teachers was held at the courthouse, the first in May of 1867. A Rockville resident became the first professional manager of the Montgomery County public schools. Captain James Anderson, a graduate of the Rockville Academy, first taught school and then was elected county surveyor before enlisting in the Confederate cavalry. After the war, the board appointed him secretary, treasurer, and examiner, titles that Captain Anderson held for eleven years.[47]

Courtesy of Montgomery County Archives and Peerless Rockville

William Veirs Bouic Sr., town commissioner, lawyer, state's attorney, leader in secessionist movement in Montgomery County, judge of Orphans' Court.

Rockville's school quickly became a centerpiece of the community. The small building provided meeting rooms and social centers for white residents. For all Rockville citizens, the public school represented aspirations and a place where home, community, and government met for the common good.

Black Identity

Education was one manner in which newly emancipated slaves could assert their independence and plan for the future. Freedmen and women began to chart new identities through religion, residential arrangements, and employment, as well as schools for their children. Frequently Freedmen's Bureau intervention was vital, as in Daniel Brogdon and Solomon Williams' successful 1866 petition to recover funds from J. M. Kilgour because the money was "much needed by the Colored people to assist in securing a church and school."[48]

Years before Maryland established a separate but equal system of free public education for black students in 1872, Rockville families provided primary education opportunities. In March of 1867, twenty Rockville black men pledged to support a school by taking responsibility for money "as may be necessary to pay the board and washing of the teacher and to provide fuel and lights for the School-house."[49] Details of these earliest schools did not survive but, like the first white schools, Rockville Colored Elementary School housed grades one through seven in a single classroom.

A second means of identity, where freedmen could steer their own course, was religion. Many former slaves remained with churches they had attended with their masters. Others formed new congregations that would help black people meet their unique needs.

Methodists in Rockville emerged from the 1860s in color-separated congregations. In the debate over whether a church member could hold slaves, whites of the Rockville Methodist Episcopal Church joined the southern branch. After the war they lost a legal battle that left the

Wood Lane church to northern black Methodists. By 1869, the Methodist Episcopal Church South had moved into a new frame church and parsonage in the block between Commerce Lane and Jefferson Street. Black parishioners, including Daniel Brogdon, renamed the old church Jerusalem.

Further refining their identity, a group of Rockville freedmen left Jerusalem Church in 1867. Solomon Williams and Alfred and Jane Ross with others founded Clinton Church, affiliating with the African Methodist Episcopal Zion movement. The Clinton congregation met in different locales in the center of Rockville, in private homes and rented space, then in a log church built in the early 1870s.[50]

After the war, with the residential options provided by emancipation, black families clustered in several areas of Rockville. Freedmen joined prewar free blacks along Washington Street, today in the area between Middle Lane and Beall Avenue, to start an enclave of homes, businesses, and common areas in the town center. Some families moved farther north toward Samuel Martin's lane or along Falls Road where Ann Davis had lived for decades. And others, such as Benjamin and Ann Smith on Judge Bowie's farm, became tenants on the properties where they had lived as slaves.

U.S. census takers in 1870 chronicled the employment status of Rockville blacks in a different light than in previous counts. Former male slaves were listed as farmers and farm laborers, and there was a barber, a carpenter, a whitewasher, and a blacksmith. Women were mostly described as keeping house or as servants, often living at the homes of whites. Attending school were children of parents recorded as illiterate.

The flames which destroyed the Rockville Presbyterian Church on Court Street in the center of town on the night of March 3, 1873, frightened the entire community. Awakened to their role in public safety, town commissioners praised "the citizens who united their efforts so efficiently and intelligently in suppressing the fire yesterday, thereby preventing what threatened to become a general conflagration." They gave "unqualified praise and thanks" to the "Colored people of the Community" for "very valuable assistance rendered so willingly" and ordered six ladders to

We, the undersigned, hereby pledge ourselves for the support of a School at Rockville, Montgomery County, Maryland and agree to hold ourselves responsible for such sum as may be necessary to pay the board and washing of the teacher and to provide fuel and lights for the School house.

Date		Signature	Witness
1867 February	14	William Kelley	N. G. Sutherford Bvt. Lt. Col. U.S.V.
"	14	Louis his mark Proctor	N. G. Sutherford " "
"	14	Reuben his mark Hill	N. G. Sutherford " "
"	15	Samuel his mark Martin	N. G. Sutherford " "
"	15	Solomon his mark Williams	N. G. Sutherford " "
"	15	Adam his mark Baker	N. G. Sutherford " "
"	15	William his mark Powell	N. G. Sutherford " "
"	19	William his mark Baker	N. G. Sutherford " "
"	21	Barney his mark Lilles	N. G. Sutherford " "
"	22	Henry Figler	N. G. Sutherford " "
"	27	Henson Norris	N. G. Sutherford " "
"	27	Alfred his mark Ross	N. G. Sutherford " "
"	28	Hezekiah Williams	N. G. Sutherford " "
"	28	Richard his mark Williams	N. G. Sutherford " "
"	28	Mason Martin	N. G. Sutherford " "
March	2	Henry his mark Dove	N. G. Sutherford " "
"	2	Levi his mark Hopkins	N. G. Sutherford " "
"	7	Israel his mark Butler	N. G. Sutherford " "
"	13	George his mark Blair	N. G. Sutherford " "
"	14	Tilghman his mark Graham	N. G. Sutherford " "

Records of the Freedmen's Bureau, National Archives

Pledge signed by twenty Rockville freedmen in 1867, guaranteeing a teacher's board and washing, as well as fuel and lights for a schoolhouse for black children.

HAITI: AN EARLY ROCKVILLE NEIGHBORHOOD

Black families began to cluster in rural settlements around Rockville after the Civil War. Former slaves who had lived in quarters or houses on the master's property found shelter among other freedmen. One settlement, united by family ties and a legacy of self-sufficiency, became one of Rockville's first neighborhoods. Haiti—pronounced *Hay-tie*—is the traditional name given by its residents to the black community on Frederick Road, a half mile north of what was then the town limits.

Haiti encompassed the Martin farm and the north end of the Beall property occupied by trusted slaves. By 1842, Samuel Martin Jr. had established a farm on eight and one-half acres, linked to the main road through "Martin's Lane." Where Martin and Beall land touched, Alfred Ross, a slave of the Bealls, built his home. As each family added a generation, Martin and Ross divided their land for additional home sites.

In the first decade after Margaret Beall emancipated her slaves, she sold homesites to several of them for five dollars each. Satisfied with the freedmen's progress, she later removed the "subject to Margaret Beall's supervision and control" clause from each deed.[52] Until her death in 1901, she maintained a close relationship with the families, employing some of them in the house and on the farm and continuing to permit burials in the farm cemetery north of the Beall-Dawson house.

Kinship, steady employment in a growing town, land ownership, and the progress of succeeding generations kept the families of freedmen Alfred and Jane Ross, Edward and Ellen Wood, and Catherine Smith in Rockville. Ross's original dwelling remains on Martin's Lane, as do second, third, fourth, and fifth generation Wood, Smith, and Ross homes. Most of the orchards, hog pens, and chicken houses are gone, but extensive gardens, outbuildings, and crazy quilt land patterns reveal the development of the community over a 170-year period.

Haiti grew and flourished in a society segregated by race. Summer visitors stayed to build permanent homes. Newlyweds built mail order cottages. Real estate speculators sold lots and homes to blacks who intermarried with the original families. Haiti residents employed local black builders to construct new homes or replace older ones and participated in civil rights activities organized by Montgomery County's sizeable black population.

Rockville extended its corporate limits in 1949 to include Haiti. Soon after, the town paved the two-lane road and brought water and sewer to the neighborhood. When Martin's Lane was widened in 1965 in order to access large subdivisions to the west, several old trees were lost, and increased traffic lessened the rural nature of the community.

The origin of the name Haiti is unknown, but there may be a link between free black farmer Samuel Martin, Rockville merchant Honoré Martin, and the symbolism of a successful Caribbean slave insurrection in 1798.[53]

be set up and stored at convenient points around town for future emergencies.[51]

In 1873, residents mourned the recent deaths of two men, Matthew Fields and Samuel Martin Jr., pillars of the community since the middle of the century. Fields, who died suddenly in 1871, had given Rockville its first successful newspaper. His widow, Rebecca Fields, took over the presses of the *Sentinel* to continue his Democratic legacy and support her six children. The refusal of the hometown paper to publish Samuel Martin's obituary occasioned caustic words from a Washington, D.C. press in 1873. The *National Republican*, in an editorial entitled "Maryland Prejudice: How the Papers of Rockville Respect the Dead," expressed dismay at this treatment by the "Democratic country paper." "The fact of [Martin's] citizenship under the law, of his long residence, of his property, of his blameless life, of his not owing a dollar to any one, were all lost sight of in the old unwarranted prejudice against his color. . . ." Samuel Martin Jr., born a slave near the spot where he died, had resided in Rockville all of his life. He left considerable property to his fourteen children.[54]

Perception and pride directed renewed civic interest and community action in the early 1870s.

The Rockville that residents referred to in 1860 as a *village* was commonly called a *town* thirteen years later. Organizations formed in an energetic spurt might founder, but the call for citizen involvement had been issued. Rockville's first neighborhoods had developed in the town center and in Haiti. Citizens augmented established institutions with new ones to meet evolving needs. The process of community-building would continue with a reconciled population governed by town commissioners who had proven response to citizen interest and to a general emergency.

By 1873, a transitional date for Rockville, the town had shaken off most of the outward effects of the Civil War. It was ready to shift attention from reconstruction and reconciliation to community-building through development in and around the town. Plans put on hold because of the war, such as the rail line through Montgomery County, were resumed. Community goals that had proceeded at a slower pace, such as education and public improvements through local government, could now receive deserved consideration.

The Rockville resident of 1873 had every reason to anticipate a bright future. Rail service was about to open, with exciting prospects for the enhancement of property values and spurring development around the growing town. Street trees planted around Court House Square were thriving. Public schools were in operation. Town government was keeping order, paving streets, and taking other steps to improve the community. Rockville had weathered the uncertainties of war and could enjoy the prospects of peace.

ROCKVILLE

Chapter Five

PEERLESS ROCKVILLE

Suburbanization and Urbanity 1873–1916

"The auspicious event occurred on Sunday last . . . [We were] assembled at the depot to witness the iron-horse as he went dashing by with his load of passengers. . . . the great work has been accomplished, and our people may bid farewell to slow coaches and muddy roads—they can now go to Washington in forty-five minutes at a cost of sixty cents."[1]

On May 25, 1873, the "auspicious event" set Rockville on a fresh track. No one who greeted the first regular passenger train that day, heard the hiss of the steam engine, exulted in the striking music of the Rockville Band, or waved the train out of town doubted the dawn of a new era.

In the last decades of the nineteenth century and the first decades of the twentieth, Rockville adjusted to new opportunities and growth. Dramatic advances in transportation enabled city dwellers to vacation or settle in Rockville and experience the suburban residential ideal. From farmland in every direction around the village, developers carved building lots, triggering a construction boom that would not be matched for another half century. New stores, hotels, and services sprang up, and local farmers benefited from expanded connections to markets.

The railroad embarked the recently incorporated town on a path of modernization. Spurred by strong leadership and the energy of newcomers, Rockville began to shift into a larger sphere. Progressive citizens and public officials revamped town government and created new institutions, both formal and informal, to address community needs ranging from sanitation to cultural activities. By 1916, in tandem with other rural communities in the Washington area, Rockville had donned some of the characteristics of an early twentieth century suburb.

NEW TRANSPORTATION CONNECTION TO WASHINGTON

The coming of the railroad through Montgomery County, passing just east of Rockville's commercial center, broadened horizons for the rural town. To the century-old functions of the town—intersection of roads connecting larger destinations, hub of county government and courts, market center for a thriving farm population—was added the role of satellite town to the larger city of Washington, D.C.

The rail line through Montgomery County took twenty years to plan and build. The Metropolitan Railroad Company had begun raising funds and determining possible routes in 1853. Due to a disappointing response from investors, labor disputes and economic downturns, and the B&O's emphasis on new lines to the Midwest, the prospect of a Georgetown-to-Hagerstown route dimmed. After the Civil War accentuated the need for rail transit, in 1865 the Maryland General Assembly granted a new charter to the B&O Railroad for its Metropolitan Branch.

While the B&O condemned land along the right-of-way, work crews graded and laid track. In 1868 and 1869, Montgomery County juries awarded eight owners a total of $7,231.01 for their properties between Rockville and Randolph, the stop above

Garrett Park. The total cost of the 42.5-mile line was $3.5 million. On September 11–12, 1872, two months after the railroad made an experimental run between Rockville and Washington, special trains brought hundreds of Washingtonians to the Rockville Fair. Following more delays, during which residents frequently complained, the B&O finally inaugurated regular passenger service on May 25, 1873.[2]

The rail connection immediately set Rockville awhirl. William Brewer, a young Rockville attorney, subdivided ten acres of his family farm behind Saint Mary's Church into twenty-one building lots, three streets, and an alley. For one thousand dollars he sold to the B&O two lots on which to erect the railroad station. Rockville's town commissioners were so delighted by this new gateway that they extended the boundaries to include Brewer's Third Addition to Rockville and built a board sidewalk from Montgomery Avenue to the depot.

B&O architect E. Francis Baldwin designed a first-class brick station house, one of four on the line, for Rockville. Baldwin (1837–1916) was a Baltimore-based architect who specialized in railroad buildings and churches. The Railroad Gothic style passenger depot—a delightful combination of red brick, white limestone, wooden gingerbread detailing, overhanging eaves, and patterned slate roof—was an architectural landmark upon completion in 1873. The building contained waiting rooms for ladies and gentlemen, an outside window to the ticket office, and upstairs living quarters for the agent and his family. In 1884, a separate freight house was added

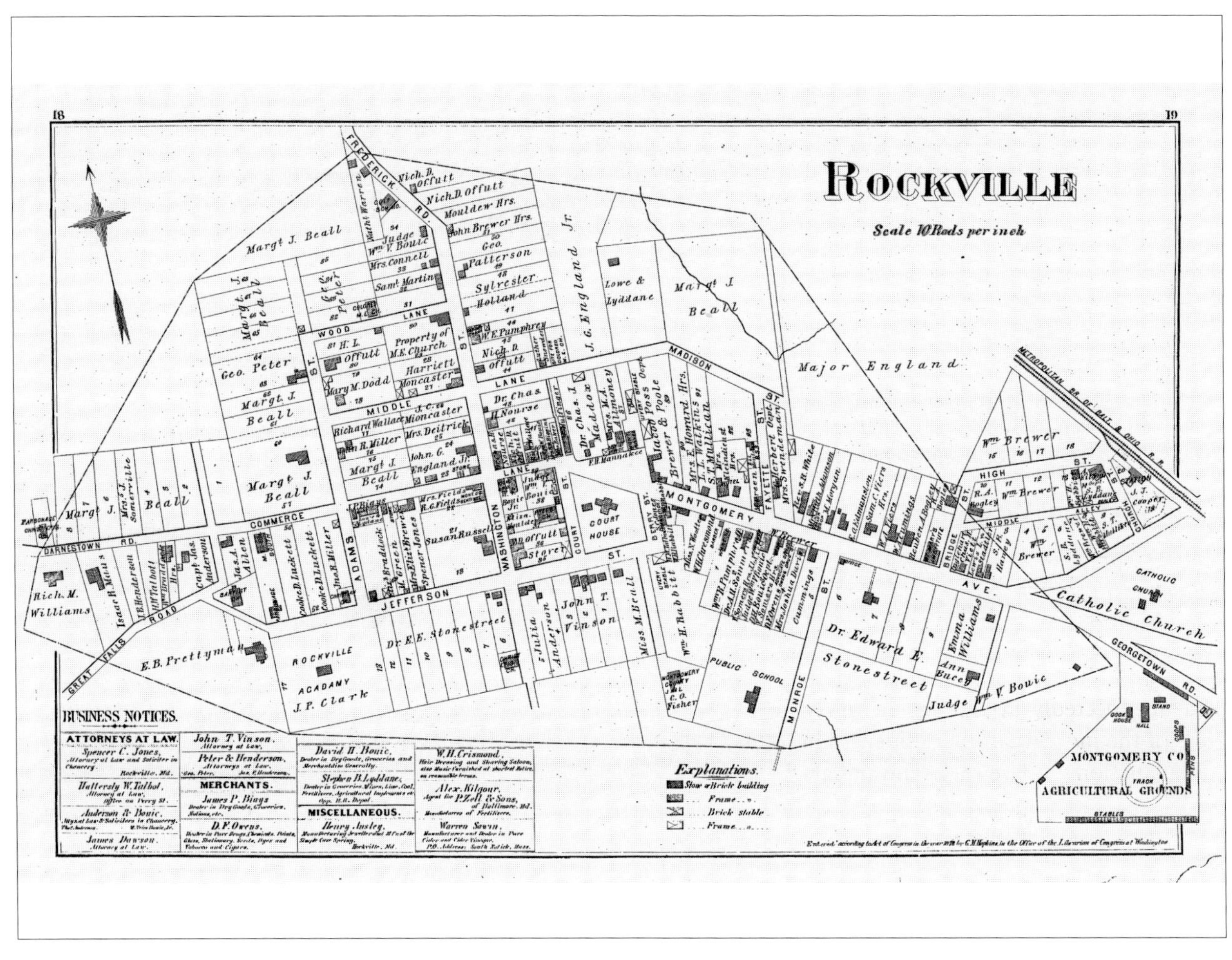

Map of Rockville 1878. From G. M. Hopkins, Atlas of Fifteen Miles Around Washington Including the County of Montgomery, Maryland.

to provide space for shipments which started or ended in Rockville.

The *Sentinel* immediately acknowledged that Rockville's connection to the federal city was greatly enhanced by the new rail line.

> The opening of the Metropolitan R.R. has brought a good many strangers to our town, while hundreds are passing by on this great thoroughfare.—Parties are continually going to Washington from this point and coming from Washington to Rockville—the two places being now in such close proximity, the interchange of friendly greetings and the transaction of business is but a trip of pleasure, when formerly a person ought to have made his will before setting out in the old stage-coach in a visit to the Metropolitan city. The member of Congress who traveled over the old road to the National Capitol ought to have back pay because he earned his money, but now the scene is changed, and instead of eight or ten mortal hours of almost unendurable agony, the trip can now be made in forty-five minutes, and at trifling cost.[3]

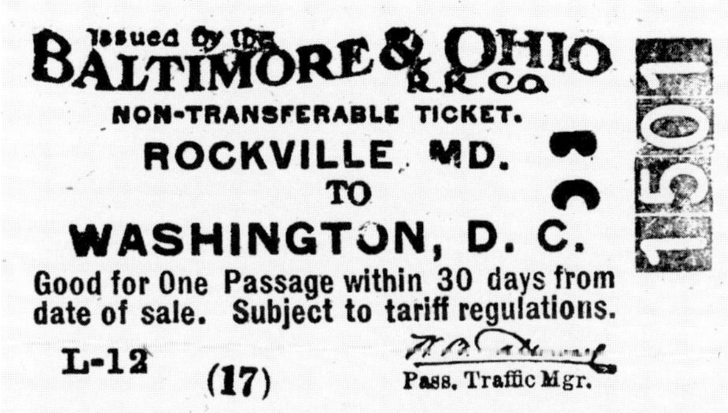
Issued by the BALTIMORE & OHIO R.R. CO.
NON-TRANSFERABLE TICKET.
ROCKVILLE, MD.
TO
WASHINGTON, D. C.
Good for One Passage within 30 days from date of sale. Subject to tariff regulations.
L-12 (17) Pass. Traffic Mgr.
1501

Courtesy of Montgomery County Historical Society

Courtesy of Peerless Rockville

TOP: B&O ticket. Trains stopped at thirteen depots or waiting stations between Rockville and Washington, D.C. BOTTOM: Earliest photo of the Rockville depot, circa 1883. The railroad opened Rockville to Washingtonians wishing to live and relax in the country and also expanded urban markets for local farmers.

The optimism of railroad boosters was quickly affirmed. William Brewer sold eleven of his twenty-one lots for two to three hundred dollars each. With other Rockville businessmen, he formed the Rockville Mutual Building Association, the first of its kind in the county, to finance construction in the county seat. The initial three loans went to purchasers of Brewer's lots near the depot.

Brewer selected Lots 5 and 6, on a slight rise commanding a view of the fairgrounds and the town, as the location of his own home. He moved into the ten-room Italianate style house in 1878. When Brewer died unexpectedly at the age of thirty-nine in 1885, "one of the most desirable residences in town" sold at public auction for five thousand dollars.[4]

The Rockville depot became the meeting place for townspeople, local farmers, and visitors. In the early morning, farmers loaded milk and produce bound for Washington. Later, commuters entrained for city jobs as up-county students disembarked for the high school. In the afternoon, the outbound trains brought traveling salesmen, vacationers, and return commuters. Visitors and urban goods bound for local stores arrived each day. Townspeople gathered to exchange the news of the day, and young women coincidentally met the trains carrying the eligible bachelors.[5] Initially six trains ran each way, three local and three express. The original nine stops on the line quickly expanded to twenty-eight as the B&O willingly established flag stops at the new mills, dairy farm stations, and suburban developments which sprang up along the route. Between

Charles Brewer collection, courtesy of Peerless Rockville

The Woodlawn Hotel was Rockville's grandest destination during the town's heyday as a summer resort. The hotel closed in 1906 to emerge four years later as Chestnut Lodge Sanitarium.

1893 and the 1920s there were eighteen passenger trains a day.

In the Rockville area, the rail line paralleled the Rockville Pike, one of the muddy roads referred to by the *Sentinel*. Stations on this section of the line were: Randolph (thirteen miles out of Washington), Halpine, Rockville, and Derwood. Windham, one quarter of a mile south of Randolph, and Westmore, on the northern edge of Rockville, functioned for a time as minor train stops but those areas never saw the development planned in the late nineteenth century.[6]

For farmers in the Rockville area, the railroad was a real boost. Most had recovered from the Civil War's physical damage, but they still owed money and faced stiff competition from larger midwestern operations. On September 6, 1876, the anniversary of the founding of Montgomery County, two thousand to three thousand people gathered at the fairgrounds. The all day celebration featured speeches by civic leaders Thomas Anderson and Judge Richard Johns Bowie, a luncheon, music and prayers, an old-fashioned picnic, and an exhibit of relics, (which included a lock of George Washington's hair, arrowheads and hatchets, flax raised near Rockville in the 1770s, and a piece of wood from the carriage in which Gen. Andrew Jackson traveled from Tennessee through Rockville to his inauguration in Washington in 1829). In his centennial address, Anderson pronounced county farms healthy, citing soil-enrichment practices with improved production, busy mills, and the impact of the new rail line. With the train, farmers could ship milk, fruit, and vegetables to market in Washington without spoiling.[7]

With the railroad providing a new gateway, Rockville and other Montgomery County towns soon began to enjoy popularity with city folk as a country resort with a high, healthy altitude. Hotels and boarding houses which had catered to court clientele and traveling salesmen advertised Rockville's attractiveness as a weekend and summer refuge. In the spring of 1889, Mary Colley, proprietress of the Clarendon Hotel in Washington, opened the Woodlawn Hotel at the far west end of town. She boasted forty guest rooms, electric bells, gas lighting, artesian water, teas, card parties and musical soirees, walks among tree-filled lawns, and breezy porches. Carriages transported summer guests from the train a mile to the Woodlawn.[8]

THE SUBURBAN IDEAL

Suburbanization—the systematic growth of fringe areas at a pace more rapid than core cities—began to change America even before the Civil War. Movement to the outskirts of cities was spurred by urban crowding, an expanding middle class that envisioned home as haven from work, and modern transportation technology that opened up less expensive real estate beyond walking distances. As horsecars and then railroads connected the countryside with the city, speculators carved farmland around New York, Boston, Philadelphia, and Baltimore into building lots and proclaimed the suburban ideal of healthy family living, home ownership, and easy access to work. Embellishing the romance of suburbia for an eager audience were Victorian cottages designed in the manner of Andrew Jackson Downing and curving, flowing landscapes patterned after the work of Frederick Law Olmsted.[9]

Washington, D.C., doubled in population from 1860 to 1873. Many of the newcomers worked for a greatly expanded federal bureaucracy recruited to administer such needs as pensions and patents, the postal service, census work, and the new Department of Agriculture. Developers initially attracted families of government clerks and service industry workers to close-in Le Droit Park and Anacostia, but soon residential suburbs sprang up in more distant areas such as Cleveland Park and Tennallytown. When the landmark Civil Service Act of 1883 established a career civil service for federal employees, the stage was set for a stable, middle-class work force that needed housing in and near the nation's capital.[10]

Rockville residents welcoming the railroad were mindful of the suburban ideal. "And this beautiful town of Rockville . . . will at the Centennial Anniversary of this Celebration be a suburban city, its streets shadowed by palatial mansions, its environing hills crowned with splendid villas," Thomas Anderson predicted in 1876.[11]

Economic downturns in the 1870s stunted local optimism for suburban residential growth. A few railroad-inspired subdivisions, such as Linden near Forest Glen and the Methodist camp meeting in Washington Grove, opened in Montgomery County in the mid-1870s. In Rockville, new dwellings materialized on the Darnestown Road (today the close-in two hundred block of West Montgomery Avenue) at the western limits of town. Margaret Beall, daughter of county clerk Upton Beall, sold lots for the new Episcopal rectory and another residence on the north side of the road. On the south side, attorneys Hattersly W. Talbott and James Henderson purchased adjacent parcels and in 1878 erected a shared windmill and barn on Falls Road behind their new Victorian cottages.

With improved economic times in the 1880s came more vigorous development along the new Metropolitan Branch. As its sponsors had predicted, the railroad brought growth and prosperity to the countryside it crossed. Rockville's population tripled as successful developments led to sharp rises in Montgomery County land values, a trend which continued for two decades. Takoma Park, Kensington, and Garrett Park exemplified the railroad suburbs. Hopeful speculators surveyed and recorded new subdivisions between the tracks and the Rockville Pike from Randolph to Rockville, which they named Spring Lake Park, Halpin, and Autrey Park. Queen Anne style homes using the balloon framing method of construction quickly appeared, made possible by mill-sawn lumber in standardized dimensions, mail order catalogs, and inexpensive machine-made nails.

Entrepreneurs scrambled to entice purchasers to Rockville. Richard Beall and G. Minor Anderson formed a partnership to sell real estate and publish a four-page pamphlet. *Cheap Lands* lauded Rockville as handsomely paved and well lighted, with lovely homes and affordable goods, and "fast becoming one of the most popular summer resorts in the country, being in reality a suburb of Washington."[12]

One individual poised to take advantage of the interest in Rockville was Rebecca T. Veirs (1833–1918). A former slaveowner whose farm is now occupied by Lakewood Country Club, she purchased two lots in a grove of oak trees west of Van Buren Street from Margaret Beall in 1883. There Mrs. Veirs built a large boarding house and a modest Victorian cottage that she rented to summer visitors and year-round tenants. Two years later, the entrepreneur laid out twenty building lots in R. T. Veirs Addition on Wall and Thomas Streets near the Woodlawn Hotel. Veirs and her son also purchased lots in other new subdivisions, in one instance borrowing two thousand dollars to build an Italianate villa at what is now 409 West Montgomery Avenue. Mrs. Veirs mortgaged these early ventures in order to obtain cash for larger investments, but in a late-century depression found herself in default. Upon her death in 1918, the *Sentinel* observed that "Mrs. Veirs was a woman of many striking and attractive traits of character. . . . and a person of natural business capacity rarely possessed by members of her sex. . . ."[13]

Enterprising bankers, lawyers, and realtors platted and promoted new residential subdivisions close to the railroad depot. Former Register of Wills Robert Carter's 269-acre farm yielded five-hundred building lots, connected by board sidewalks and streets now known as Washington, Maryland, Fleet, Monroe, and Mt. Vernon. Charles J. Maddox, a physician and farmer, sold one third of an acre lots for one hundred dollars in Janeta, around First Street on the road to Wheaton. Dr. Maddox offered free alternate lots to

Three New Rockville Neighborhoods

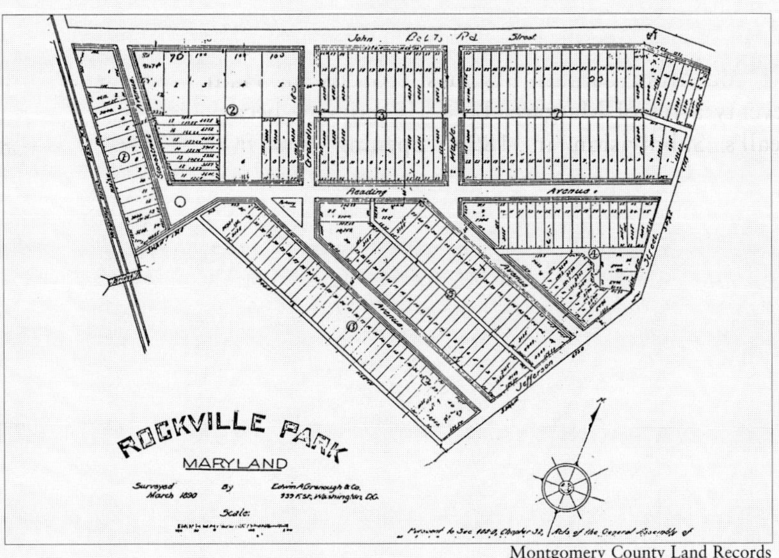

Montgomery County Land Records

Plat of Rockville Park, one of Rockville's late-nineteenth century residential subdivisions.

The coming of the railroad produced a flurry of speculative activity in Rockville. As a suburb of Washington, Rockville could provide the growing middle class with healthy family living, home ownership, and easy access to city jobs. Farm land, valued by proximity to the railroad, yielded hundreds of building lots on paper. City dwellers paid \$150 to \$500 for one-quarter to one-acre lots, on which they built Victorian cottages of all imaginable sizes and styles in the 1880s and early 1890s.

From gleams in the eyes of real estate promoters emerged several attractive nineteenth century Rockville neighborhoods. Three new subdivisions did much to change the face of Rockville: Rockville Park, Lincoln Park, and West End Park.

In 1884 William Reading, a Washington lumber and coal merchant, purchased twenty-eight acres of land near the B&O Station from Dr. E. E. Stonestreet for \$4,293. Reading laid out fifty-six large-sized building lots, six of which were built upon before he sold Readington to another D.C. speculator for \$10,000. Washington Danenhower, who also laid out Spring Lake Park near Halpine, resurveyed the area in 1890 as Rockville Park. Stylish homes, built for local merchants and city commuters, stand today on Baltimore Road and Grandin and Reading Avenues.

Lincoln Park was one of the first real estate ventures in Montgomery County intended for sale to blacks. William Wallace Welsh, proprietor of a general store next to the depot, purchased eight acres of land and divided it into fifty-three building lots, which he sold for eighty dollars each. Lincoln Park, outside the town limits, was close to five black families already in the area. Sales were brisk. In 1899 the *Sentinel* advertised a property in Lincoln Park "with a well of good drinking water at the kitchen door, and . . . convenient to the Rockville depot. The property is situated in a very highly improved community. . . ."[14] Welsh erected a number of homes for sale and rental. The narrow, deep lots in Lincoln Park allowed space behind the house for the well, privy, gardens, trees, and farm animals. Many of the men labored on nearby farms and industries, on the railroad, or at Welsh's store. The women worked as domestics in Rockville homes and hotels.[15]

West End Park may have been named for its location or for Julius West. In 1890, Washington attorney Henry Copp purchased close to five hundred acres and planned an elaborate suburban neighborhood. Quarter-acre lots sold quickly at three hundred and four hundred dollars, and large Victorian homes arose along the Darnestown Road. In the promotional booklet *Peerless Rockville*, Copp extolled Rockville's virtues. "To live in the midst of a cultivated population is an advantage not to be overlooked."[16] Copp built several houses in West End Park and lived for a time on Beall Avenue. Economic depressions coupled with lawsuits led to default and abandonment of his grand plans. All but 220 lots of West End Park were auctioned at the courthouse door in 1900.[17]

those who would build substantial houses. Two white entrepreneurs, Nathan Bickford of Washington and William Wallace Welsh of Rockville, fashioned building lots to sell exclusively to blacks. Welsh opened the first section of Lincoln Park in 1890, the second in 1892, the same year Bickford carved twenty-five lots from Samuel Martin's property in Haiti. Seventy acres of Margaret Beall's inheritance became Beall's Subdivision in 1893, opening lots from Harrison to North Street and from the Frederick Road west to Forest Avenue.[18]

By far the most ambitious subdivision in nineteenth century Rockville was Henry Copp and Reuben Detrick's West End Park, a multi-sectioned mixed-use plan for the former Julius West farm. Its grand boulevard, prominent hotel sites, and separate residential and business sections represented the epitome of the suburban ideal. In the 1880s, Copp had developed Ken Gar and Garrett Park. Copp's silver-tongued brochure, *Peerless Rockville: What It Offers to Homeseekers and Investors*, captured the excitement in 1890:

> Do you want Health? Do you expect to keep or secure it for yourself, your wife, or your children within city limits? . . . While Washington is beyond dispute the healthiest and handsomest city in the United States, it has many of the disadvantages that are common to all cities. . . . Do you want wealth? . . . The wisest patrimony a man can leave his family is a good sized lot or lots in a growing village near Washington. . . . Do you want comfort? . . . The society in these villages is desirable, and the moral tone of the children is decidedly improved by removing them from the streets of Washington. . . .
>
> Like an eagle on its eyry, Rockville looks down upon the National Capital from an altitude of five hundred feet. . . . As a winter sanitarium, summer resort, and all-the-year-round place of residence, Rockville stands without a rival. An altitude of five hundred feet, unapproached train service, and an organized community of about fifteen hundred people, are the claims upon which its superiority is based.

Rockville's first suburban building boom peaked about 1890 and concluded a decade later. The bubble of activity that spawned exclusive subdivisions all around the town boundary burst with economic downturns and saturation of the market along the railroad line. When the first train arrived in 1873, Rockville counted about 670 residents, up from 365 in 1860. The 1890 census noted 1,568 residents, although a decade later the number had declined to 1,110. Land area nearly doubled, from 134 to more than 200 acres. Homes erected in the boom years in Rockville's railroad subdivisions are still admired as excellent representatives of nineteenth century architecture, but it was left to later generations to fill in the surrounding lots.

TRANSPORTATION REVOLUTION

Before 1873, methods of getting into and away from Rockville were limited. An extensive but crude road system in place for nearly a century directed foot, horseback, carriage, and stage travelers toward Georgetown, Baltimore, Great Falls and the canal, Frederick, Annapolis, or west toward Poolesville and Monocacy. Rockville's direct link to the nation's capital was the Rockville Turnpike.

In the late nineteenth and early twentieth century, the alternatives greatly expanded. The steam railroad came into Montgomery County in 1873, connecting remote areas to markets in Washington and triggering a real estate boom that dramatically changed the size, appearance, and character of Rockville. Two decades later, the electric trolley opened another connection to the nation's capital. This comfortable and inexpensive mode of public transit encouraged additional residential and commercial development along the Rockville Pike, connecting tiny communities such as Montrose and Halpine to Rockville's stores, government offices, and schools.

By the last decade of the nineteenth century, the Washington Turnpike Company had lost all incentive to maintain the Rockville Pike. The road was rutted and muddy, particularly during winter. Users paid insufficient tolls to warrant keeping the tollbooths open. The turnpike company declared bankruptcy and deeded the roadway to the Montgomery County commissioners. In the twentieth century, the Pike was revived by Maryland's new system of state-maintained roads and by the increasing popularity of the automobile.

ROCKVILLE MASTER BUILDERS

Paralleling Rockville's construction boom was the success of four local builders. Edwin West, Reuben Hill Sr. and Jr., and Thomas C. Groomes turned their carpentry talents into design and house-building skills to take advantage of the flurry of activity. Three of the men were carpenter-builders, while the fourth advertised himself as an architect.

Edwin M. West (1862–1928) came to Rockville about 1886. He cut ice, sawed lumber, and operated a mule-driven thrashing machine. West aided the suburban ideal by purchasing lots from developers and erecting charming houses on them. Between 1888 and 1895 he constructed the new Rockville Academy building and at least fifteen homes and churches in Rockville, including a handsome house for his own family. West's house, at the present-day address of 114 West Montgomery Avenue, featured a variety of shapes and exterior materials in the Queen Anne style as well as exquisite interior woodwork and fireplaces. It incorporated many of the architectural details he offered his clients. West, who served on the town council 1892–96, moved to a farm in Alexandria in 1909.[19]

Thomas C. Groomes (1845–1937) began his career in the Mechanicsville (Olney) area as a carpenter and undertaker. In 1879 he built his first house, Rock Spring, for Roger Farquhar. He constructed three more large homes in Rockville before relocating to the town in 1888. There he continued to design, construct, enlarge, and remodel more than forty homes, businesses, and churches, many of which stand today. Perhaps his grandest product is 100 Forest Avenue, built for Hattersly Talbott (attorney and state senator) and Laura Talbott (niece of Judge Bowie) in 1890 at a cost of $4,950. Groomes, the first in Rockville to describe himself as an architect, also designed public schools for Rockville and Montrose. Groomes left Rockville in 1922 to live in Washington, secured his driver's license at age eighty-four, and died in 1937 at age ninety-two.[20]

Reuben Hill Sr. (1829–1915) and Reuben Hill Jr. (1859–1936) were farm laborers and carpenters who lived in the area which is now Lincoln Park. When Reuben Sr. agreed in 1867 to support a school for black students, he likely honored that pledge in skilled labor. A slave until his mid-thirties, in 1880 Reuben Sr. purchased land and teamed with former Confederate soldier and fence builder Simeon Berry to build a house northeast of Rockville. That year, Berry bequeathed to Hill his tools, furniture, and the house. Reuben Sr. also helped to build a brick dwelling in the new subdivision of Lincoln Park in 1897. When he died in 1915, the *Sentinel* noted that "Uncle Reuben" greeted friends with an old-fashioned, courteous bow and had "gained the respect and confidence of both races in this community." Reuben Thomas Hill, or Reuben Jr., inherited his father's tools and talents. He enlarged the family home, built household furniture and tiny houses for children, and helped to erect other homes in Lincoln Park. The Reuben Hill house on Lincoln Avenue is still owned by the family.[21]

Richard Andrews collection, courtesy of Peerless Rockville

Courtesy of Montgomery County Historical Society

TOP: Edwin West, one of Rockville's master builders in the "boom" period, chose the Queen Anne style for his family house on Commerce Lane. BOTTOM: Thomas C. Groomes designed many houses, businesses, and schools in the Rockville area. Groomes posed at his office on Commerce Lane near the courthouse.

THE TROLLEY ARRIVES IN ROCKVILLE

The railroad's success whetted appetites for additional transportation connections that would open more land for development. Beginning in the late 1880s, new street railway companies organized to foster development in suburban Chevy Chase and Bethesda. Soon, trolleys also connected Washington with Cabin John, Takoma Park, and Tennallytown. In July 1891, the Tenallytown & Rockville Railway Company opened electric rail service on Wisconsin Avenue, through Bethesda, and along Old Georgetown Road to Bethesda Park, an amusement park near Alta Vista. After the Washington & Rockville Electric Railway Company was chartered in 1897, talk of extending the line to Rockville became serious.

The first trolley rolled up the Rockville Pike to the fairgrounds at the eastern limits of the town in January 1900, but it went no further. It had traveled a distance of sixteen miles from Georgetown in fifty-five minutes. In the previous eighteen months, the Washington & Rockville had obtained permission from Montgomery County for a right-of-way along the Rockville Pike and from the Mayor and Council to enter Rockville. The town granted the franchise and right-of-way under the condition that the company construct a double track to the courthouse and then a single-track rail to the western limits of the town. The company requested changes, and a special town election was set for July 23, 1900, to vote on the issue.

Trolley service for Rockville was not welcomed by all. By vote of sixty-four in favor and thirty-two against, Rockville residents approved a revised ordinance permitting the W&R to lay single track through Rockville from the eastern to western boundaries. At the same time, the Mayor and Council imposed speed limits, prohibited steam engines, and required service to the Woodlawn Hotel. The W&R began laying track from the fairgrounds to the courthouse in 1900. However, through 1901 and 1902, the rail company claimed that financial conditions for extending the Rockville line farther west "were not sunshiny."[22] It was not convinced there were sufficient customers. After legal huddles and raucous citizen meetings, the town fathers revoked the ordinance in January 1903. When the company threatened to tear up its track, the Mayor and Council covered the in-town track with macadam. The impasse continued until November 1905 when the town readmitted W&R into Rockville on a single track from the fairgrounds past the courthouse to Laird Street, with a siding near the fairgrounds. The law ran through January 1, 1935. Service on the main street to the west end did not begin until the spring of 1908, after the owners of the Woodlawn Hotel had declared bankruptcy and sold the property.[23]

Trolleys received power from an overhead electric wire. Once out of Washington and carrying fewer passengers, they rode a single track. Motormen manually operated switches and signal lights so cars could wait on side tracks to pass in opposite directions, or to ensure safe intersection with other tracks. The cars could be driven from either end. With speed limits in Rockville of twelve miles per hour (six miles per hour at intersections), trolley operators would make up time through open country at speeds of up to sixty miles per

Charles Brewer collection, courtesy of Peerless Rockville

Photo by Lewis Reed, Charles Brewer collection, courtesy of Peerless Rockville

TOP: Lewis Reed took this photo of a trolley bound for Rockville with a five-by-four box camera which produced an image on a glass plate. Note the cow-catcher on the trolley. BOTTOM: The tracks met the Rockville Pike among farmland between Old Georgetown Road and Montrose Road. The trolley in the center of this 1910 photograph is headed south.

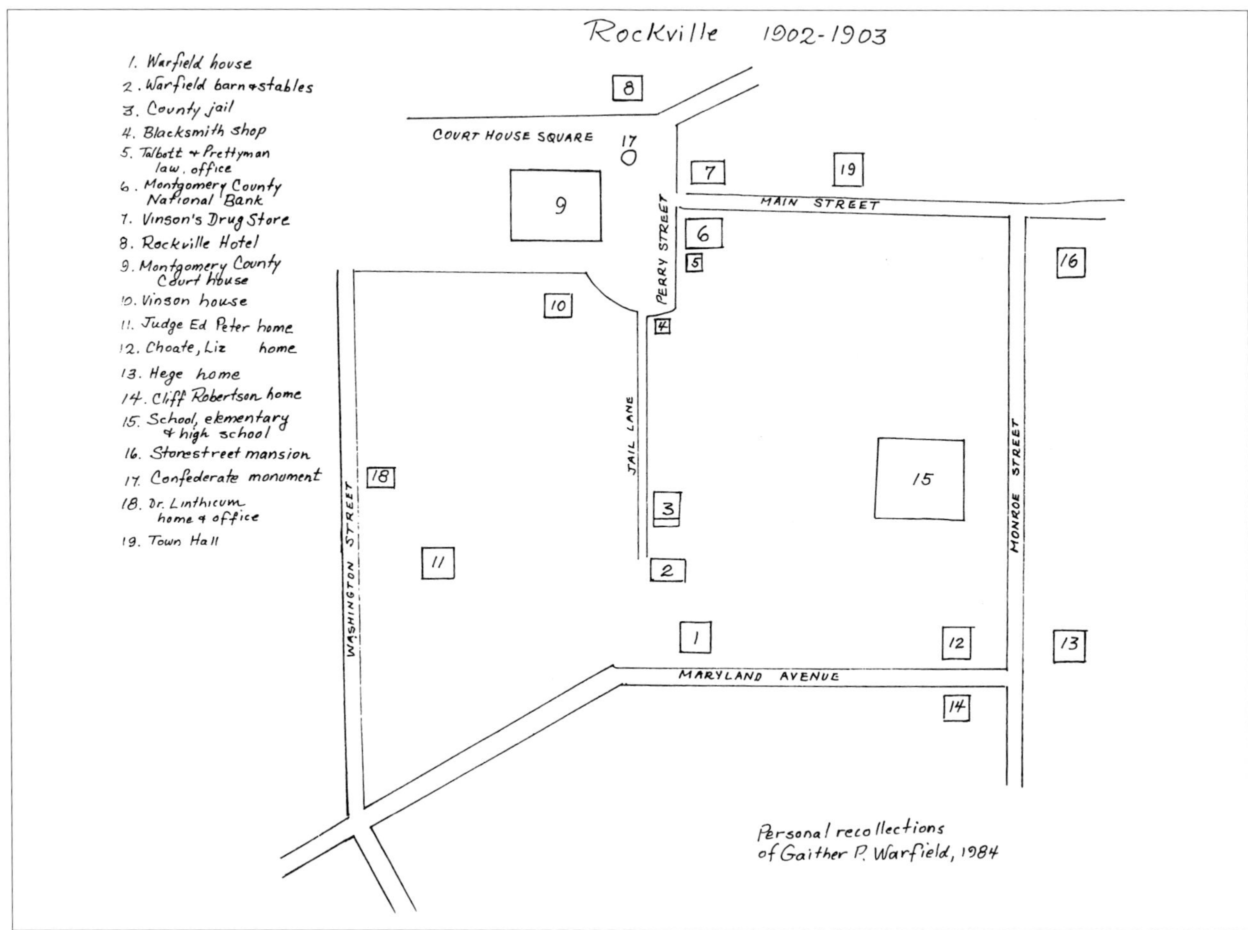

Hand-drawn map of Rockville, 1902–3, as recalled by Gaither P. Warfield eighty years later. Number seventeen is an error as the Confederate Monument was not erected until 1913.

hour on the Pike or in the woods between Grosvenor and Montrose.

Washington commuters and county farmers used the railroad, but Rockville residents took to the trolley. They used it for short trips to work or school, to shop in Washington for items not available locally, for deliveries of all kinds, and just for fun. Georgetown Preparatory School students arrived from Washington in droves each morning. Trolleys rolled through Rockville between 6:30 A.M. and 12:30 A.M.; the last run was nicknamed the Owl. Cars left Rockville and Georgetown every thirty minutes. The trip cost fifty cents and took almost an hour. Cars paralleled Wisconsin Avenue, Old Georgetown Road, and the Rockville Pike, with local stops at Montrose, Halpine, the fairgrounds, courthouse, and Woodlawn, although passengers could pull the cord for special requests. Rockville shoppers arranged with Washington stores to send purchases by trolley, so it was not unusual to see a wood stove or a piece of furniture on the back platform of the car. In 1905, the company added a freight car to carry perishables such as cakes of ice, butter, or milk.[24] The route of the W&R can still be seen to the east of the Pike near Georgetown Preparatory School and in the rusted trestle near Tuckerman Lane.

ROCKVILLE IN 1900

Improvement in transportation was but one influence on the character of Rockville. Changing demographics and the philosophy of the Progressive movement also helped to alter the town. A visitor in 1900 would have noted some progressive rumblings yet recognized that no amount of innovative technology, aggressive real estate marketing, or demographic realignment could easily stir the town from its customary ways. Although Rockville in 1900 differed significantly from the county seat of 1800 or 1860, its routine changed little between those times. The pace of life for most Rockville residents was as slow as their Southern-accented speech.

Between incorporation and 1900, Rockville nearly tripled in area and in population. In 1860, the town contained 134 acres and 365 residents. Four decades later, 354 acres of land housed 1,110 people, nearly half of them newcomers in new homes in new subdivisions on all sides of the original town.

Courtesty of Montgomery County Historical Society

Three homes, built 1890–91, on Forest Avenue.

Mid-nineteenth century Rockville was a *walking town*—a clearly bounded settlement mixing residential and commercial functions, whose inhabitants lived a short distance from work, and where the most fashionable addresses were located close to the center of town. By 1900, Rockville had taken on characteristics of a Washington, D.C., suburb. The best residential addresses, affordable to the middle class, were on the fringes of the town, and Rockville looked to Washington for much of its employment and shopping.[25]

The demographic mix of the area had expanded by the new century. Joining earlier English, Scots, and Irish settlers were German immigrants John and Dorothy Reisinger, Henry Viett, a tinsmith, and his wife Helen, and liveryman Jacob Poss. Benjamin and Annie Lenowitz left Russia to open a general store at Halpine on the Rockville Pike. Charles Hoy and Moy Toy, natives of China, operated a laundry near the courthouse.[26]

The U.S. Census of 1900 reported about thirty Rockville residents employed by the federal government, with the majority in the Post Office, War Department, or Census Bureau. An equal number worked for the courts, county government, or the railroad. Representative of federal employees were Agnes Matlock, a clerk at the Census Bureau, and Edwin Smith, of the Coast and Geodetic Survey, who studied variations of latitude from a temporary observatory behind his home on Forest Avenue and later in Gaithersburg. The Smiths had summered in Rockville in 1888 and two years later hired Edwin West to build a sixteen-room year-round residence on Forest Avenue. County and court workers residing in Rockville included Henry C. Allnutt, register of wills, who lived near the circle on Beall Avenue, public school Superintendent Willis Burdette, and Circuit Court Judge James B. Henderson.

The Census listed most black men as day laborers, although Rockville also claimed a black upholsterer, post office clerk, carpenter, mail carrier, plasterer, stone mason, liveryman, well-digger, and blacksmith. Black women earned money in domestic work, taking in laundry, sewing, and cooking in private homes or at local business establishments.[27]

Schedule of electric light rates, January 22, 1898, from Minutes of the Mayor and Council of Rockville.

SCHEDULE OF RATES.

4 lights or less, - - -	$1.25	per	month.
5 or 6 lights, - - -	1.89	"	"
7 " 8 " - - -	2.30	"	"
9 " 10 " - - -	2.75	"	"
11 " 12 " - - -	3.15	"	"
13, 14, or 15 lights, - -	3.70	"	"
More than 15 lights, - -	3.70	"	"

and 15 cents additional for each light in excess of 15 per month.

Charles Brewer collection, courtesy of Peerless Rockville

Courtesy of Edward, Bonne, and Becky Prettyman

TOP: Looking east on West Montgomery Avenue (then called Darnestown Road), in 1917.
BOTTOM: Law office of Talbott and Prettyman on Court Street. Posed at their law office about 1900 are Charles W. Prettyman and his son William F. Prettyman, both future presidents of the Montgomery County Bar Association, and an unidentified man. Sons often followed their fathers' occupations; Albert Bouic noted that his family practiced law in Rockville for 120 years.

The accelerating pace of technology gradually, yet dramatically, altered lifestyles in Rockville. The addition of a town waterworks and electric light plant in 1897 put modern conveniences within the reach of residents and businesses, although it would take decades before all properties were connected. By 1900, electricity provided the means for artificial light in churches and residences in the West End as well as the trolley, but the Red Brick Courthouse waited until 1913 to be connected to the power grid. The house at 301 Baltimore Road, built in 1906 for Roger and Catherine Shaw, may have been the first new home with electric wiring.[28] Although Rockville had a very deep well and water mains in place throughout the town in 1900, very few residents had indoor plumbing. They paid a monthly fee for the scavenger, who cleaned out the privies. Mayor William Veirs Bouic Jr. claimed the first indoor bathroom for his house on Commerce Lane. The Bouic boys pumped water from the attic water tank to the third floor bathtub, where Mrs. Bouic invited the ladies of the neighborhood to partake of the novelty.[29]

Telephone service arrived in Rockville in 1889 in the form of a public toll station set up by Chesapeake & Potomac Telephone Company (C&P) in Ernest Fearon's drug store near the courthouse. In 1895, the Mayor and Council permitted C&P to erect poles and string wires in Rockville, in return obtaining free use of a phone. The company installed a switchboard in 1906, which allowed twelve lines in Rockville, each shared with six telephones. In 1900, a call from Rockville to Washington, which cost twenty cents, could be overheard by the operator and anyone who wished to listen in.[30]

Even with electricity, housekeeping was a full-time job. Washing—including heating the water, scrubbing, wringing, starching, drying, and ironing—was an all-day affair. Those who could afford to send out their laundry did. Women made clothing at home, so for most, an occasional store purchase, an order from a Sears Roebuck catalog, or a trolley trip to a Washington store was a special occasion. Food came from local farmers or the family's backyard garden, and block ice was delivered several times a week by the Rockville Ice Company. Bread could be made from packaged flour purchased at a local store,

Courtesy of Historical Society of Washington, D.C.

or from fresh-ground Veirs Mill wheat, or could be purchased ready-made from Mrs. Reisinger's bakery for four cents a loaf. Storekeeper David H. Bouic advertised new breakfast foods called "Grape-Nuts, a food for brain and nerve centres," Pillsbury's Vitos, and Cream of Wheat.[31]

The center of Rockville bustled with activity. Shops sold groceries, baked goods, meats, bicycles, carriages, furniture, sewing machines, hats, lumber, and hardware. Families lived above their stores, renting extra rooms to others. By 1900, the *Montgomery Advocate* had joined the *Sentinel* to report the weekly news. A dentist, two druggists, and four physicians who made house calls tended to the health of Rockville residents. Those seeking a barber, plumber, undertaker, blacksmith, shoemaker, or attorney need not leave town.

Courtesy of Montgomery County Historical Society

TOP: North side of Commerce Lane near the courthouse, about 1920.
BOTTOM: Looking from the yard of W. Guy Hicks toward the triangular public park in front of the courthouse, June 1914. In the triangle were the Confederate Monument and a kiosk which contained the weather report.

Two hotels on Commerce Lane, the main street—the Corcoran and the Montgomery House—catered to those with court business, to the county commissioners who met on Tuesdays, to people setting up exhibits at the fairgrounds, to summer visitors who would stay for three weeks or a month, and to local folks seeking a special meal. Traveling salesmen and wholesalers also took rooms, arriving in buggies and later in Ford runabouts, as they fanned out to the country stores for new orders. The Montgomery House, owned by Jarrett Almoney during the Civil War, was completely renovated by John Kelchner in 1883. Beginning as operator of a line of carriages from the C&O Canal and Washington, Kelchner also became the sheriff of Montgomery County. He and his family lived and worked at the hotel, charging $2.50 per day for a room and three meals. The hotel had two big parlors on one side, a center entrance hall, steam heat, and a ten-pin bowling alley. Two baths served twenty-eight people, but each room had a bowl and pitcher.[32]

The Corcoran, less than a block from the Montgomery House, had long been owned by the Kleindienst family when William H. Carr rented it in 1882. Carr died soon after building a new three-story Mansard-roofed hotel, so his wife Emma took over. She raised ten children in the hotel before selling it to her manager, Lawrence Flack, for fifty-six hundred dollars in 1908. It was about that time that the Rockville school became so crowded that the first and second grades set up in the hotel's front rooms. Transportation from the railroad to the hotels, or elsewhere in town, was arranged by Poss Livery. Arrivals would be met by a driver with two horses and a large "bus" entered in the rear by two steps. Jacob Poss, Mrs. Carr's father, charged ten cents a ride but was usually tolerant of the boys who hitched a free ride.[33]

On Montgomery Avenue, opposite the Kleindienst Hotel, ROCKVILLE, MD.

THE subscriber would respectfully inform his old customers and the public generally that he has just completed his

NEW SHOP AND WAREROOM,

and is now prepared to attend to all calls in his line of business, on short notice and reasonable terms.

Trimmings and Ornaments of all kinds, for Burial Cases. kept constantly on hand, and everything furnished in as good style as in the cities, and at much lower prices.

BURIAL ROBES, of different styles, kept constantly on hand.

READY-MADE COFFINS, of all sizes and of various styles, including full and half glass tops, constantly on hand. Personal attention given at funerals, and satisfaction guaranteed in all cases. A call is respectfully solicited.

jan 11-tf* W. R. PUMPHREY.

Pumphrey advertisement in the Sentinel, *March 18, 1881.*

A third guest house, the Woodlawn Hotel, still served summer visitors, but by 1900 it no longer held the attraction it once had. In 1906 the Woodlawn's owners, heavily in debt, sold their grand hotel at public auction. The four-story brick hotel, stable, carriage house, laundry and servants quarters, and 125 chestnut trees on eight acres appealed to Dr. Ernest L. Bullard, of Milwaukee, Wisconsin. A surgeon and professor of psychiatry and neurology, Dr. Bullard purchased the Woodlawn and renovated it. In 1910 he opened Chestnut Lodge as a private sanitarium for the care of nervous and mental diseases. Three generations of Bullards built up a nationally recognized institution and maintained an outstanding reputation for treating mental illness for more than seventy-five years.[34]

Five separate Rockville establishments dispensed general merchandise. One owner, William W. Welsh, located his store near the railroad station for warehousing, delivery, and customer convenience. When a fire destroyed the original store in 1895, Welsh reopened quickly in a new cast-iron-front brick building. He offered local residents a range of items from meats to feed grains and coal to clothing and shoes. Residential and business customers wrote requests on fancy letterheads and scraps of paper to Welsh, who usually delivered the goods the same day.[35]

Early attempts to establish banks were more successful elsewhere in Montgomery County than in Rockville. Upton Beall twice failed in the early nineteenth century to organize a Rockville bank. By 1900, two local banking institutions had offices in town. Montgomery County National Bank of Rockville was founded in 1884.[36] Farmers Banking and Trust Company opened in a small rented room in 1900 with capital stock of fifty thousand dollars and, while its new building was being constructed, carried cash in a tin box each afternoon to the National Bank for safekeeping. People could also borrow from attorneys such as Philip Laird and Frank Higgins, who specialized in real estate and farm securities, respectively.[37]

Another enterprise that flourished in Rockville prior to World War I—the marriage business—soon earned the town a reputation as a "Gretna Green." Gretna Green was a Scottish border town known in the nineteenth century for its instant marriages. According to Maryland law, women only had to be sixteen to marry without parental permission. There was a shorter waiting period for a marriage license than in other states, and Rockville clergy were most accommodating. Couples from stricter nearby jurisdictions obtained a license from the clerk of the court in

Rockville, then found a local minister willing to obtain witnesses and perform a ceremony. The clergymen were paid minimal fees or, sometimes, with wood, bags of potatoes, or farm products. Reverend S. R. White, a retired Baptist minister, conducted at least one hundred nuptuals annually between 1910 and 1916. Washington and Baltimore newspapers criticized this local business, asserting that couples were often hurried or drunk.[38]

Courtesy of Robert S. Cohen

Shaw-Bride collection, courtesy of Peerless Rockville

TOP: Bank note issued 1903 by the Montgomery County National Bank of Rockville. With charter #3187, MCNB was the first local bank to circulate national currency. After 1929, American paper money went to a smaller size.
BOTTOM: William H. and Emma Carr and children posed for a family portrait at the Corcoran Hotel in 1885.

Town government in 1900 operated simply, with a policy-making Mayor and Council who supervised seven part-time employees. Citizens paid taxes on real estate and personal property, and were required to pay a corporation tax as well as a scavenger tax. Rockville buildings were protected by three fire engines that were located in an engine house leased from Jacob Poss. In 1900, the town spent what it received—$8,327.79. Clerk John L. Brunett reported that town expenditures included employee salaries, work on streets, and operating the waterworks and electric light plant.[39]

Life in Rockville centered around home, work, and church. Most of Rockville's marriages occurred at home, doctors delivered children at home, folks entertained at home, and all expected to die at home. Work for men consumed six days a week, with the seventh day dedicated to religion, rest, and play. Most Rockville residents attended church regularly, and much of their social lives revolved around the church.

Black and white people in Rockville, like the rest of America at the time, were segregated in their lives and activities. Whether longtime residents or newcomers, they lived in different neighborhoods, attended separate schools, and met in independent social halls. They were cordial on the streets and often maintained close relationships as they worked together in homes or shops, but an unwritten code kept lives parallel and separate.

By 1900, segregated residential patterns were firmly in place. With the exception of Lincoln Park, the new subdivisions were open only to whites. Black families and individuals settled near the town in clusters near existing dwellings, which were not quickly annexed by the town. Lincoln Park grew up around properties owned by five black families—Hill, Sedgewick, Williams, Powers, and Hebron. Haiti, the community on Martin's Lane, expanded around the Martin, Ross, Powell, Wood, Smith, Carroll, and Johnson homes.

Within town boundaries, blocks from the courthouse and Commerce Lane, blacks settled in a concentration of homes and businesses after the Civil War. White owners sold or leased land and loaned cash to freedmen and women who came to Rockville for jobs as domestics and laborers. By the 1890s, large and small dwellings spilled from Washington Street and Middle Lane into smaller streets named Cairo and Sarah. Frog Run, a small stream, ran through the back fields. On either side were shanties, many of which were built for multifamily use. Here, in cramped conditions, life expectancy stayed below national and state levels. By 1920, the entire block—from Middle Lane north to what is now Beall Avenue, and from Washington Street east to what became Hungerford Drive—teemed with shops, gathering places, an elementary school, Clinton A.M.E. Zion Church, and a variety of dwellings that accommodated more than a hundred people. This humming black community in the center of Rockville became known as Middle Lane, The Lane, and disparagingly, Monkey Run.[40]

Shaw-Bride collection, courtesy of Peerless Rockville

Shaw-Bride collection, courtesy of Peerless Rockville

TOP: View of Middle Lane, looking north from the backyard of the Corcoran Hotel. Date unknown. BOTTOM: Farmhouse built 1872 at Woodbine, owned by the Shaw family. Woodbine is now the site of RedGate Golf Course.

The largest black community in Rockville was also the poorest. Blacks with greater resources lived in Haiti or purchased lots in Lincoln Park rather than settling on Middle Lane. Lane families often took in boarders to bolster their limited wages. However, the central location was ideal, for nearby whites depended upon black Rockvillians to help run their businesses, their homes, and their farms. On Saturday night, Middle Lane was filled with people, shooting craps, playing cards, or just sitting on porches and talking. On Sundays, after attending nearby Jerusalem or Clinton church, they played baseball and other games in the field behind the schoolhouse.

Out of this setting and into national notoriety came George Baker Jr., who would later become known as Father Divine. His mother, Nancy Smith, formerly a slave in Gaithersburg, settled in Rockville after the war and took a position as a domestic servant. With her young daughters and two other families, she lived on Middle Lane. In the 1870s she married George Baker, a farm laborer, and together they saved to buy a lot for sixty-five dollars[41] and build an inexpensive house on it. George Jr., born in 1879, absorbed his parents' hopes while experiencing the despair of a small-town ghetto. He and his sisters worked to supplement the family income. They attended Rockville Colored Elementary School and the black Methodist churches near their home. The *Sentinel* reported Nancy Baker's death in May 1897 for the drama of a five foot tall, 480 pound woman needing an extra large coffin, ten pall bearers, and the door of her home to be cut away to remove her for burial.[42]

Within a year, young George left Rockville, making his way as a gardener and assistant preacher in Baltimore. He relocated to New York, where he founded peace missions he called *heavens* and

PLAYTIME IN 1900

Leisure time activities in Rockville in 1900 included sports, excursions, picnics, hikes, fishing, and visiting. Rockville boys spent hours with their dogs hunting rabbits, squirrels, and birds in fields within blocks of the courthouse. Kids swam in summers in Ten Foot Hole on Rock Creek and in Watts Branch. They skated in winter on the pond left on the Rockville Pike near First Street when Wallace Cromwell closed his brick-making operation. Annual community highlights were the amateur baseball league summer season, Chautauqua week in August, and the Agricultural Fair in September.

Base ball developed a strong following after the Civil War. Black and white players formed teams that represented the town. The Rockville Base Ball Club, organized in April 1899, scheduled games with amateur teams from Washington and Maryland. Much of the town came out to the fairgrounds to cheer the home team. The 1900 season started on June 1 with a double-header with the YMCA team of Washington.[43] Rockville lost both games. Each summer Rockville's black community fielded players, who also played teams throughout the area. Once a year, Rockville's black and white teams faced off, to the delight of the entire town.[44]

Courtesy of Rosie and William Wood, Black History collection, Peerless Rockville

Charles Brewer collection, courtesy of Peerless Rockville

TOP: Rockville black baseball team posed at the stadium at 15th and H Street N.E., in Washington about 1900. BOTTOM: Rockville baseball champions of 1893 posed in front of the railroad station.

attracted followers to his social and religious charismatic movement. In 1930, Baker changed his name to Father Divine. His charismatic leadership appealed to poor blacks, wealthy whites, and the thousands who depended upon his business enterprises and free meals in East Coast cities. Baker was the most famous black native Rockvillian of the 1920s and 1930s, although he never acknowledged his origins.[45]

Farms of all sizes abounded around Rockville. The three hundred-acre Dawson farm stretched from the Pike west to Seven Locks Road. Henry (Hal) and Fannie Dawson returned to Rockville and Rocky Glen in 1911 with western ideas after thirty years in the Dakota Territory. Fannie designed their new home on the hill to reflect Frank Lloyd Wright's prairie style. Hal updated the farm operation and invested in a variety of local innovations, including a shoe heel factory. He imported western beef cattle, which arrived on the railroad and were then driven down the Pike to Rocky Glen. Once the wild cattle spilled out of the railroad cars and ran toward the center of town. Hal called his four children who, yelling and whistling, dashed about Rockville on their cow ponies until they drove the herd to the farm.[46]

Other farms thrived in areas now within Rockville corporate limits. Just south of Rocky Glen, the Bradleys farmed 430 acres left after breaking off 152 for the subdivision of Autrey Park. Dairying became important along the entire length of the railroad, and many Rockville area farmers depended on milk and vegetable sales for their income. Northeast of

Charles Brewer collection, courtesy of Peerless Rockville

TOP: The Rockville Fair was a community institution at summer's end for nearly a century, from 1846 to 1932. Competitions, entertainment, food, and socialization attracted people from Montgomery County and Washington, D.C. This 1917 photo shows grandstand, judges stand, track, and fairgoers.
RIGHT: The Town Hall corporation formed to bring culture to Rockville and to provide space for community events.

Rockville and the railroad was Woodbine, a farm operated by George Shaw and his son Roger. The Shaws rotated crops of corn, hay, and wheat on their 103 acres, while keeping other fields for grazing milking cows. Woodbine farm is now the site of RedGate Golf Course.[47]

DEVELOPMENT OF URBAN INSTITUTIONS

Active citizens working to improve their community became a Rockville tradition in the late nineteenth and early twentieth centuries. Longtime residents joined with newcomers from Washington for cultural and civic activities. Having a larger number of people with leisure time and civic interest encouraged the development of organizations beyond the church and school. Local attorneys, accustomed to leading in law and politics, turned to create community institutions. Freed by the availability of domestic help, Rockville residents, particularly white middle-class women and men, found the small town ripe for an injection of culture.[48]

Photo from *Peerless Rockville* brochure, 1890

Cultural Organizations

Groups formed for literary pursuits dominated cultural life in Rockville in the nineteenth century.

Before the Civil War, residents of the town created the Rockville Lyceum. Otis C. Wright, principal of the Rockville Academy, was the first president. The Lyceum opened a reading room in June of 1846 and sponsored debates and entertainment for townspeople.[49] In 1869, a group of attorneys and public officials formed the Rockville Library Association to "procure books . . . and preserve them for the use and benefit of its members," who were "any white person" purchasing at least one share of stock. Located in the rear of Anderson and Bouic's law office and open on Wednesday and Saturday afternoons, the library offered histories, romances, and adventure fiction. Despite initial enthusiasm, the group dissolved in 1876.[50] Rockville attorneys revived the Lyceum as a literary organization four years later. It met in the courtroom.[51] In the late 1880s the Rockville Literary Society met in members' homes for "the promotion of literary culture and social habits."[52] Longtime and newly arrived Rockvillians who called themselves "the Pythosophians" enjoyed recitations, vocal and instrumental music, and poetry readings.

Hoping to coordinate efforts, several men involved with the library incorporated the Rockville Town Hall Company in 1881 to "improve the educational, moral, scientific, literary and social condition of the community."[53] Stock sold at ten dollars per share raised most of the six thousand dollars needed to erect a handsome two-story brick building on Montgomery Avenue.[54] The Town Hall opened on Tuesday evening, July 18, 1882, with the Comus Club presenting the play, *Our American Cousin*. Afterward the room was cleared, the band set up, and "handsomely attired couples engaged in the dance" until 3:00 A.M. For the next half century, the Town Hall operated as a small-town cultural center, with a four hundred-seat auditorium on the second floor, a stage, balcony, and dressing rooms, a ticket office on the lower level, and seven leased offices. The community used the facility for visiting lecturers, theatrical and musical performances, high school graduations, dances, and other suitable "instruction and amusement."[55] More staid gatherings were held in the courtroom.

Rockvillians loved music. Brass bands became popular after the Civil War, and several towns organized

WOMAN'S CLUB OF ROCKVILLE

In 1900, Margaret C. Welsh, wife of merchant William Wallace Welsh, and her sister, Sophia Higgins, founded the Woman's Club of Rockville. With the motto, "All for the Common Good of Woman Kind," the original seven women met once a week to "promote the intellectual growth of its members, and to quicken a deeper interest in civics among the people of Rockville." Early programs focused on art, literature, music, travel, and critiquing one another's presentations. Dues were fifty cents a year. The women formed a museum committee to keep local history items in the tiny building that was formerly Dr. Stonestreet's office. Later, the tiny building became Rockville's library.

Courtesy of Helen Welsh

Margaret Ann Claggett Higgins Welsh, "Miss Maggie," (1856–1955), founder of the Woman's Club of Rockville.

The Woman's Club soon shifted from a social to a service club. In the nineteen-teens and twenties, the club sponsored Chautauqua in Rockville and raised funds for the Red Cross. As an early member club of the Montgomery County Federation of Women's Clubs, the ladies actively advocated reform in public welfare, education, and in the courts. Once, to raise money, members put on a "Leg Show." Their stocking-covered legs appeared when the curtain was raised to the level of their knees. Whose legs were selected as the most shapely by the three judges has been lost to posterity.

Through one hundred years the Woman's Club of Rockville has given numerous scholarships and aided in beautifying the town. Other women's groups followed its example, and several have spun off from the Rockville club. In 1975, the Woman's Club worked with Scottie Fitzgerald to move her parents from Rockville to Saint Mary's Cemetery. The club celebrated its golden anniversary with a luncheon and party on March 10, 2000.[56]

Courtesy of Saint Mary's

Courtesy of Peerless Rockville

Charles Brewer collection, courtesy of Peerless Rockville

TOP: Saint Mary's Church and rectory, 1899.
MIDDLE: Jerusalem Methodist Episcopal Church, from a postcard, circa 1906.
BOTTOM: Christ Episcopal Church survived the hurricane which crashed through Mongomery County on September 29, 1896, but its steeple was shorn off.

cornet bands in the early 1900s.[57] Rockville had sufficient musical talent to muster two brass bands, one comprised of white and one of black residents. Both bands played at summer picnics and gave concerts in the winter. They provided music for temperance and grange affairs, dances, and school events. In 1877, the county commissioners permitted Rockville to erect a music stand in the courthouse yard, "provided they do not interfere with the shade trees. And that they will not permit it to be used when it would interfere with the transaction of business in the Court House."[58] The *Sentinel* opined that since townspeople had helped to purchase implements, the Rockville Brass Band should play more frequently in Court House Square "for the pleasure of the people" on summer evenings.[59]

Women's Organizations

Voluntary associations channeled the considerable energies of white middle-class women of the Progressive Era. They sought to learn from one another, to better their community, and to form social connections. One of the earliest groups was the Woman's Club of Rockville, formed in 1900, followed and complemented by the Inquiry Club. Founded in 1911 as the Club of Present Day, the Inquiry Club raised money for the Library Fund and for women's scholarships and was concerned with such issues as sanitation in food handling and enforcement of the dog nuisance ordinance.

Women also formed patriotic and charitable clubs. The ladies of the Rockville Civic League persuaded the council to allow them to place waste paper boxes at different locations as a beautification measure.[60] Ten women formed the Burden Bearer Circle of the King's Daughters in 1890 to assist sick and needy individuals. In 1909, a group of ladies organized the first Daughters of the American Revolution (DAR) chapter in the county. The town donated twenty dollars to help mark the Braddock Trail. Rockville women opened a chapter of the Daughters of the Confederacy in 1911.

Churches and Cemeteries

Churches dominated Rockville's charitable and social life. Each denomination sponsored socials, and fundraisers such as strawberry festivals, box suppers, and lawn fetes were well attended. Ladies' aid societies displayed varying degrees of sociability and welfare. This arena was particularly important for black residents, who had few other outlets. For them, the church was the center of society. They organized pageants, picnics, lawn parties, and contests. The highlight of the year was the Decoration (Memorial) Day parade and picnic.

In 1900, Rockville Christians had their choice of ten churches to attend—A.M.E. Zion, Baptist, Christian, Episcopal, Methodist Episcopal (black), Methodist Episcopal, South, Presbyterian, Roman Catholic, and two new congregations that accommodated the town's changing demographics. In 1902, the First Colored Baptist Church of Rockville purchased land in Lincoln Park, having met in the homes of members for a brief time. The congregation, comprised of local families, erected a church building on Horner's Lane, a newly cut road connecting Baltimore Road with the B&O Railroad's Westmore station. In 1910, the name changed to Mt. Calvary Baptist Church.[61] The white Rockville Free Methodist Church organized in 1900, at first drawing adherents to tent revivals and home

ROCKVILLE CEMETERY

Rockville Cemetery on Baltimore Road, in addition to being the community's oldest burying ground, is significant as a classic rural cemetery as well as for the many individuals prominent in local history interred there.

Rockville Cemetery began as a colonial burying ground associated with a tiny chapel of ease established by Prince George's (Anglican) Parish in 1738. After 1822, when the congregation moved Christ Episcopal Church into the town of Rockville, it continued to use the graveyard but paid less attention to maintenance than it had.

Establishment of a community cemetery in Rockville coincided with the desire of the vestry of Christ Episcopal Church to reverse the ravages time had taken in the old burial ground. Local citizens had discussed the concept of a public cemetery prior to the Civil War, but took no action until 1880. That year, Judge Richard Johns Bowie donated five acres of land to the vestry, which deeded the cemetery to the newly incorporated Rockville Cemetery Association. The association was formed to maintain "a public Cemetery for the burial of all persons, irrespective of religious denominations." The original board of directors—all prosperous well-respected men—included William Veirs Bouic Jr. and David H. Bouic (Baptists), E. Barrett Prettyman and Dr. E. E. Stonestreet (Methodists), Hezekiah Trail (Christian), James B. Henderson (Presbyterian), and several Episcopalians, including Judge Bowie.[62]

The neglected cemetery's future brightened under new stewardship. In 1889 the association built a tenant house for the grounds supervisor. Judge Bowie's widow, Catharine Bowie, added two more acres, making a total of nine acres. Visible improvement came in 1894, when the board appointed an executive committee comprised of women. Under the leadership of Rebecca T. Veirs, the Rockville Union Cemetery Society cleared the grounds, planted trees, and transformed the burying ground "from a veritable wilderness into a spot of unusual beauty."[63]

Rockville Cemetery is a striking example of the rural cemetery movement. This concept began in large eastern American cities in the 1830s as a reaction to space and sanitation issues as well as the disruption caused by growth. Influenced by cemetery architects and landscape gardeners, the movement filtered down to small towns such as Rockville as a picturesque, safe burial ground that symbolized community unity. Curving roads, attractive plantings, three-dimensional monuments, an isolated yet accessible location, and family-controlled plots carried out the rural cemetery philosophy.[64] Through the years, Rockville Cemetery continued to expand, and the adjacent farmland was developed into residential and institutional uses.

The roster of persons buried at Rockville Cemetery reads like a Who's Who of Montgomery County and Rockville. Examples are Upton Beall and E. Barrett Prettyman (clerks of the court), Walter "Big Train" Johnson (baseball great and county commissioner), Judge and Mrs. Richard Johns Bowie (who lived next door), the Pumphrey family (carpenters and undertakers), veterans from the Revolutionary, Civil, Spanish-American, Korean, Vietnam, and both World Wars. For thirty-five years author F. Scott Fitzgerald and his wife Zelda were interred there. The earliest remaining stone marker is that of John Harding (1685–1752), longtime vestryman and owner of a nearby farm.

worship. Ministers split their time among Spencerville, Avery, Lay Hill, and Rockville. In 1904, the congregation built a small church at First Street and Grandin Avenue in Janeta.[65]

Rockville residents created two community burial grounds in the 1880s. For 130 years, local residents had buried their family members in rural plots or in the town's Episcopal, Baptist, or Catholic graveyards. White Rockville churchmen united to incorporate the Rockville Cemetery Association to maintain the deteriorated Anglican burial ground on Baltimore Road. Dedicated volunteers over the following twenty years upgraded the graveyard to reflect the rural cemetery movement then popular in America. Haiti Cemetery was started by Agatha Smith, a black homeowner on Martin's Lane who buried her sister, Charlotte Penny, in 1889. The women had inherited the property from their grandfather, Samuel Martin Jr. Agatha and Dennis Smith began making burial plots available to other local families, for there was no cemetery for black residents in Rockville at the time. Haiti Cemetery is still in use today, altough the number of burials there slowed considerably after 1917, when the Galilean Fishermen opened a cemetery in Lincoln Park.[66]

Civic and Self-Improvement Organizations

Temperance—control of alcoholic beverage abuse—was a major issue in the post-Civil War period. Several societies organized between 1830 and 1872, led by Rockville residents Thomas G. Allen, rector of Christ Episcopal Church, miller Samuel C. Veirs, Rev. William McClenahan, and Lycurgus Eagle. John M. Kilgour helped start the Young Men's Total Abstinence Society in 1846.[67] The Rockville Division, No. 49, Sons of Temperance operated for many years, and in 1897 the Women's Christian Temperance Union (WCTU) opened a lunch room above Reading's Drug Store. Led by E. Barrett Prettyman—clerk of the circuit court, Maryland superintendent of schools, and Methodist layman who lived on Jefferson Street—black and white Methodists from Montgomery County repeatedly petitioned the General Assembly to allow communities to prohibit the sale of alcohol if a majority of voters agreed. They succeeded in 1884, from which date until 1933 Montgomery County was legally dry.[68] The Anti-Saloon League, represented by Rockville attorney Frank Higgins, continuously presented evidence of illegal activities to the grand

From a postcard, circa 1906. Courtesy of Peerless Rockville

Courtesy of Rosalie M. Campbell, Black History collection, Peerless Rockville

TOP: Fishermen's Hall, located on North Washington Street, hosted many meetings, concerts, and social events between 1912 and 1966.
BOTTOM: Members of Rockville's black band marched on unpaved Washington Street, circa 1910. This annual Decoration Day celebration was the forerunner of Rockville's Memorial Day parade.

Charles Brewer collection, courtesy of Peerless Rockville

Charles Brewer collection, courtesy of Peerless Rockville

LEFT: The Rockville Academy, rebuilt in 1890, in a photo taken on December 13, 1914, well after the institution had become coeducational. Private schools, primary and secondary, became less popular as public school education improved. To the two-room public elementary school for white students in 1892, the Board of Education added a wing for the high school—the first in Montgomery County.

RIGHT: In 1905, the new Rockville High School opened on Monroe Street, for grades one through eleven.

jury. Higgins attempted "to suppress the great evil of open saloons and unrestricted sale of liquor," fought for federal prohibition, and ran for governor under that banner.[69]

One of Rockville's longest-lived and most effective organizations was the Order of Galilean Fishermen. Rockville's chapter of the statewide organization formed in 1912[70] as a sick and burial society so people could care for their own at a time when insurance companies refused to sell policies to blacks. Men and women residing in Lincoln Park and Haiti, serving as officers of Eureka Tabernacle No. 29, collected payments from members. When injury or illness prevented work, the society paid benefits up to $150 per year. It also paid funeral expenses. In 1917, the Fishermen purchased land in Lincoln Park and began selling burial plots to black families.[71]

The Fishermen erected a frame building on Washington Street just north of Wood Lane. Fisherman's Hall was the scene of meetings, performances, dances, oyster suppers, and Christmas dinners for the poor. It was a focus for the annual Decoration Day gathering in Rockville and for a parade on Washington Street followed by a homecoming picnic. By the mid-twentieth century there were more opportunities for black residents, and the organization lost its urgency. Although membership declined and the organization gradually died out, from this fraternal and charitable organization came one of Rockville's most cherished traditions—the Memorial Day parade.[72]

Other organizations also made their mark on Rockville. All of the officers and most of the founding members of the Bar Association of Montgomery County in 1894 were Rockville residents.[73] The Montgomery Masonic Lodge No. 195 organized in 1893 with twenty-seven members. When the group outgrew rented rooms and offices, they moved into a handsome brick building on Commerce Lane near the corner of Washington Street.[74] Rockville was home to Pythagoras Lodge No. 74 of the Free and Accepted Masons (Prince Hall Affiliated) and the Odd Fellows, a black chapter of the international benefit and social organization. Rockville farmers met for thirty years as a local unit of the Patrons of Husbandry, commonly known as the Grange.[75] Sixty Rockvillians opened the Montgomery Country Club in 1907 on Forest Avenue for dances, pool, games, and other entertainment.[76] Less formal was the Anonymous Club, a group of men and women from Rockville's old families who met every other Friday evening for literary and social activities. And even more casual was the Polecat Club of sixty-five to ninety-year-old men who gathered each morning in the lobby of the Montgomery House Hotel before attending Police Court sessions in the courthouse.[77]

LOCAL GOVERNMENT COMES OF AGE

In February and March of 1888, Rockville citizens met at the Town Hall to adopt a new charter. The General Assembly approved, and voters selected the first Mayor and Council of Rockville in May. All of the existing ordinances passed by the town commissioners 1860–1888 remained in effect, but the new governing body gained additional powers that the town would need through the next century of phenomenal growth.

The new charter recognized the increasing complexity of Rockville. Since incorporation in 1860, its population had multiplied four fold, and its land area had nearly doubled. The charter delineated and enlarged the town boundary and increased the number of men on the council by two. It authorized the Mayor and Council to regulate construction and issue building permits, to place a tax on dogs and other animals, to preserve health and cleanliness, and to establish and regulate markets and all offensive trades. The council could incur debt up to five thousand dollars beyond the annual revenue of the town, but it had to be repaid within five years. It also was required to publish an annual statement of receipts and expenses.[78]

In a letter published by the *Montgomery County Sentinel*, soon-to-become-mayor William Veirs Bouic Jr. outlined his dreams for Rockville and a bit of philosophy about government:

> It is truly grand for a man to come out from the atmosphere of self into the broad sunlight of Public Good. Rockville has by the energy and enterprise of its citizens become already a very attractive little town. . . . But whilst all this is true, yet there is much, very much to be done.
>
> We have no protection in case of fire. . . . The wells must of necessity become more or less impure as the population increases. There is no sufficient drainage and sewerage. . . . There are grave-yards in our town that . . . are unhealthy. More streets should be opened in order that we may expand laterally and not have our town stretching itself for a mile or two along the county roads. . . . We must, in all things, endeavor to put ourselves thoroughly in accord with the progressive spirit of the age and thus obtain increased population and wealth by offering tempting inducements to strangers to settle in our midst. And above all things, we should curb our differences of opinion, and instead of wrangling work harmoniously together for the general good. . . .[79]

Bouic, who served as town commissioner for fourteen years before becoming mayor, symbolized the transition between the nineteenth century village mentality and the progressive public servant of the early twentieth century. The new charter started Rockville on its path to modernization.

Elected to govern Rockville in May 1888 were Bouic (attorney and Democratic party leader), Reuben A. Bogley (Baptist deacon, incorporator of Mutual Building Association of Montgomery County, and Master Mason), Hattersly W. Talbott (attorney, later state senator), John H. Kelchner (proprietor of Montgomery House Hotel and livery stable), and Dr. E. E. Stonestreet (physician).[80] Mayor Bouic and the four councilmen were not paid for their duties, but were reimbursed for expenses. The town clerk, attorney Charles W. Prettyman, recorded council actions and took care of correspondence for a salary of one hundred dollars

The Red Brick Courthouse, built in 1891 for a growing county. The third courthouse on this site was designed in Richardsonian Romanesque style by Frank E. Davis and built by Thomas P. Johns, both of Baltimore. Rockville's importance as the seat of county government was enhanced by the new building, which housed all county courts, offices, records, and a single courtroom.

Postcard circa 1920, courtesy of Peerless Rockville

annually. Implementing the daily business of the town was the bailiff, merchant Melchisdec Green, who received $175 per year to collect taxes and fines, enforce ordinances, preserve order, and attend all public gatherings and council meetings. Assisting was a supervisor of streets, who was compensated $1.75 per day when working. Another essential employee was the scavenger, responsible for cleaning the privies of each house, at a salary of $35 per month. A lamplighter, at $125 annually, rounded out the town's workforce. Other specialties, such as surveying, day labor, or legal services, were engaged as needed. In the first month, the council ordered a survey of the town by George M. Anderson, asked Dr. Stonestreet to study the sanitary condition of the town, and directed the clerk to purchase supplies needed to start tagging dogs.[81]

Rockville's elected officials faced, as did other growing towns, three difficult issues: how to provide public services such as sanitation, roads, and street lighting; how to keep order; and how to pay for it all. The Mayor and Council met monthly, and in special session as necessary, to attend to a multiplicity of concerns including maintaining and installing kerosene lamps, enforcing ordinances, prohibiting pigs, requiring building permits and dog tags, setting the annual tax rate, repairing and surfacing roadways, addressing citizen complaints and requests, and developing specific rules for council sessions and for the scavenger's duties. Topics for discussion ranged from the minutia of approving each submitted invoice to long-range planning for street lights. Councilmen, assigned to oversee specific road projects or to report on larger issues, were usually willing, but many of them resigned under the weight of the workload. Rockville's public officials were volunteers taking time from their businesses and lives for community service. Their employees were part-timers who often needed to be reminded of their duties and who sometimes left before completing their terms.

The first councils accomplished much in a short time. Initially, the men addressed many of the issues Bouic had identified, with varying degrees of success. In 1888, they set standards for new brick sidewalks, plank boardwalks, and grading and macadamizing (or piking) town streets. They purchased three fire engines and built an engine house. They addressed health concerns by closely supervising the town scavenger. In 1890–91, the year five of their number resigned, the council drafted its first annual work plan, which

Charles Brewer collection, courtesy of Peerless Rockville

Stonecutter John Heagy, seated, with a coworker in his shop on the south side of East Montgomery Avenue, shortly before World War I.

outlined lighting, tax collection, and other duties assumed by the town. They attempted to hire a full-time bailiff to supervise all employees and work of the corporation, but no one would accept the job. That year, the first building permit was granted to "Thomas Dawson as per application filed and it is ordered that henceforth the ordinance requiring building permits be strictly enforced. The Clerk is directed to have proper forms of applications and permits printed."[82]

By 1892, brick sidewalks, in herringbone style laid in sand and curbed with white oak, had been installed on many of the streets west of the commercial center, and Forest Avenue had been named. New kerosene lamps lit up the town after dark. In April of 1894, when four hundred unemployed workmen marched through Rockville on their way to Washington, the town ordered extra bailiffs in case of trouble and appointed a committee to provide food for "Coxey's Army" (veterans protesting unemployment). By the end of 1895, The Park, a new subdivision near the fairgrounds, had been annexed, merchant Welsh had received permission to place coal and hay scales next to his new store across from the depot, and the town had borrowed $1,450 to purchase a new Howe combined Chemical and Water Engine for fire protection.[83]

In 1896, the town fathers took a bold step. The new mayor was Joseph Reading, a druggist whose

THREE ROCKVILLE MAYORS

In a period of decision making, change, and increased community activism, Rockville's elected officials did not always feel successful or appreciated. Three Rockville mayors added personal style to their leadership.

William Veirs Bouic Jr. (1846–1906) served as a town commissioner from 1872 through 1881, then 1882 through 1888. Raised at Meadow Hall, a large farm on Veirs Mill Road near Rock Creek, he followed his father into law practice and as a Democratic political leader in Rockville and Montgomery County. He was the first mayor under the new town charter, serving a two-year term and part of another. From 1898 to 1901, Bouic was the state senator from Montgomery County. Bouic and his wife Alice raised six children in a ten-room brick house on Commerce Lane where the gray courthouse is now. Later, they built a new home on Montgomery Avenue. Two Bouic sons joined their father in the law firm of Bouic and Anderson. Bouic's fox terrier, Bulger, accompanied his master to the office and frequently into court.[84]

Courtesy of Montgomery County Archives and Peerless Rockville

William Veirs Bouic Jr. served as town commissioner for fourteen years. He was Rockville's first mayor under the new charter of 1888.

Spencer C. Jones (1836–1915) was a prominent public figure in Maryland for nearly half a century. The grandson of Rockville's first Baptist minister, Jones left as a youngster but returned after serving in the First Maryland Confederate Cavalry to establish a law office. A Democrat, he was elected state's attorney of Montgomery County 1871–1879, clerk of the Maryland Court of Appeals 1879–1889, then state treasurer 1892–1896. In 1898 he became mayor of Rockville but resigned in 1901 to become state senator, and was president of the senate in 1904. Jones donated land to the Baptist Church for a parsonage on North Adams Street and a new church on South Washington Street. He was secretary of the Rockville Library Association, president of Montgomery County National Bank of Rockville, a Mason, and a Knight of Pythias. Jones was master of ceremonies at the unveiling of the Confederate Monument in 1913. Tradition says that because he contributed the most money, the cavalryman's head was modeled in Jones's likeness.[85]

Lee Offutt (1862–1929) served on the town council a total of twenty years between 1890 and 1920. Son of a merchant from an old Montgomery County family, he grew up in Rockville and became a farmer. Offutt's marriage to Mary Clements produced three children, none of whom lived to adulthood, and a lifelong close connection to Saint Mary's Church. First elected in 1890, he served four nonconsecutive two-year terms on the council before becoming mayor in 1906. Offutt's mayoral years saw electric lines and a central telephone switchboard installed in Rockville. Construction of a sewer system in Rockville, following a typhoid epidemic in 1913–14 which killed his teenage son Lemuel and numerous others, was one of Offutt's achievements. The Offutts lived for many years at 8 Baltimore Road, the former Brewer home near the depot. In later years, the house became the WINX radio station, but was razed in 1995.

father had opened east Rockville and whose house was on the hill overlooking the depot. Councilman S. B. Hege, passenger agent for the B&O, offered the following resolution, which the council supported:

> Whereas: Rockville, the County Seat of Montgomery County, Maryland, is situated 16 miles North West of Washington, and is within 30 minutes ride by rail of the capital city. It enjoys the advantages of an altitude of 500 feet, pure water, splendid natural drainage, and the healthfulness attendant upon these attributes. It is moreover in a charming and beautiful country, and thus offers not only unusual attractions as a place of residence, but peculiar and advantageous inducements

> for the establishment of manufacturing enterprises, because of the very reasonable cost of living, and the easy accessibility of the markets of the country, while land is cheap, and the direct connection with the coal mines of Maryland, guarantees cheap and abundant fuel.
>
> To the student of literature, or of the arts or the sciences, Rockville affords the quiet suited to a reflective mind while at the same time it is convenient to the great storehouses of learning with which the National Capital abounds.
>
> Its citizens invite, and be it Resolved: That the Board of Town Commissioners will encourage the investment of Capital, and the Establishment of factories.[86]

Despite this encouragement, industry did not flock to Rockville. Three local mills held their own. On Rock Creek, both Veirs and Muncaster sawed lumber and ground grain using water power. About 1908, brothers Lindsey and Clarence Hickerson built a steam-powered mill on the east side of the tracks at Baltimore Road. Wootton's mill on Watts Branch had ceased operation by then, and the property was taken over by renowned archeologist William Henry Holmes and his wife Kate as a summer place. Stonecutter John Heagy fashioned and sold marble monuments at his shop on Montgomery Avenue. Just south of Rockville on the Pike were located the Rockville Manufacturing Company, organized in 1904 to produce wrappers, the short-lived Rockville Shoe Heel factory, Wallace Cornwell's brickyard, and the Rockville Ice Company, a necessary industry in Rockville through the 1920s.

A major hindrance to growth was Rockville's water and sewer system, as Mayor Bouic had predicted. Artesian wells and cisterns once were sufficient to supply water for the small town and protect it in case of fire, but the postrailroad building and population explosion rendered this system obsolete. The Mayor and Council ordered a census and survey of the town and looked into the practicality of introducing a waterworks system in Rockville.

Once decided, action came rapid-fire. The census, accomplished in June 1896, reported 1,261 inhabitants. In October, the council approved plans and specifications for a waterworks and electric light plant. In December, it asked the General Assembly for bonds totalling twenty thousand dollars and purchased two lots in Rockville Park from Mayor Reading. That winter, Rosser & Castoe, of Bellaire, Ohio, dug a new 225-foot well and constructed the waterworks and plant north of Baltimore Road. When more funds were necessary, the five individual councilmen advanced six thousand dollars to complete the job. In April, a schedule of water and electric rates was adopted, and the council confidently traded the Baptist Church water and lights free for five years in exchange for permission to cut Van Buren Street through the graveyard. By May, sixteen bodies had been moved to Rockville Cemetery, and water mains had been constructed in many town streets. In August, the council accepted the plant and selected James B. Adams

Schedule of water rates set by the town council soon after the waterworks and electric light plant were installed.

SCHEDULE OF WATER RATES.

	Per annum.
BATH TUBS—Public, with hot and cold water	$5 00
Each additional tub	2 50
BAKERIES—In addition to regular rates for dwelling	2 00
BARBER SHOPS—For two chairs or less	3 00
Each additional chair	2 00
COWS—Each	1 00
FOUNTAINS—Average daily use of six hours during season, aperture of 1-16 inch	10 00
Aperture of 1-8 inch	20 00
FORGES—Blacksmith with one forge without other draw in shop	6 00
With other draw	2 00
Each additional forge	2 00
HOTELS & DWELLINGS—One family occupying 10 rooms or less, one draw	6 00
Each additional room	50
Each additional draw	2 00
(One spiggot each hot and cold water reckoned as one draw, and bath tub and wash basin in same room, one draw.)	
HYDRANT—For lawn sprinkling, watering garden and other out-door use, including one draw in house, for lot not exceeding 10,000 square feet	8 00
For each additional 5000 square feet or part thereof	1 00
Hotels and boarding houses not open more than six months in the year will be charged proportionate rates for the time actually open, with an addition of 10 per cent.	
LAUNDRIES—Not in private dwelling	10.00
OFFICES	3 00
OYSTER & EATING SALOONS	6 00
SODA FOUNTAINS—In addition to other draws	3 00
STORES and SHOPS—Without dwelling	4 00
With dwelling (in addition)	2 00
STABLES—Livery, for each horse, including use of hose for washing vehicles, ten horses or less	1 00
Each additional horse	50
Private, for each horse, including use of hose for washing vehicles	1 00
METER RATES—(Meter to be furnished by consumers) less than 1000 gallons per day, per 1000 gallons	30
Over 1000 gallons per day, per 1000 gallons	20

All bills payable semi-annually, June 15th and December 15th. If not paid before end of month in which rendered, 10 per cent. will be added. If not paid on or before 15th of succeeding month, water will be cut off, and charges collected as other taxes.

In case of extravagant use or waste of water by any consumer, the Board reserves the right to furnish a meter and charge meter rates.

On and after July 1, 1897, a fee of $3 will be charged persons desiring to tap a main on the side nearest the curb, and a fee of $1 on the side farthest from the curb. A permit must first be obtained from the clerk to the Water Board. 5-8 inch and 3-4 inch taps only allowed unless by special permission of the Council.

From Minutes of Mayor and Council, April 6, 1897

as engineer and superintendent of the Water Works and Electric Light Plant for one year at a salary of sixty dollars per month.

During the following year, 1898, Rockville opened the waterworks and pumping station. It determined that electric current would be supplied "from one half hour before sunset until 1 o'clock A.M." It placed hydrants on the streets and negotiated water costs for individuals, churches, and businesses. Edwin West, who lived on Commerce Lane next to the Methodist Church, paid "Draw in Kitchen $6.00; Bath $2.00; Six horses to be watered at Hydrant in yard $6.00 per year." Although welcomed by townpeople as sanitary and convenient, these new services subjected the Mayor and Council to years of detailed management.[87]

The town fathers were slower to comprehensively address the problem of waste disposal. This cleanliness issue was the responsibility of the scavenger, who cleaned individual privies once a month in winter, twice in summer, and removed dead animals from the streets. Rockville physicians were more concerned about a proposed tuberculosis sanitarium, while other citizens demanded enforcement of the law prohibiting cesspools within the corporate limits. In 1906, Montgomery County's health officer closed two Rockville wells polluted by nearby privies. The following year seventy citizens petitioned the Mayor and Council to appoint a health officer for Rockville. Dr. Claiborne H. Mannar was so named.

In the first decade of the twentieth century, health still took a back seat to other concerns. Rockville had concentrated its energies on telephone wire installation, safety at the B&O crossing, an explosion in 1901 that destroyed the electric light plant, and an ongoing battle with the W&R Electric Railway Company over completion of trolley tracks to the western limits of the town. A crisis was necessary to focus attention on public health.

The crisis came in the form of a typhoid epidemic in the winter of 1913–14, when townspeople reported twenty-eight cases in less than a month. One of them was eighteen-year-old Lemuel Clements Offutt, son of Mayor and Mrs. Lee Offutt. He died at Mount Saint Mary's College, where he was a third-year student, after contracting typhoid at home in Rockville.

U.S. Public Health Service Bulletin #65, *dated May 1914, included a drawing which showed the progression of Rockville's 1913–14 typhoid fever epidemic.*

ILLUSTRATION OF PUMPING STATION AT ROCKVILLE, MD., AND ITS SURROUNDINGS.

A. House in which a typhoid fever patient was treated in December and January: B. Privy; C. Garden; D. Spring branch; E. Point at which uranine was applied; F. Point at which Spring branch enters secret ditch; G. Pumping station.

Alarmed, the U.S. Public Health Service dispatched investigators to Rockville on February 2, 1914. Dr. L. L. Lumsden and his assistants wasted no time. By the following evening, the team had interviewed the families of typhoid victims, assessed conditions in Rockville, and reported to the Mayor and Council. The experts found that most Rockville residences had "crude and dangerous" methods of waste disposal.[88] Only twenty dwellings had water closets that discharged into septic tanks. The public water supply, which served ninety percent of the population, pumped eighteen thousand pounds of water daily from two deep wells near the pumping station in east Rockville. There were still twenty-five private wells in the town. Dr. Lumsden determined the source of contamination as a residence on Baltimore Road, located within four hundred feet of the town wells and pumping station. A typhus-infected guest staying there had polluted the well, and the infection had been distributed through the public water supply. The team urged the Mayor and Council to advise Rockville residents to boil water for drinking and cooking, to treat the public water with lime, to appoint a visiting nurse to aid victims and inoculate others, and to radically improve the general sanitary conditions of the town "as soon as practicable."[89]

Within days the first three recommendations had been followed, and the Mayor and Council moved to construct a state-of-the-art sewerage system. By 1916, using a state bond issue, the new technology was in place, the scavenger was relieved of his duties, and all Rockville houses were required to connect to the system.

In May, 1914, the Public Health Service published *Public Health Bulletin No. 65*, entitled "Typhoid Fever in Rockville, Md." It chronicled the fast-paced epidemiological investigation, noting that it was confirmed by the results of bacteriological examinations of the water supply and would only be continued with Rockville's current disposal practices, and praised the town's quick actions. The bulletin concluded with advice for other communities. "The important lessons to be learned from the Rockville outbreak have a wide range of applicability in the United States."[90]

Rockville's typhoid epidemic and sanitation crisis encouraged similar action in the town of Kensington. Soon after, Montgomery and Prince George's Counties formed the Washington Suburban Sanitary Commission (WSSC) to provide sewer for fast-growing down-county areas such as Bethesda and Silver Spring. In its report to the Maryland General Assembly in 1918, the WSSC described Rockville's methods of night soil disposal as "mediaeval" and noted that, "It has too often been the practice to wait until an epidemic of disease has occurred before taking remedial measures to improve water supply and sewerage conditions."[91]

Although Rockville by 1916 had become a suburb of Washington, D.C., it also was a vigorous settlement in the center of rural Montgomery County. The thriving business district was supported by residential areas of varying economic and social composition. Newer areas were distinguishable by their singular residential function and by a marked change in architectural style. Residents and institutions were segregated by race. Improved technology in transportation and daily living made life easier. The Rockville Fair, Memorial Day parade, and picnic became established traditions. Attempts to unite the community—through private and public organizations, civic causes, and community participation—succeeded in bringing together old and new residents.

Thus, by 1916, through a combination of solid leadership and unfortunate experience, transportation improvements and unprecedented growth, Rockville became a more modern place. Not quite a suburb, it absorbed suburban characteristics in tandem with other Washington area population centers. Between 1888 and 1916, the small town values which had seen Rockville through the nineteenth century were melding with those more suited to a metropolitan world. Rockville's tightly knit society opened up to include newcomers, mostly middle class, identified more by skills than family and wealth. Town government evolved from setting narrow goals to a continuously involved institution with a capacity to effectively respond to citizen concerns and manage affairs within its boundaries. Although some new ideas did not work, the town government in this period did its best to maintain its country charm while improving its economic base and public services. Broadening its vision, the Mayor and Council emerged from the Progressive Era with a small staff of professional bureaucrats and a private citizenry who increasingly looked to local government to better their lives.

Malcolm Walter collection, courtesy of Peerless Rockville

Chapter Six

Connecting with the World 1917–1945

"Rockville, the county seat . . . Its long Main Street, lined on both sides with low buildings, no one of which has the slightest relation to its neighbors in size, design, material, or color, is an example of how far bad planning or lack of planning may go. In this respect it is very American. At any rate it has the merit of variety; it has so much variety that a modern painter would find it an interesting subject for his brush."[1]

The period between the two world wars was one of balance for Rockville—striving for modernity yet struggling to maintain the status quo of small town life. Between America's entry into World War I in 1917 and the end of World War II in 1945, Rockville became part of a changing urbanized nation, making adjustments in life at home, responding with new institutions and a maturing local government, and planting seeds for future change. The relatively quiet interwar years enabled the small municipality to further solidify community ties it would need in the modern world.

ROCKVILLE IN WORLD WAR I

Rockville residents improved their knowledge of world geography as they pumped up patriotic fervor. The nine-month whirlwind known as the Spanish-American War had taken young Rockville men to Cuba and Puerto Rico with Maryland infantry units in 1898. But it was World War I that caught American imagination and provoked horror not seen since the Civil War. The "War to End All Wars" mobilized American men, arms, ships, and provisions to aid the Allies, who had been fighting the Central Powers for three years.

Montgomery County's first sixty recruits, eight from the county seat, left Rockville by train for Camp Meade, Maryland, on September 28, 1917. They each received a package of smoking tobacco and a rousing send-off from two thousand people after speeches at the courthouse, dinner at the Montgomery House Hotel, and a parade to the depot.[2] About 160 Rockville men served in the eighteen-month war. Three—Robert Lindsay Edmonds, Frederick Neel Henderson, and Theron Eaton Smith—gave their lives.

Patriotism challenged all to do their part at home. Local residents sacrificed personal luxuries, agreed to government controls, and increased production on their farms. Flags flew from Rockville homes and businesses. As with previous wars, the nation's capital swelled with the mobilization effort, and Rockville business picked up as well. Robert G. Hilton, president of Farmers Bank, headed the committee to encourage Liberty Bond sales. Rockville residents participated in the Woman's Section and Colored Division of the Council of Defense to coordinate war operations around Maryland. Local women knitted sweaters and sent books to troops overseas. A Rockville unit of the Woman's Land Army trained women to fill agricultural jobs left by men going to war. In 1917, Rockville women formed a local auxiliary of the American Red Cross and also helped organize a Montgomery County chapter. Many joined the Rockville Woman's Club Kitchen Band to tour army camps during the war and raise funds for the Red Cross.[3]

During the fall of 1918, as young men crammed onto troop ships bound for Europe, the deadliest epidemic ever recorded was at its peak. An estimated twenty-one million people around the world died of the Spanish influenza in three waves in 1918–19, including about six hundred thousand in the United States. Places of assembly closed, including Rockville churches. William R. Pumphrey Jr. traveled house to house with a buggy equipped with embalming materials, instruments, and caskets. The *Sentinel* maintained a column entitled "Death's toll," reporting more than two hundred cases in Rockville and the vicinity.[4]

Photo by Marvin W. Simmons, courtesy of Robert Khuen, Houston Hancock, and Peerless Rockville

Troops on East Montgomery Avenue during World War I.

In April 1920, Rockville residents and veterans of the Great War formed American Legion Post 86, naming it Henderson-Smith-Edmonds Post in honor of the three Rockville men who did not return. Its first commander was Dr. George E. Lewis, a homeopathic physician and a veteran of both the Spanish-American and World Wars. Through the years, the American Legion (and its women's auxiliary) sponsored patriotic programs, sports teams, commemorations, carnivals, flag-raisings, and other community projects. One of the post's earliest programs was dedication of a German field cannon, which for many years sat on the lawn of the Red Brick Courthouse.[5]

ROCKVILLE CONNECTS TO THE NATION

After the sacrifices of the war, Americans craved peace, prosperity, and progress. By 1920 more Americans lived in cities than on farms. Urbanization, technology such as electricity, and inventions such as the automobile and the radio dramatically altered daily lives. Home appliances, personal travel, consumer goods and information, manners, and morals would never again be the same.

In the small town of Rockville, citizens found themselves increasingly tied to a national economy. Residents clamored for consumer goods. Businesses scurried to offer the latest products described on the radio and seen on the moving picture screen. Town officials scrambled to keep up with demands for public services, for controlling the motor car, and for managing growth.

Rockville citizens and elected officials met some of the challenges of change, but failed to address or conquer others. They continued traditional, comfortable ways even as they invited technological improvements. They also understood the communication and economic links that Rockville had forged to other urban areas, and began using them to plant seeds for future change.[6]

THE MARVEL OF THE AUTOMOBILE

The excitement of the train and the trolley faded with the coming of the automobile. In addition to improving connections to Washington, D.C., and within Montgomery County, the private car opened up vast areas to development and revolutionized personal life styles, consumer attitudes, and leisure time. With increased use of the automobile, America's landscape and outlook took a dramatic turn.[7]

The popularity of the car coincided with the improvement of public roads around Rockville. The Pike's reputation as "one of the worst pieces of main highway in the state"[8] helped initiate Maryland's Good Roads Movement. Responding to citizen demands, the newly created State Roads Commission incorporated the Pike into the state highway system.

The road took on new life after World War I to handle farm vehicles, recreational bicycles, and the increasingly affordable private automobile. By 1929, when Montgomery County residents owned thirteen thousand cars, the Pike and Montgomery Avenue had been paved, but less-traveled routes such as Veirs Mill remained narrow dirt roads for decades.[9]

Rockville took some time to get used to the automobile. According to local lore, the first two cars in town collided head-on when neighbors Dr. Otis Linthicum and Albert Bouic both attempted to use a narrow alley off South Washington Street. Other early Rockville cars were William R. Pumphrey Jr.'s one-cylinder Cadillac, Dr. George E. Lewis's two-cylinder Maxwell, and Rev. Thomas J. Packard's Studebaker. Jim Kelchner bought the parts and assembled one for himself. The motorcar frightened horses, broke down frequently, and was noisy and uncomfortable.[10]

As it evolved from toy of the wealthy to household necessity, the automobile dramatically altered Rockville's economy and appearance. Throughout town, auto-related businesses sprang up. In 1923, there were sixteen garages and dealers in Rockville. By the late 1920s, one could purchase a Chevrolet, Dodge, Essex, Ford, Hudson, Hupmobile, Lincoln, Nash, or Packard in town. Willys Overland, Oldsmobile, Plymouth, and Terraplane cars were added to the list in the 1930s. When prices of cars came within reach of average people, sales turned brisk.

Businesses opened in the 1920s and 1930s to cater solely to the automobiles, while outdated livery stables, carriage factories, and harness makers closed their doors or shifted to new services. On Montgomery Avenue at Washington Street, the Fergusons pumped Esso gasoline. On the other side of town, Ward Brothers sold Texaco under a new canopy at Welsh's former general store.

Land along the Rockville Pike remained agricultural for decades to come but, as dirt and ruts gave way to pavement, surroundings changed. Farmers sold road frontage to enthusiastic operators of new restaurants, tourist cabins, and general stores. In season, farmers offered produce at roadside stands. In the short span between Randolph Road and White Flint Golf Course, Waverley Sanitorium opened for convalescents, the

Charles Brewer photo, courtesy of Peerless Rockville

LEFT: Veirs Mill Road, prior to paving.
BOTTOM LEFT: A lone car heads north on the Rockville Pike, south of Strathmore Avenue, 1924.
BOTTOM RIGHT: Waverley Sanitorium, on the Rockville Pike, was a popular country destination for rest and convalescence.

Courtesy of Montgomery County Historical Society

From a postcard, courtesy of Lew Dronenburg and Peerless Rockville

Malcolm Walter photo, courtesy of Peerless Rockville

Courtesy of John Hickman

Courtesy of Gilbert Gude

TOP LEFT: The Brosius brothers and J. Harry Gormley sold and serviced Hudson, Essex, and Hupmobile cars from their dealership on East Montgomery Avenue in the 1920s and 1930s.
BOTTOM LEFT: W. C. Ferguson operated the Esso service station at the corner of Washington Street and Montgomery Avenue before selling the business to John Hickman. Ferguson is behind the vehicle, to the left of the tire, wearing a dark hat.
RIGHT: Brothers Gilbert Gude and Adolph Gude Jr. in a field of football mums at the family nursery north of Rockville.

Ingleside and Rainbow Inns welcomed visitors, Blandy's tourist cabins provided facilities for travelers, and the Villa Roma Club offered dining and entertainment in the country.[11]

A lane north of Rockville on the east side of Frederick Road (where Gude Drive is now) marked the approximate entrance of A. Gude Sons Company nurseries, which bloomed in Rockville from 1925 to 1989. Adolph Gude Sr. had established a florist business in southeast Washington in 1886. In 1925, interested in greenhouses and a nursery, he purchased 371 acres on the railroad line. On the property was a brick mansion which previous owner Judson Welliver, press secretary to President Warren Harding, had named Four Winds. The Gudes lived at Four Winds, raising, in addition to ornamental trees and shrubs, wheat and corn. Adolph Sr. had a passion for English boxwood, maintained a two-acre iris garden, and installed a dirt airstrip for son Adolph Jr. In addition to the suburban market, Gude supplied plants for the Lincoln Memorial and the 1939 New York World's Fair. In 1981, the Gudes donated the house and five acres to the American Society of Plant Physiologists.[12]

Two Rockville Pike farms hosted another transportation innovation of the twentieth century—the flying machine. In the winter of 1919–20, Emile and Henry Berliner experimented with their gyrocopter at the Corby farm (now Strathmore Hall). The father and son inventor team later successfully flew a predecessor of the helicopter at the College Park airport.

Nearly a decade later, after Charles Lindbergh's trans-Atlantic flight captured the world's imagination, a young pilot named Arthur C. Hyde came to Montgomery County. In 1929, Hyde purchased 269 acres of the Wagner farm on the Rockville Pike for a private airfield. The only such facility in Montgomery County, Congressional Airport and School of Aeronautics opened long before an airfield existed to serve Washington, D.C.

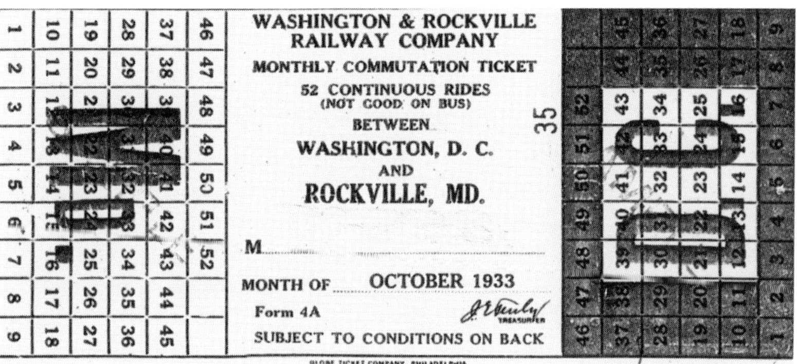

Courtesy of Francis Tosh

Trolley ticket for the Rockville line, dated 1933.

The new use initially frightened local residents, who formed the Rockville Pike Citizens Association to protest "undesirable encroachments of business in this residential area,"[13] but they soon caught Hyde's enthusiasm. By the mid-1930s, in addition to the flying school, Congressional had a restaurant and overnight accommodations. About sixty-five small aircraft, including gliders, were based in steel hangars. Pilots were guided by a twenty-four inch revolving beacon atop a tower, but had to watch the high tension wires along the Pike. Flyers L. Ron Hubbard and Arthur Godfrey mixed with local aviators who occasionally got into trouble for buzzing nearby Rockville. On Sunday afternoons, local families laid blankets out on the grass to watch small airplanes take off and land from a grass strip with a dip in the middle.[14]

Arthur Hyde operated Congressional Airport on the Rockville Pike from 1928 to 1958. This photo is dated 1931.

Courtesy of Major Joseph Bergling, Houston Hancock, and Peerless Rockville

TROLLEY TO BUS

The automobile soon eclipsed other forms of transportation. Without fanfare, the last trolley rolled down Montgomery Avenue in Rockville on the night of August 4, 1935. Trolley service had declined in the 1920s and early 1930s, through cost-cutting measures such as eliminating trips and conductors. Automobiles competed with the trolley for ridership and for space on the streets. After 1923, many trolley lines in the Washington area were closed in favor of the more flexible, gasoline-driven bus. Capital Transit Company, which took over the line in 1933, claimed that the Rockville bus operated at a substantial loss, but agreed to continue with fewer trips per day. The Blue Ridge Transportation Company also provided bus service in Montgomery County from 1924 to 1955. Even so, many Rockville residents invested in cars because of inadequate bus services and schedules.[15]

RESIDENTIAL GROWTH

"Washington is so close that hundreds of jobholders there can commute to their homes in Rockville in a few minutes. . . . clerks or officials in the national whirligig who find it pleasant to live in Rockville."[16]

Rockville's population, which had declined between 1890 and 1920, climbed again in the 1920s and 1930s. From 1,568 residents in 1890, the numbers fell to 1,110 in 1900, 1,181 in 1910, and 1,145 in 1920. With construction booms in Montgomery County in the mid-1920s and mid-1930s, Rockville's population rose to 1,422 in 1930, to 1,550 in 1935, then to 2,047 in 1940.[17]

The automobile greatly enlarged the area around Rockville where people could reside, work, and play. City commuters and their families could live a greater distance from the rail lines. As additional development occurred, new subdivisions opened in Rockville to fill areas inaccessible in the age of train and trolley yet close enough to Washington, D.C., jobs.

In the first half of the twentieth century, Rockville still embodied the suburban ideal of a bucolic residential setting within urban commuting range. However, the appearance of single-family dwellings changed. The huge, ornate Victorian succumbed to the compact, open bungalow and then to revival styles that evoked earlier times. Modest dwellings built from the 1910s through the 1940s—bungalows in large and small versions, small cottages, craftsman, and Cape Cod styles—nestled into smaller lots throughout Rockville neighborhoods. Mail order homes, selected from Sears Roebuck, Aladdin, or Montgomery Ward catalogs, arrived by rail to be erected by local contractors.

Covenants to protect residents from encroachment by nonresidential uses or minority races or religions were sometimes used to sustain desired standards. In

Inset from Bower's Map of Washington and Environs, *Robert F. Bower, Washington, D.C., 1934.*

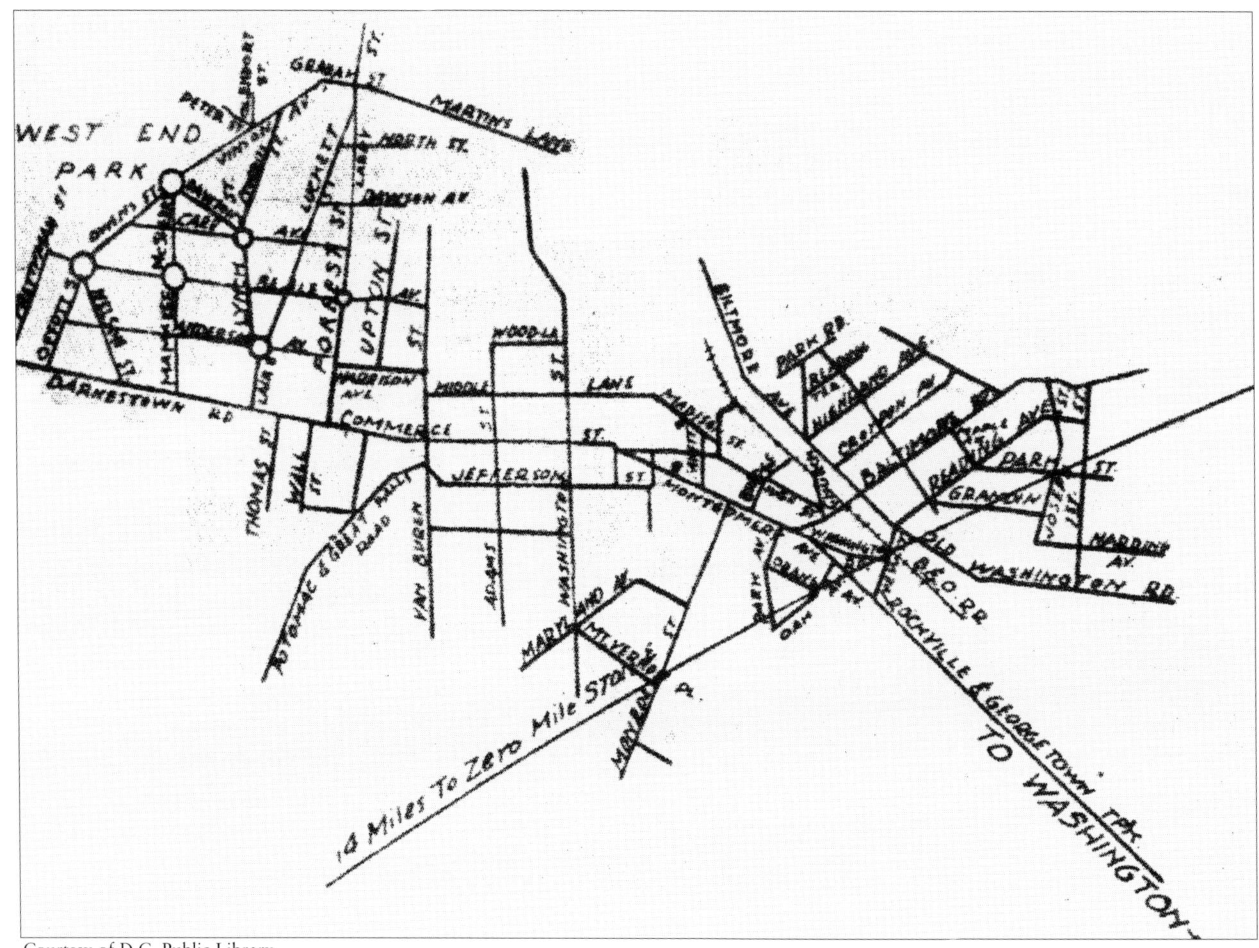

Courtesy of D.C. Public Library

an effort to contain the black settlement of Middle Lane east of Washington Street, owners of frontage on both sides of Washington Street between Wood and Commerce Lanes agreed not to sell or lease to anyone "of African descent or having negro blood." The covenant ran for fifty years, from 1925 to 1975.[18]

Courtesy of Harold and Ellen Pskowski

Three residential areas of the 1920s and 1930s were Beall's Subdivision, South Adams Street, and Croydon Park. West of the town center, Margaret Beall's heirs sold lots on Harrison, Upton, and Van Buren Streets. W. Valentine Wilson—merchant, movie theatre operator, and a founder of the Volunteer Fire Department—bought a romantic brick house at Harrison and Upton Street in 1932. Around the corner on Van Buren Street, Judge Charles W. Woodward Sr. built a classical Georgian style brick home in 1936.[19]

Courtesy of Elizabeth Tuel Jacques, granddaughter of Harrison L. England

TOP: This large bungalow was built in 1923 as a summer home for Waring and Kate Evans on Prettyman's Lane. Then just beyond town limits, the house faced onto Great Falls Road. Its current address is South Van Buren Street. Early 1930s photo, taken from the meadow that later became Evans subdivision.
BOTTOM: Scene in Lincoln Park, on Stonestreet near Frederick Avenue before WWII.

Between the world wars, the one hundred block of South Adams Street filled in with modest homes in a variety of architectural styles. Across from the Rockville Academy, the Christian Church built a parsonage. For decades, local boys hunted birds and squirrels in the intervening fields and woods, and wild strawberries reigned at the south end of the block where two large homes stood at the meeting of Adams and Maryland Avenue. Rockville merchants, professionals, and speculators—some of them second and third generation townspeople—built Colonial Revival, American Foursquare, Arts and Crafts, and Bungalow style cottages. Some deeds stated that the lots were "for exclusive residential use, and the building must cost at least $4,000." Construction activity continued through the 1940s, although a proposal for an apartment building next to the academy was withdrawn by the property owner in 1938 because of local opposition.[20] Around this time South Adams Street was paved, but homeowners still raised chickens at this edge of town.

Rockville developer Joseph Reading, mayor 1896–98, opened a subdivision for white families of modest means on the east side of the B&O tracks in the 1920s. Laying out streets and 180 lots in the field north of Baltimore Road, he named it Croydon Park.[21] At the time, Baltimore Road had two lanes with a ditch on either side and a few older homes, with gardens and farm animals, remained on large lots. Although soon annexed into the town, it took some years for public services to reach Croydon Park—a lively neighborhood of cottages connected by dirt roads and surrounded by fields.[22]

Just north of Croydon Park, Harrison L. England divided a parcel of land to record two subdivisions in 1926. He developed the southern half, adjacent to

Courtesy of City of Rockville

Aerial view of Glenview farm, between 1926 and 1938. Note rectangular rose garden on front lawn and the rolling hillside.

Reading's lots, for white families, the northern half next to Lincoln Park for blacks.[23] Distinctly separating the two areas was a break in Biltmore, now Stonestreet, Avenue. A sixth-generation Rockvillian, England named new streets for his family—England, Crabb, Howard, Elizabeth, Virginia—and original home, Ashley. England's real estate company, Suburban Properties, continued selling lots and houses in the two subdivisions for forty years.

England's addition to Lincoln Park doubled the area of Welsh's original subdivision with 186 new lots. The new development was designed for blacks who had migrated from the rural South to the North after the World War I labor shortage had created urban jobs. Many families relocated in Washington, D.C., to participate in the postwar expansion of the federal workforce and the accompanying market of service oriented occupations. In semirural Lincoln Park, constricted by segregation and outside of the town, residents opened tiny shops to sell groceries or give haircuts. Through the 1940s, many of the older homes continued to operate with pumped well water, kerosene lamps, dirt roads, and outhouses.[24]

The Isreal family migrated to Rockville from Georgia in 1923 seeking a better life. Frank Isreal initially worked as a caretaker and handyman at Chestnut Lodge, and Violet Isreal kept house at Rose Hill farm on Falls Road. The family purchased a lot from Harrison England for $250 and built a home in Lincoln Park, where they raised chickens, hogs, and vegetables. Their twelve children attended segregated schools in Rockville and Washington.[25]

THE ESTATE ERA

The coming of the automobile and improvement in the condition of the Rockville Pike inspired a trend begun by rail transit—that of city dwellers moving to the countryside around Rockville. Wealthy Washingtonians purchased farms along the Pike as country summer refuges. John E. Wilkins, a former publisher of the *Washington Post*, created such a country estate in the 1920s. Architect John Russell Pope used stone quarried on the property to build a Classical Revival mansion, gardens, and outbuildings. From the Pike, Wilkins turned at a stone gatehouse, then traversed bridges and streams to reach the house, which he called Norwood. Today the property is Parklawn Cemetery.

Herman Hollerith, inventor of a data encoding system and punch card machine, received a patent in 1889 and founded a company that was a predecessor to IBM Corporation. Hollerith heated his summer place near Halpine with stove coal delivered by William Wallace Welsh's store in Rockville.[26] Other summer estates on the Pike were Strathmore Hall (owned by the Corby brothers) and Wild Acres (built for Gilbert Grosvenor of the National Geographic Society).[27]

Other nearby areas also became summer destinations. Meadow Hall, the former Veirs/Bouic farm on Veirs Mill Road, became a summer residence for

GLENVIEW, THE LYON ESTATE

Glenview is one of several farms in the Rockville area that became summer estates for wealthy Washingtonians in the early twentieth century. Heiress Irene Moore Smith purchased parts of the former Bowie farm, starting in 1917. Five years later, she married former Army surgeon James Alexander Lyon, a heart specialist who practiced, taught, and wrote in Washington. The couple engaged James A. Lochie and Irwin S. Porter of Washington, D.C., to design a large country home.

The architects retained the old farmhouse as the central block of a five-part Classical Revival mansion, replacing its Victorian features with a majestic portico and columns. New side wings and a rear section added space for entertaining, elegant living, healthful sleeping, and service areas. The interior, notable for its large spaces and fine materials, featured a huge entry foyer with an elegant staircase, a walnut paneled dining room that opened to a terrace overlooking formal boxwood gardens, and a marble floored conservatory holding fountains and Mrs. Lyon's collection of exotic birds.

On the grounds, the Lyons planted specimen trees, rose and vegetable gardens, and a vineyard above the rolling farmland. They built a greenhouse, walkways, a cottage playhouse for their daughter Betsy, and a deer enclosure. Lion head motifs graced the mansion and gardens. Cars approached the house through wrought iron gates at Avery and Baltimore Roads.

Although Dr. and Mrs. Lyon maintained a large apartment in Washington, D.C., Glenview was their home. They frequently opened the beautiful estate for functions such as a reception following dedication of Rockville's new post office in July 1939. The following year, they hosted delegates to the twentieth anniversary convention of the Military Order of the World War. A caravan of cars left the Hotel Mayflower to be escorted by motorcycle police from Washington and then Maryland, arriving at Glenview for a garden party. During World War II, because of gas rationing, the Lyons wintered in Washington.[28]

Photo from June Hall Lovell, courtesy of City of Rockville

Glenview after 1918 and before 1926 remodeling.

Roy Perry collection, courtesy of Peerless Rockville

Agricultural scene less than a mile from the center of Rockville, early 1940s.

Donald Woodward, president of Woodward and Lothrop department store. Dr. and Mrs. James A. Lyon bought the former Bowie farm on Baltimore Road. Architect Warwick Montgomery built his stone and brick country house in what is now Fallsmead, and the Scotts built Horizon Hill on Falls Road. William Henry Holmes, a prominent archeologist, ethnologist, and illustrator, and his artist and teacher wife Kate left Washington to summer in Rockville. They enlarged the former miller's house and established a formal garden above Watts Branch, but allowed the old mill to deteriorate. To the east of Rockville, a Washington syndicate opened Manor Club and Manor Park on 431 acres in 1922. They promoted four hundred house lots with social and recreational facilities in an exclusive country club setting.[29]

FARMING IN ROCKVILLE BETWEEN THE WARS

Most of Montgomery County's population increase between 1920 and 1940 occurred in suburban areas in the lower region of the county. North of Bethesda, Silver Spring, and Takoma Park, small enclaves such as Rockville, Gaithersburg, and Poolesville punctuated the rural landscape. Town residents, farmers, and suburbanites shared wartime restrictions, the prosperity of the 1920s, and belt-tightening in the 1930s. Electricity, telephones, and indoor plumbing were available in towns and suburban areas before the 1920s, but these services did not reach most farms until later.

Fifteen dairy farms were within a mile of Rockville's boundaries. Much of Rockville's milk came from Sycamore Farms at Norbeck. On the Pike, south of the Dawson farm (present-day Hungerford-Stoneridge and New Mark Commons) and the Bradley farm (now Woodmont Country Club), there were so many families of German extraction that the Montrose area was known as Dutch Tussle.[30] North of Rockville was the Anderson farm (present-day College Gardens and Montgomery College), and to the west was the Trail farm (now Fallsmead). Out Great Falls Road, the Scotts operated the Rockville Fruit Farm with apple and peach orchards,[31] and the Poor Farm (Alms House) still grew crops to support the inmates. James and Rose Armstrong Dawson farmed Rose Hill, which they had received as a wedding gift in 1910. In 1935, they sold the forty-acre farm to Dr. and Mrs. Dexter Bullard Sr. The Bullards modernized the house, and Anne Bullard kept seven cows to provide milk for adjacent Chestnut Lodge Sanitarium.[32]

The area in northern Rockville now known as King Farm was assembled by William Lawson King between 1925 and 1942. An upcounty farmer and businessman in Gaithersburg and Rockville, he purchased four parcels which had been farmed by the Graff, Ricketts, Watkins, and Fields families. King named the operation Irvington Farms, raising Guernsey and then Holstein herds to become the largest single shipper of milk to Washington, D.C., in the 1930s. The huge forty-cow barn sported "milk for Thompson's Dairy" on its roof.[33]

Numerous tiny rural communities, once self-sufficient, are now part of Rockville. Street signs still carry their names, such as Hunting Hill and Montrose, and court records chronicle the high hopes of the old subdivisions of Avery Lodge, Halpine, and Westmore. Building lots in Avery Lodge faced Avery Road, which connected Baltimore and Muncaster Mill roads, near the crossing of Beantown Road (now

Southlawn Lane). There were a few homes, a Free Methodist Church, a one-room school, a blacksmith shop, and a garage. Melvin Penn ran a general merchandise store near Avery which his family lived above. Penn purchased flour from Hickerson Brothers in Rockville, tobacco from Washington, shoes and biscuits from out-of-town makers, and other items for resale at Avery. On seventy-six acres of land, the Penn family also maintained farm animals, fields, an icehouse, and orchards.[34]

LIFE IN TOWN

"Rockville, up until say, 1941, was a sleepy, charming, Southern community. . . . the people, to a large extent, . . . didn't agitate very much for causes. The status quo didn't bother them too much. . . . It was a very happy place with lots of characters," recalled Valentine C. Wilson.[35] Still, housekeeping, work, and leisure in Rockville did change incrementally through the installation of utilities, availability of modern technology and products, and desire of citizens to better their environment.

Modern conveniences came to town first, then gradually spread to outlying farms. By World War I, most townspeople had electricity and running water. In 1939 there were six hundred electricity customers within the town limits who were supplied from eleven and a half miles of lines. Local plumber Louis J. Ryan advertised in 1926 that "the bathroom is no longer the luxury of the city man alone."[36] By 1929, Rockville had 572 telephones; the *Sentinel* installed one the following year when the newspaper changed ownership. Washington Gas Light Company extended gas mains to the town in 1930.[37]

Social life in Rockville continued to be dominated by the churches. The interwar period saw a proliferation of church suppers, pageants, plays, and picnics. Denominations cooperated to form the Layperson's Association and an interdenominational choir. In the 1920s, Christ Episcopal and Saint Mary's Churches built parish halls to meet the growing demand for social space. Rockville Methodist Episcopal Church, South (now Rockville United Methodist) suffered a disastrous fire in 1942. The building was so badly damaged that the congregation met at the courthouse for a year while the church was modernized and veneered with stone. In this small town, helping neighbors superceded the separation between church and state.

By 1920, six Jewish families had settled in Rockville. Competing in friendly fashion with other local businesses, their shops became meeting places

TOP: Rockville Methodist Episcopal Church, South, looking from grounds of the Beall-Dawson House on West Montgomery Avenue, in the 1920s.
BOTTOM: The 30 Club, so named for the date of its organization. Dances with live orchestras, oyster suppers, the traditional May 30 parade and picnic, and dinners for the poor were popular in the 1930s.

Charles Brewer collection, courtesy of Peerless Rockville

Malcolm Walter photo, courtesy of Peerless Rockville

Roy Perry photo, courtesy of Peerless Rockville

From photo album of Virginia Hudson Simmons, courtesy of Cecilia Hudson Khuen and Bob Khuen

TOP: A girls' softball game at Welsh Field in the early 1940s. The community field, only a block from the courthouse, was replaced by the County Office Building in 1953. BOTTOM: Janeta youngsters cool off in the swimming hole at Rock Creek, 1922.

for the small Jewish community. The families bought kosher meats in Washington and arranged for a rabbi to instruct their children twice a week.[38] On the main street, the Steinbergs operated clothing and grocery stores, while two unrelated families of Wolfsons ran a tailor shop and Rockville Clothing Store.[39] For the *minyan* (the required ten adults necessary for religious events) at small ceremonies, they pulled in local merchants and traveling salesmen. High Holidays found Jewish-owned stores closed and families attending services in Baltimore or Washington. For the predominantly Protestant town, the *Sentinel* explained the traditions of Rosh Hashanah and Yom Kippur.[40]

Segregation—in residency, schools, churches, and places of public accommodation—was part of Maryland's status quo. The number of black residents changed little but was declining in proportion to the growing white population. Relationships between black and white citizens were prescribed by custom and situation. Persons of one race could live, work, shop, attend school, and have an active social life without contact with the other. Pre–World War II strategies of local blacks ran the gamut from harmony and respectful distance to anger and making do. Generally, the situation was peaceful, major change was not an issue, and no one thought seriously of breaking the pattern.[41] Rockville's churches, Fisherman's Hall, the Odd Fellows, and the Masons provided pleasant events and respectable meeting places for black people from the Rockville area.

Rockville individuals, organizations, and local government tried to provide a variety of cultural and social experiences. Chautauqua, scouting, civic groups, and local interest organizations exposed Rockville to new ideas and brought the outside world to town. One influential group began in 1917 when Kate O. Holmes, the wife of scientist William Henry Holmes, issued an invitation to the first meeting of the Society of Amateur Gardeners. Later renamed the Community Garden Club, they sponsored beautification projects, educational programs, and juvenile offshoots. The gardeners, who numbered 165 in the 1920s, held flower shows at the courthouse and firehouse and planted a tree each time a member had a baby.[42]

Following in the traditions of the Lyceum and Town Hall Company, the Woman's Club and other groups sponsored annual visits under the tent of the Chautauqua Association, Swarthmore circuit. An institution which began in New York State in the 1870s and set up in Glen Echo 1891–1903, Chautauqua also traveled to small towns. Each summer, from 1912 through 1926, Rockville residents gathered under the tent for "seven joyous days"[43] of lectures, performances, concerts, demonstrations, and oratory. The tent was pitched near what is now the intersection of Fleet and Monroe Streets. For two dollars, one could attend a variety of afternoon and evening sessions. Interest in Chautauqua declined in the mid-1920s, about the time the Town Hall Company dissolved. Radio, moving pictures, and automobiles proved to be enduring entertainment, and community guarantors tired of covering the shortfall caused by a decline in ticket sales.[44]

Rockville's library became a cherished community institution during this period. Some decades after the failure of an all-male venture, women revived the town's interest. The timing was right, and by 1921 Dr. Stonestreet's tiny former medical office was pressed into service. In August 1937, the library moved into the vacant Rockville Academy building. Rockville Library Association officers, including women and men, hired Allison Chapin as librarian for nine hundred dollars annually. By 1939, five-thousand volumes, including magazines, were available for circulation to 1,161 borrowers who paid one dollar a year. Children and clergy could read free of charge.[45]

Courtesy of Robert Isreal

Clarence "Pint" Isreal learned baseball from Rockville undertaker Robert "Mike" Snowden. Isreal played in the Negro League for the Newark Eagles and the Homestead Grays.

Outside of school and town teams, no organized recreation programs existed in Rockville. F. Barnard Welsh, an attorney, asked his friend Dr. Edwin Broome for permission to build an athletic field on the Board of Education's property. Welsh devoted the summer of 1925 to digging out a two-acre field and constructing bleachers. Electric lights came later. Welsh Field hosted many games of baseball, soccer, and football over nearly three decades.[46] In April 1929, fifty Rockville men met at the firehouse to organize the Rockville Athletic Association (RAA). Open to "any male white citizen of Rockville or vicinity" over the age of sixteen who acted "in courteous and gentlemanly manner"[47] and paid his dues, the group fielded baseball, soccer, and basketball teams which played teams from other Montgomery County towns. Later, RAA opened to girls' sports.

Two Rockville athletes made national news. Welsh's son, Barnard T. Welsh, proceeded to win every major tennis tournament on the east coast during the 1930s. The lanky lawyer beat world-famous professional Bill Tilden on the court on Harrison Street. Clarence "Pint" Isreal was Rockville's baseball hero. Growing up in Lincoln Park, he was signed in 1933 by the semipro traveling team, the Washington Royals. Isreal later moved to the Negro League to play for the Newark Eagles and the Homestead Grays, Washington's team. When their sports careers ended, both athletes returned to Rockville to raise their families and assist upcoming generations.

The interwar years continued the trend of civic activity begun at the end of the nineteenth century. Civic and social organizations provided the opportunity for intellectual pursuits, community service, and social control. Between the wars, Rockville men formed the Knights of Columbus (1921), Ku Klux Klan (1922),[48] Rockville Volunteer Fire Department (1921), Rockville Rotary Club (1929), Rockville Chapter of the Izaak Walton League (1933), and the Upper Montgomery County Lions Club (1938). In addition to the earlier Woman's and Inquiry clubs, civic-minded Rockville women organized a chapter of the American Red Cross (1917), Homemakers club (1922), and the Order of the Eastern Star (1930). Scouting for boys and for girls also came to Rockville in the 1930s.[49]

DOING BUSINESS IN ROCKVILLE

Rockville's small main street offered a full range of goods and services. Businesses depended upon long-term relationships and on customers who could not easily get to Washington, D.C. In the town center, mom and pop shops thrived beside new chain retail stores. Grossman Bros. Meat Market shared customers with the new Sanitary Grocery Store. Murphy's Five and Ten competed with Vinson's Pharmacy.

A variety of establishments catered to differing tastes. Frugal parents could outfit a child for an entire school year for ten dollars at Steinberg's store.

Rockville Volunteer Fire Department

Fire protection in Rockville began in 1806, when the Maryland General Assembly authorized a lottery to purchase a fire engine, a hand-drawn barrel on wheels. By adding more sophisticated equipment later on, the town managed to avoid major conflagrations.[50]

By the turn of the twentieth century, Rockville's safety was in the hands of black uniformed volunteers supervised by George Meads. The men used hoses reeled on carts to pump water from the two deep town wells. Meads, a delivery man and deputy sheriff, refused payment for his services as fireman. Periodic attempts at a more structured arrangement went nowhere until Rockville's business district was nearly lost on a bleak night in February 1921.

That night, Meads fired a pistol and others yelled "Fire!" From John Collins's store on East Montgomery Avenue—beloved by local children for Cracker Jacks and penny candy—flames reached toward the sky. Volunteers arrived with buckets while others operated the hose reels and hook and ladder truck. The main street was saved with help from men and equipment of Washington, D.C., but Collins's store was a smouldering ruin.

A few weeks later, fifty concerned townspeople elected officers of the new organization. The council voted "that whereas—A number of public spirited citizens of our Town have organized a volunteer Fire Department . . . be it resolved—That we, the Mayor and Council of Rockville, highly commend the public spirit thereby manifested by the members of the organization and that we approve their plans to date." Soon, a house-to-house campaign raised two thousand dollars for fire apparatus and an alarm system that included a siren in the courthouse tower. The town purchased a Waterous Fire Engine, kept in the Red Brick Courthouse basement, and painted the fire plugs. Rockville was divided into three wards, each with a captain and ten men.[51]

The momentum continued. The Mayor and Council bought fire-fighting equipment and contributed to a building fund, conditional upon "protection to all persons and property within Rockville corporate limits." The new firehouse on Perry Street, completed in 1925, had an engine room, meeting room, and a number of rentable offices. The following year, the town conveyed all engines and equipment to the volunteers and began an annual appropriation for fire protection.[52]

Rockville volunteers enjoyed themselves while serving the community. For decades, they sponsored an annual carnival. Other fund-raisers were a supper and "He Night," a male-only extravaganza. In 1938, Rockville Volunteer Fire Department had fifty-two volunteers.

Charles Brewer collection, courtesy of Peerless Rockville

RVFD in front of new firehouse on Perry Street (now Maryland Avenue at the Judicial Center) in the 1920s.

The man most widely associated with the fire department in the early years was local businessman W. Valentine Wilson. Chief from 1931 to 1951, he was in charge of the Rockville Rescue Squad in 1935, when a train hit a school bus from Williamsport, Maryland.

Volunteer fire companies began to change dramatically in the 1950s, when Montgomery County created a board to oversee and coordinate paid and volunteer firefighters. Afterwards, service and training became more uniform, fire prevention received more attention, and women were admitted. In the 1960s, Rockville added three more fire stations. Fire fighters today still proudly polish their engines and participate in parades around the state. Residents from all walks of life serve as volunteers. In 1995, Rockville dedicated a memorial at Vinson Park to the Rockville Volunteer Fire Department.

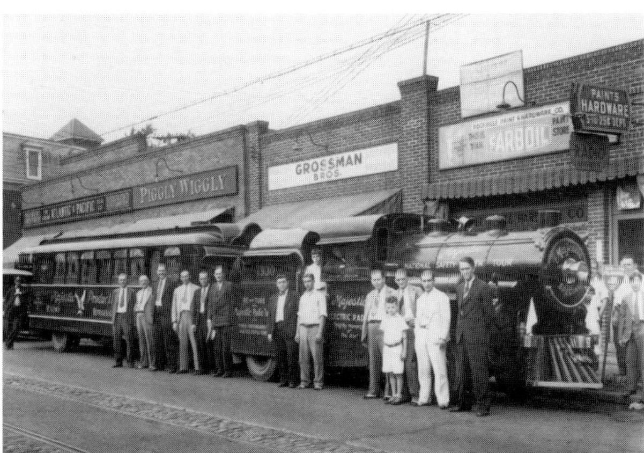

Malcolm Walter photo, courtesy of Peerless Rockville

A promotional train for Majestic products rolled into Rockville in 1930. In the background are two chain grocery stores, The Great Atlantic and Pacific Tea Company and Piggly Wiggly, next to Grossman Bros. market. From their location on Montgomery Avenue, the Grossmans delivered meats and groceries twice a day to local customers from 1920 through 1960.

Charles Brewer collection, courtesy of Peerless Rockville

Charles Brewer collection, courtesy of Peerless Rockville

TOP: Albert Wolfson came to Rockville in the early 1920s and opened a tailor's shop on East Montgomery Avenue. A few years later, he built a dry cleaning plant nearby, which the family lived above. 1924 photo.
BOTTOM: Washington Hicks (third man from left) opened a dry goods store on Montgomery Avenue early in the twentieth century. Late 1920s photo.

Across from the courthouse, the Little Dutch Inn featured a special green plate lunch for thirty-five cents, and the Dixie Tavern sold frog legs on toast for seventy-five cents. During Prohibition, people in Rockville knew where, when, how, and from whom to purchase illegal liquor. Bootleggers were likely to be located in the less-populated countryside, but one who used the Runyonesque name of "Mink Hide" regularly sold in town. The SECO Theatre brought Tom Mix to Rockville. For accompaniment, Len Meads played the piano, and employees banged horseshoes for percussion. Kids loved Jack's Store with its nickelodeon and A. F. "Seen" Beane's confectionary.[53]

Even during the depression, Rockville's town center held its own. Goodwill Industries opened a store in town in 1938. Rockville had a bakery, candy stores, barbers, a fruit vendor, The Great Atlantic and Pacific Tea Company, a jeweler, and a telephone exchange. General merchandise stores were scattered throughout the town. The *Sentinel* continued to publish under new owners after the death of Rebecca Fields in 1930. In 1939, there were 116 places of business near the town center. Thirty-one attorneys practiced in Rockville, thirteen of whom were residents. The town had six physicians, a dentist, and thirty agents of various insurance companies.[54]

The heart of Rockville's business district was Vinson's Pharmacy. Dr. Daniel F. Owens had bedazzled the town in 1886 with a handsome new brick store across from the courthouse, from which he offered medical supplies, vegetable seeds, and household articles. Joseph Reading next took over, then E. T. Fearon, both from Washington. Robert W. Vinson bought the business in 1901, the building in 1909, and for the following half century operated one of the most popular shops in town.

"Doc" Willie Vinson's drug store became a local legend. From behind his fancy soda fountain, Doc served up flavors and advice. Rockville children stopped for candy, local residents frequented the telephone booth (which had no door, so Doc could listen), lawyers negotiated a last time before crossing the street to court, and bailiffs found additional jurors. President Woodrow Wilson stopped in for his favorite horehound drops. Long after the modern People's Drug Store chain came to town (1935), Vinson's hung on as a warm and familiar gathering place for Rockvillians of all ages. After Vinson's death in 1958, a new owner replaced the old brick store with a three-story, modern office building.

A popular black-owned business was Mr. T's. A young George Johnson once stopped at a Rockville store for a cake of soap and, watching the white proprietor wait on five persons who arrived after him, he decided that blacks needed a store of their own. Johnson opened on Washington Street in 1918, selling candy, ice cream, and lunches. Forty years later, Mr. T's on the Pike was a Rockville landmark as a tavern, a restaurant, and a gathering place. Johnson's interests extended to politics, church and fraternal circles, and philanthropy. The first black member of the Rockville Chamber of Commerce, Johnson also attracted a local white clientele.

Industries and building supply companies clustered along the rail line. After water-powered mills went out of business, the Hickerson Brothers operated a steam-powered (fired first with coal, then with oil, and later converted to electric power) flour and feed mill across the tracks from Saint Mary's. Porter and Frank Ward succeeded William Wallace Welsh at the general store and lumber yard, owning it from 1923 to 1944, when Paul Wire and Ben Lanier took over. Holland and Clark offered seeds, implements, equipment, and other goods to local farmers. Nearby, Oscar Johnson sold his lumber yard in 1921 to his cousin, Douglas Blandford, who built up the business through the next quarter century. Rockville Fuel and Feed used its siding on the west side of the tracks to ship coal and feed.[55]

Rockville businessmen formed the Chamber of Commerce in 1925. The group attempted to resolve traffic and parking problems, advocate public improvements, and generally upgrade the town. Chamber members served on the town council and generously supported the Rockville Volunteer Fire Department. Under the leadership of W. Valentine Wilson and others, the group espoused progressive ideas on behalf of improved education, economic development, and civic improvement. In 1926, Wilson commissioned a twelve-minute-long movie featuring the best of Rockville—its business establishments, new firehouse, and dairy production, boasting "clean

TOP: "Doc" Vinson's pharmacy at the corner of Perry Street (now Maryland Avenue) and Montgomery Avenue was a landmark for fifty-seven years. A mortar and pestle perched atop the turret that faced Perry Street. BOTTOM: Rockville residents stopped at Mr. T's on the Pike for lunch, conversation, and groceries for half a century. Rabbit was on the menu every Friday. Hickman's Exxon is now on the site.

Charles Brewer collection, courtesy of Peerless Rockville

Charles Brewer collection, courtesy of Peerless Rockville

Malcolm Walter photo, courtesy of Peerless Rockville

Two hundred merchants closed their Rockville, Bethesda, and Silver Spring doors to bring their families to the first annual Rockville Chamber of Commerce outing on July 21, 1927. County police escorted the group fifty miles to Chapel Point on the Potomac River. Roger Shaw, on the far right, chaired the outing committee.

cows—clean udders—clean milk." Organizing the Chamber marked a coming of age of Rockville's business community. Common ground for the merchants further bonded the small town.

PLANTING SEEDS FOR CHANGE—THE COUNTY INFLUENCE

"A great deal of the life and activity of the town centers about the Courthouse and the police headquarters. The town is Courthouse conscious. . . ." observed a writer for the *Sun* in 1938.[56]

Demographic changes and strong leadership in Montgomery County in the first half of the twentieth century profoundly altered its governance. The divide between up-county rural interests (including Rockville) and down-county concerns widened, as increasing numbers of suburban newcomers pushed for expanded public facilities and services. Colonel E. Brooke Lee, who had commanded county men during World War I and was Maryland Comptroller and local political boss between the wars, guided the growth explosion. With Lee's leadership, the Maryland General Assembly created the Maryland-National Capital Park and Planning Commission to control zoning and land use and the Washington Suburban Sanitary Commission to extend water and sewer lines for future development. A modern tax system funded schools, roads, parks, and other public services in the down-county area, but elected officials found citizens unwilling to pay higher property taxes. The intense growth ended with the depression, followed by a movement to reorganize county government.[57]

These trends affected the county seat. The Red Brick Courthouse, venue of county government since 1891, struggled to accommodate space and personnel required by the growing county. The newly created Montgomery County Police Department moved into the courthouse in 1922, installing a red signal light in the tower and posting an officer there each day at 2:00 P.M. The new Health Department kept offices at Rockville High School. Continued growth reinforced Rockville's position as the center of local government, even as the lower county grew more rapidly in population and residential construction activity.

Farmers Banking and Trust Company dazzled Rockville with its Art Deco style in 1931. Forced to make way for the new courthouse, the business relocated across the street on Commerce Lane.

Malcolm Walter photo, courtesy of Peerless Rockville

FAMILY-OWNED BUSINESSES IN ROCKVILLE

Rockville businesses survived by adapting to changing times while maintaining traditions. Three such companies—Snowden Funeral Home, Rockville Fuel and Feed, and Pumphrey's Funeral Home—have served the needs of Rockville residents for many decades. Their combined three hundred years of business in Rockville provide anchors for the town.

George R. Snowden moved his mortuary business to Rockville from Howard County in 1926. Local blacks appreciated his professional knowledge, respect for tradition, and a hearse drawn by four white horses. Snowden passed his prosperous business to a second generation in 1936. A decade later, the family replaced the original frame building on Washington Street with a brick structure. Today, third and fourth generations operate the funeral home.[58]

Malcolm Walter photo, courtesy of Peerless Rockville

A hearse in front of Pumphrey's Funeral Home on West Montgomery Avenue. The new concept of a funeral home altered the traditional practice of visiting the deceased's family at home to viewing and visiting in a home-like setting.

In 1926, Rockville Fuel and Feed opened its doors just north of the Rockville depot. Founders Curtis L. Ward, G. Edington Bell, and W. Scott Collins named the company for the coal and wood it sold to residents, straw and feed to farmers, and stone hauled from Rockville to Washington, D.C. Between the wars, brothers Curtis and G. Dudley Ward added partners and broadened to include cement block manufacturing. Today, the second and third generations of Wards continue to operate the company on Southlawn Lane.[59]

William Reuben Pumphrey Jr. purchased a large house on West Montgomery Avenue in 1928 to begin Pumphrey's Colonial Funeral Home. His grandfather, William E. Pumphrey, had established a successful carpentry, house-joining, coffin-making, and undertaking business in Rockville nearly a century before. A subsequent generation added embalming services and horse-driven ambulances. Today, Pumphrey's sixth generation helps to operate the business.[60]

Recommendations for a courthouse addition led to state funding for a new building. In 1930, crews began to demolish buildings in the block bounded by Court, Jefferson, Washington Street and Montgomery Avenue—the old Bouic house, Farmers Banking and Trust Company, the Presbyterian Church, and several law offices. Workmen hauled the brick Masonic Lodge across Washington Street to safety. Presbyterians salvaged the rose window for their new sanctuary on Commerce Street (now West Montgomery Avenue). The bank rebuilt across from the new courthouse.[61]

The gray limestone Neoclassical-style courthouse contained larger offices for the county commissioners and clerk of the court, rooms for judges and records, a large courtroom, and jail cells on the top floor. The original plan, as the county grew, was for future extensions on either side of the new building, one of which would replace the old courthouse.[62] When the stone jail southeast of the courthouse was razed, the jail alley and adjacent athletic field were widened, preparing the area for future expansion of government or business at the east end of Jefferson Street.

The increase in county employees and in visiting citizens produced more daytime activity in Rockville, more traffic, and greater demand for parking, particularly around Court House Square. This necessitated better coordination between town and county on land use, public space, and roadway logistics. Nearby businesses seized the opportunity to modernize. Older restaurants upgraded and new ones opened for additional patrons. General merchandise and specialty stores on the main street delighted in the increased sales.

Another area where Rockville and Montgomery County intersected was the public school system. Rockville men continued leadership roles in education. E. Barrett Prettyman directed the State Normal School at Towson. Reverend S. R. White, George H. Lamar,

Malcolm Walter photo, courtesy of Peerless Rockville

Malcolm Walter collection, courtesy of Peerless Rockville

Montgomery County hired Kensington photographer Malcolm Walter to chronicle construction of the 1931 county building. For nearly a year in 1930–31, Walter photographed older structures being moved or razed, then completion of the Neoclassical-style gray courthouse.

and Dr. George Edmonds served on the Board of School Commissioners. Most superintendents were Rockville residents. Edwin W. Broome, the superintendent from 1917 until 1953 who lived on Monroe Street near his office in the high school, brought a modern school system to Montgomery County before World War II. Influenced by educator John Dewey and assisted by E. Brooke Lee, Broome put into practice visionary ideas—junior high schools, a twelve-year system, Parent-Teacher Associations (PTAs), a teachers' retirement plan, employment of married women and, later, junior colleges.[63]

In this era, students from grades one through eleven attended the public school at Montgomery Avenue and Monroe Street. Named Montgomery County High School with the addition of upper grades in 1892, as the school board opened other facilities it became Rockville High School and then, in 1935, Richard Montgomery High School. Students arrived by train, trolley, and later by school bus from points throughout the county. Local schools improved as Washington, D.C., barred nonresident students and the private academies closed. Rockville parents and teachers organized a Home and School Club to supply extras and helped form a Federation of Home and School Associations for county-wide issues. After an exploding boiler destroyed the high school in 1940, students attended other county schools for eighteen months. In November, 1942, students paraded to the new high school built on the former fairgrounds. The presence of a single public school for the entire community joined Rockville residents of all ages in the common cause of educating the next generation.[64]

Elementary and high school students were separated in the 1930s. The school board closed rural elementary schools such as Avery and Travilah and bused students to Rockville. The board purchased the fairgrounds in 1933 and built Rockville Elementary School, with four classrooms, at the corner of Park Street. Local builder Bradley C. Karn had barely finished when the board ordered additional classrooms. A decade after its 1935 opening, with the aid of federal and local funds, the school had been enlarged three times.

Each spring from 1917 through 1940, thousands of Montgomery County students descended upon Rockville to compete for badges and cash prizes in athletic and field meets. Rockville schools, largest in the county, usually won most of the meets. Grace Beall Howes and her students at tiny Montrose Elementary School trained hard and took great pride in fielding competitive teams. White and black students competed on separate days.

Schools for black children continued to receive second-class treatment from Montgomery County. As with facilities for whites, tiny schools that failed to meet minimum attendance requirements were gradually consolidated into two- and three-room buildings. Scotland, on Seven Locks Road, was the exception, remaining open until 1954. Rockville Colored Elementary School students crowded into Jerusalem Church and Fisherman's Hall for nine years after their

Courtesy of Nina H. Clarke and Peerless Rockville

Courtesy of Jane Ward Petrosewicz

TOP: The first graduating class of Rockville Colored High School posed with the bus that brought them to Rockville each day. Each month, families paid three to five dollars per student, depending on distance from Rockville, to operate the blue Ford bus. Photo circa 1931.
BOTTOM: Rockville Elementary School opened in September 1935 in a Georgian-style building with four classrooms. It was Rockville's only public primary school for white students until Lone Oak opened fifteen years later. Used as a junior high school in the 1950s, the name became Park Street School before the county took it over for offices. Photo from The Rocket, 1936, *a yearbook published by the students of Richard Montgomery High School, Rockville, Maryland.*

school on Washington Street burned, moving to a new four-room school in 1921. Local youngsters competed county wide on field day at the nearby Oddfellows field at the close of each school year.

Until 1927, black children wishing to attend school beyond seventh grade had to commute or live with relatives in Washington. That year, parents and trustees matched funding from the Rosenwald Fund (Sears, Roebuck & Company) to add two rooms and a library to the elementary school on Washington Street for use of grades eight through eleven. Teens traveled for hours in a school bus, supported by fees from their parents, to take advantage of Montgomery County's first secondary school for black students. Half-day sessions and the makeshift arrangement soon proved inadequate, so the school board opened Lincoln High School on Stonestreet Avenue (outside of town limits) in 1935.[65] Lincoln's student population skyrocketed as the economic status of blacks and school bus transportation improved. The school board later added steel quonset huts for use as a gymnasium, auditorium, home economics, woodworking, and other programs.[66]

In 1936, Rockville Colored Elementary School was the setting for an historic event. Teacher-principal William B. Gibbs Jr. volunteered as a litigant to challenge Montgomery County's practice of paying black teachers half that of whites with equal qualifications. Gibbs earned $612 annually, compared with an average white teacher's salary of $1,362. Attorneys for the Maryland Teachers' Association, the black teachers' organization, and the National Association for the Advancement of Colored People (NAACP), among them Thurgood Marshall, filed suit in circuit court. Several property owners in Haiti pledged their house mortgages as collateral, should it be needed, and also helped to found the Montgomery County Chapter of the NAACP at Jerusalem Church. In 1937, the school board settled out of court. The following year black teachers received a pay raise equal to 50 percent of the discrepancy and, beginning in 1938, all teachers were on the same salary scale. The victory was gained at a cost, however. Gibbs was fired on a technicality regarding his principal's certificate, and he never taught in Maryland again.[67]

MANAGING THE TOWN

As Rockville connected with the nation, its citizens and public officials charted the path of change. The transition was slow; it was interrupted by jolts and crises, new opportunities, and imposition of new ideas. The years between the wars saw Rockville consider a variety of public services for the increasingly urban community. The town opted to plot its own growth rather than to embrace regional planning with the lower county. Continuously grappling with issues of water and sewer supply, recreation, social services, and comprehensive economic development, Rockville developed patterns during the transition years of 1917 to 1945 that steered it through the rest of the twentieth century.

The town's most troublesome problems were adequate water supplies and sewage disposal. The water distribution system and sewer plant, to which almost all Rockville had been connected by October 1916, could not accommodate the growth that occurred between the wars. From 1920 to 1940, through residential construction and annexation, the population within Rockville's corporate boundaries rose by 78 percent. In 1917, the town council decreed that outside property owners could connect to town water and sewer if they paid for it. Town services became so attractive that twenty years later the council voted not to issue any water or sewer permits on properties outside the corporate limits. The *Sentinel* declared that the only way development could be controlled was by extending town limits. Between the world wars the council, appreciating the favorable addition to the taxable base of the town, usually granted requests by builders and developers to build lines to their new construction.[68]

The Mayor and Council's ambitions for growth stumbled on the supply of water. Following years of shortages, the town purchased water from the Agricultural Society's wells at the fairgrounds in the 1920s. In the 1930s and 1940s, contracts with William McBain, owner of the ice plant on the Pike, provided water for residential, business, and fire protection needs. The town held serious discussions with the State Board of Health and Washington Suburban Sanitary Commission in the mid-1920s, but saw no advantage to placing Rockville in the Suburban Sanitary District. Instead it continued to replace and chlorinate wells as needed. A fifty thousand dollar state bond in 1931 enabled Rockville to enlarge the town's water distribution system and sewage disposal plant, including a new one hundred thousand gallon steel water tank in West End. In 1937, outsiders were charged for the use of town water and sewer. Rockville used federal funds to erect a new water tower in 1938 and a new sewer plant in 1939. In an interplay of politics, it also convinced the General Assembly to require the largest user of the town's system, Montgomery County, to help finance the capital investment.

As Rockville grew, so did concerns with garbage and trash disposal. In the 1920s, local hog farms took some of the garbage, and burning was still legal, although the town discouraged it as a nuisance and fire hazard. Merchants pushed trash from the sidewalks into the main street, which was swept early on Saturday mornings. The municipal dump was located northeast of town in a rural area called Beantown. Increasingly, citizens complained about waste water

Traffic congestion on Rockville's main street in 1931. To the right is the courthouse lawn.

Photo by Harrison England, Charles Brewer collection, Peerless Rockville

from gasoline stations and dry cleaners. The Mayor and Council considered a municipal garbage collection in 1934 and 1935, but decided that "they could not involve the Town in any private enterprise and that the Town was not in a position to furnish the taxpayers with garbage collection service. . . .[69] If some individual would take up this line of work and do it in a proper manner the Town would cooperate with him. . . ."[70]

A growth management strategy that did interest Rockville was the new concept of zoning. With the help of Irving Root, engineer for the Maryland-National Capital Park and Planning Commission, and a three-man zoning commission, the town adopted its first zoning ordinance on August 3, 1932. The new rules regulated "the height, bulk, and location of buildings . . . and the areas of yards and open spaces" and divided Rockville into five zones: *A* for single family residential, churches, farms, schools, aviation fields, cemeteries; *B* for two-family dwellings; *C* for apartments not to exceed six stories high; *D* for commercial uses, including bakery, bowling alley, gas station, cooperage, and horseshoeing; and *E* for industrial uses. The E zone required assent of the council, which was concerned about manufacturing that "may become so noxious or offensive by reason of the emission of odor, dust, smoke, gas, or noise."[71] The council appointed Charles E. West as building inspector, and included his fees in the charge for permits issued.

Population growth and the increasing presence of the automobile also required controls. In the 1920s, the Mayor and Council introduced a stop-and-go electric traffic signal at the corner of Washington Street and Montgomery Avenue, where the main road turned north toward Gaithersburg and Frederick. Failure to obey the signal drew fines of five dollars to twenty-five dollars. Streets in the commercial center frequently clogged, so in the 1930s the town petitioned the State Roads Commission and Montgomery County commissioners to widen Commerce Lane as "a necessity to the traveling public and to the sane and safe growth of the Town."[72]

The
Mayor and Council
of
Rockville - Maryland

TOWN
ORDINANCE FOR ZONING

1931

Courtesy of Peerless Rockville

Rockville's first zoning ordinance.

Courtesy of Dr. William A. Linthicum, reproduced by the Montgomery County Archives

The corn cob pipe of Douglas M. Blandford, mayor 1932–46, was his trademark. Photo from History of the Rockville Rotary Club, *reproduced by the Montgomery County Archives.*

As time went on, the problem appeared to be caused as much by through traffic as by cars with Rockville destinations. The council installed state route markers, created parking lanes on Montgomery Avenue, and endlessly discussed road conditions and widenings. It passed numerous laws to regulate cars, parking, and persons distributing literature to passing vehicles. A *Sentinel* columnist declared: "Rockville has an acute parking problem. Week-end visitors to the local theatre and stores have but scant chance to park their automobiles anywhere near their destination."[73] In 1945, the town installed parking meters.

Town councils between the wars increased beautification and modernization efforts initiated by their predecessors. With ideas from *American City* magazine and from other urban areas, the Mayor and Council planted street trees in the 1920s and accepted a town clock for the main street in 1939. When house-to-house postal delivery began in 1926, Rockville installed street signs and devised a numbering system for buildings. The town supported garden, women's, business, and civic clubs with specific projects and contributed toward early recreation efforts such as Welsh Field. Rockville paid particular attention to the triangular public park in Court House Square.

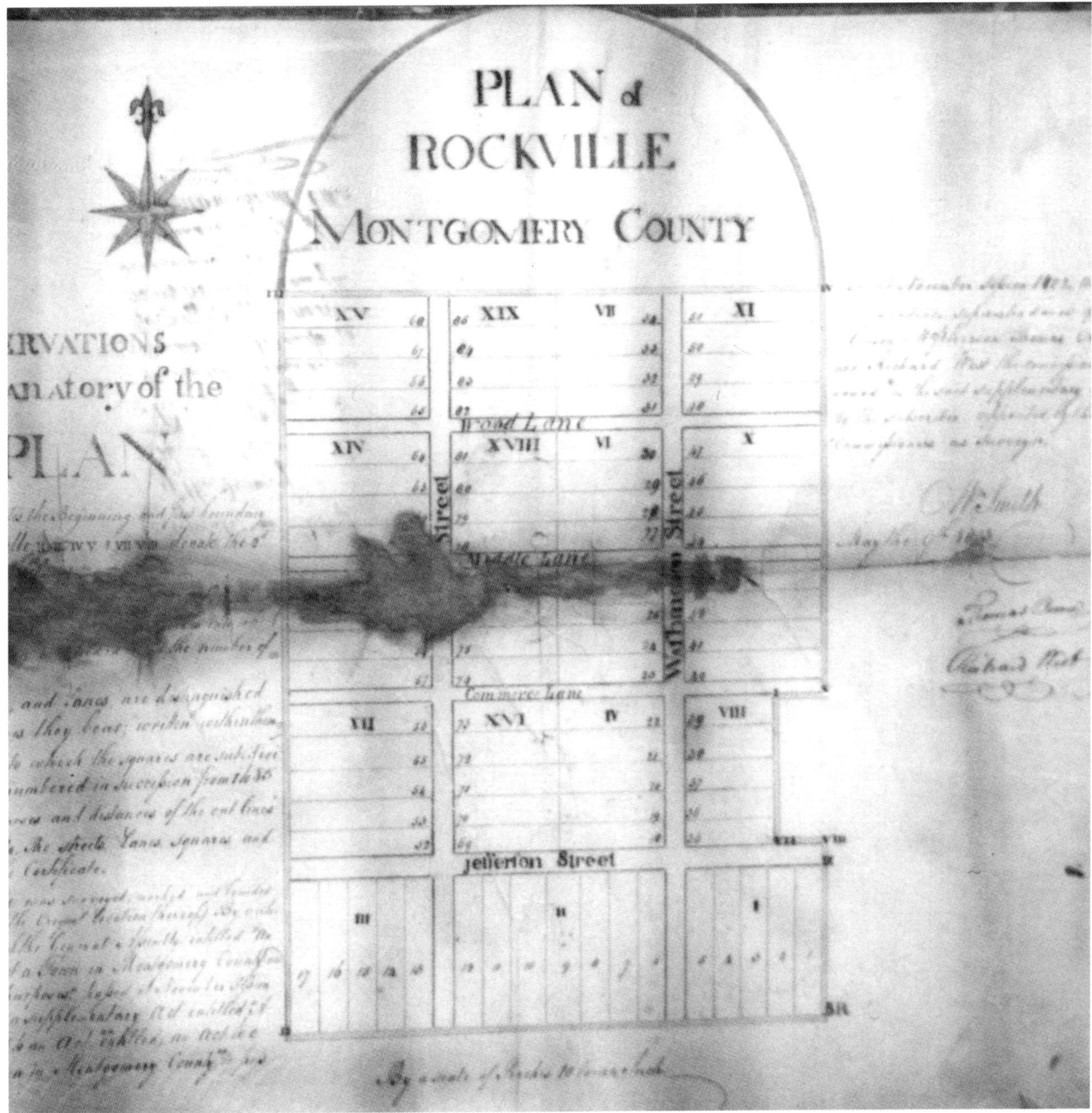

Photo by Dean Evangelista

Plate 1: *In 1801, the Maryland General Assembly authorized a survey of lots near the courthouse and erection of a town, "to be called and known by the name of Rockville." This Plan of Rockville, dated May 9, 1803, was recorded in the Land Records of Montgomery County.*

Photo by Dean Evangelista

Plate 2: *Twinbrook street scene.*

Photo by Dean Evangelista

Plate 3: *Bethany House Apartments.*

Photo by Dean Evangelista

Plate 4: *King Farm street scene.*

Painting by Connie Ward Woolard

Plate 5: *Victorian houses in West End.*

Photo by Dean Evangelista

Plate 6: *Lincoln Park mural.*

Photo by Dean Evangelista

Plate 7: *Three county buildings in 2000: Judicial Center, Executive Office Building, and County Office Building.*

Photo by Dean Evangelista

Plate 8: *Three courthouses.*

Photo by Dean Evangelista

Plate 9: *Red Brick Courthouse.*

Charles Brewer collection, courtesy Peerless Rockville

Plate 10: *North side of East Montgomery Avenue as seen in 1917.*

Charles Brewer collection, courtesy Peerless Rockville

Plate 11: *North side of East Montgomery Avenue as seen in 1966.*

Photo by Dean Evangelista

Plate 12: *North side of East Montgomery Avenue as seen in 2000.*

Painting by Houston Edward Hancock

Plate 13: *Painting of East Montgomery Avenue, looking west, 1950.*

Photo by Dean Evangelista

Plate 14: *Night scene, East Montgomery Avenue, 2000.*

Courtesy City of Rockville

Plate 15: *Farmers' market.*

People Make the City

Photo by Dean Evangelista

Plate 16: *Twinbrook Metro.*

Photo courtesy Joyce Staub, Rockville Senior Center

Plate 17: *Seniors playing cards.*

Photo by Dean Evangelista

Plate 18: *Playing softball at King Farm.*

Courtesy City of Rockville

Plate 19: *Spirit of Rockville—a celebration of cultures, 1998.*

Courtesy City of Rockville

Plate 20: *Walking town meeting.*

Photo by Dean Evangelista

Plate 21: *Outdoor dining at Congressional Plaza.*

Courtesy Dickran Y. Hovsepian

Plate 22: *1957 view southeast from East Montgomery Avenue, at the intersection of Veirs Mill Road and the Rockville Pike.*

Painting by Connie Ward Woolard

Plate 23: *Same view of the Rockville Pike, 1989 painting.*

Photo by Dean Evangelista

Plate 24: *Public park at the "mixing bowl" intersection in 2000.*

Commerce and Industry

Walter Smalling photograph, courtesy Celera Genomics

Plate 25: *Lab techs at Celera gene sequencing laboratory.*

Photo by Dean Evangelista

Plate 26: *King Farm-Irvington office building.*

Photo by Dean Evangelista

Plate 27: *125th anniversary of the Rockville B&O Railroad Station.*

MEMORIAL DAY PARADE

Mural by William Woodward.

Plate 28: *Mural at City Hall depicts Rockville's Memorial Day parade.*

Courtesy City of Rockville

Plate 29: *Rockville High School marching band, circa 1980.*

Courtesy Rosalie Campbell and Peerless Rockville

Plate 30: *Black residents on Washington Street, circa 1910.*

Courtesy Montgomery County Historical Society

Plate 31: *1950s parade down Montgomery Avenue.*

Plate 32: *American Legion Post 86 Color Guard, circa 1990.*

Courtesy City of Rockville

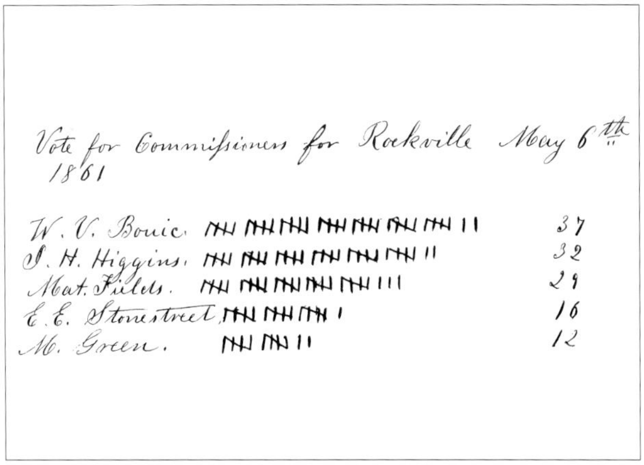

Vote for Commissioners for Rockville May 6th 1861

W. V. Bouic	37
J. H. Higgins	32
Mat. Fields	29
E. E. Stonestreet	16
M. Green	12

City of Rockville document at Montgomery County Archives

Plate 33: *1861 election tally sheet.*

Photo by Dean Evangelista

Plate 34: *City Hall sign.*

Plate 35: *Rockville Antique & Classic Car Show Millennium Display, 2000.*

Photo by Edward R. Vaughan, courtesy City of Rockville

Photo by Dean Evangelista

Plate 36: *Twinbrook Community Recreation Center.*

Courtesy City of Rockville

Plate 37: *Hometown Holidays laser light show.*

Views of Rockville

Courtesy City of Rockville

Plate 38: *Glenview Mansion in the snow.*

Courtesy City of Rockville

Plate 39: *View from the second floor balcony window at Glenview.*

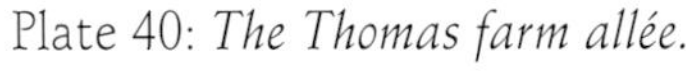

Plate 40: *The Thomas farm allée.*

Photo by Bill Gray, courtesy of Burt Hall

CLOSING THE RAILROAD CROSSING

A horrific accident on April 11, 1935 shocked the community and forever altered traffic patterns in Rockville. At 11:30 P.M., a train bound for Union Station in Washington slammed into a blue school bus as it crossed the B&O Railroad tracks at Baltimore Road. Fourteen seniors from Williamsport High School in Western Maryland were killed and thirteen others injured as they returned from a chemistry fair at the University of Maryland. Neither train nor bus had warning because the B&O Railroad watchman had left his post in the telegraph tower at the crossing when his shift ended at 10:00 P.M. Nearby residents, including priests at Saint Mary's, rushed to help. The Rockville Volunteer Fire Department worked through the night to pull victims out of the wreckage. Despite the best efforts of local physicians, students died on the scene, in ambulances, and en route to hospitals. Less seriously injured students were comforted in nearby homes. Rescue workers took bodies to the morgue at Pumphrey's Funeral Home, where Williamsport families came to identify their children.

Courtesy of The Maryland Historical Society, Baltimore, Maryland

Newly constructed bridge on Veirs Mill Road, 1937

The tragedy shook Williamsport and Rockville and attracted national attention. Rockville officials and rescue workers attended a memorial service at Williamsport High School on April 17. President Franklin D. Roosevelt immediately pledged public works funds to eliminate at-grade crossings, the B&O inaugurated a twenty-four hour watch service at the crossing, Maryland legislators and the school board wrote new rules, and suits were filed in court. In 1937, the Federal Works Progress Administration built a bridge on Veirs Mill Road over the tracks.[74]

Between the wars, public drinking fountains and a board on which to post daily weather reports were installed, and the garden club planted flowers around the Confederate statue. The town center was the pride of Rockville.

After World War I, Rockville's government intensified its presence, although it continued to operate in an informal way. In 1919, the town opened an office in a room over Vinson's drug store at a cost of eight dollars per month. Six years later, the council rented a room in the new firehouse for seventeen dollars, later increasing the space and the rent. In 1945, Mrs. Allnutt kept office hours at the firehouse from 10:00 A.M. to 4:00 P.M., except Saturday when she closed at noon. Rockville kept a town horse for snow plowing and other chores until about 1932, when it purchased an automobile. It borrowed road machinery from the county, and rented the town's street roller to citizens. The town alternated its bank account yearly between Montgomery County National and Farmers banks. It set the property tax rate and reported to the public annually, but needed General Assembly authorization for bonds to be issued for construction projects. In keeping with the times, and with no public comment, the Mayor and Council regularly purchased needed items, such as building supplies and automobiles, from sitting councilmen. The town closed streets and provided utility connections for prominent citizens and for those outside corporate boundaries who would aid the tax base.

In seven terms as mayor of Rockville, Douglas M. Blandford (1877–1956) came to personify local government. Blandford came to Rockville in 1921 and purchased Oscar Johnson's lumberyard. A good businessman, careful with the dollar, he often wore old clothes. From 1932 to 1946 he pushed to maintain the

A four-sided clock arrived in Rockville in 1939, courtesy of the estate of Washington confectioner Walter Brownley. Chased off the public triangle by indignant Daughters of the Confederacy in favor of the Civil War monument, the clock came to rest on the grassy street divider in front of the 1931 courthouse. There it helped people attend court on time for years, until a hurried fireman lost control of his car on a rainy night in 1957. The city installed a replacement clock, this time two-sided, the following year. At the time this photo appeared in the Washington Star, *the Milo Theatre was also new in town.*

tax rate while enlarging the boundaries and the tax base of the town. He encouraged construction projects, took aggressive stands against utility and transportation companies on behalf of the town, and supported groups who worked to improve Rockville. He could be stubborn in defense of the town, such as when he went head-to-head with Police Court Judge Harold C. Smith (about parking his car in a restricted zone) or set his chair in the middle of the trolley tracks (in a dispute with Capital Transit Company).[75] In addition to his home on South Washington Street, Blandford owned considerable real estate in Rockville. He was vice president of Montgomery County National Bank, a charter member of the Rockville Rotary Club, and a legendary poker player.[76]

Assisting the public officials was a small staff increasingly characterized by expertise. Town clerks, who served part-time at the pleasure of the council, were men until the appointment of Mrs. Leigh Allnutt in April 1945. William F. Disney and John McDonald were town engineers, at varying times responsible for the water and sewer systems, streets, and other projects. As they had since 1803, two bailiffs performed police duties, with periodic help from county, state, and deputy bailiffs. A building inspector and plumbing inspector processed permits, and day laborers did road work and maintenance. In the late 1930s when the council set the annual salary of its street foreman, it agreed to deduct ten dollars each month that he appeared intoxicated, then proceeded to evaluate his performance closely. An Auditing Committee in 1932 recommended that the town pay employees by check and to "keep a better check on Town labor."[77] Despite this attention to detail, the governing body recognized that a small town could not provide every service for its citizens.

THE GREAT DEPRESSION

While the depression was difficult for the people of Rockville, proximity to Washington, D.C., softened the pain. President Franklin D. Roosevelt's New Deal programs and construction of new federal institutions (National Institutes of Health, David Taylor Model Basin, Public Health Service) attracted people to the area. Population growth in the metropolitan area necessitated construction of housing, schools, and government buildings close to Rockville. The building and development industries revived to participate in a building boom in 1935, rivaling Montgomery County's peak of the mid-1920s.[78] The Civil Works and Works Progress Administrations (WPA) sent federal funds for several public construction projects in Rockville—a new water tower, elementary school, post office, sewage treatment plant, street work, and extension of sewer and water lines.

Several Rockville businesses closed their doors during the depression. Some suffered from modern competition, and the economic downturn finished them off. Val Wilson's 1929 purchase of a new organ to accompany silent movies at his SECO Theatre was the final straw for an enterprise losing ground to the *talkies*. The mill operated by Clarence and Lindsey Hickerson near the depot gave way to packaged flour and feed. After an abbreviated fair in 1932, the historic Rockville fairgrounds were auctioned off in August 1933 and purchased by the Montgomery County Board of Education for a school site. The Villa Roma Club and restaurant on the Pike, managed by Frank Abbo, succumbed in 1934. The following year, when R. E. Milor razed the Dixie Tavern, which briefly took the place of the renowned Montgomery House, Rockville was left without a hotel.

Rockville's two banks survived the depression. When President Roosevelt declared a holiday in March 1933, bank examiners told Farmers Banking and Trust Company of Montgomery County to reopen if it secured $75,000 from its depositors. The bank's directors, having decided to remain closed unless it raised twice that amount, met with depositors to explain the situation. Farmers reopened on April 25 with $125,000 cash on hand and continued operating for many years under the stewardship of

Rockville's first permanent post office opened in 1939. The following year, WPA artist Judson Smith painted the mural in the lobby of the building. The use of Sugarloaf Mountain, located outside of Montgomery County, caused local disapproval at the time.

Postcard courtesy of Bonne Prettyman

Records of the Public Building Service, National Archives

Aerial of center of Rockville, looking south, 1938. Courthouses appear in center of photograph.

Richard F. Green. Montgomery County National Bank took longer to reopen, but it also recovered. It remained in its handsome brick building on a prominent corner across Perry Street from the Red Brick Courthouse until the 1970s.[79]

The 1930s did bring new construction and new businesses to Rockville. The classical limestone courthouse kept contractors and the town center busy in 1930 and 1931, and the handsome Farmers Bank building introduced Art Deco design to town. Two other mid-decade main street construction projects brought out the *Sentinel*'s boosterism. "Rockville is being placed on the map by the large-scale construction work now in progress,"[80] the paper reported in 1935, referring to Mrs. Ida Wolfson's office and apartment building on the site of the old Town Hall and to the Milo Theatre complex, both within sight of the courthouses.

"The bright lights from the marquee of the new Milo Theatre will soon add their modern glow to the many others in fast growing downtown Rockville."[81] Designed by John Zink for the Sidney Lust Theatre chain, the Milo featured "springy and well upholstered" orchestra seating for 600, a balcony for 150 black patrons with outside access, a modern restroom, and parking for 300 cars behind the building. Soon after the Milo opened on October 12, 1935, lines formed to see Clark Gable, Jean Harlow, and Wallace Beery in *China Seas*. Gable telegrammed "All Hollywood wishes you the best of success with your new Venture," and Shirley Temple wrote "Hello to you and all the children of Rockville. Watch for me in *The Littlest Rebel* about Christmas Time."[82]

Rockville's finest legacy of the depression was a permanent post office building. For 145 years, the post office moved approximately every five years from one rented commercial space to another in the town center. In town delivery did not begin until 1926. The Rockville postal address covered a huge outlying territory, extending to the Kent estate on Darnestown Road and the Fitzgerald farm on Clopper Road.

In 1937, the Rockville Chamber of Commerce proposed a new post office, and soon WPA gave its approval. The old *Sentinel* and PEPCO buildings were condemned and bulldozed in November 1938, so construction could begin. Designed by architects Louis Simon and R. Stanley-Brown in the English Georgian style, Rockville's post office was more modest in appearance than those in faster-growing Bethesda and Silver Spring. The limestone building's two-story hexagonal entrance tower marked the intersection of Rockville's most important streets. Inside were terrazzo floors, brass and glass bulletin boards and postal boxes, a lookout gallery, and a handsome mural of Sugarloaf Mountain.[83]

Three thousand people celebrated the dedication of the post office on July 22, 1939. A colorful parade from the fairgrounds led to ceremonies on the courthouse lawn, followed by a smaller reception at the Glenview estate of Dr. and Mrs. James A. Lyon. The day was further enlivened by two protesting heirs of the Fields family who erected a No Trespassing sign on the post office lawn. The new public building then settled down to business, led by postmaster Dr. George L. Edmonds, his assistant Joe Dawson, six clerks, two city carriers, and three rural carriers.[84]

Economic recovery coincided with harbingers of Rockville's busy future. Construction began in 1939 for Bethesda Naval Hospital, another federal installation within easy commuting distance of Rockville. As the new decade opened, Thomas O. deBeck planned a development for land he had acquired in the late 1930s, using Federal Housing Administration financing. In the fall of 1940, deBeck received approvals from county and state agencies and filed three subdivision plats for seven blocks of Rockcrest, a new development south of First Street. Soon the new streets were dotted with small cottages on six thousand-square-foot lots.[85] DeBeck negotiated an agreement with the town of Rockville to furnish water and sewer facilities and to annex the new subdivision. The town policy makers proceeded cautiously, perhaps knowing this would be the first of many such requests.

ROXBORO

ROCKVILLE'S NEW DEVELOPMENT

NEW HOMES

$6,000

5 Rooms - Bath - Oil Heat - Insulated - Screened - Weather Stripped - Garage.

★

$7,000

6 Rooms - Bath - Oil Heat - Insulated - Screened - Weather Stripped - Garage.

★

Open Sunday Afternoons
Call Rockville 288

★

Mr. & Mrs. Porter N. Butt
Developers.

★

MORE HOMES TO BE CONSTRUCTED

Porter and Emma Butt subdivided fourteen acres in the west end of Rockville into building lots and advertised affordable Roxboro homes for sale in the Sentinel *in the spring of 1940.*

WORLD WAR II

On an unusually warm December 7, 1941, many of Rockville's two thousand residents attended church, then returned home for family dinner and a leisurely Sunday afternoon. When President Roosevelt's radio announcement of the Japanese bombing came at about 2:00 P.M., few knew the location of Pearl Harbor. Most were worried about Europe and if the United States might be dragged into the conflict. That evening, church bells rang and people congregated to pray. The following day, long lines formed at the recruiting station. The Japanese attack had united Americans.

Rockville mobilized with the nation. Young men joined the armed forces, and women took over their jobs. The Civilian Defense Council quickly geared up, for the Washington area had been preparing for war for some time. "Victory begins at home!" inspired rationing of sugar, meat, butter, canned food, coffee, shoes, and gasoline. Tons of newspaper, tires, cardboard, and scrap metal, including the Baptist Cemetery fence, were salvaged for the war effort. Baseball hero Walter Johnson spoke at a bond rally at Montrose School. Rockville farmers increased production. Town residents and school children led by elementary teacher Lucy Barnsley planted Victory Gardens. High school students, members of the Victory Corps, drilled younger children on Park Street. Dimes collected for savings stamps culminated in students dedicating a jeep, "The Rockville Bumper." The Civil Air Patrol used the Congressional air field for its home base, and student flyers trained there under the civilian pilot training program in 1942. Children wrote to local servicemen in Europe and the Pacific. Rockville cut off lights to the town clock and imposed a fifty dollar fine for inside or

F. SCOTT FITZGERALD AND ROCKVILLE

On December 27, 1940, two dozen people gathered at Rockville Cemetery to attend a short, simple graveside service for F. Scott Fitzgerald. The author of *The Great Gatsby*, *Flappers and Philosophers*, *This Side of Paradise*, and *The Beautiful and Damned* and other icons of twentieth century literature was buried at the young age of forty-four in the community with which he had maintained a life-long connection.

Fitzgerald learned about Rockville through the Civil War stories of his father, Edward Fitzgerald, who grew up on Locust Grove farm. Young Scott visited his paternal relatives frequently and in 1903 carried the ring at his cousin Cecilia Delihant's wedding in their home on Randolph Road. Cousins Scott and Ceci corresponded frequently throughout their lives.

Fitzgerald became one of America's most-read twentieth century writers. Born in St. Paul, Minnesota, he attended Princeton University and married beautiful Zelda Sayre of Montgomery, Alabama, soon after publishing his first short story. As they lived and played in America and Europe, the Fitzgeralds embodied the headiness of the 1920s, coining the phrase "the Jazz Age."

Scott Fitzgerald kept in touch with Rockville through his diary, letters, and writings. He returned from Paris in 1931 to attend his father's funeral at Saint Mary's Church. At the time Fitzgerald was writing *Tender Is the Night*, published in 1934, where the bereaved Dick Diver spoke for him: "It was very friendly leaving him there with all his relations around him. . . . Dick had no more ties here now and did not believe he would come back. . . . 'Good-by, my father—good-by, all my fathers."

Fitzgerald was too ill five years later to be present at his mother's burial at Saint Mary's. Always concerned about Zelda's mental condition and their daughter Scottie's upbringing and education, Fitzgerald's health declined. He was in Hollywood writing screenplays, short stories, and *The Last Tycoon* when he suffered a fatal heart attack. His Princeton classmate, Judge John Biggs, arranged for Fitzgerald's body to be sent by train to Pumphrey's Funeral Home in Rockville and attempted to have him laid to rest near his parents, grandparents, and great-grandparents. A series of errors sent Fitzgerald's body to Pumphrey's in Bethesda, then to a simple service conducted by Rev. Raymond P. Black of Christ Episcopal Church at Rockville Cemetery.

Eventually, all was set right. Zelda Fitzgerald died in 1948 and was buried next to her husband. In 1975, their daughter Scottie teamed with the Woman's Club of Rockville to relocate Scott and Zelda Fitzgerald to Saint Mary's cemetery next to the historic chapel. There they rest under elegant oak trees with other Fitzgerald relatives interred there long ago.[86]

outside lights during air-raid blackouts. To complicate matters, when nearly seventy cases of rabies were confirmed in 1944, police were ordered to shoot any dog acting suspiciously and local veterinarians dispensed vaccine from the hoods of their cars.[87]

In the summer of 1942, Rockville organized two companies of Minute Men. Once a week, older men trained to protect Congressional air field and to block the enemy from entering through local roads. As the men drilled and crawled over Welsh Field and through Cabin John Creek, the children of Rockville watched and on the sidelines played soldier.[88] The Colored Businessmen's Association of Montgomery County, assisted by the Fishermen and the Elks of Rockville, erected an honor roll board on Washington Street to list the names of black servicemen and women. After the war, black veterans would form American Legion Post 151 in Rockville.

The *Sentinel*, *Star*, *Post*, and other local papers published detailed news of Rockville's servicemen—reporting to the induction center in Baltimore, completing training and receiving orders, participating in landings and actions, being wounded, recuperating from long weeks of combat, being taken prisoner, earning medals, and parents receiving word from the War Department that their sons had been killed in action.

At 10:00 A.M. on June 6, 1944, the bell at Christ Episcopal Church began to toll. Within minutes, towns-people of all denominations gathered in the sanctuary. Reverend G. Freeland Peter, retired Canon of the Cathedral, substituting while Rev. Raymond Black served as a Navy chaplain, led the overflow crowd in a special prayer service for the safety of the men attempting to land at Normandy. One of those at the D-Day landing was nineteen-year-old Stephen Cromwell Jr., a Navy corpsman in the first waves at Omaha Beach. No local man lost his life that day.[89]

On September 3, 1945, residents gathered on Rockville's main street to celebrate V-J Day—victory over Japan. Speeches and a grand parade marked the official end of nearly four years of war and sacrifice.

The years 1917 to 1945 saw Rockville overtaken by modern trends in the nation and the world. Innovations in transportation and communication technology multiplied the rate of change. Locally, issues generated by growth in and around the small town and by proliferation of the automobile dominated the period. Rockville officials found that attempts at managing utilities, annexation, and traffic problems often led to new concerns, so much remained unsettled. Civic and social organizations proliferated, many with the purpose of community improvement. Patterns developed in the years between the two world wars—expectations of public services and of community participation—became sources of local pride.

Rockville connected with the world and the nation between the World Wars, but it did so as a maturing small town. Two thousand generally homogeneous residents bonded through daily contact, through the presence of a single public educational facility for their children, through interdenominational activities, and through organizations formed to improve the community. The informality of local government helped solidify the personal ties that existed throughout the small population.

Despite continuing attempts by town government and citizens to maintain the status quo, the flow from town to small city was set in motion. Issues of growth and social change that urban areas had wrestled with for some time were about to enter the consciousness of Rockville residents. Planning for growth, recreation and social services, and comprehensive economic development would come with the next boom of 1945–60.

TOP: Siblings Gordon Rosenberger, Margaret Rosenberger Byrd, and Douglas Rosenberger in WW II uniforms. They posed in front of the parsonage on Jefferson Street, as their father was the Methodist minister.
BOTTOM: Roy Perry photographed the festivities in Rockville on V-J Day, September 3, 1945.

Courtesy of Bonne Prettyman

Roy Perry collection, Peerless Rockville

Chapter Seven

From Town to City

The Emergence of Modern Rockville 1945–1960

"Washington has expanded so rapidly and so extensively that even the suburban towns are developing suburbs of their own. . . . One such expanding community is Rockville, which has been spreading rapidly since the war along Viers Mills [sic] road towards Wheaton. It has been one of the scenes of considerable mass-building in the District area, with emphasis on medium-cost homes."[1]

One July morning in the hot, dry summer of 1953, Dickran Hovsepian turned on the shower and . . . nothing happened. Rockville's wells had again gone dry. The water shortage, and the indignation of residents at their government's response, launched Hovsepian and his compatriots into small-town politics and started Rockville on a path toward modernization. Ironically, the Hovsepians' new home and Twin-Brook neighborhood were part of the problem.

Dick and Viola Hovsepian met during World War II, married, and came to work in Washington. In 1950, they saw a newspaper ad for a house they could afford in a new subdivision along Veirs Mill Road. That same day they put down the required $250 deposit and bought a house. The couple soon found kindred young professionals in Twinbrook who were charmed by Rockville's small-town atmosphere, but missed the recreation programs and well-managed urban services they enjoyed growing up elsewhere. Their concerns became urgent when Rockville ran out of water. For decades, the town had connected new homes to a piecemeal water and sewage system of uncertain capacity. The new citizens scrutinized the operations and philosophy of the town government and found it as inadequate for post–World War II growth as the water supply.[2]

THE QUINTESSENTIAL POSTWAR SUBURB

After the war, Rockville returned to the serious business of growing. Washington, D.C., had expanded, as it had during previous wars. Federal agencies created during the Great Depression and in wartime crises enlarged a government work force that remained after the ticker tape of V-J Day parades had been swept away.

The acute housing shortage in the metropolitan area after World War II set the stage for new suburban developments. Returning veterans drew concentric circles on maps of Washington to consider Rockville on the basis of housing affordability and distance. The most intense growth was along Veirs Mill Road. In addition to Rockcrest, which started before the war, new subdivisions were Harriett Park, Twinbrook, Silver Rock, Rockland, the Burgundies, and others. Buses and automobiles made commuting easy.

Federal programs affected Rockville as much as employment opportunities. Most houses in postwar Rockville were financed with Federal Housing Administration (FHA) loans—created in 1934 by the National Housing Act—which were biased toward new single family residential developments on city edges. The 1944 GI Bill supplemented FHA and made possible the popular American dream of home ownership. The

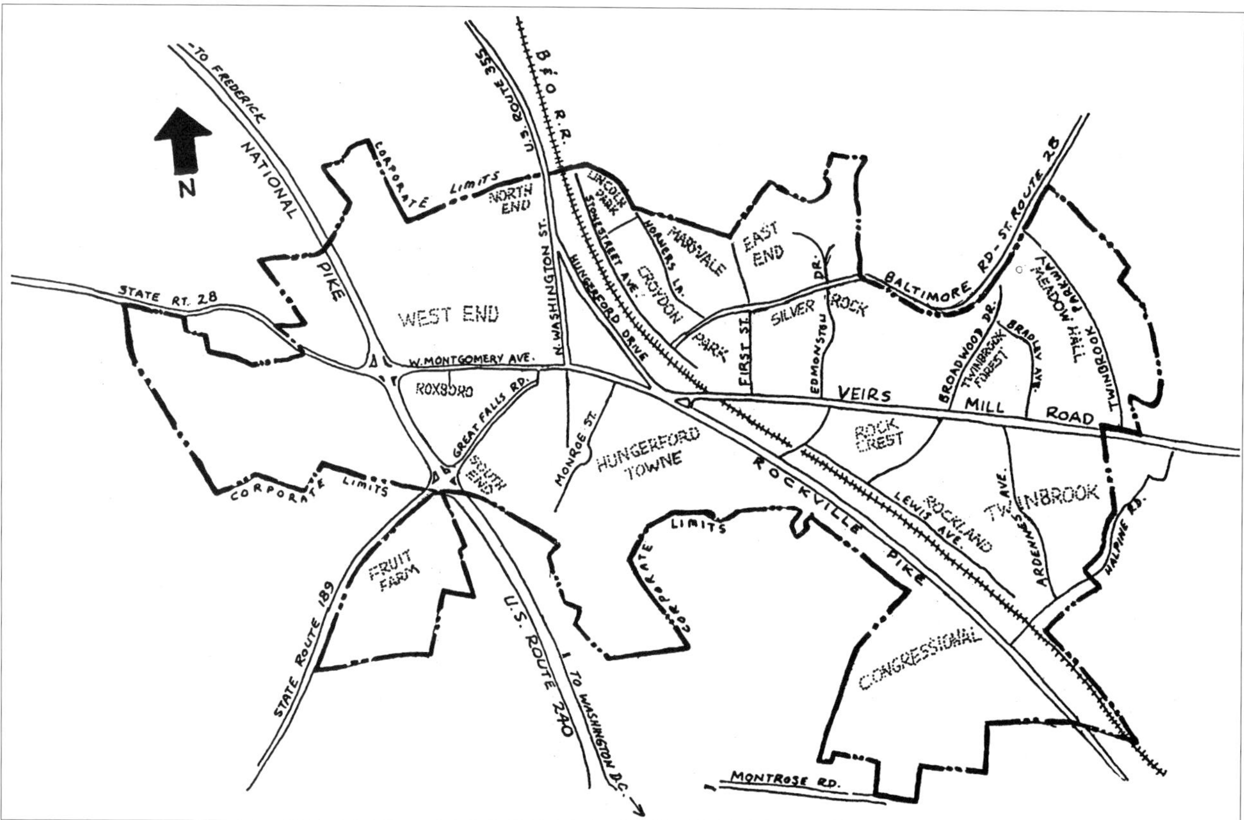

From *Citizen's Handbook, City of Rockville, Maryland, 1959–60*

Map of Rockville neighborhoods.

FHA stimulated postwar construction needed to house sixteen million returning servicemen and their families by insuring long-term mortgage loans made by private lenders. It further influenced Rockville's development by proposing minimum lot size and setback standards for new subdivisions and by discouraging racial mixing.[3]

In 1946, four builders (Joseph L. Geeraert, Roland E. Simmons, Wesley J. Sauter, and Donald E. Gingery) formed Twin-Brook and purchased 202 acres known as Walnut Hill Farm, wedged between the B&O Railroad tracks and Veirs Mill Road, from Lillian Small of Washington, D.C. At first, the developers planned half-acre lots needed for septic fields. When the State Board of Health approved plans for a sewer plant and the town agreed to annex the development, the builders substantially reduced lot sizes and raised the number of homes. By Christmas of 1948, seventeen families had moved in.

The development of Twinbrook, named for two streams flowing from the Small property into Rock Creek, became the Washington metropolitan area's quintessential postwar middle-class suburb. The new homes employed cost-saving techniques inspired by Frank Lloyd Wright's Usonian modular house of the 1930s and put into practice by William Levitt in Levittown on Long Island immediately after the war. Twinbrook represented a departure from earlier Rockville residential development in concept and appearance of the dwellings, in lot configuration and size, and in the dimension of the demands it would place upon local government to provide public services. Like Levittown, Twinbrook abandoned the traditional grid pattern of streets and lots in favor of irregular side and rear lot lines that followed the contours of the land and streams. To discourage through-traffic, only a few streets connected to major roads.[4] Geeraert had visited Levittown and, while impressed by the design and size of the homes planned for moderate-income buyers, he chose not to employ Levitt's preassembly techniques for his Rockville development.[5]

Courtesy of Peerless Rockville

View from Twinbrook Elementary School, 1956. "A Typical Housing Subdivision in Rockville, Md." from the North America Fieldman, *November 1956.*

Courtesy of Margaret S. Sante

Courtesy of Margaret S. Sante

TOP: Mr. and Mrs. J. Pete Sante purchased this house at 12800 Atlantic Avenue in Twinbrook, in 1953. The developer issued six shrubs to each new homeowner. BOTTOM: Peg Sante and children, Easter Sunday, 1957.

Twinbrook was most notable for its rhythmic rows of nearly identical houses—the typical tract streetscape that became popular in Rockville. House design varied little from the basic model—turned 90 to 180 degrees on the lot—with roof, window, and door modifications. The lure of a new, detached home with modern appliances, brick fireplace, knotty pine paneling, tile bath, large window wall, and expandable attic that cost less than $10,000 was irresistible. Veterans quickly signed contracts ranging from $9,250 to $11,500—$50 down and 100 percent GI loans, with monthly payments set at $42 to $60.[6]

For young postwar couples, Twinbrook promised starter homes, built for expansion as income and the number of children grew. "The homes are just what you have been looking for, room enough now for your present needs. May be easily and economically made into a three or four bedroom, or two bath house," declared the developers.[7] Section One houses were modest, with two bedrooms and a bath on the first floor, no basement, and an upper level to be finished or added to later. Young government workers, nuclear physicists, lawyers, and clerks—most of whom commuted to Washington—purchased homes as rapidly as they could be built. By 1952, despite an early lack of telephones or paved streets, three hundred homes were occupied. Every afternoon a city worker would come to prime the pump of the well at the corner of Atlantic and Vandegrift. Each treeless lot received six bushes but no sod or grass.[8] There were so many children that Twinbrook Elementary School opened that September. The following year, additional classrooms doubled the school's capacity. The last section of the original development opened in 1954.

Geeraert and Gingery, having bought out their partners, continued to buy land and build homes on the north side of Veirs Mill Road. From 1951 to 1953, they opened streets to add to Broadwood Manor. In 1952, they branched out to Twinbrook Forest, a huge

Courtesy of Mr. and Mrs. Anthony Morella

Connie, Tony, and Paul Morella moved into their new home on Twinbrook Parkway in 1959. With assistance from the GI Bill, they paid $18,500 for the house. This photograph appeared in the Washington Star.

tract in which only the tiny Willow Tree graveyard hinted at past habitation. Besides honoring Generals Marshall and Bradley and Admiral Farragut, Geeraert named streets for his daughters Dorothy and Rosanne, and wife Marcia. In Twinbrook Forest, Geeraert added split levels, small colonials, and ramblers, incorporating new features such as cathedral ceilings and spacious kitchens. Halpine Village, south of Veirs Mill Road, was built in 1955–56, and Twinbrook Forest Condominiums opened around the old Meadow Hall mansion in 1964. After his daughter's wedding reception at the mansion, Geeraert offered the nineteenth century home of Samuel Clark Veirs for institutional use, but there were no takers and the house was razed. Only a brick patio, pool and bath house, gatehouse, and terraced gardens remain.

Geeraert promised to build a complete community that would instill pride in its residents. Twinbrook streets, named for military heroes such as Halsey, LeMay, Stillwell, Wainwright and battles such as Ardennes, Coral Sea, Okinawa, Midway, and St. Lo, reinforced bonds among the veterans. The neighborhood was self-contained and strengthened with its own social, civic, commercial, educational, and religious opportunities. In 1949, the Twinbrook Citizens Association (TCA) emerged to tackle such issues as street lights and recreation programs. TCA printed a newsletter and a community directory. Residents formed a 4-H club, scout troops, Campfire girls, Boys Club, and three Homemakers clubs. By the mid-1950s, a swimming pool and community center were planned.[9]

Twinbrook residents shopped in Rockville or Silver Spring until retail shops opened on the south side of Veirs Mill Road in 1956. In addition to the A&P grocery store, the newcomers patronized People's Drug Store, Ward's, and branches of the Rockville post office and library. In 1958, new stores opened on the north side: Safeway, G. C. Murphy Company, a bowling alley, Wenger's Bakery, Drug Fair, Farmers Bank, and several smaller shops.[10] The interest of chain stores measured the impact of new Rockville subdivisions.

The newcomers required additional services and amenities to complete the quintessential suburban subdivision picture. Attempting to keep up with the school-age baby boomers, the Board of Education opened four elementary schools in the east side of Rockville between 1950 and 1956.[11] Twinbrookers swelled the ranks of Rockville's established churches and initiated new groups that planned for future buildings. But the framework and mind-set of Rockville's town government were unprepared for the increased expectations and demands. When the time came, new residents of the postwar subdivisions—chiefly those of Rockcrest and Twinbrook—sparked the revolution that turned Rockville's government upside down.

FROM TOWN TO CITY

New postwar housing developments, combined with continuing construction on vacant lots in Rockville, overwhelmed the town's capacity to provide services. This difficulty did not happen suddenly. Most meetings of the Mayor and Council from 1925 through 1960 had some discussion of sewer and water issues—drilling for new town wells, requests for water and sewer connections, bond bills to finance construction of water towers and sewage pumping stations, negotiations with the Washington Suburban Sanitary Commission (WSSC), borrowing purifying chlorine from Fort Belvoir, correctness of water bills, or dealing with new subdivisions.

Citizens pitched in to help with the frequent crises that resulted. During the drought of 1946 when Rockville's artesian wells failed, local black leaders sent a large contingent to help the all-white fire department bring in water. Together, white and black volunteers laid more than one and a half miles of fire hose from Rock Creek on Veirs Mill Road to the nearest standpipe within the town limits. The operation used all of the hose owned by the Rockville Volunteer Fire Department as well as additional hose borrowed from Gaithersburg and Kensington.[12]

In 1951, Mayor G. LaMar Kelly described to visitors from Hagerstown and Annapolis how Rockville dealt with new subdivisions outside of its boundaries. When a development neared completion, the town would extend water and sewer mains only if there was a signed agreement that the area would be annexed at the next Maryland General Assembly session and that the owner of each lot would pay the full town tax rate. When these conditions were met, the Mayor and Council would grant the developer's petition and proceed to finance the extension by issuing bonds. The town repaid the bonds under a Front Foot Benefit Assessment system that billed homeowners annually for thirty years for the connection to public water and sewer. In concept this sounded progressive, but in reality Rockville proved unable to provide adequate services to postwar subdivisions.

In the late 1940s and early 1950s, the Mayor and Council (all local businessmen) came under increasing pressure to act on a variety of problems—mostly parking and traffic, and water and sewer issues. They refused to raise the tax rate for a staff and budget that would keep up with the population. When forty-three merchants petitioned for parking meters, the council purchased meters for the main commercial streets and hired a patrolman to enforce payment of ten cents for two hours of parking. This opened doors for biweekly deliberations on whether to invalidate parking tickets issued to people on public business, irate or elderly citizens, double-parked cars, and out-of-town motorists. The town leased a parking lot on Commerce Lane, which quickly filled. Mayor Kelly commented on how parking had aided the tremendous growth of Silver Spring and asked merchants for ideas. He assigned Rockville police to traffic detail from 4:00 to 6:00 P.M. and requested help from state and county police at other times.

Painfully, Rockville outgrew the system of local government that had served for more than half a century. The town encouraged development but did not provide adequate infrastructure to serve the growing population. Unpaid and untrained in town management, some men reluctantly took a turn at public office. Elected officials were increasingly frustrated by their inability to resolve recurring problems.

One new idea adopted by the postwar Mayor and Council set the stage for later change. The council-manager system of government had emerged from progressive reforms early in the century, but it best suited communities with populations larger than Rockville's. The council's attempt to delegate personnel responsibilities to a professional manager as early as 1890 had met with failure. However, in April 1948, the council created a position to attend "to all matters of administrative nature in the maintenance and operation of the government of the Town of Rockville . . . [and to be] empowered to retain such personnel as he deems necessary. . . ." It appointed John McDonald as Rockville's first town manager, since he "in the function of Town Engineer has acted in this capacity since 1938."[13] A Rockville resident and officer of Standard Supplies, of which company Mayor Kelly was president, McDonald had numbered houses and recorded sewer maps for the town in 1926. He served on the Board of Zoning Appeals, then was hired as building inspector and subsequently promoted to town engineer.

Although mayors and councils usually favored recreation, the postwar residential subdivisions changed the playing field. Before 1950, children's lives were less organized, and a small town got by with school athletic programs and facilities. Kids played in nearby woods and creeks, drank in the drama of the courtroom, or joined pickup games in local fields. With the newcomers, huge numbers of children lived far from existing facilities. In 1948, the council began a seven-week summer program for white children at Rockville Elementary School and for black children in

ROCKVILLE'S POSTWAR GROWTH

Year	Population	Population Increase	Land Area
1940	2,047	44.0 percent	466
1950	6,934	238.7 percent	2,753
1960	26,090	276.3 percent	4,473

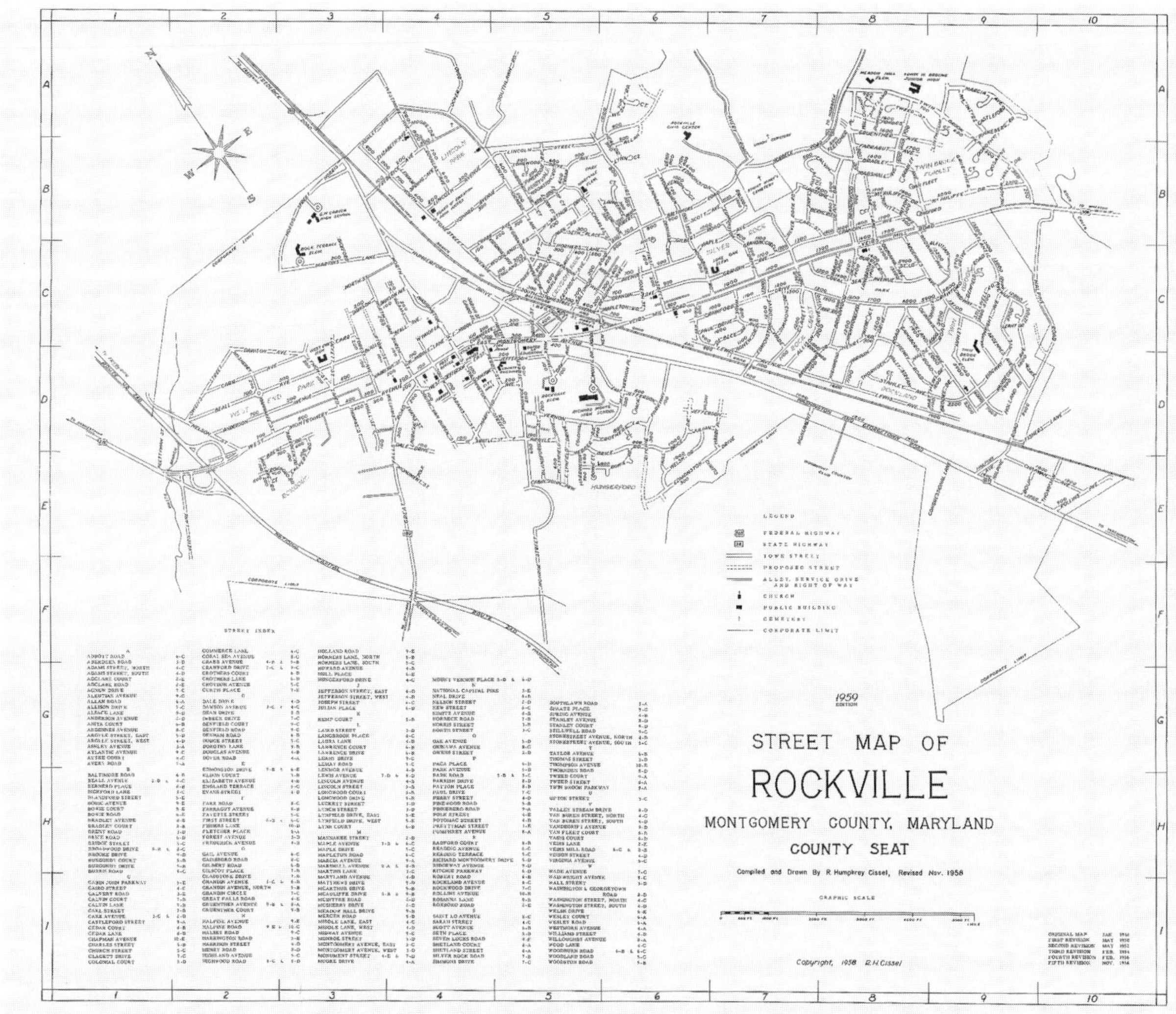

Courtesy of Peerless Rockville

Street Map of Rockville, *R. Humphrey Cissel, 1959 edition.*

Lincoln Park. More than two hundred youngsters played games, engaged in crafts, and swam in local segregated swimming pools in Glen Echo or Washington, D.C. The town surveyed taxpayers in 1949 as to whether they would favor a tax increase "in order to guarantee an annual recreation program."[14] Receiving a two to one vote against it, the Mayor and Council instead approved modest amounts for supervised summer recreation programs, including assistance to those organized by neighborhood groups.

In 1947, a new group formed "to make Rockville a better place to live"[15] and set up what would become the prototype for Rockville's nonpartisan activists. The Rockville Civic Association (RCA), under the leadership of Pat Axtell, Leslie Abbe, Boyd Ladd, Ralph Williams, Watson Phillips, and others, approached the Mayor and Council from 1947 through 1953 with a barrage of requests and recommendations "for the good of the entire community."[16]

RCA was the lightning rod that attracted advocates of change in Rockville. The association's first efforts focused on reducing residency requirements for voters and permitting federal government employees to take part in nonpartisan town elections. Working with neighborhood civic associations, RCA assembled facts, provided information to Rockville taxpayers, and boldly took positions on issues in the rapidly growing town. For example, RCA supplemented the town's postcard mailings on recreation programs with a two-page mimeographed fact sheet, mailed out information on voter registration and proposed town legislation, and compiled comparative financial data for 1950–53. Activist Boyd Ladd of Rockcrest ran unsuccessfully for town council in 1950. As the first candidate from an area annexed since 1940 and the sole nonincumbent, he found Rockville unready for change.

One of RCA's most fruitful suggestions came in January 1950 when it convinced the Mayor and Council to contract with the Bureau of Public Administration at the University of Maryland to "survey . . . the Town of Rockville to determine what and if any changes should be made in the Town's administration."[17] The resulting report bluntly concluded that while "Rockville [was] serving its citizens well," the growth in population and land area made change imperative. "It must be recognized that the informal, cozy, and personalized governmental arrangements which served Rockville excellently when the population totaled only about 2,000 are not equally satisfactory for a municipality of 7,000 population. This is a penalty of growth."[18]

The University of Maryland report, published in 1950, made seventeen specific recommendations. It decried the "unwise arrangement" of having matters affecting only Rockville settled by state legislative action in Annapolis and proposed that Rockville prepare an official charter document leading to home rule. The town's tradition of ignoring outmoded and obsolete laws rather than eliminating them should not be tolerated, the report said. It also suggested changes concerning town personnel, fiscal management procedures, the fire department and library, liquor sales, annual reporting to citizens, and Rockville's relationship with the county. Finally, the university administration professionals opined that "Rockville needs a city hall building."[19]

ROCKVILLE IN 1950

As the report noted, Rockville had changed. The town included 6,934 residents in 1950, three times its 1940 population. Most of the increase resulted from the new residential subdivisions of the 1940s and the town's mass annexation of 2,210 acres in 1949 of Lincoln Park, Haiti, Twinbrook, Broadwood Manor, and land to the north and west of town. Acknowledging growth that had occurred in the 1940s and identifying areas next likely to develop gave the town control.

The five-member Mayor and Council guided the town, with the help of an appointed clerk, manager, bailiff, and attorney. Mayor G. LaMar Kelly, reelected in May of 1950, was the president-elect of the Maryland Municipal League and owner of Standard Supplies, a building supply company on Middle Lane. Unopposed for his third two-year term, Kelly's slogan was "Greater

TOP: Looking east toward Rockville Pike on East Montgomery Avenue.
BOTTOM: East Montgomery Avenue, the main street, in the 1940s looking west toward the courthouse.

Roy Perry photo, courtesy of Peerless Rockville

Charles Brewer photo, courtesy of Peerless Rockville

Rockville for Better Living at No Tax Penalty." Four other businessmen served on the council: Frank Higgins, owner of a fuel oil company, Murray Bradshaw, manager of the Western Auto store, Samuel "Pete" Hersperger, an employee of Kelly's at Standard Supplies, and Daniel Weddle, the manager of the Rockville PEPCO office.

The government was still very small and informal. The Mayor and Council met twice monthly at their two-room office at 110 Commerce Lane and frequently borrowed chairs from Mrs. Pumphrey, who lived nearby. When expecting more than a few visitors, they convened in the courthouse. Clerk Leigh Allnutt kept the office open for the few townspeople who dropped in. Town Manager and Engineer John McDonald supervised about fifteen employees, many of whom served in two or more capacities and were based at the pump house on Horner's Lane. In 1950, Rockville had 150 parking meters and two uniformed policemen. By 1950, more people called Rockville a *city*, but to its elected officials and most residents it was still a *town*.

By the mid-twentieth century, Rockville had become primarily a residential suburban community. Farmers around Rockville found it more profitable to

Aerial of Rockville Fuel and Feed Company before 1950. Industrial and building supply companies clustered along the rail line. Rockville Fuel and Feed began in 1926 selling coal and wood to residents, straw and feed to farmers, and stone hauled from Rockville to Washington. Note railroad siding. Dirt road in foreground parallels future alignment of Hungerford Drive.

Courtesy of Rockville Fuel and Feed Company

sell to developers than to continue agricultural operations. The town's traditional functions as a market center for the region and as a seat of government for Montgomery County remained in the center of the town. From this base, concentric circles of residential subdivisions expanded into farmland. Rockville was a core for banking, light industry, local government and court-related occupations, and small, mostly family-owned businesses. Roads leading to Rockville, including the Rockville Pike and Veirs Mill Road, were two lanes wide. About 50 percent of Rockville's residents in 1950 worked in Washington, D.C., or for federal agencies in Bethesda and Carderock. New residents commuted to their jobs by bus, train, and automobile.[20]

Charles Brewer collection, courtesy of Peerless Rockville

Lawyers' row and courthouse, looking north from Perry Street(now Maryland Avenue), across Jefferson Street, circa 1950.

Rockville homes were comfortable. Many people had converted coal furnaces to oil or installed gas systems, particularly since construction of the Transco pipeline across the county in 1948. Local merchants offered electric home appliances. A. G. Watkins, who in the 1920s sold generators and milking machines, now kept a store with the latest in cooking, heating, and cleaning devices. Sears employee Ben Lanier teamed with Paul Wire to sell Frigidaire appliances from an addition to the old coal and feed store near the railroad depot. The Postal Service cut door-to-door delivery to once a day, but telephone service improved in 1946 with a dial system in a new C&P Telephone Company building on Jefferson Street, and local usage jumped from one thousand to twenty-three hundred lines. A typical telephone number in 1950 was "Rockville 3988."

Returning veterans and government employees rapidly purchased the midpriced postwar single-family homes, but a shortage of low-cost housing and apartments existed. Reluctantly, Rockville allowed multifamily housing. Since the early nineteenth century, rooms had been available for whites on the upper floors of shops and homes along the main streets and for blacks along Middle Lane and Washington Street. Neighborhood opposition and the town's zoning ordinance rebuffed attempts by developers to construct new apartments. However, the housing shortage led Rockville to accept federal rent controls, allow division of large old houses, and permit two developers to build apartments in the decade after the war. Former mayor Douglas Blandford, in partnership with developer Eugene Casey, built 190 units on land near Rockville Elementary School in stages between 1947 and 1953. Joseph Berlin used FHA funds to construct a 15-building, 169-unit complex at Dawson, Adams, and Van Buren Streets in 1950–51. Young white teachers and police officers quickly moved into both developments, but these crumbs of supply did not alleviate the demand.

The business center of Rockville ran east to west on State Route 240, from the Rockville Pike through town to Washington Street. The area around the courthouses was simply Rockville. The main street—East Montgomery Avenue—contained a variety of buildings, mostly two or three stories in height. Many of the wood frame buildings had two or more facades applied over the original. The streetscape presented a variety of materials, shapes, styles, setbacks, and degrees of upkeep. The town clock and the Confederate statue were fixed prominently near the two courthouses. On the back and side streets—Commerce Lane and Jefferson, Perry and Fayette Streets—buildings were less attractive and less maintained.

The business district contained an eclectic mix of uses. Within a few blocks were shops, offices, homes, churches, manufacturing, places of assembly, an athletic field, a movie theatre, the post office, and a firehouse. Rockville stores sold all necessary personal and household items, but shopping in Silver Spring or Washington was considered a special treat. Stores owned by blacks, housing, churches, and the elementary school clustered on both sides of Middle Lane and Washington Street. Light industry existed on the back streets, although most of Rockville's seven auto dealers had main street addresses.[21]

Rockville's business district, although not keeping pace with the residential dynamic, attempted to stay flexible. In 1950, the Needle Craft Shop and Bill Heflin's radio and television repair store opened, G. C. Murphy's Five and Ten Cent Store was remodeled with a modern luncheonette and forty-eight departments, and a shoemaker became the Shoe Hospital. The Rockville Chamber of Commerce sponsored a Miss Rockville contest won by Jenny LaTona and a December in Rockville campaign that displayed a new Ford on the courthouse lawn before awarding it to a local farmer.

On the fringes of the main street, industry turned out products useful to the expanding economy. Companies related to building and construction led the way—A. B. Veirs Paving, Standard Supplies, Leland Fisher Lumber Yard, Maryland Cast Stone, and numerous contractors. Rockville enterprises manufactured cabinets, furniture, ice, recreation equipment, and some unique items such as aluminum crutch handles. Rockville Fuel and Feed, founded in 1926 to sell and haul coal, wood, straw, feed, and stone, took advantage of the changing times. Owners Dudley Ward and Frank Jenkins began to manufacture cinder blocks and to sell sand, stone, and cement. In the 1950s, the company poured ready-mix concrete for many of the housing developments, school and commercial construction, and road paving projects in the Rockville area.[22]

Dominating the center of Rockville was Montgomery County government. By 1950, the two courthouses were bursting with court personnel, court records, the jail, and county employees. Nearby buildings contained offices of attorneys, bondsmen, insurance agents, transcribers, title companies, and others associated with public business. On South Perry Street (now Maryland Avenue) just east of the Red Brick Courthouse, the two-story buildings known as Lawyers' Row housed a collection of storied and storytelling legal talent. When the noon fire siren blared,

TOP: Notice for Rockville Little Theatre performance in the Sentinel, *February 9, 1950.*
BOTTOM: Clinton A.M.E. Zion Church on North Washington Street. Roy Perry stood approximately where Beall Avenue now crosses Washington Street to photograph this scene in 1948. The curve in Washington Street was straightened a few years later.

rockville little THEATRE

INVITES YOU TO THE OPEN CASTING For The Comedy "DEAR RUTH"

MONDAY, FEB. 13 - 8 P.M. - EPISCOPAL PARISH HALL

OPENINGS IN ACTING, COSTUMING, SET DESIGN, PUBLICITY, MAKE-UP, ETC.

If Interested Call ROCKVILLE 2772

Courtesy of Peerless Rockville

Courtesy of Peerless Rockville

Dedication of the new Edmonston Drive bridge over the railroad tracks was cause for a parade in August of 1950. The bridge permitted Rockcrest residents access to the Rockville Pike. Photo by Balfour O. Lytton, organizer of the festivities.

restaurants filled up with employees and visitors. Restaurants ranged from musty hangouts to fine foods—Roy's Place, Budd's Deli, the counter at People's Drug Store, Tastee Diner (which had moved from Silver Spring in 1946), Crader's, the Hungerford's Tavern restaurant, Miller's Dutch Tavern, Tol-Mur Restaurant, or Mary Anna's Fine Foods, which was famous for its lobster newburg sandwiches.[23]

Cars and trucks clogged Rockville's narrow streets all day long. Drivers en route to Gaithersburg or Washington eagerly awaited completion of the state road project that would bypass Rockville and straighten the dangerous curve on Washington Street. Parking was permitted on most streets, although Rockville's finest closely monitored the meters. Parking could be found off the streets behind some of the buildings, such as the A&P and Safeway grocery stores and the Milo Theatre. The two taxi stands were well marked, but the bus lines that served Rockville lacked consistent daily routes. Despite the proliferation of cars, Rockville was still a walkable, pedestrian-oriented town.

Rockville in 1950 had a bustling social, cultural, and religious life. The Milo showed six films each week, and Cheetah, a star in many Tarzan movies, came to visit. The community delighted in performances at Christ Church parish hall. There were three shows a year by Rockville Little Theatre (founded in 1947) and Rev. Raymond P. Black's productions of Gilbert and Sullivan operettas. The same year also marked the start of the Junior Woman's and Kiwanis Clubs in Rockville. Churches in town blossomed with the newcomers. Presbyterians broke ground for a new educational

Courtesy of Dora Demma

Introduction of pizza at the Rockville Drive-In made the front of the Society page in the December 10, 1954, Washington Post and Times Herald. *The theatre had a capacity for eight hundred cars.*

building on Montgomery Avenue. Reverend Benjamin Slye conducted services at the Highway Tabernacle on Veirs Mill Road near First Street, and Saint Mary's had sufficient volunteers to hold a spring carnival for the first time in fourteen years.[24]

Rockville's growth fostered civic activity. Representatives from Lincoln Park, Rockcrest, and East Rockville civic associations regularly addressed the Mayor and Council. Nine groups formed the Rockville Community Federation in 1950 as a clearinghouse for issues and to foster participation in civic affairs. School PTAs provided opportunities for parents to work together. The *Sentinel* published weekly columns with Twinbrook, Rockcrest, and Rockville and vicinity news. Croydon Park had a Homemakers club. Rockvillians helped fight polio with the March of Dimes, and joined Planned Parenthood, Alcoholics Anonymous, and the Woman's Temperance Union. At the Rotary Club's annual Farmers Day luncheon at Normandy Farm, each member brought a farmer from the surrounding area as his guest. The Woman's Club celebrated its fiftieth anniversary and raised funds to benefit a boy in the Netherlands. Rockville's only high school, Richard Montgomery, began its year with a tea for teachers hosted by the Inquiry Club.

The Cold War cast a shadow over the Washington area in 1950. News from Asia became more personal after local men fought in Korea. When the new bridge over the B&O Railroad tracks that connected Rockcrest with the Rockville Pike opened on August 12, 1950, it was named for John C. Brown. Corporal Brown, Maryland's first fatality in the Korean War, died in a plane crash on June 30, 1950, one week after the conflict began.[25] National defense and disaster preparedness measures involved Rockville men (many of them associated with the fire department) in planning and public education. Toward the end of 1950, the council appointed Justice Chambers and James Miller to organize civil and military personnel in a Civil Defense program. They scheduled first aid courses, registered local nurses, and outfitted bomb shelters.[26]

ELECTING CHANGE— THE REVOLUTION OF 1954

With the old order still in control in 1953, the year started out quietly. Activity continued much as it had since the end of the war. Dan Weddle, two-term councilman, had been elected mayor when LaMar Kelly stepped down in 1952. Despite problems caused by rapid growth, he and the council enjoyed the headiness of the times and letters such as this from a Roxboro resident: "Our little ones have shown much improvement in health in the short period of time we have been members of this delightful suburban community."[27] Mindful of traditional areas where black citizens lived, the town scheduled installation of street lights and water mains in Haiti on Martin's Lane and Lincoln Park. It encouraged local merchant Morris Stern to build apartments in the former Madden Theatre and twenty-two new duplex houses on Lenmore Avenue in Lincoln Park "since the colored people . . . do not have the freedom of location" and there was a shortage of "colored housing" for teachers who commuted from Washington.[28]

The commercial limelight moved to small shopping centers on the east and north parts of town. Developers built shops on Horner's Lane in Maryvale, stores on North Washington Street, and a shopping center for the convenience of Burgundy Hills, Burgundy Estates, and Burgundy Knolls residents. Creative minds considered possibilities along newly opened Hungerford Drive, but for now, fruit stands, temporary snack bars, and expansion of existing industrial enterprises sufficed. The Mayor and Council established a five-person zoning board, which included a woman and a black man, to suggest revisions to the code and propose use classifications for new property taken into the town limits.

A huge annexation in 1953 extended Rockville's eastern tilt begun by the 1940s residential subdivisions. Business property owners around Halpine and Congressional Airport petitioned for inclusion of 660 acres of land into the city limits. Tapping into city water and sewer facilities when feasible (with no taxation until benefits were available) made annexation attractive. However, Woodmont Country Club (which had moved from Bethesda to the Rockville Pike) and some residential owners were opposed to the annexation. Delegate Anders Lofstrand Jr. was so enthusiastic about promoting growth in Rockville that he introduced the annexation bill in the General Assembly prior to city approval. Mayor and Council approval was unanimous, but one councilman observed that "if there were no developments soon in the West and North section of Rockville the heart of Rockville would soon be around . . . Halpine Road."[29] Rezoning and even more intense development were soon to come.

Relieving the development intensity in March of 1953 was a proposed new concept in recreation for Montgomery County. Kogod-Burka, owners of five theatres in the Washington, D.C., area, purchased eleven acres on the Frederick Road near Martin's Lane and requested rezoning for an "out door theatre." Fred Burka told public officials that drive-in theatres are "the cheapest entertainment for a man and his family. They can keep the children in the car or they can get out and walk around or play in the playground. There is no sitter problem. It is basically a family enterprise."[30] Burka explained that people wanted open-air movies where individual speakers in the car allowed each group to adjust the volume. Local attorney Barney Welsh, who represented Burka and allowed that he was "getting paid a substantial fee," called the theatre "the last hope for Rockville recreation." Councilman Warren Milor agreed. "Rockville is twenty years behind the times and should wake up. There are no recreation facilities."[31] The Rockville Drive-In opened on March 25, 1954, with Alan Ladd in *Deep Six* and Randolph Scott in *Tall Men Riding*.

Theatre supervisor and former vaudeville dancer Charlie Demma brought first-run movies to the 125-feet wide, 63-feet high screen. He hosted Easter egg hunts, raffled used cars, and gave a gallon of gas to each car on chilly nights for car heaters. A snack bar served hamburgers, hot dogs, drinks, ice cream, popcorn, and candy. Demma evicted couples whose heads he couldn't see. Admission cost sixty cents for adults and twenty-five cents for children aged five and over.[32]

City officials, following one of the University of Maryland recommendations, appointed a committee to locate potential sites for a municipal building. In 1953, the committee suggested the home property of J. Vinson Peter. The 1.3 acres fronting South Washington Street contained a nine-room house that met current personnel needs and had a parking lot close by. The property cost fifty thousand dollars, and Peter took back a mortgage at 4.5 percent.

As the hot summer produced no rain and the ground water table dropped, an alarmed government met in special session on Saturday morning, June 27, "to protect the Public Health and Welfare."[33] The Mayor and Council passed an ordinance effective through October 31, 1953, making it unlawful to sprinkle lawns, wash cars, or water gardens between noon and midnight. When the group reconvened on Sunday, Rockville had been without water for several hours on Saturday night. City Manager McDonald explained that people in the newer subdivisions had used water faster than the wells could pump and refill the tanks. He believed an unanticipated jump in water use—for new washers, lawns, and shrubbery—combined with an early seasonal drought caused the problem. The council authorized him to order new pumps and pipelines and asked City Clerk Sara Mortimer to mimeograph copies of the water restriction ordinance for immediate distribution throughout the town. It then prepared a news release for a waiting reporter and arranged for Mayor Weddle to appear on a WTOP radio newscast on Monday morning.

The crisis worsened. Six weeks passed without rain. The council extended conservation coverage to twenty-four hours and banned citizens from filling swimming or wading pools. It wrote letters, arranged to dig more wells, and agreed to educate citizens about water conservation. The *Sentinel* editorialized that "Rockville's place in the sun shouldn't be allowed to dry out for lack of water."[34] Twenty-five Rockville residents petitioned for a public meeting, deploring the "evasiveness and lack of candor of Rockville officials."[35] Heightening resident concern was news of a polio outbreak, which led the county health officer to order city officials to repair a leaking sewage line at Chestnut Lodge. Nearly four hundred residents—some with dirty babies to make their point—jammed into the sweltering circuit courtroom on July 29 to hear Mayor Weddle report on the situation and tell them to water their plants with dishwater. Stanley Smigel, head of the newly formed Rockville Citizens' Action Committee, charged that "the city lacks a concrete plan for providing sufficient water to care for the needs of the inhabitants."[36]

By the end of August, WSSC agreed to sell water to Rockville, and Smigel had appointed a Citizens' Water Committee at the suggestion of Mayor Weddle. On October 21, the mayor announced that the water use ban would expire but asked continued voluntary cooperation to practice conservation of water in every way possible. However, by then many citizens had lost confidence in town government, questioning any actions of the council such as purchasing the Peter property, zoning regulations, billboards, voter registration, and "unannounced meetings behind locked doors."

The water emergency emphasized the obsolete practice of digging a new well for every two hundred new houses built. In the fall of 1953, new housing construction overloaded Rockville's sewer plant. When the State Board of Health expressed concern, McDonald explained that the city was waiting for WSSC to extend a sewer line close enough for Rockville to connect. Developers Donald E. Gingery and J. Wesley Buchanan had prepared to build a large subdivision on part of the Dawson farm on the Pike for some time. Due to the crisis, their plans to build the first two hundred homes in Hungerford Towne were put on hold.

A somber city council convened on December 1, 1953, to hear McDonald explain the injunction served on Rockville the previous day by the Board of Health. All development west of the railroad tracks, the state agency said, must halt until adequate sewer service was available. The council adjourned after forty-five minutes, having authorized the city manager to obtain cost figures and to coordinate with WSSC and the city's consulting engineers. Days later when they met with the consultants, Whitman Requart and Associates, the Mayor and Council agreed to pursue extension of WSSC's Cabin John Branch trunk sewer line to Rockville's sewage treatment plant. Whitman Requart believed that Rockville's current arrangements and plans for additional pumping lines could handle the immediate issue of Cabin John Branch valley area sewerage. Combined with WSSC's offer to furnish water along the Rockville Pike, this arrangement could accommodate Rockville for about one year.[37]

The municipal election of 1954 was among the most exciting in Rockville's history. The water crisis of the previous summer energized longtime residents and newcomers from all sections of the city. A huge advertisement in the *Sentinel* on February 4 announced the birth of a new non-partisan political group. Citizens for Good Government (CGG) called for an updated local government "responsive to the wishes of its citizens."[38] The following week, delegates selected five men to run as a slate for public office. Dickran Hovsepian, Alexander Greene, and James Robertson worked for the federal government. John Oxley practiced law in Rockville, and Wendell Turner owned a small business in Washington. The candidates were convinced they could make Rockville a better place.

CGG met again on February 22 to adopt a platform, emphasizing open, progressive government. Planks included formulation of a master plan to guide orderly development, a promise to improve transportation and parking, more recreation programs and park facilities, more efficient city operations, and review of financial practices. Most of these issues had been identified by the University of Maryland surveyors in 1950, but they had not been implemented by the city government.

Mayor Weddle declined to run again, but two other slates soon formed. Incumbents J. Warren Milor and Murray W. Bradshaw joined opposing slates mostly composed of businessmen. At candidates' forums, political rhetoric was red hot. CGG candidates accused previous town officials of choosing not to borrow money for water and sewer projects, and of making it difficult for citizens to vote in local elections. Candidates on the Milor and Hitt slates charged that CGG contained power-hungry men who earned their livings in Washington and used Rockville as an experimental laboratory for their ideas. These radicals would summarily dismiss all city employees.

As March turned into April, the campaign intensified. Responding to litigation initiated by CGG and citizen pressure, the Mayor and Council divided Rockville into three wards to facilitate voting and extended registration dates to four full days and three evenings from March 29 to April 5. CGG volunteers organized workers to knock on doors and make telephone calls. By April 5, about seventeen hundred new voters had registered, making a total of nearly thirty-one hundred eligible to vote. Milor questioned the legality of CGG's campaign funding and whether local government service would conflict with federal jobs. He asked the U.S. Attorney in Baltimore to investigate possible violations of the Corrupt Practices Act by three CGG candidates and five supporters—charges pursued by FBI agents for months after the election. Hitt, Milor, and Mayor Weddle joined to level political bossism charges at CGG campaign chairman Herman Hartman. Just before the election, CGG held a rally and the *Sentinel* reminded voters—including those 40 percent polled as undecided—that "life in Rockville during the next two years will be real and it will be earnest. The next Mayor and Council will have a tough row to hoe. . . . What you elect will be what you'll get—and for two, long years."[39]

Eighty percent of eligible voters pulled levers on the new voting machines on Monday, May 3, 1954. By nightfall, CGG claimed victory by a margin of two to one. Mayoral candidate Hovsepian polled 1,479 votes to 610 for Hitt and 347 for Milor. John Oxley led all candidates with 1,640. *Sentinel* editor Lila Thomson remarked that the campaign had not been a fight between old and new Rockville, but rather about "new and old approaches to solving the same old problems." She attributed CGG's victory to party organization and a well-thought-out plan for running the town.[40]

When the five men took their oaths on May 5, they knew only a fraction of the problems they would uncover. The University of Maryland study and CGG's platform articulated major municipal issues—planning, ordinances, budget, zoning—but the new Mayor and Council soon encountered the complexities of each.

The newly elected councilmen brought different strengths to the task of modernizing the city. Only one had political experience. John Oxley, a Montgomery County native and Rockville attorney for thirty years, had served as a county commissioner from 1938 to 1942. A naval architect with the U.S. Coast Guard, James Robertson also was president of the Lone Oak PTA. Wendell Turner operated a scientific laboratory equipment supply business in Washington. Dickran Hovsepian, a Philadelphia native and civil engineer for the Army Mapping Service, had an acute interest in planning. Alexander Greene was a budget examiner at the Bureau of the Budget.

TOP: The Peter house at 120 South Washington Street served as Rockville City Hall from 1954 to 1962. BOTTOM: CGG sample ballot, Rockville city election, May 3, 1954.

The *Washington Star* photo, copyright the *Washington Post*, reprinted by permission of D.C. Public Library

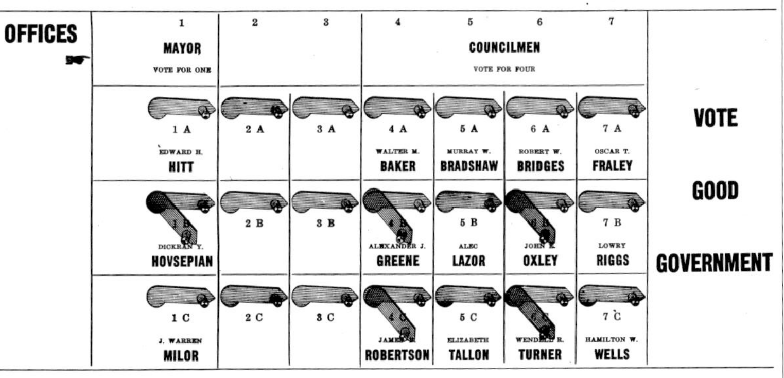

GOOD GOVERNMENT SAMPLE BALLOT

ROCKVILLE CITY ELECTION – MAY 3, 1954 – 7 A.M. TO 7 P.M.

OFFICES	1	2	3	4	5	6	7	
	MAYOR VOTE FOR ONE			COUNCILMEN VOTE FOR FOUR				
	1 A EDWARD H. HITT	2 A	3 A	4 A WALTER M. BAKER	5 A MURRAY W. BRADSHAW	6 A ROBERT W. BRIDGES	7 A OSCAR T. FRALEY	VOTE
	1 B DICKRAN Y. HOVSEPIAN	2 B	3 B	4 B ALEXANDER J. GREENE	5 B ALEC LAZOR	6 B JOHN OXLEY	7 B LOWRY RIGGS	GOOD
	1 C J. WARREN MILOR	2 C	3 C	4 C JAMES ROBERTSON	5 C ELIZABETH TALLON	6 C WENDELL R. TURNER	7 C HAMILTON W. WELLS	GOVERNMENT

Dickran Hovsepian collection, courtesy of Peerless Rockville

Alexander Greene collection, courtesy of Peerless Rockville

The Rockville All-America City banner flew from City Hall's flagpole throughout 1955. From presentation program, All-America City Award, February 1, 1955.

"The first days in city government were absolutely astounding," recalled Greene. "It really was a . . . primitive kind of government."[41] As the new Mayor and Council met three times during their first week in office to initiate their programs, they learned how city government operated. Front foot benefit ordinances went unrecorded, with payments due. Neither a map of water and sewer lines nor systematic personnel rules existed. Black residents seemed unaware that they could speak at public meetings. Decisions had been made behind closed doors, and purchases were made without bids. As there were few copies of the zoning ordinance, citizens relied on the clerk's interpretation. The city carried twenty separate insurance policies. The Mayor and Council approved every invoice, and too many people had keys to the city gasoline pumps.

Efficient administration was the priority, to which professional personnel held the key. The Mayor and Council appointed David L. Cahoon as acting city clerk and city attorney and elevated John Markland from engineer to acting city manager. The council requested a new system for paying bills, new laws to regulate bidding for supplies and contracts, and codification of all city ordinances. After three public hearings, the council adopted its 1954–55 budget by ordinance for the first time, then published and distributed it. Insurance coverage was consolidated and sent out to bid. Staff inventoried equipment and materials owned by the city. In early August, the council issued the thirteen-page *Report to the People* on actions and activities during its first three months in office.[42]

Rockville's flurry of modernization was quickly noticed. The National Municipal League and *Look Magazine*'s All-America Cities Awards program (presented for citizen action directed toward improving local government or other areas of civic welfare) was tailor-made for Rockville's experience of 1953–54. Herman Hartman orchestrated the nomination, based upon the wave of citizen involvement that began with the Rockville Civic Association and carried through recent election successes. Five months into office, the reformers had revamped practices and rules embraced for more than sixty years and cut the tax rate by five cents. They had appointed a professional manager and permanent clerk, Joseph Blocher. Ten volunteer committees and commissions—to study and advise on youth activities, home rule legislation, traffic and transportation, housing, recreation and parks, Memorial Day, Independence Day, Rockville's centenary, fire prevention, and beautification—augmented the small city staff. The council began aggressive clean-up measures and ordered a street-sweeping machine. Changes occurred so quickly that the nomination was updated right to the deadline. As one of twenty-two finalists, Rockville sent a delegation to Kansas City, Missouri, in November to present its case. Word soon arrived that Rockville had been selected to receive the prestigious award.

Rockville proudly claimed its first All-America City Award at ceremonies at Richard Montgomery High School on February 1, 1955. *Look Magazine* credited Rockville citizens for their grueling campaign to "elect a government with modern ideas to fit the town's rapidly growing population."[43] President Dwight D. Eisenhower wrote: "My congratulations to the people of Rockville on their aggressive work to promote community improvement. They have given an outstanding example of initiative and united citizen action."[44]

Mindful of the major issue that sparked the revolt, Hovsepian and the council moved quickly to deal with the city's water supply. WSSC supplemented Rockville's thirty-nine wells with a twelve-inch water line on the Rockville Pike between Waverley Sanitorium (near White Flint) and the city limits, and an appeal for voluntary conservation averted a water shortage in the summer of 1954. Councilman Oxley suggested that the city itself go to the Potomac River for water. In a special advisory referendum, 92 percent of city voters agreed that Rockville should retain an independent water supply. The new system opened four years later, on the night of October 17, 1958, when a valve on Sandy Landing Road was turned on to fill the drinking fountain at the corner of Court House Square and Montgomery Avenue.

Sewer lines were a different, albeit concurrent, issue. The State Board of Health banned Rockville from issuing building permits in the Cabin John drainage area because of insufficient capacity at the treatment plant (located on the Dawson farm). In 1939, the plant could handle 325,000 gallons of sewage daily, but by 1953 its capacity was greatly overloaded. The state agreed to permit five hundred new housing units, but only if Rockville built a new facility. Gingery and Buchanan paid for sewer facilities for the first two hundred homes in Hungerford. However, the Mayor and Council elected to participate with WSSC in a regional linking of trunk sewers designed to protect Washington's water supply at Dalcarlia. In 1955, WSSC began constructing a line to link Rockville to Washington, D.C.'s treatment plant by way of the Cabin John valley. The city paid two-thirds of the $900,000 project cost. Subsequently, Rockville set up a Water and Sewer Authority, pledging revenues from front foot benefit charges and water and sewer fees. With a predictable future, the city's bond rating rose.[45]

MODERNIZATION CONTINUES APACE

Development picked up in the mid-1950s, with water and sewer lines planned in a more orderly way. Completion of the last sections of Twinbrook and conversion of the Dawson farm into Hungerford Towne carried on the tradition of postwar residential development on the east side of the city. While the earliest of Hungerford's fourteen hundred homes were delayed by the state injunction, after the city's agreement with WSSC, model homes and some sale houses appeared. A promotional booklet declared: "Out of the fertile countryside of Maryland's Montgomery County is being carved a completely new town. Dedicated by its builders, Buchanan and Gingery, to serve and glorify that greatest of all American edifices, our ever rising standard of living. . . ."[46]

The immediacy of postwar housing having been met by other developments, Hungerford emphasized design and amenities. Large kitchens, living rooms with a brick fireplace and picture window, first-floor bedrooms with sliding door closets, seasoned oak floors, pastel bath fixtures, and a carport led the list of desirable features. Cape Cods, which started at $12,950—no down payment to qualified veterans, new FHA terms available for others—followed the theme of future expandability.

Officials dedicated Rockville's new $2.6 million water system in 1958 with a drink from the new fountain on the courthouse lawn. Left to right: Dickran Y. Hovsepian, former mayor; Colonel G. B. Sumner, Washington district engineer; Mayor Alexander J. Greene; State Senator Edward S. Northrop.

Photo by Brooks, in Alexander Greene collection, courtesy of Peerless Rockville

Courtesy of Naomi Ellison

Courtesy of of Mary Dawson Gray

TOP: "Hungerford Towne's unique design," from At Hungerford Towne *brochure.*
BOTTOM: Rocky Glen, the Dawson farm, as seen from a field near the fairgrounds, late 1940s.

Rockville—the community as well as location—was a prime selling point. "An investment in the future of a rapidly growing progressive community in one of the most prosperous counties in the country! In addition to this, because of its unsurpassed location Hungerford assures a remarkable sound and steadily increasing resale value. . . ."[47] Traditional and new roadways sped commuters to downtown Washington.

Hungerford, like Twinbrook, quickly developed cherished neighborhood institutions. A civic association formed, then a new park area, and finally a column in the *Sentinel.* Hungerford Elementary opened in 1960 to relieve overcrowding at Park Street School. "In a sincere effort to provide every means for a happy and care-free way of life,"[48] neighbors incorporated to build the community pool, which was open from 1964 until 1990.

A memorable relationship grew between the newcomers and Rose K. Dawson. She and her brother Walter remained at Rocky Glen (the Dawson farm) after the deaths of their parents, Hal and Fannie Dawson, selling off parcels of land over a period of decades for the disposal plant, Richard Montgomery High School, and residential and business development. Walter W. Dawson, known as "Mr. Republican" in an overwhelmingly Democratic county, served in the House of Delegates and as State's Attorney from 1946 to 1955. Rose K. Dawson also became a political institution as clerk of the county Board of Election Supervisors for thirty years. Rocky Glen's fields and woods delighted Hungerford children, and Rose Dawson kept horses in the front field between the house and the Rockville Pike. Best of all, Miss Dawson invited children to see her Indian room, an intriguing array of artifacts collected when the family lived in the Dakota Territory. Rose Dawson lived to see Hungerford built in stages, the last of which—in the mid-1960s—was named Stoneridge.[49]

One fortuitous reform came to all Maryland municipalities in 1955 and forever changed the ground rules of managing Rockville's future. In a referendum on November 2, 1954, Maryland voters ratified an amendment to the state constitution that granted home rule to incorporated cities and towns. Enacted by the General Assembly in its 1955 session, this reform marked a major change in the way Rockville would conduct business. Since incorporation in 1860, Rockville needed General Assembly authorization to pass a law on the most ordinary issues, such as sign placement or barking dogs, as well as annexation of land into the corporate boundaries. Home rule, coupled with the ability to manage utilities, gave the city greater power with regard to annexations, planning, zoning, and a spectrum of issues that might come before the Mayor and Council.[50]

What those issues might be was still unfolding between 1955 and 1960. In a few areas, the CGGers built upon the work of previous elected officials, but clearly the sweep had been necessary for wholesale modernization and reform. "We never had a notion of full service government," recalled Alex Greene. "Our attitude . . . was: we ought to do those things that we can do best. Where you truly had a rationale for local involvement, keep it local . . . but where you couldn't do as good a job, let's join the most efficient system. Well, the first test was the library."[51]

Rockville's library, like most others in the county, was a homey institution operated by volunteers and part-time staff. Reeling under the demand for expanded services, in 1949 the Rockville Library Association approached the town for assistance. Finding it "in the best interest of the inhabitants of the Town of Rockville that said library continue in operation as a local endeavor,"[52] the Mayor and Council appropriated thirty-six hundred dollars. Soon the town included the free library in its budget and required the library board to report annually. When Montgomery County created a Department of Public Libraries in 1951, the city and the Library Association agreed to continue under the current arrangement, at the Rockville Academy on South Adams Street. As county libraries became better funded, Rockville officials became increasingly aware of advantages to joining the county system. For several years, the parties negotiated without agreement, Rockville citizens paid a county library tax, and the county added services such as bookmobiles to serve the growing city population. Finally, one Rockville official noted, "we decided it was time that the library grew up."[53] The Library Association transferred its books and equipment to the county for a one-year trial period in 1956, after which Rockville became the seventh independent library association to join the system. The library remained in its musty quarters for another decade, then moved into the bank building at 255 North Washington Street for a

The Rockville Allstars played for teams sponsored by lumber companies, builders, and service organizations. 1955 photo from Houston Edward Hancock, who is third from the left in the first row.

Courtesy of Peerless Rockville

few years. The county opened a second library facility in the Twinbrook shopping center in 1959.

With the large numbers of children, improving youth recreation programs ranked high on the reform council's list. In the mid-fifties, Rockville maintained nine playgrounds and parks on nearly forty-three acres. A small field house was built in Rockcrest. Local businesses and service organizations sponsored teams of Rockville boys, and in 1954 Rockville Boys Baseball Association organized as a sports league. Ballplayers, coaches, and parents celebrated opening day with a parade of decorated pickup trucks and convertibles through the town. New fields at Broome Junior High School, which opened in 1957, greatly increased opportunities for league play. Eugene P. Moran, vice principal of Rockville Junior High School and part-time recreation director, boasted: "If you live in Rockville, there is a park, playground, or recreation area within half a mile of your home." In 1956, twenty-four hundred youngsters registered at summer playgrounds. Boys and girls learned ballroom dancing in Richard Montgomery's gym on Saturday afternoons. Girls took baton twirling classes, while boys teamed up for touch football and basketball. The following year, the Mayor and Council spent $41,500 on recreation programs and hired a full-time director, Bert Kurland.[54]

Rockville's teens were not neglected. Autumn Saturday afternoons found much of Rockville at Richard Montgomery or Carver High School rooting for the home teams. The city operated teen canteens at both high schools. In 1959, the city built a center at Harrington and Mercer Roads in Hungerford for junior and senior high students.

The exuberance of peacetime, economic prosperity, phenomenal population growth, shared visions of the American dream, and postwar optimism combined to make the 1950s a decade of organizations. Individuals with notions of intellectual and business pursuits, community service, or sociality joined like-minded people to form new groups or invigorate established ones. Vibrant groups organized in Rockville between 1950 and 1960 included the Jaycees, Civitan, Junior Woman's Club, American Association of University Women, Kiwanis, the Young in Heart Club, and Town and Country Woman's Club. Immediately after receiving a charter in January 1955, the Rockville Jaycees jumped into community projects. In 1955 they sponsored a spring clean-up campaign and the following year initiated for teens the popular Road-e-o, an automobile obstacle course laid out in a parking lot on Jefferson Street. Many projects introduced to Rockville by the Jaycees over the years—toy drives, junior miss pageants, bicycle safety campaigns, large-item trash collections, civic awards—became community traditions. Catching the spirit of the times, Rockville merchants regrouped as the Board of Trade, then

TOP: Elwood Smith Center was named in honor of a Rockville volunteer fireman who lost his life in 1956 while performing a rescue mission. Teens met at the center six days a week for classes, sports, dances, and other recreation activities.
BOTTOM: Rockville Jaycees float in Memorial Day parade, 1965.

From *Mayor and Manager*, February, 1961

Courtesy of Tricia Gallalee, historian, Rockville Jaycees

incorporated in 1957 as the Rockville Chamber of Commerce, Inc., with attorney Jim Miller as president.

The spate of new residents enhanced Rockville's church attendance and spurred building campaigns. In the 1950s, Crusader Lutheran and Assembly of God churches opened on Veirs Mill Road. Local residents attended Faith United, Twinbrook Baptist, and Church of God in Rockville. Clinton A.M.E. Zion moved from North Washington Street to a new church and parsonage in Lincoln Park in 1956. Christ Episcopal purchased a rectory next to the church, enlarged the parish hall and Sunday School, and opened the Bargain Box thrift shop, then began planning a second phase to expand the church and improve the educational building for Christ Episcopal Day School. Rockville's Presbyterian and Methodist churches added large education wings. The congregation of Jerusalem Methodist renovated the church, covered the exterior brick with stucco, and lopped off the top of the steeple. Saint Mary's built a school and convent and added an auditorium to accommodate larger numbers at worship. Mount Calvary Baptist Church raised funds to construct a new building. Unitarians organized a Rockville fellowship in 1957 as an offshoot of Cedar Lane Church in Bethesda, meeting at West Rockville Elementary School until they built a church on Mannakee Street. Seventh-Day Adventists met at the Rockville Christian Church, then built a house of worship on West Montgomery Avenue. With this burst of activity, by 1960 Rockville claimed twice the number of religious organizations as it had before the war.

Charles Brewer collection, courtesy of Peerless Rockville

The Rockville Baptist Church on South Washington and Jefferson Streets reached out to the community with services and hymn sings. A bank building replaced the church and parsonage in 1974.

Even as Rockville celebrated selection as an All-America City, elected officials and community groups began to think about a civic center. Rockville Little Theatre, outgrowing Christ Church parish hall, was the first to offer cash toward the project. The Junior Woman's Club surveyed sixteen hundred taxpayers in the fall of 1955; 83.9 percent favored the idea.[55] City staff whittled down forty-two suggested locations to four. The Mayor and Council sponsored a contest to help the Advisory Committee on Parks and Recreation decide what kind of center was most wanted and practical, and budgeted money with an eye to starting construction in 1958–59. Ninety-two students entered the Junior Woman's essay contest on "Why I Want Rockville to Have a Community Center." The April 30, 1956, election included a referendum on whether the city could spend up to $250,000 for a new center that would include an all-purpose auditorium, meeting room, and youth center. No location was specified. The idea won by a narrow margin of forty votes, but CGG candidates, favorable to the idea, were voted in handily.

Meanwhile, after the death of Irene Lyon in 1950, Dr. James Lyon sold more than one hundred acres of Glenview estate on Baltimore Road to developers for the Burgundy Estates and Burgundy Knolls subdivisions. The Montgomery County Historical Society purchased the mansion and twenty-eight acres from Dr. Lyon in March 1954. Formed a decade earlier, the group wanted a home for museum exhibits, a research library, and activities. The cash-strapped organization resorted to digging up plants and selling them and leasing classrooms for overcrowded Twinbrook Elementary School to support the property.

The Historical Society voted to sell Glenview in September 1956—four months after Rockville's referendum on a civic center. The Mayor and Council conducted a public hearing on October 2, where City Manager Markland reported on the building's condition and some possibilities for the grounds. Representatives of the Civic Center Advisory Committee pointed out disadvantages of the proposed site: the large portion of gardens, lawns, and shrubbery would reduce room for expansion. The building, while beautiful, would not be as functional as a modern one and "might become a white elephant for the City."[56] But the majority of citizens spoke in favor. At the council meeting of October 23, Markland compared costs of purchasing the Lyon estate with estimates for constructing a new civic center and recommended the purchase. A unanimous Mayor and Council voted to buy Glenview for $125,000.[57] On February 22, 1957, the Mayor and Council formally opened the thirty-room mansion as Rockville's community center.

The road to converting a residential estate into a community center which met the needs of a surging suburban population was shorter than Glenview's

A CIVIC CENTER FOR ROCKVILLE

Congratulate us!! We have just come into a fortune! We now own a Mansion, complete with Grounds, in other words, we have inherited an Estate! . . . Marble halls are ours; and crystal chandeliers; and countless Balconies with Views! . . . That we share ownership with 17,000 other Rockvillians bothers us not. . . . To our poor friends who are so unfortunate as to live outside Rockville, we now extend a gracious invitation. Do drop in some time. Any time. Just come out Baltimore Road . . . and that long winding driveway on the left with those lovely old trees is Our Driveway.[58]

Courtesy of City of Rockville

Glenview Mansion, purchased by the Mayor and Council in 1957.

The Mayor and Council purchased Glenview Mansion and twenty-eight acres for $125,000 in 1957. On the property at the time were the Lyon residence (a thirty-room mansion dramatically remodeled in 1926), a greenhouse and a dairy barn, streams, and beautiful plantings.

Glenview quickly became "the public's country club."[59] In the 1950s, when Rockville's population increased at a faster rate than in any decade before or since, neighborhoods outgrew facilities as soon as they could be built. Glenview filled an immediate need, and traditional community events fit nicely there. Cultural and civic groups flourished as they held meetings, concerts, and art shows in the elegant setting. City-sponsored recreation classes used rooms throughout the building. The grounds, including the six-hundred-foot lawn in front of the mansion, became the venue for city-wide picnics, egg hunts, summer concerts, and other activities. Outdoor rituals, such as Easter dawn services, formerly held on the courthouse grounds, relocated to Glenview's formal gardens. Betsy Lyon's playhouse, built in 1938, saw regular use by scout and recreation groups.

The acquisition of a civic center was a major milestone in Rockville's emergence as a modern city. As a potential magnet for community events, as a facility for use by the increasing numbers of local organizations emerging in the postwar period, as a venue for cultural activities, and as a locale where the entire population could celebrate together, Glenview proved to be the bargain of the century.

tree-lined driveway. Cultural and social organizations of all sizes clamored for space before financial and use issues could be resolved. Glenview immediately became a base for meetings, special events, and activities, and the city's small recreation staff moved in. The Historical Society continued to meet and keep museum artifacts at Glenview, including the Lyons' huge round table. The Rockville Art League, founded in 1957 with eighteen members, held its first show in the mansion. Civil Defense headquarters set up in the basement, and classes of children from nearby schools picnicked on the grounds.

Alexander Greene collection, courtesy of Peerless Rockville

The new Rockville Civic Auditorium was dedicated on August 28, 1960. Drawing from dedication program.

With a public facility, and organized leisure playing an increasingly important role in suburban lifestyles, the city offered recreation programs for adults as well as youngsters. Recreation Director Kurland arranged for Young in Heart, a senior citizens' group formed in 1952, to meet at Glenview each month. Art and square dancing lessons were popular. One early instructor was Virginia Moore (Mrs. Maryland in 1960), who taught aerobics and dance to Rockville homemakers wanting to stay fit and to get out of the house. The city charged ten dollars for ten one-hour sessions of Moore's popular exercise classes.[60]

The city wasted no time in constructing an additional building and using Glenview's expansive grounds. From its grand opening in 1960, the Civic Auditorium was popular. The 504-seat theatre provided a sparkling venue for Rockville Little Theatre, the new Rockville Municipal Band, and a variety of music, dance, and theater groups. The social hall on the lower level accommodated large social gatherings, wedding receptions, and civic and political functions. In 1963, the city added tennis courts, a public works building, and an animal shelter on land below the mansion. And, over the years, the city acquired additional acreage beyond the original purchase of twenty-eight acres.

Rockville's civic center proved to be the magnet the community imagined it would be. Glenview's gracious setting, augmented by programs and facilities added through half a century of public use, provided a municipal focus and united Rockville as few other undertakings could have done. Seeing the success of Glenview, developers offered city officials other mansions caught amidst modern subdivisions. In the 1960s, the Mayor and Council declined to purchase Meadow Hall mansion in Twinbrook or Horizon Hill on Falls Road. By then, many residential developments had recreation facilities, and local schools provided meeting space.

ROCKVILLE'S SISTER CITY

In the spirit of the time, the Mayor and Council pursued international interests. While a move to celebrate United Nations Day in Rockville fell flat, at the end of 1954 Mayor Hovsepian explored adoption of a "sister city." The matched-cities program began during the Eisenhower Administration as part of a people-to-people concept to promote good will and understanding between countries. In mid-1956, the council agreed that "an affiliation of the City of Rockville with some overseas city of similar size, and with similar municipal problems, would be a desirable and very worthwhile relationship, both to the cities themselves and to the effort at international understanding"[61] and established a five-member Sister City Advisory Committee. The U.S. Information Agency, working with the U.S.

Courtesy of City of Rockville

Pinneberg Burgermeister Henrich Glissmann visited stores in Twinbrook Shopping Center in May 1958. He tasted watermelon and tried his hand at bowling. Shown here with his Memorial Day parade car and Mayor Greene.

Department of State, proposed three German cities—Kleve, Siegburg, and Pinneberg.

On October 13, 1957, a group gathered at Glenview Mansion to mark Rockville's sister city relationship with Pinneberg. A suburb of Hamburg in Schleswig-Holstein in northern Germany, Pinneberg was an old city with a 1957 population that, like Rockville's, had doubled in the previous decade to about twenty-five thousand. Mayor Hovsepian had business in Germany the following month and visited Pinneberg for a few days. Burgermeister Henry Glissmann and the people of Pinneberg prepared tours, social and publicity events, and special dinners to welcome Hovsepian, who bore gifts in return. Before the mayor left Pinneberg, he placed a wreath in the city's cemetery and invited his German counterpart to visit Rockville. Herr Glissmann's arrival in May 1958 strengthened the ties. New mayor Alex Greene led him on tours of schools, businesses, farms, public buildings, and Twinbrook Shopping Center, where all stores had new signs written in German. On Memorial Day, the Burgermeister reciprocated Hovsepian's wreath-laying to establish an annual ritual. At Glenview, Glissmann planted the first of one hundred rose bushes as a gift from his "City of Roses," and Mayor Greene handed Glissmann the symbolic key to the city.[62]

For a decade, the Sister Cities maintained the original momentum, exchanging visits by dignitaries and committee members and encouraging student pen pal correspondence. After a break in the 1970s, interest revived during Mayor John Freeland's administration. Rockville established a Sister Cities Task Force, which orchestrated a visit from Pinneberg and a mutual list of future partnership actions of interest to both cities. A group of three students, including fourteen-year-old Emily McGuckian, and two teachers in 1983 became the first in a series of annual student exchanges. In 1984, Pinneberg citizens founded Deutsch-Amerikanische Gesellschaft Rockville-Pinneberg. Rockville followed two years later by establishing the corresponding Rockville Sister City Corporation (RSCC). Since that time, the relationship has been solidified and enlivened by additional contacts with local groups and occupational representatives, student and sports exchanges, and RSCC activities.[63] A sculpture in Welsh Park from Pinneberg and two clocks in City Hall, set at Rockville and Pinneberg times, provide daily reminders of the relationship.

PUBLIC HOUSING

Decent housing for Rockville's poorest residents had not been addressed by pre-1954 officials. Sanitation and building codes were unevenly enforced in the city. With little support, Montgomery County created a Housing Authority in 1939, but it clung to conducting surveys and educating the public. Restrictive covenants, high land prices, and social customs kept blacks of all income levels in Lincoln Park, Haiti, and North Washington Street, in tiny enclaves across from Rose Hill on Falls Road and near Chestnut Lodge on Montgomery Avenue, and on East Middle Lane in the area degradingly called "Monkey Run." In 1934 and 1948, concerned county groups called the town's attention to deplorable conditions in that area, but the council turned a deaf ear. A contentious meeting in 1952 pitted John Pratt, head of the County Housing Authority, against a defensive Mayor and Council. When Pratt stated that black people were living in deplorable conditions, deteriorating houses with no sewer or water, and no units available for rent and little ground to buy, councilmen replied that Middle Lane residents refused to connect to sewer and water. As proof that they "did not want nice conditions but were happy to live in their own backward way," one councilman cited the 290 blacks who had signed a petition opposing a shopping center on North Washington Street.[64]

In the postwar years Rockville blacks, eyeing residential construction elsewhere, requested improvements in their neighborhoods. Knowing that under segregation "desirable dwellings and home sites in residential areas were not available to Negroes elsewhere in the town,"[65] men such as Simon Smith of Martin's Lane, "Mr. T." Johnson of North Washington Street, Raymond Smith, president of the Progressive Citizens Association, and Reverend Davis of Lincoln Park lobbied tirelessly for paved streets, utility lines, and police protection. After annexing Lincoln Park and Haiti in 1949, the old-order councils incrementally budgeted funds to lay water and sewer lines in Lincoln Park and to pave streets and install street lights in both neighborhoods. Only two blocks from the courthouse, Wood Lane was one of the last streets to obtain water, sewer, and paving—after the newcomers took over.

The reform council bristled at conditions on Middle Lane and in the back lanes of Haiti and Lincoln Park. "People were living in the black community in shacks . . . in garages and chicken coops. No heating; they had kerosene stoves, no water, no sewer,"[66] the new officials marveled. "People who had no furniture, living . . . in packing boxes, black people mostly . . . conditions that were unbelievable, and . . . no program that was reasonably able to take them out of that situation."[67] In 1955, the council appointed a Housing Advisory Committee to study the issue and in November of that year accepted its suggestion to create a Housing Authority. The new agency was asked to start a program "to erase permanently Rockville's substandard dwellings and provide new, adequate housing."[68]

Public housing was not easily sold in Rockville. In the 1950s, it was seen as an underclass program, one that had never been tried in Montgomery County. Councilmembers received abusive telephone calls. Some black citizens—particularly middle-class homeowners in Lincoln Park and Haiti—worried that low-rent housing would attract the wrong kind of people. A representative of the Home Builders Association wrote: "Since when does a new and prosperous community like Rockville need low cost housing other than they have at present? . . . Public housing is un-American. . . ."[69]

The Mayor and Council moved ahead nonetheless. They took care to appoint prominent citizens, black and white, to the first Rockville Housing Authority. Twinbrook resident Stanley Smigel chaired the independent authority, which received city funding for the first year. The council allayed fears of an invasion of undesirables from Washington, D.C., with the reminder that state law kept projects local. It took three years to apply for funding and issue bonds, to purchase vacant land on Moore Drive in Lincoln Park, and for Rockville contractor Sydney Fishman to construct ten two-story buildings containing sixty-five apartments and an eleventh building for offices and a community meeting hall. Black churches, in cooperation with city and county officials, furnished a demonstration apartment to aid new tenants in their transition from substandard housing to modern housekeeping. The first families moved into Lincoln Terrace in April 1959.

Public housing came to Rockville none too soon. Some of the black neighborhoods had been cleared for the new commercial construction on Washington Street. Concurrently, the city stepped up its efforts to remove seriously substandard housing. Families evicted from city-condemned houses on North Street and Frederick Avenue received priority for the new apartments. By September 1959, all units were occupied, with a waiting list of more than one hundred eligible families. Only six of the original sixty-five families came from outside of Rockville, accepted at the urging of the county Welfare Department. All families were black, as the project was segregated pursuant to local, state, and national practice in 1959. At the same time, Rockville began to vigorously enforce its housing code. City Manager Walter A. Scheiber reported in 1960 that in the previous two years, more than 100 existing homes were connected to water and sewer, 117 substandard buildings had been razed, and 63 had been condemned.[70]

Lincoln Terrace helped accommodate an overdue community need, but much remained to be done.

More units were needed; the Housing Authority applied to the U.S. Public Housing Administration for another 125 apartments and discussed a future project for white families. Segregation did not cease to be an issue; a decade later, after racial restrictions were lifted, critics attempted to block another project near Lincoln Park. Public housing still was unpopular; despite Lincoln Terrace's relatively small size and scale, it did not fit in with Lincoln Park's single-family house tradition. Other slum conditions existed; some would be addressed by other public programs.

COUNTY SERVICES

The Rockville resident who demanded the most space and caused the most change was the Montgomery County government. The county's unprecedented growth in the postwar period led to expansion of county buildings and services in Rockville. County population nearly doubled from 1946 to 1950, then more than doubled again between 1950 and 1960. It jumped from 87,777 residents in 1946 to 340,928 in 1960, as the area became a bedroom suburb for Washington, D.C.[71] With record numbers of school-age children in new homes in new

George Washington Carver High School and Junior College symbolized the end of substandard facilities for black students. The first county school to be named for a black person, the name Carver was selected by students in a contest. Pictured here is the graduating class of 1953. In 1961, the Board of Education converted Carver to office use.

Courtesy of Warren G. Crutchfield and Peerless Rockville

subdivisions, the school board added hundreds of new classrooms and teachers to serve thousands of additional students. Five elementary schools for white youngsters opened in Rockville in the 1950s—Lone Oak, Twinbrook, Maryvale, West Rockville (later renamed Beall), and Meadow Hall—but the bumper crop of children still necessitated double sessions in several schools. Crowded conditions at Rockville Junior High School (formerly Park Street Elementary) led to the building of Broome Junior High, in Twinbrook, which opened in 1957.

Although the county's black population decreased in relative size, improved educational facilities were long overdue. Consolidating small country schools, the school board moved black students from Quince Orchard, Scotland, Rockville, and Norbeck into the new Rock Terrace Elementary School. Sharing the thirty-acre campus with Rock Terrace was Carver High School and Junior College—the first, last, and only institution for post-secondary black education in Montgomery County. By day, Carver was a high school; at night, a junior college. Carver and Rock Terrace opened in September 1951, in a racially segregated school system that foresaw no change in the separate but equal philosophy of the times. School buses collected black students, many of whom rode three or four hours daily to attend Carver or Lincoln (which became a junior high). After the 1954 landmark U.S. Supreme Court decision, the Board of Education transferred Carver students to formerly all-white schools throughout the county in a staged integration process from 1955 to 1961. Lincoln was closed, and Carver Junior College merged with white-only Montgomery Junior College. In 1961, the Board of Education moved its administrative offices into Carver and converted Rock Terrace into a facility for special education students.[72]

Postwar expansion also strained space for county and court workers. The County Council, whose staff had outgrown the 1931 gray courthouse, replaced Welsh athletic field with a large office building at the corner of Maryland Avenue and Jefferson Street. Even so, additions were needed to the courthouse for circuit and peoples courts, and plans were made to tear down the Red Brick Courthouse for further expansion. The county relocated the last nine inmates from the Poor Farm and demolished the old buildings to make way for a state-of-the-art detention center.

ROADS

The vigorous postwar period placed pressure on traditional roadways and triggered new construction. In the 1950s, a solution to traffic problems in the business district, wider paths to jobs in Washington, and a swath through the western countryside reoriented vehicular traffic in mid-Montgomery County and brought new uses to roads in and around Rockville.

Excess traffic and inadequacy of parking had troubled Rockville shoppers and merchants for decades. The business community, Mayor and Council, and the State Roads Commission agreed by 1949 to separate through-traffic from vehicles having a Rockville destination. Maryland Route 240—Rockville Pike through the business district and north on Frederick Road—would no longer jog west onto Montgomery Avenue, pass the courthouse, then turn north on Washington Street. Instead, a new 1.4 mile roadway, starting at Saint Mary's Church, would parallel the railroad tracks northward and bypass the center of town. The Rockville Bypass opened for traffic in September 1951. A year later, the Mayor and Council accepted a citizen committee's recommendation to name it Hungerford Drive. From the start, the bypass did exactly what was intended—to direct traffic away from Rockville's traditional business district on the main street. One business to open on the new stretch was Hechinger's "do-it-yourself hardware supermarket."[73]

Next came a project of national importance and far-reaching local implications. A new limited access highway—known as the Washington National Pike, or National Bypass, and planned by federal and state officials for many years—would include some thirty-one hundred feet of roadway within the corporate limits of Rockville. The city's interests, handled through the State Roads Commission and Montgomery County, involved selecting interchanges to service Rockville and ensuring the safety of residents along the proposed route. The road was part of the National System of Interstate and Defense Highways that connected major American cities and provided an escape route for federal officials in case of an attack on Washington, D.C. Some wags suggested that President Eisenhower wished to avoid a repeat of the incident where he received a speeding ticket in Rockville en route to the presidential retreat

THE WASHINGTON NATIONAL PIKE

Groundwork for the National System of Interstate and Defense Highways was laid in the postwar period. In case of nuclear attack on the nation's capital, modern four-lane roads would provide evacuation routes for essential personnel, urban populations, and crucial industries. In addition, policy makers planned to relocate key federal agencies along the routes.

The limited-access highway from Washington to Frederick—known as the Washington National Pike—was initiated in the early 1950s. For years, city lawmakers negotiated with county and state officials, finally designating Route 28 and Montrose Road as the city's interchanges.[74] Rockville received a bridge across the highway on Great Falls Road, but Monroe Street was closed until future development warranted entry directly into the business district.

Map from advertising brochure for Rockville Plaza Motor Hotel shows new U.S. Route 240, the Washington National Pike (now I-270).

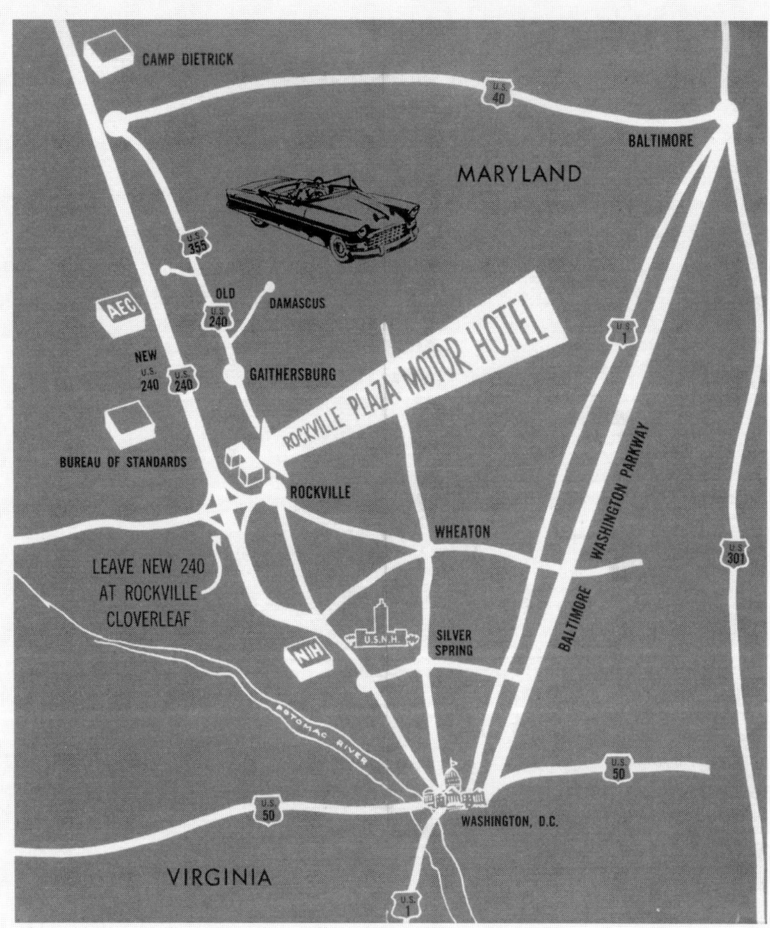

Alexander Greene collection, courtesy of Peerless Rockville

The first federal agency to move from Washington to upper Montgomery County spurred highway construction. Atomic Energy Commission (AEC) Chairman Lewis Straus moved the agency into new quarters in Germantown in 1957. Paving crews completed the National Pike between Shady Grove Road and Pooks Hill after AEC employees occupied the building.

Even before the move, the highway's impact on Rockville was felt. City officials met with AEC representatives about employee road use and housing needs. Developers assessed the potential of the additional corridor from the suburbs to Washington, adjusting their marketing accordingly. Gingery and Buchanan touted the congestion-free expressway which would speed Hungerford residents to downtown Washington in twenty minutes. Merrimack Construction Corporation provided a map to show its new subdivision of Montrose within "easy and fast access" to federal jobs.[75] In the $22,000 dollar range, Montrose homes attracted Germantown- and Washington-bound bureaucrats in the early 1960s. The National Bureau of Standards opened its first building along the new highway in 1962.

Regional planners designated the Washington National Pike as a corridor radiating from the District of Columbia, along which would be located new population centers. In between would be large wedges of open space. To the south was the highway encircling Washington, built between 1957 and 1964 as the Capital Beltway.

Courtesy of City of Rockville

Courtesy of City of Rockville

TOP: Washington National Pike, at Route 28 interchange. BOTTOM: Rockville Pike had two lanes in each direction in 1962.

at Camp David.[76] When the last segment between Shady Grove Road and Pooks Hill opened in 1957, the Washington National Pike became new U.S. Route 240 (later 70-S, then I-270).

Around the same time, the State Roads Commission improved older roads connecting Rockville with Washington. With new development occurring along Veirs Mill Road on both sides of Rock Creek, increased usage of the roadway necessitated rebuilding. Montgomery County's oldest street, the Rockville Pike, also was overdue for improvement. By the end of 1957, both Veirs Mill and the Pike had been reconstructed and widened to four lanes with concrete islands.

The city continued its own road program. Commerce Lane was broadened to please the merchants and county officials. Access to the northeast was improved by widening and paving Horners and Southlawn Lanes. Norris (now Mannakee) Street opened. Paving, curbs and gutters, and other improvements reached older areas as well as new developments. Requests for stop signs, traffic lights, and speed limit postings came to officials in a steady stream. In 1958, Rockville's Planning Commission published *A Master Plan of Principal Highways*. The slim document classified primary and secondary roads and identified the railroad crossing at Halpine Road as the worst hazard in Rockville. Anticipating traffic jams, it also proposed a loop arterial route around the city.

A traveler familiar with the Rockville Pike before World War II would have been shocked upon returning in 1960. Not only had the ancient thoroughfare become a four-lane divided roadway, but commercial enterprises of every type had replaced farms and mileposts. On the east side, Kraft's general store and Montrose Motors sat beside Dixie Cream donut shop, a crab house, and two drive-in restaurants—Morrell's and McDonald's. Bradley's dairy farm on the west side had been bought by Woodmont Country Club. There were the Rainbow Motel, Hank Dietle's tavern, and Tyson Wheeler's funeral home.[77] The most striking change was the huge modern shopping center on the site of Congressional Airport. Congressional Plaza opened in November 1959 with seventy-five stores and parking for four thousand cars. Arthur Hyde, who had operated the airfield for thirty years, brought in national and local chains—J. C. Penney, S. B. Kresge, and Giant Food. Shoppers from the new subdivisions quickly transferred loyalty to the regional retail center, guaranteeing immediate success.[78]

Two new businesses symbolized twentieth century suburbia as well as the altered but continued importance of the Rockville Pike. McDonald's, with

Roy Perry collection, courtesy of Peerless Rockville

Roy Perry collection, courtesy of Peerless Rockville

Congressional Plaza, circa 1960.

its low prices and standardized menu, led the fast-food industry to locate near substantial family neighborhoods. Young Rockville customers turned at the twin arches to purchase carry-out meals. The Hot Shoppes, Rockville's place in the Marriott world, featured Mighty Mos delivered by tray-carrying carhops.[79]

A MASTER PLAN FOR ROCKVILLE

The concept of a master plan was not new with the CGG council, but the revolution of 1954 accelerated its preparation. Mayor Kelly's request that city staff write a plan "with particular attention to zoning"[80] got lost in the flurry of development in the early 1950s. CGG candidates, who promised a document that would anticipate issues and coordinate development, created an advisory committee in December 1954. The following year the city hired a full-time planner, Robert L. Plavnick, and appointed the first Planning Commission with longtime activist Leslie Abbe as chairman.[81]

Rockville's future began in earnest with a federal 701 grant to prepare a comprehensive plan for the future growth and development of the city. The resulting *Master Plan*, a thirty-two-page document produced by consultants and city staff and adopted by the Planning Commission in September 1960, analyzed Rockville's economic health and projected its population. It surveyed housing needs, commercial facilities, and industrial potential. Solutions for traffic and parking problems were proposed, and needs for community facilities such as schools, parks, recreation areas, and public buildings were addressed. The plan included a six-year capital improvement expenditure program and a land use map delineating zones. Part of the planning concept was to provide a diversity of housing—apartments as well as higher-priced homes—so people could meet their housing needs within corporate limits. Rockville's *Master Plan*, the first comprehensive community plan in Maryland, sought to balance residential and commercial properties and to prevent suburban sprawl, but it did not claim to be a cure-all.[82]

A vital feature of the plan was the concept of maximum expansion limits. This delineation allowed the city to enlarge in an orderly way to a boundary with Montgomery County. Within these lines, Rockville could guide development and the roadways, community facilities, and utility capacity needed for the forecasted population of sixty-two thousand by 1980. The city was so anxious to demonstrate the integrity of this concept that it declined to include property on the Pike that became Super Giant and Montrose Crossing. Mayor Greene reasoned that limiting Rockville's size would maintain the sense of community that had developed in the independent municipality since 1860.[83] Reviewing the original document a decade later, citizens and officials concurred that while Rockville had outgrown its first master plan, the document had generally accomplished what its creators had hoped.

Roy Perry collection, courtesy of Peerless Rockville

Hamburgers at McDonald's, 1960s.

CAUSES FOR CELEBRATION

In 1960, Rockville took time out to celebrate one hundred years of incorporation. The centennial kicked off on March 10—exactly one hundred years after Rockville became an independent municipality. Maryland Governor J. Millard Tawes praised the city for its enthusiasm, progress, and prosperity. Mayor Greene purchased the first shares of stock from Rockville Centennial, Inc., the nonprofit corporation formed to raise funds for the commemoration.

A committee of residents and merchants, headed by Judge Stedman Prescott and attorney J. Hodge Smith, organized an array of activities. Rockvillians of all ages attended events, visited displays, and took advantage of special sales. Men challenged one another in a beard-growing contest, and women and girls participated in beauty contests. Wooden nickels were redeemable at local stores or at either of Rockville's banks. Celebratory events came together during the week of August 27 to September 3. Weekend special events, evening concerts, games, a parade of antique cars, a street dance, and a costume ball kept the city awhirl. The Mayor and Council dedicated the new civic auditorium and marked the recently unearthed 1803 BR boundary stone. Each night from Monday through Saturday, thousands of people descended on Broome Junior High School athletic field to watch *The Thin Gray Line*. This "pageant spectacle" (as described by its producers, French and Maryhelen Sansabaugh) was a monumental undertaking involving a cast of hundreds. Four episodes, eleven scenes, and a grand finale took onlookers through a review of American and local history from 1860 to 1960. Fireworks followed each dramatic performance.[84]

Rockville continued celebrating into the following year. For the second time, *Look Magazine* and the National Municipal League selected Rockville as an All-America City. The 1961 award cited Rockville's achievements in completing a city-owned water system and safe sewage disposal, adopting a master plan, developing a year-round recreation program including the Teen Center, acquiring the Civic Center and constructing the auditorium, sponsoring a public housing project, comprehensively revising the charter and codifying all city ordinances, achieving an "A" credit rating, and reducing the tax rate. Again, broad citizen participation was a major factor in the award. The judges honored Rockville "as a community where excellent citizen-governmental cooperation has brought steady progress [and] an extraordinary display of civic responsibility. . . . Rockville citizens exemplify the finest traditions of constructive participation in the affairs of a community."[85]

Between 1945 and 1960 Rockville emerged as a modern city. Its phenomenal growth was a major factor. From 1945 to 1960, the population increased almost nine fold. New residents and more youngsters brought

MAYORS G. LAMAR KELLY AND ALEXANDER J. GREENE

The dynamic mayors who anchored postwar Rockville provide a study in contrasts. G. LaMar Kelly Jr. symbolizes local government before explosive growth rendered the traditional ways of governing a town obsolete. Alexander J. Greene represents the reformers who took on the challenge of maintaining traditions while bringing the city to modern standards.

G. LaMar Kelly Jr. came to Rockville in 1927. A graduate of Johns Hopkins University with a degree in chemical engineering, he settled into the family business of his wife, Verna Viett. LaMar and Verna formed a new construction supply company, Standard Supplies, on East Middle Lane. The Kellys built a brick house on Baltimore Road, where they lived with their daughter. Kelly served on the town council from 1934 to 1942. As new town wells were always needed, he tried his skill at dowsing—locating water by pacing the ground with a forked stick. Kelly didn't attempt to explain the phenomenon. "I just accept it," he said.[86]

When Kelly returned after four years in the Coast Guard, the stocky, fiery, voluble Irishman ran for mayor. In six years as mayor, from 1946 to 1952, Kelly became passionate about his adopted town. "Don't throw away the heritage that is Rockville,"[87] he cautioned newcomers, pointing out that it is a mistake to plan too far into the future. Kelly ran for Montgomery County Council as a Democrat from the third district in 1950, but lost to reformer Lathrop Smith in a crucial referendum on the county's recent charter. He retired from city government two years later.

Alexander Greene collection, courtesy of Peerless Rockville

Courtesy of City of Rockville

TOP: Mayor G. LaMar Kelly served 1946–1952.
BOTTOM: Mayor Alexander J. Greene served 1958–1962.

Alexander J. Greene came to Rockville with his wife Jayne after they met in the army during World War II and moved to Washington. They purchased acreage in Potomac on which they planned to build and rented a house on Randolph Road. Involvement in Rockville Little Theatre led to friendships in the small town, and the Greenes soon sold the acreage to buy a house in Roxboro. Alex worked for the Bureau of the Budget, while Jayne covered Rockville for local and Washington newspapers. "In a sense, it was a whole generation looking for some roots. Most of us had been in the army, had come from other places. This is where we were going . . . to raise our [five] kids."[88]

Greene joined Rockville Civic Association and, as a budgeteer, looked closely at city finances. He was tapped by CGG to run in 1954 because of his budget experience. He claimed the reform movement wasn't started to "throw the rascals out" but rather to update the city by blending old and new. "It was an attempt to . . . get modern without destroying what was the focus of city life."[89] After four years on the council, Greene served two terms as mayor, from 1958 to 1962. As mayor, Greene continued reforms and worked to maintain Rockville's autonomy and sense of community amidst sprawl and larger government. His proudest mayoral accomplishment was acquisition of Glenview as Rockville's civic center.

additional needs. Rockville's land area grew from less than one square mile to more than seven. Capacious vacant land surrounding a municipality with its own utility systems attracted a total of twenty-two annexation petitions. Postwar development—the burst of residential construction in east and south Rockville and commercial improvements around the business district—was the most prolific and profitable in Rockville's history.[90]

In 1954, residents—many of whom had migrated to the Washington area—worked to replace the traditional government, which they considered backward, inefficient, and inappropriate for the city they wanted to make their home. The water crisis of 1953 prompted individuals to confront local officials they perceived as uncaring and incompetent. The newcomers organized a groundswell of indignation to capture city hall in May 1954. Adept new leadership moved quickly to professionalize Rockville's government and channel enthusiastic talent to develop a modern, workable city.

For the first time in its history, Rockville's leadership came from outside the region. The newcomers shared wartime experiences, youthful dreams, and a common interest in making Rockville home. They brought with them a variety of traditions different from those who grew up in rural Rockville, and by sheer numbers changed the culture of the town. The newcomers may have been enchanted by a town where some residents still kept hogs and chickens, but not for long. They wanted to remake Rockville into the mid-twentieth century American suburban ideal.

These new citizens captured control over Rockville's future. Prereform mayors and councils governed their community with limited information and limited resources. Their piecemeal, reactive approach to issues of growth at first seemed adequate, but was soon overwhelmed. In the 1953–54 municipal campaign, citizens scrutinized the operations and philosophy of the old order of government and found it wanting. Once set on a path of modernization, longtime residents joined the newcomers to revise almost every aspect of city government in a whirlwind of activity lasting nearly a decade. The foundations for change were home rule, planning, a professional staff, citizen participation, and municipal services. Lack of professional expertise on the city payroll emphasized the importance of the civic clubs, cultural organizations, and citizen advisory committees that blossomed in the mid-1950s. The overriding objective was to maintain a professionally managed municipality that would respond quickly to questions of growth and change.

The 1950s set the stage for the Rockville of a half-century later. Amidst profound change in surroundings and in governance, citizens retained a viable municipality with the atmosphere and lifestyle that had originally attracted them to the city.

NO PARKING ANY TIME
TO
OUR HEROES
OF
MONTGOMERY CO.
MARYLAND
THAT WE THROUGH LIFE
MAY NOT FORGET TO LOVE
THE THIN GRAY LINE
1861
1865

Chapter Eight

LOCAL GOVERNMENT TAKES THE LEAD

1961–1984

"A proposed city of the future that would wipe out the tired heart of Rockville and transform it into a pulsing commercial and high rise apartment center, peopled daily by thousands of bustling shoppers and workers. . . ."[1]

On Saturday, April 7, 1962, Mayor Alexander J. Greene was feeling justifiably proud. Serving his final month in public office, the two-term mayor greeted Rockville taxpayers who streamed into the newly opened City Hall. He watched approvingly as City Manager Walter A. Scheiber (1958–64) answered questions and showed off the new offices and meeting space. On the flagpole was Rockville's second All-America City flag.

Better city government offices had been recommended by the 1950 University of Maryland study. In February 1954 the Mayor and Council relocated from a two-room office on Commerce Lane into the Peter house, on South Washington Street. However, the old house soon proved unwieldy. City staff reported in 1960 that "the municipal operation has grown substantially both in the range of activities which it performs and in its size." The Mayor and Council razed the house and asked architect Donald N. Coupard to design Rockville's first municipal office building. The 18,300-square foot, two-story building, reoriented to Perry Street (now Maryland Avenue) and Vinson Street, cost nearly $250,000 and housed half of Rockville's 120 employees.

While the sleek new City Hall filled a practical need, it also symbolized the modern City of Rockville. The physical appearance of the city had changed since World War II, but other issues waited in the wings. Elected officials focused on population growth and geographic expansions in the fifteen years since the war. Citizens, demanding a better living environment, stepped in to assist the policy makers. Reform mayors and councils set in place the physical infrastructure, planning tools, and professional staff to implement the philosophy that brought Rockville to the forefront of modern small-city government. However, Rockville did not escape the consequences of urban decay and social inequality that led to upheaval in small cities as well as large. Faced with a deteriorating business district and a minority population demanding equal rights, city officials could not rely upon piecemeal approaches. By 1961, the historic crossroads community of Rockville had itself arrived at a crossroads. City government took the lead.

CIVIL RIGHTS

Race relations in Rockville reached a turning point in the early 1960s. Not only had black residents seen advancement on long sought objectives, but postwar newcomers had brought progressive attitudes from other places into Rockville. Within a segregated society, blacks in Montgomery County had struggled for a century to obtain adequate school facilities for their children. However, despite some progress and school desegregation, black students returned home to segregated neighborhoods, and their teachers commuted from Washington or rented

Photo courtesy of City of Rockville

Rockville's new City Hall.

rooms in Haiti or Lincoln Park. Few blacks felt comfortable in the majority of business establishments. Because local restaurants sold to black patrons only from the back door, or not at all, Rockville blacks patronized black businesses. These included printers Jesse and Celestine Hebron on Wood Lane, Mr. T's on the Pike, Snowden Funeral Home, Mead's taxi service, and Claude Prather's pool hall, barber shop, and ice business.

Black Rockville residents who made their living as government employees and school teachers teamed with black businessmen to change the way life had always been. A local man with a long career of civil rights activism was Alphonzo Lee (1883–1974). Born in Washington, he graduated from Dunbar High School and carried mail in the District of Columbia for thirty years. Lee was a handsome man with a commanding voice and a talent for cabinet making and photography. In 1925, he and his family moved into a new house on Martin's Lane. An organizer of the Montgomery County Branch of the National Association for the Advancement of Colored People (NAACP) in 1937, he later served as its president and worked to equalize conditions for all students and teachers.[2] Into the ranks of local black activists Lee welcomed white newcomers from other places who were appalled by "Colored" and "White" signs over courthouse and railroad station doors. During 1958–59, Lee, Florence Orbach, and Verna Motley surveyed Rockville eating places on behalf of the NAACP. They published lists of places that served without discrimination and persuaded three drug stores and two variety stores in Rockville to change their practices.[3]

An incident in the autumn of 1959 became a rallying point for equality. One evening, Mary Williams and her two young daughters sat down at the HiBoy restaurant on Route 355. They had walked from their home in Lincoln Park after receiving a flyer from the eatery, but Williams—the new president of the Montgomery County Branch of the NAACP—was denied service in the dining room. Failing to come to terms with HiBoy's attorney, NAACP took a cue from the boycotts in Montgomery, Alabama. By December, activists distributed five thousand flyers in Rockville asking people to "stay away from Hi-Boy [*sic*] and tell the management why."[4] Police later arrested twenty-five black and white demonstrators who refused to leave the restaurant. Church leaders organized written protests against HiBoy's racist policy, and George Lincoln Rockwell's American Nazi party, based in Virginia, staged a counterprotest at HiBoy. Rockville Mayor Greene stated that although the city lacked authority to "require desegregation in public eating establishments, personally I think it is wrong to advertise a restaurant or any business for use of the general public and then turn away a part of that public when it comes to be served."[5] The HiBoy sit-in was one moment in a trend spreading across America. Not long after, four black college students refused to leave a lunch counter in Greensboro, North Carolina, protesters picketed Glen Echo Amusement Park's denial of entry to blacks, and Edward Johnson, a black man, was arrested when he insisted on being served at the Tastee Diner on East Montgomery Avenue.[6]

The protesters at HiBoy and Glen Echo emboldened rights activists and opened others' eyes to segregation in public places. An alliance of black and white citizens pressed for the county council to ban segregation in Montgomery County. NAACP members were arrested for trespassing at the Congressional Roller Skating Rink in 1961. The Mayor and Council maintained a policy of encouraging integration, including considering building a swimming pool open to all and rebuffing boycott threats and counter-threats aimed at local businesses.[7] In January 1962, the Montgomery County Council enacted a public accommodations law that would prohibit discrimination in places open to the public. To secure a deciding vote, they exempted taverns. The Mayor and Council followed with their own law, including the exemption. Both were the first such legislation in Maryland. At its session in 1963, the Maryland General Assembly enacted a state law which also included the tavern exemption. A huge outcry by activists and embarrassed federal officials who hosted international patrons defeated an attempt to repeal the county's public accommodations law the following year.

In 1963, Rockville established a Human Relations Study Group, chaired by Rupert Curry, to identify and rebuff recurring discrimination in local establishments. The next year, the group recommended creation of a Human Relations Commission that would draft ordinances prohibiting discrimination in employment and housing. The Mayor and Council soon appointed a commission which succeeded in overturning the tavern exemption. The commission then tackled other issues,[8] bolstered by the Federal Civil Rights Act of 1964 and Edith M. Throckmorton, a school teacher who took over the helm of the NAACP. In this decade of high-profile civil rights marches, assassinations, urban riots, and black power, Mrs. Throckmorton quietly and forcefully worked with Alphonzo Lee to educate and register voters, connect blacks with job opportunities, and call attention to injustice. This measured approach helped Rockville to remain calm when fifteen robed and hooded Ku Klux Klansmen strutted around Court House Square for an hour on an August Saturday in 1966. Whether the Klan targeted Rockville for its symbolism as the county seat or because of the city's activism, it left disappointed with the lack of interest aroused.[9]

Rockville officials responded to the recommendations of the Human Relations Commission in 1966. Chairman Joseph Jeffs led the commission through a study of the practices of realtors, apartment owners, builders, and house sellers to learn that discrimination was common. Of the 10,000 dwelling units in Rockville, 402 of the 409 occupied by black families were located in black neighborhoods or rural areas.

TOP: Alphonzo Lee battled for civil rights in Montgomery County for half a century.
BOTTOM: Members of the Montgomery County Branch of the NAACP distributed protest flyers to the community in the early 1960s.

Courtesy of Peerless Rockville

STOP!

•

We are asking your support in an effort to bring real democracy to Rockville.

Rockville has won an award as an All-American City We Are Proud Of This Award. We Know You Are.

* * *

This store will not serve ALL OF ITS CUSTOMERS AT ITS FOOD COUNTERS will you help us to change this policy and make this truly an ALL-AMERICAN CITY, a wonderful place in which to live.

Shop at stores like Murphy's that serve everyone alike.

Montgomery Civic Unity Committee
V. F. W. Post 9863
N A A C P Rockville Branch

PLEASE FILL OUT THE BLANK BELOW AND RETURN TO
The person who gave you this flyer or

From Florence Orbach materials at the Montgomery County Historical Society

The few black families who moved into Twinbrook, Hungerford, and New Mark Commons found church groups and advocate Suburban Maryland Fair Housing more helpful than realtors or lenders. City clergy and other demonstrators marched through Rockville demanding action by the county council. Ultimately, the city enacted its fair housing law simultaneously with Montgomery County in July 1967. Both predated Title VIII of the landmark Federal Civil Rights Act of 1968, which prohibited discrimination in housing. The first rental complex in the area to practice open occupancy was the Summit Apartments (now Fireside Apartments), owned by Dr. Leonard Kapiloff, publisher of the *Montgomery County Sentinel*.[10]

Courtesy of Community Ministries of Rockville

The burning bush and God's revelation to Moses motivate Community Ministries of Rockville. CMR provides and coordinates a broad spectrum of human programs in the city.

The general upheaval of the 1960s generated other private and public responses. To assist local families, Rockville church women started the Interfaith Clothing Store in an empty store on Montgomery Avenue. Two Rockville churches formed the United Church Center for Community Ministries in 1967, under the guidance of Rev. Donald Maccallum. In a teen-oriented club and counseling center called Risque, Community Ministries demonstrated the need for compassionate public services. In the next few years, the city created the roving youth leader program and a unit concerned with special problems and opportunities for young people. In addition, the city opened Experiment 1 in the former Woolworth store on North Washington Street as a center for youth programs.

Identification of community needs and successes of early programs created interest in increased services. Community Ministries of Rockville, under Rev. Alfred Winham (1972–79) and then Rev. Mansfield Kaseman (1979–2000) built upon the work of the NAACP and the Rockville Human Relations Commission to address issues of discrimination, adequate housing, and equal access to jobs and education. Community Ministries (now expanded to an interfaith coalition of twenty congregations) moved to provide direct service to minorities, the poor, homeless, and the hungry. Programs established or nurtured by the organization include Manna Food Center, Rockville Emergency Assistance Program, Rockville FISH, Latino Outreach Program, Meals on Wheels, and shelters for families, men, and women. By the mid-1980s, a public-private partnership of Community Ministries and the city had an enormous impact on Rockville citizens.[11]

The City of Rockville expanded and consolidated its human resources programs over the next three decades. The Human Relations Commission became the Human Rights Commission and took on new responsibilities under a comprehensive ordinance. The commission investigated discrimination complaints, initiated an annual Martin Luther King Jr. observance, and put information out to the community. A new Department of Community Resources coordinated service programs. Youth Services reached out with new tutoring and counseling programs, and the Rockville Free Clinic offered medical and mental health services. Together with the courts and State's Attorney Andrew Sonner, Rockville began an Alternative Community Service program for first time offenders, one of the first such programs in the country.

The Mayor and Council instituted other services during the 1960s that today are taken for granted. After decades of controversy, the city established a municipal refuse collection program for single-family residences in October 1965. Seven modern compactor trucks made pickups twice a week and special collections once a month, at a cost to residents of thirty dollars per year. The city newsletter, which began in 1957 as a mimeographed monthly report entitled *Speaking of Rockville*, settled into an attractive format bearing information about past and future city activities. "An informed citizen is a better citizen," declared the masthead. The tradition of Citizens' Forum—where anyone could address the Mayor and Council at its regular meeting—began in 1964. Each innovation contributed to citizen identification with Rockville.

Photograph by Dean Evangelista

Growth spurred new faith congregations in Rockville. Local Jewish families built Beth Tikva, Rockville's first synagogue, on Baltimore Road in 1965. The First Church of Christ, Scientist, opened on Nelson Street on Thanksgiving Day, 1970. Older churches also grew. Saint Mary's removed its old rectory and social hall to build a larger church in 1966. The Baptist and Christian congregations relocated to new edifices in the 1970s.

MANAGING GROWTH

Planning shaped and interpreted the future growth of Rockville. The Planning Commission and professional planners produced a new *Master Plan* in 1970 which elaborated on the first document of a decade before and set the tone for the remainder of the century. The plan stated the goal of making Rockville the "best possible residential community" at a time when most thought of the city as a bedroom community. A general document outlining a balanced community of residential, commercial, civic, and open spaces, the *Master Plan* called for development of detailed neighborhood plans in fifteen study areas. Beginning with Twinbrook and Croydon Park, the Planning Commission appointed neighborhood advisory groups to help identify local problems and propose land use. By 1984, the Mayor and Council had adopted plans for Town Center, Croydon Park, Twinbrook, and Lincoln Park.

The 1970 *Master Plan* also touched on two subjects that had arisen in the postwar period. The

THE COLD WAR COMES TO ROCKVILLE

City Hall also took on the role of coordinating local civil defense efforts. In the Cold War atmosphere of the 1950s and 1960s, a small group of citizens dedicated years to planning for any natural or military disaster.

Concluding that it was safer to remain in Rockville in the event of an attack on Washington than to try to get out, the Rockville Civil Defense Organization (CD) focused on educating the populace to help itself and on organizing specialized units of volunteers. Within a total survival plan for the Washington area and Montgomery County, Rockville was divided into five areas. Volunteers trained residents in first aid, home protection, and bomb shelter construction. Rockville's CD headquarters and largest bomb shelter was in the basement of Glenview Mansion, in communication with Montgomery County CD control in the County Office Building. Some fifteen other shelters existed around the city, in solid structures such as banks and churches and also in private homes. The Civil Air Patrol planned to use the interstate highway as a landing strip for delivering supplies or blood to waiting vehicles. Two Nike missile launcher sites were located near Rockville on Muddy Branch and Snouffer School Roads. Intricate plans were maintained through the mid-1970s.[12]

Courtesy of Henry Rapalus

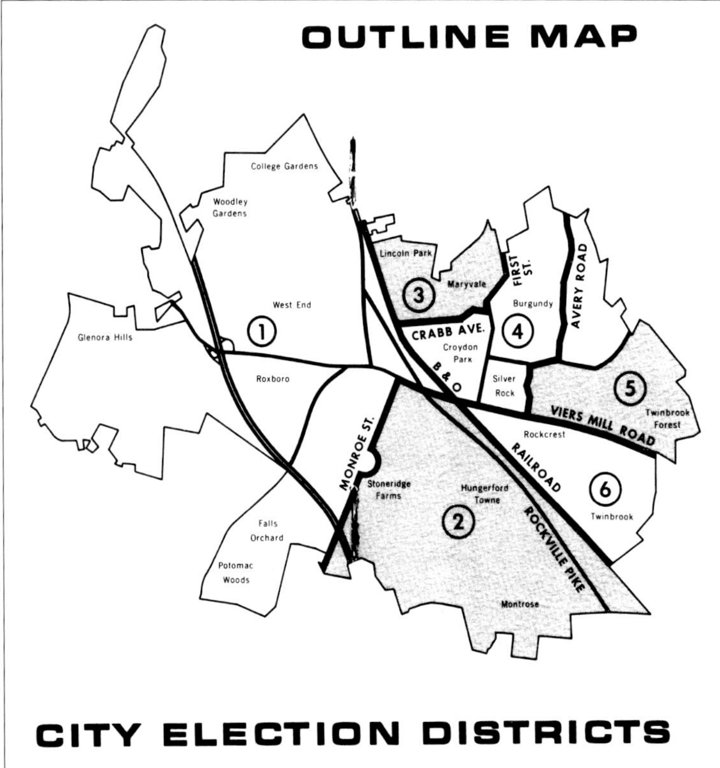

From *Citizen's Handbook*, City of Rockville, 1966 edition

The number of Rockville neighborhoods continued to grow. Map of city election districts in 1966 shows new subdivisions.

rapid growth of commercial space along Rockville highways and in shopping centers serving neighborhoods in outlying areas led planners to suggest that existing facilities sufficed. No additional land should be rezoned to provide for neighborhood and convenience shopping. In a more oblique manner, the plan touched on providing a transition between the central business district and adjacent residential areas. Older buildings on South Washington Street, Adams Street, and Jefferson Street were threatened by more intense uses in the center of town. Soon, planners introduced transitional office zones, O-1 and O-2. The latter classification specifically targeted historic buildings close to the Town Center that were too cumbersome to heat, too large for modern family size, or on streets less conducive to residential enjoyment. Owners could convert a building for office use, provided they did not enlarge it. This had the effect of encouraging maintenance of the existing building, at least on the exterior. The first conversion to O-2 was the Brown sisters' residence on North Adams Street in 1972. Within a decade, most of the houses on the east side of North Adams Street and both sides of South Washington Street had been classified for transitional office use.

Crucial to guiding the location of growth was road access. The 1970 *Master Plan* built upon concepts introduced in 1958 and 1960, which designated roadways needed to move traffic around Rockville and through the city for specific residential, industrial, or commercial areas.[13] During the period 1960–1984, most of the circumferential highway around Rockville was built and two railroad grade crossings were closed. Ritchie Parkway (now Wootton Parkway) opened between Falls Road and Route 28. Improvements on Route 28 (First Street and Norbeck Road) bypassed a section of ancient Baltimore Road and cut rural Avery Road in two. The Falls Road interchange of the interstate was constructed in the 1970s, as was East Gude Drive between Route 355 and the relocated Route 28. In 1964, the county closed the railroad crossing at Halpine Road, cited as a danger as early as 1958, and constructed a bridge across the tracks for the new Twinbrook Parkway. Closing the railroad crossing at Frederick Avenue caused deep concern in Lincoln Park about access to the main part of town. As a compromise, Metro constructed a pedestrian bridge at Frederick Avenue and widened the rail underpass at Park Road to three lanes.

INDUSTRY, 1960–1984

Part of urban planning was the city's desire to maintain light industry within its boundaries. Mayors and councils in 1896 and again in 1959 issued statements encouraging investment of capital and establishment of local industry. However, industry found itself more and more set apart in the twentieth century. Prohibited by covenant in some residential sections—separation of uses was a tenet of the suburban ideal—the town's 1931 Zoning Ordinance relegated manufacturing to areas where odor, dust, smoke, and noise would be less offensive to residents. Thus, by World War II Rockville's industrial concerns had located along the railroad tracks from Derwood south to Halpine and on the northeastern fringe of the business district close to the tracks.

During the Greene administration, the city took stock of its industry and liked what it found. In 1959, 2,154 employees worked in nintey-seven industrial establishments. Nearly half were construction-based (a product of the postwar home-building boom) while others engaged in manufacturing or research.[14] One was WINX, Rockville's own radio broadcasting station. IBM opened a division headquarters on East Montgomery Avenue. The Rockville Development Council, a citizens committee chaired by Richard M. Cooperman, executive director of the Rockville Chamber of Commerce, produced a brochure and helped the city institute the I-3 Restricted Industrial Zone, designed for high-tech research and development. The 1960 *Master Plan* encouraged light industry in order to strengthen Rockville's economy and lessen the city's reliance on residential property taxes.[15]

Between 1960 and 1970, industry grew at a faster rate than any other type of land use in Rockville, and the city's tax-assessable base grew commensurately. City plans and assistance—including a successful petition to the Interstate Commerce Commission resulting in lower motor transport rates—led to Rockville's strong position in the I-270 corridor and set patterns for local industry. The 1970 *Master Plan* confirmed the presence of small industry in the Stonestreet Avenue area where it had existed since the 1930s, and encouraged it between the Pike and the railroad tracks around Halpine. It recommended new high-tech industrial enclaves along what is now Research Boulevard and below the new Detention Center (now Fortune Terrace). The plan also sanctioned continuation of an industrial trend at the northern boundary of the city east of Route 355.[16] In April 1970 the Mayor and Council established a fifteen-member Economic Development Council to study issues, suggest programs, and act as a liaison between businesses and city government.

Responding to city encouragement and to the proximity of federal facilities in the I-270 corridor, more than one hundred new industries moved into Rockville in the 1960s and 1970s. Rockville's first light industrial park on Research Boulevard came as a result of a trade-off in 1960 whereby sixty-four acres on Great Falls Road became residential, and fifty acres along Route 28 and I-270 were rezoned to I-3.[17] Donohoe Construction Company of Washington developed the tract for research and scientific firms. The first firm to locate

TOP: NUS building (now COMSYS and Government Institutes) in Research Park, as seen from the interstate in 1970.
BOTTOM: National Plate Grainers in Halpine Industrial Park, 1964.

Courtesy of City of Rockville

Brooks Photographers image from the *Washington Star*, copyright the *Washington Post*, reprinted by permission of the D.C. Public Library

Photo by David Kelsey, courtesy of Peerless Rockville

N. Richard Kimmel nestled a modern office building in the woods as part of city's RedGate Industrial Park development. The pentagonal structure, designed by Thomas O'Reilly, is located on East Gude Drive.

there was Rabinow Engineering Company. Jacob Rabinow, formerly a mechanical engineer with the National Bureau of Standards (now NIST), patented 230 mechanical and electrical devices and founded several other companies.[18] Later came Meloy Laboratories, Gillette Company, Westat Research, Aspen Systems, and others. Large office buildings arose on Piccard Drive and Shady Grove Road from the late 1960s into the early 1980s. General Motors, Ward Development, Litton Bionetics, Bradford National, Tektronix, Calculon, Eastman Kodak, Danac Associates, NUS, and other companies moved into attractive modern buildings bordering the interstate highway.[19]

An older industrial area, Halpine expanded with new companies brought in by developer Dermot A. Nee in the 1950s. After Washington Technological Associates opened a multimillion dollar research and development center on Rollins Avenue in 1961, other large and small companies moved in.[20] Along the Pike and rail line, new owners built offices for small research and scientific concerns. Haynes Lithograph, the radiological laboratory of the U.S. Public Health Service, and Pepsi-Cola Bottling Company built facilities nearby. In 1965, closure of the grade crossing at Halpine and construction of Twinbrook Parkway over the tracks split the industrial area into sections. The U.S. Department of Health, Education and Welfare opened in the Parklawn Building in 1970.

The northeastern part of Rockville, beyond Lincoln Park and Maryvale into Beantown, had remained rural for many years, but it began to change rapidly. Into the 1960s, a few large farms existed along Southlawn Lane and Avery Road, separated by small residential tracts in the woods and fields.[21] Anders Lofstrand Sr. and Jr. operated a factory near Horners and Southlawn Lanes as early as the 1930s, manufacturing products as varied as prostheses, commercial dishwashers, and equipment for Nike guided missile stations.[22] In 1962, Lofstrand Jr. teamed with other investors to subdivide fifty-seven acres of his farm into lots and start Southlawn-Lofstrand Industrial Park.[23] By 1965, Taft Street, Lofstrand Lane, and First Street were in place, and some industrial buildings were under construction. Sulzer Laboratories, Electronics for Life Sciences, Inc., and Teddington Aircraft were among the first firms to locate there. Within a decade, numerous other businesses bought or leased space. Farther north, Montgomery County operated a solid waste landfill and incinerator on forty acres of the former Gude farm from 1965 until Rockville citizens and government pressure helped to force its closure more than two decades later.[24]

As Gude Drive east of Route 355 opened in sections in the early 1970s, more commercial and industrial buildings obliterated the fields and woods. The east end of Gude Drive, ending at realigned Norbeck Road, was annexed into the city. The area around Southlawn and Gude attracted a variety of businesses and uses. In 1968, the Rockville Housing Authority built a second housing project with seventy-six units called David Scull Courts (named for a champion of public housing in Montgomery County). Later, the county opened an animal shelter, and the city added a public works maintenance complex. Nearby, Rockville developed RedGate Industrial Park, where C. I. Mitchell & Best and

William Rickman built sizeable buildings for growing businesses like Vitro, the Elks Club erected a lodge, and Wheel-a-While skating rink operated.

Older Rockville industrial concerns began an exodus from the outskirts of the old business district as plans for urban renewal and the Rockville metro station solidified. Rockville Fuel and Feed purchased land on Southlawn Lane and relocated its plant there over a five-year period in the late 1970s. Other construction-related companies followed: Jack Irwin, Montgomery Concrete, Grove Lime Company and Rockville Excavating. Longtime businessman Leland Fisher, selling lumber, millwork, and building supplies, moved to Gude Drive in 1980.

Courtesy of Jennie and Bill Forehand

Ad for new homes in Woodley Gardens from the Washington Post *(May 2, 1964).*

DEVELOPMENT OF WEST ROCKVILLE

The rules and direction of residential growth in Rockville changed in the early 1960s. Postwar growth for the most part had occurred to the east of the old town—down Veirs Mill Road and the Rockville Pike—where water and sewer were easily added and land annexed. With adoption of a new zoning ordinance and comprehensive map amendment in 1957 and of the *Master Plan* in 1960, city officials could review proposals for residential development as a whole neighborhood. At the same time, extension of the Watts Branch trunk sewer enabled the city to expand westward, across the interstate. Proximity to this highway assured the popularity of new subdivisions that soon would arise.

In the early 1960s, the Mayor and Council approved several rezoning applications under an innovative concept that defined residential development for the remainder of the century. Initially termed the Planned Community Group, the Planned Residential Unit (PRU) quickly captured the imaginations of developer and planner alike, for it permitted flexibility and encouraged creativity in planning total neighborhoods rather than merely groupings of individual lots. Lot sizes and housing types could vary, community needs such as apartments could be addressed, and additional open space could be created within the development using land saved by clustering. Other goals included preserving natural features and undergrounding utilities. Early PRU developments in Rockville included Meadow Hall,[25] Woodley Gardens, College Gardens, New Mark Commons, Fallsmead, Rockshire, North Farm, and Carter Hill.[26]

One of the first PRU applications was from Monroe Warren Sr. and Jr., veteran Washington builders responsible for hundreds of houses in Rockcrest in the 1950s. The Warrens purchased 220 acres of the Milor farm straddling Watts Branch and worked with city planners Robert Plavnik and William Hussmann to develop "Montgomery County's first preplanned community," Woodley Gardens. Under the PRU concept, the cohesive design of Woodley Gardens included single-family homes, rental town houses, apartments, an elementary school, commercial area, and a pool. Roughly 15 percent of the land area in the development became public parkland. Prices began around twenty-five thousand dollars for single-family homes with a variety of floor plans and styles. Officials were delighted to have higher-priced housing options within city limits, although FHA at first refused to approve plans for houses costing more than twenty-one thousand dollars because they considered Rockville a working-class suburb.[27] The Warrens advertised "Woodley Gardens, the country club community" as "conveniently located . . . less than 10 minutes via a non-stop divided highway to the heart of Bethesda and the District Line." They sold off sections to other builders as Woodley Gardens filled out to 234 homes over the following decade.[28]

To the north of Woodley Gardens, the neighborhood of College Gardens sprouted on the former Anderson farm. Andersons had lived at Vallombrosa for nearly two centuries, but members of the family moved into town, razed the old house and, in the 1930s, let the farm to tenants. After it was sold to Polinger Corporation, part of the acreage became the campus of Montgomery Junior College in 1965. The city negotiated for years with Polinger on issues of density distribution, sewer connections, and commercial development before annexing the 333 acres and finally approving the subdivision plans in 1964.[29] Artery Organization built the first houses in 1967, and continued construction for five years. Using the marketing name "Plymouth Village," Artery Organization built colonial-style single-family homes in the thirty-six to forty-two thousand dollar price range as well as townhouses and apartments. Couples with young families arrived in such great numbers that College Gardens Elementary School opened in 1967.[30]

New Mark Commons, Edmund J. Bennett's planned residential community, opened on ninety-six wooded acres in 1967. Aerial photograph from the early 1980s shows the lake and recreational facilities in addition to the variety of housing.

Courtesy of New Mark Commons Homeowners Association

Protection of upper Watts Branch—the creek flowing through Woodley and College Gardens—spurred local environmentalists into action. Developers of both subdivisions dedicated the wooded stream valley to the city and, when combined with open space acquisitions, Upper Watts Branch Park became the largest park in Rockville. Much of the credit goes to an early conservationist and Woodley Gardens resident, Judy French. As vice chair of the Maryland Environmental Trust, French was tireless in identifying the consequences of past and future development on the watershed and in pushing for a storm water management program. Years after she dissuaded officials from crossing the creekbed seven times with a sewer line, others joined her advocacy. Bolstering French's warnings of the destruction of the beautiful stream valley was a study by Luna B. Leopold.[31] The hydrologist studied water flow, siltation, and configuration of the Watts Branch channel over a twenty-year period, determining that ravagement of the stream escalated about 1967, when the sewer line was laid and development activity in the area was at its peak. A twenty-acre wooded site immediately adjacent to the stream—originally set aside for construction of a junior high school—became a rallying point for the neighborhoods in the 1980s. College and Woodley Gardens activists effected a land swap between the city and county and, ultimately, Mayor and Council designation of Upper Watts Branch Park Forest Preserve.[32] Battles fought by subdivisions created neighborhoods.

PRU-5 was Rockville's planning designation for Edmund J. Bennett's subdivision of New Mark Commons. Bennett filed an exploratory application in 1965 for the ninety-six-acre wooded site, but the final configuration and types of residential development took years to work out. A local builder of homes in Reston, Columbia, Carderock Springs, and Potomac Overlook, Bennett had in mind a planned community. He admired the work of Ebenezer Howard, a nineteenth-century builder of English garden cities, small urban communities of thirty thousand or fewer people, as alternatives to the continued growth of large cities. Once New Mark was built, the names of garden cities around the world—Letchworth, Farsta, Don Mills, Welwyn, and others—found their way onto its street signs. Like Howard, Bennett wished to "find an unspoiled piece of land inside an established town or small city and create a village. . . . [It has to do] with the use of land and the combining of amenities to create a sense of village life."[33]

The architectural firm of Keyes, Lethbridge, and Condon helped Bennett conduct a complete tree survey and to design houses to respect the rolling wooded terrain. Houses clustered on cul-de-sacs, vehicles traveled on one main road looped for interest and speed control, and pedestrians enjoyed a network of footpaths to reach the tennis courts, a swimming pool, and the clubhouse. Two city parks, Monument and Dogwood, were nearby. Eventually, Bennett and two successor builders sold 384 houses in three basic types—single-family detached dwellings in contemporary and traditional designs, contemporary townhouses, and lakefront townhouses. Because of objections from residents in 1985, the originally planned small commercial "Village Green" instead became thirteen townhouses.

Professional, technical, and management employees—evenly divided between the private and government sectors—eagerly sought homes in New Mark Commons, initially paying an average of forty-five thousand dollars for a single-family home. Patricia and Fielding Ogburn became the first family to settle in 1967. Location added to the attraction as New Mark had easy access to Washington, D.C. Bennett and the residents governed the New Mark Commons Homes Association, settling problems concerned with Lake New Mark, the common land, pool, clubhouse, street maintenance, bike paths, and other community issues. An architectural control committee enforced the deed covenants, and residents started a monthly newsletter originally called the *New Mark Commonist*. Popular activities such as Sunday softball games, shrimp feasts, chess and scrabble tournaments, and holiday children's parties solidified the neighborhood.

With the new trunk sewer, I-270 ceased to be a barrier to development. Kettler Brothers developed Fallsmead in the mid-1960s, incorporating parcels once farmed by people named Trail, Jones, Rabbitt, Duncan, Ewing, and Betts. Annexed into Rockville, Fallsmead soon sprouted homes, schools, a park and pond, bike paths, a pool, and tennis courts. From 1968 through 1973, three hundred families moved into houses priced in the mid-forty-thousand-dollar range. A corporation governed the community's common areas. Residents published the *Fallsmead Forum* newsletter, organized clubs for various interests, and formed a citizens association.[34]

Residential subdivisions of the 1960s, 1970s, and into the 1980s continued the suburban ideal in Rockville. With larger homes on winding roads and cul-de-sacs away from the center of Rockville, the developments of Carter Hill, Flint Ledge, Glenora, Potomac Woods, and Rockshire Village invited dependence upon the automobile. Increasing numbers of youngsters inspired a host of new city parks and county schools.

A sewer moratorium imposed by the state secretary of health and mental hygiene from 1971 to 1973 halted new construction in the Cabin John and Watts Branch drainage basins, as well as elsewhere in Montgomery County. Neither WSSC nor the City of Rockville could permit connections to their sewer systems except in restricted circumstances.[35] For several years, until the regional Blue Plains Waste Water Treatment Plant was enlarged and improved, the city approved no new subdivisions, although construction did proceed on infill lots in existing Rockville developments. When the moratorium was lifted, growth continued.[36] The latter half of the 1970s saw construction of Potomac Springs,

THE HANNA ERA: 1974–1982

An early Woodley Gardens resident who came to the Washington area to work for the National Aeronautics and Space Administration, William E. Hanna Jr. was first elected to the council in 1968. He helped to form Independents for Rockville (IFR) because he was concerned about economic development and believed the city should appreciate the business community more. As mayor, Hanna demanded fiscal responsibility and a better balance between business and residential sectors. He was a strong advocate for neighborhoods, the arts and humanities, programs for senior citizens, and planning. "A past and continuing strength of Rockville is its willingness to move ahead to meet change, rather than waiting for change to overtake it," he declared.[37] He worked to attract R&D companies, touting Rockville's educated population, good quality of life, and access to major roads.

Courtesy of City of Rockville

Mayor William E. Hanna Jr. carefully holding the city mascot, the rock hawk.

Hanna's interest in municipalities led him to seek ideas from other places. During his regime, Rockville designed a new city flag and seal. The city adopted a mascot, the rock hawk (better known as the peregrine falcon). Hanna delighted in celebrating America's bicentennial with local projects and programs.

Rockville received two All-America City Awards during Mayor Hanna's administration. In 1977, the National Municipal League cited Rockville for grassroots initiative and involvement. Citizens who served on nineteen advisory boards and commissions, volunteered for the Free Clinic and other city programs, participated in twenty-four civic associations and the Chamber of Commerce, preserved historic buildings, presented awards for beautification, and helped set priorities for the development of park land and Block Grant funding were mentioned, as were bicentennial projects. Two years later, Rockville became the only four-time winner. Its achievements were the community goal-setting process, the development of a comprehensive program for senior citizens, and the creation of a community arts program.[38]

Rockshire, Carter Hill, Watts Branch Meadows, Fallsridge, Saddlebrook, Fallsbend, Horizon Hill, Fallswood, Rock Falls, and Glen Hills Club. The Rockville Fruit Farm, a local enterprise at Falls and Seven Locks Roads that was in business from 1919 to the 1950s, gave its name in the late 1970s to Orchard Ridge subdivision.

EXPANSION OF MUNICIPAL SERVICES

By and large contented with local government, Rockville residents nevertheless expected more and more. The revolution of 1954 produced public officials who prided themselves on progressiveness and responsiveness to constituents. City reliance on citizen committees to complement the work of staff and to assist the Mayor and Council in making policy reinforced the comfort level of taxpayers.

But no coalition could last forever. By the 1960s, political groups splintered off from Citizens for Good Government. Mayors Frank A. Ecker, Achilles M. Tuchtan, and Matthew J. McCartin mostly followed the political philosophies of their predecessors, Hovsepian and Greene. Ecker (1962–68) emphasized solid planning and quality recreation programs as numerous subdivisions opened. Tuchtan (1968–72), the first mayor to live west of the interstate, guided Rockville as it continued to grow in residential acreage and to develop a reputation friendly to research and development companies. The first crack in CGG became public when Dickran Hovsepian, John Rausch, Herman Hartman, and others formed the nonpartisan Federation of Independent Voters (FIV). Fielding a full set of candidates in 1962 and 1964 with no success, they opposed "government by smoke-filled car pool" and the "interlocking clique"[39] (CGG) who ran the city. FIV folded into Rockville Voters for Responsible Government (RVRG), which called for breaking up the ruling party and speeding up the urban renewal program. In 1968, McCartin won a council seat as an independent, shattering the fourteen-year-old adage that nomination by CGG was tantamount to election. By 1970, opposition to CGG coalesced around Independents for Rockville (IFR), which in the following election ran a full slate, headed by sitting councilman Rupert Curry. Curry, an IBM manager, made his mark in areas of youth athletics and human relations and as Rockville's first black councilmember (1968–72).

The 1972–74 Mayor and Council split politically and often. Mayor McCartin, back in the CGG fold with councilmen Robert Bryan and George Northway, often differed with IFR members William E. Hanna Jr. (who had challenged McCartin for mayor at the CGG convention) and Jean Horneck, the city clerk from 1957 to 1972 and the first woman on the council. Still, McCartin—with the assistance of new City Manager Larry N. Blick—maintained the direction of previous administrations and took advantage of the sewer moratorium to address long-term concerns. One was the Rockville Gardens apartment complex, fifteen buildings of low-cost housing that had been plagued by crime, drugs, and owner-tenant conflicts since passage of fair housing legislation. The city purchased the apartments from Joseph Berlin in 1973, but it took years to relocate tenants, raze the buildings, get multiple levels of government to agree on funding, and to find a developer to construct replacement housing.[40] In 1974, the Mayor and Council also designated three historic districts, the first in Montgomery County.

William E. Hanna Jr. headed the IFR ticket in 1974 in a sweeping defeat of CGG candidates. City Hall took a conservative turn. Concerned about park safety, the Mayor and Council hired a professional police chief, Charles Wall, and more officers. They were aided by the General Assembly, which authorized Rockville to ban drinking in parks and in store parking lots. Staff also arranged for sports teams and youngsters to help clean up the parks. Often taking advantage of outside funding and assistance, the city addressed problems of older neighborhoods through

TOP: Rockville celebrated America's bicentennial with activities and patriotic flower gardens. Rockville children helped to restore the town clock .
BOTTOM: Rockville Day continued the fourth All-America City Award celebration, shown here in 1979. Each May for fifteen years, city residents gathered on the civic center grounds for picnics, family games and contests, pony rides, music, a conga line, and a celebration of community.

Photo from City of Rockville, *Annual Report*, fiscal year 1976

Stuart Pohost photo, courtesy of City of Rockville

code enforcement, removal of old vehicles, street upgrades, property maintenance programs and, later, Community Development Block Grants.[41]

CGG never revived after the divisive conventions and election of an opposition party. Shadowed by increasingly negative feelings about the progress of downtown revitalization, the group failed to attract sufficient candidates and suffered total defeat at the polls. Its effectiveness was also reduced by a controversy over cable television, a service newly available to local jurisdictions. In the mid-1970s, two private companies—TelcoR and Mitre, each including prominent Rockville residents as investors and officers—competed for the city's cable television franchise. The Mayor and Council passed an ordinance to enable the city to grant a franchise, but deadlocked on selecting a company, so granted none.[42] Years later, Rockville joined Montgomery County's cable system. On November 11, 1976, members of CGG voted to permit the organization to die a graceful death near its birthplace in Twinbrook. They voted to transfer its remaining assets to a new historic preservation organization "which benefits the city enormously"—Peerless Rockville.[43] Two months later, Ken Kisiel, Bob Namovicz, and Naomi Josephs invited Rockville voters to explore an alternative. The New Group, which soon became the Alliance for Rockville Citizens (ARC), fielded candidates and won two seats (Ken Sullivan in 1978 and Viola Hovsepian in 1982) in elections where candidates debated issues relating to the coming of the metro, leashing cats, and responsiveness to voters.

Another area in which city government stepped up its level of activity was beautification. In 1969, the Mayor and Council created the Civic Improvement Advisory Commission (CIAC) to recommend programs that would improve the city's appearance. One of the energetic group's first projects was to place seven "Welcome to Rockville" entrance signs. CIAC assisted the Rockville Woman's Club in relocating F. Scott and Zelda Fitzgerald from Rockville Cemetery to Saint Mary's Cemetery on November 7, 1975, and planted flowers in the F. Scott Fitzgerald triangle at Veirs Mill Road and Rockville Pike. Led by Jennie Forehand for many years, CIAC also helped rewrite the city's sign ordinance, which phased out billboards.

Photo by Ronnie N. Haber, courtesy of Peerless Rockville

Courtesy of Jayne L. Greene, Peerless Rockville

TOP: On November 7, 1975, F. Scott and Zelda Fitzgerald were removed from Rockville Cemetery and reinterred in the family plot at Saint Mary's churchyard. Scottie Fitzgerald Smith requested the move, recalling her father's letter: "I wouldn't mind a bit if in a few years Zelda and I could snuggle up together under a stone in some old graveyard here. That is really a happy thought and not melancholy at all."
BOTTOM: Woodley Gardens Park, on Nelson Street, was acquired by the city 1960–63 in three parcels totaling 45.7 acres. State-of-the-art when it opened in the spring of 1964, the park included a fountain and sitting area, two all-weather tennis courts, a tot lot, two ball fields, and a functional shelter. A picnic area and two foot bridges were built on Watts Branch behind the shelter.[44]

ART IN PUBLIC PLACES

"The arts and humanities are not a luxury . . . they are the things that dreams are made of. . . . While a city's buildings and facilities constitute its structure, the arts and humanities constitute its soul," declared Mayor William E. Hanna Jr.[45] Under his leadership, the Mayor and Council established the Cultural Arts Commission in 1976 and the Humanities Commission in 1979. As with planning, beautification, civil rights, and human resources, the city shaped its active role in enhancing the physical environment of Rockville.

In 1978, Rockville created Art in Public Places (AIPP) to design works of art for specific sites in the city. The Cultural Arts Commission was charged with coordinating selection of sites, interaction with neighborhoods, selection of artists or artwork, and recommendations to the Mayor and Council for decisions. The city funded the program from two sources—by allocating one dollar per year per resident in the Capital Improvements Program budget and by assigning one percent of the construction cost of city buildings. By 1984, AIPP had produced thirteen pieces of art, the first being a sculpture by William Calfee in front of the Civic Center Auditorium. A favorite of many is the mural in the atrium of City Hall, completed in 1983 after the building was expanded. A total of twenty-nine works of art have been commissioned or purchased under AIPP between 1978 and 2000.[46]

Courtesy of City of Rockville

This abstract sculpture was the first purchase under AIPP. William Calfee, working with bronze, brass, and granite, created it for the front lawn of the Civic Center Theatre in view of Glenview Mansion.

Rockville expanded immensely between 1961 and 1984, adding nearly twenty thousand new residents and annexing three thousand acres of land. In the 1960s, Rockville overtook Cumberland and Hagerstown to become Maryland's second largest city. Besides enlarging City Hall and land area around the civic center, Rockville added a public swim center, golf course, senior center, and acres of parkland. With the addition of 226 employees, city staff grew by almost 300 percent between 1960 and 1980.[47]

In the context of increases in population, citizen needs, and government activity, the 1960 *Master Plan* provoked expansion of Rockville's park and recreation system by emphasizing the inadequacy of small playgrounds and parks and proposing an aggressive program to acquire land throughout the city.[48] With advice from Neil Ofsthun, director of recreation from 1960–72, and a fifteen-member Recreation and Park Advisory Board, the Mayor and Council purchased 102 acres in the first three years of the decade. Dedication of parkland as a component of development approval for a new neighborhood became standard procedure. Thus, Monroe Warren set aside roughly 15 percent of the land area in Woodley Gardens for public park land in the 1960s, and Kettler Brothers donated 5.5 acres in North Farm in the 1970s. By 1984, Rockville claimed 648 acres of green space in thirty-six parks.

Funding from federal and the state governments proved crucial to Rockville's recreation plans. Three separate grants, from 1963 to 1974, from the Federal Open Space Land Program, covered 30 percent of land costs for new green space in the city. Beginning in the early 1970s, Program Open Space, through the state, provided funds to purchase other parcels. When open space became an eligible activity of the Community Development Block Grant (CDBG) program in 1974, Rockville developed existing parks and playgrounds as well. Between 1963 and 1984, federal and state funds enabled the city to add playground equipment at Montrose, Welsh, and Lincoln Park; to build tennis courts and a picnic area at the Civic Center as well as shelters at Twinbrook and Woodley Gardens; to design bikeways near Rock Creek; and to improve facilities at Hillcrest, Lincoln Park, Maryvale, and Potomac Woods. Public money helped purchase land around the Rockville Academy, along Watts Branch (Wootton's Mill Park) west of the interstate, and in Woodley Gardens and Hungerford-Stoneridge. It helped buy the beautiful

Photo from *Sentinel* 1977, courtesy of Margaret Welsh May

Photo courtesy of Virginia Moser

TOP: Local attorney Barnard T. Welsh with his 1938 Packard. The Rockville Antique and Classic Car Show began as an event of the 1960 centennial, organized by Welsh in remembrance of such shows at the Lofstrand farm in the 1950s. In the early years, a line of cars wended their way through the streets of central Rockville before facing the judges' reviews on Glenview's lawn. Welsh wrote, "I have my theory. It is very simple. It is fun to drive a classic car." BOTTOM: Nancy Grosshans and Lee Norris in Rockville Little Theatre's 1984 production of Come Back, Little Sheba.

Shapiro tract on Rock Creek, near Glenview.[49] In 1965, Rockville took title to the 1815 Beall-Dawson House. The cost of $92,500 for the historic house and 1.5 acres fronting on West Montgomery Avenue came from Federal Open Space funds, a contribution from the Montgomery County Historical Society (which leased the house for programs and a museum), and city monies.[50]

Rockville families—with more leisure time to participate in recreation programs—demanded high quality services and were willing to support them with taxes. The number of neighborhood playgrounds supervised by the Recreation Department increased from thirteen in 1963 to seventeen in 1984. Playschool programs for four year olds operated at recreation centers for many years. By the 1980s, thousands of children and teens registered for classes and participated in summer and after-school programs. The city teamed with the Board of Education to open community schools after hours at Rock Terrace, Southlawn, and Twinbrook. Special events like the Easter egg hunt, Aprilfest, Memorial Day parade, Independence Day celebration, Summer in the Square, and the Antique and Classic Car Show continued to grow in spectator numbers and complexity. According to Director Ofsthun, special events took a lot of time and staff work, but they were significant "because they [gave] a community identity."[51]

Expanding its scope, the Recreation and Parks Department also nurtured the arts. The city upgraded the Civic Center Auditorium based on advice from Rockville Little Theatre (RLT, formed in 1947), Rockville Musical Theater (founded in 1974), and other user groups. Rockville Art League expanded membership with juried shows in the gallery at Glenview, youth art shows, a cooperative gallery, and scholarships. In 1966, the *City Newsletter* introduced a quarterly cultural arts calendar. June Allen, city supervisor in charge of performing arts, organized Street 70 with a talented group of fourteen to twenty-four year olds who performed throughout the city. RLT president John Moser formed the Arts Council of Rockville in 1965 to coordinate cultural activities and support local groups. For eight years, the Arts Council, with help from the city and local business, sponsored a Spring Arts Festival—a two-week extravaganza that combined local talent with outside names. Drama, music, and dance performances stimulated the public's appetite for the arts. The Arts Division of the Department of Recreation and Parks provided opportunities to showcase the city's Civic Ballet, Community Chorus, and Concert Band.

The Hanna administration also paid particular attention to senior citizens, an increasing percentage of Rockville's population. New senior clubs formed, and the city provided a bus that transported participants to social and recreational activities coordinated by the Recreation and Parks Department. The city's old Pump House on Horners Lane became a special gathering place for seniors, but the increased attendance soon sent coordinators looking for larger space. The opportunity arose when the school board closed Woodley Gardens Elementary School in 1979. The state matched Rockville's funds to convert the building into a senior citizens' activity center. When the Senior Center opened in 1982, it brought in programs from around the city. The Senior Citizens Commission and Rockville Seniors Inc., a nonprofit that raised funds for the center, sponsored activities of senior clubs, social agencies, service organizations, and a multitude of ongoing programs.

Sports programs expanded as city parks improved. Dogwood Park (near the old Poor Farm burial grounds), opened in 1968 as the city's largest developed playfield, and included lighted baseball and football fields, tennis and basketball courts, and areas for sledding, skiing, picnics, and a playground.[52] Sports teams and local businesses pitched in to add scoreboards and a concession stand. Through the 1960s and into the 1970s, the vast majority of sports were geared to boys. With Title IX of the Federal Educational Amendments Act of 1972, girls' soccer, softball, and basketball programs came into their own. By 1984, more than six thousand boys and girls participated in sports programs managed by more than five hundred volunteer coaches.

In the late 1960s, youngsters who participated in the early Rockville recreation programs were in their teens and playing sports at the city's only high school—Richard Montgomery. Under coach Roy Lester, the RM Rockets dominated high school football in the Washington metropolitan area for a decade. Saturday's football game was a community event, with thousands watching the game and the spectacular halftime shows choreographed by band director Kenneth Dahlin. The enthusiasm spawned the Rockville Football League. Rockets football teams compiled a 104-12-1 record from 1959 until 1970, with a state-record thirty-four-game winning streak, and nine county titles. Two noted alumni of Rockville programs were Gordy Coleman and Mike Curtis. Coleman (Richard Montgomery 1952) played first base for the Cincinnati Reds and averaged .273 at bat. Curtis (1961) led Richard Montgomery in baseball and football and later played linebacker for Duke University and the Baltimore Colts. The city's

TOP: RedGate Golf Course opened in 1974 as a par seventy-two, eighteen-hole municipal course.
BOTTOM: The Municipal Swim Center opened in 1968 in Welsh Park and is Rockville's most-used facility.

Courtesy of City of Rockville

Courtesy of City of Rockville

Courtesy of City of Rockville

Crews applying SmoothSeal, a resurfacing technique invented in 1959 by John Gray, director of Public Works, working with the Asphalt Institute. The formula is used throughout the world. Photo taken on Monroe Street in 1966.

growth led to the end of Richard Montgomery's reign, as Wootton and Rockville high schools drew from sports-minded areas of the city.[53] The field hockey team at Richard Montgomery, coached by Sissy Natoli with Rachel McGuckian as goalie, captured the state championship in 1984.[54]

Two new facilities rounded out the city's recreation program. The Municipal Swim Center opened in 1968 in Welsh Park with an Olympic-size outdoor pool and year-round indoor pool. Since then enlarged several times, it became Rockville's most-used facility. About this time, Director of Planning Robert Lanham proposed an innovative approach to develop the former Shaw and Nagle farm on Avery Road into a public golf course. After purchasing the 133-acre property from developer Milton Polinger, the city designed an eighteen-hole, par seventy-two golf course. Expenses for constructing RedGate Golf Course, which opened in 1974, were recouped by selling 34 excess acres for industrial and office use as the RedGate Industrial Park.

Reflecting the city's growth, numerous public buildings opened in Rockville during this period: seven new elementary and eight secondary schools, the Judicial Center, the Executive Office Building, four new fire stations, two public libraries (Rockville and Twinbrook), the Montgomery County Detention Center, and three post offices. Montgomery Junior College opened a Rockville campus in 1965. As the little 1939 station at Washington Street and Montgomery Avenue was overwhelmed, a new main post office was built at 500 North Washington Street in 1965. The Rockville Volunteer Fire Department relocated from its original station on South Perry Street into a new building on Hungerford Drive in 1966. The county created a Rockville fire tax district in the 1960s, for the first time combining volunteer and paid career personnel.

REVITALIZATION OF ROCKVILLE'S BUSINESS DISTRICT

The location, character, and configuration of Rockville's commercial district was set by 1830. By then shops, manufacturing establishments, hotels, and residences great and small had augmented the wayside taverns and crude stores of the 1770s. The original town grid of blocks, lots, and streets provided a central square for the county court and jail as well as some public space. The road from Frederick came south on Washington Street, turned east onto Montgomery Avenue, then ran the length of the main street to the rise at Saint Mary's Church, from which it continued south on the Rockville Turnpike into Georgetown and Washington, D.C. Because of the road, the business district developed in a linear fashion.

Thus established, the business district continued to evolve and mature. Between 1830 and 1940, around one hundred businesses opened and closed. Owners periodically updated the appearance of their buildings with larger storefront windows, a change of materials, or a new facade. Occasionally, a building was demolished and replaced with another of more modern design. Assemblage of land for construction projects, such as the gray courthouse or the Milo (later Villa Theatre) complex, wiped out sections of blocks and precipitated a reordering of Rockville's central core.

After World War II, East Montgomery Avenue merchants struggled to keep the patronage of the expanding residential population while the competition increased. Between 1951 and 1957, George R. Kimmel, a Washington attorney, built three strip shopping centers on the northwestern edge of the area, demolishing a number of old homes and businesses as well as much of the black settlement along Washington Street and Middle Lane. The new stores quickly filled with a combination of older establishments (such as Treasure Chest Jewelers and Transcolor Photo) and others new to Rockville (the Co-op Food Store, Woolworth's, and W. T. Grant's). Small commercial centers opened near new subdivisions around Rockville. Twinbrook families supported shopping centers on both sides of Veirs Mill Road. Safeway, G. C. Murphy, and People's Drug Store maintained stores in Twinbrook and in Rockville. Developers negotiated for newly rezoned commercial land in the triangle opened by construction of Hungerford Drive and down the Rockville Pike.

Congressional Plaza, which opened in 1959 with thirty-five stores, was the first regional shopping center to drain customers from downtown Rockville. Close by was Wheaton Plaza, with fifty stores. Silver Spring's business district had expanded considerably since the war, and new stores came to Friendship Heights. Montgomery Mall opened in 1968, and Gaithersburg Square opened in 1972. Common to these new centers, small or large, was the availability of less expensive land on which to build, plenty of adjacent parking for customers, and the ability to include a variety of retailers.[55]

Rockville's business district was only three blocks in length, but it shared problems with larger urban areas of the 1950s. Competition from modern shopping centers and department stores dealt a mighty blow. The old buildings, commercial and residential, had deteriorated to a point where those businesses that could move elsewhere did, and banks stopped lending money for improvements within the business district. Vagrants moved in, and small fires were common. Decline in tax revenues helped to perpetuate the cycle. Ownership—much of it absentee—was numerous and divided, reflecting the small parcels under the shops. Further, traffic had difficulty getting in and out of the city, as the century-old street pattern could not accommodate growth. Finally, parking in downtown Rockville was almost nonexistent.[56]

TOP: Warren Beatty, Jean Seberg, Peter Fonda, and Gene Hackman stirred up the town with the filming of Lilith *in 1963. Rockville residents snagged roles as extras, and Miss Lucy Smith, here with Beatty in a scene from the movie, played Beatty's grandmother. Parts of the movie were filmed in downtown Rockville and in Miss Lucy's home on Forest Avenue.*
BOTTOM: In September 1971, the new library on South Perry Street opened with a book collection of one hundred thousand volumes. The building was designed by Stanley H. Arthur and built by Gardiner and Van Epp.

Photo from the *Washington Star*, November 10, 1963, courtesy of Montgomery County Historical Society

Montgomery County Archives, Records of Facilities and Services Department

Courtesy of City of Rockville

Courtesy of City of Rockville

ABOVE AND NEXT PAGE: Within the Mid-City Urban Renewal Project area were 120 structures of all sizes, shapes, vintage, and architectural merit. Maryland National Bank, designed by E. Francis Baldwin in 1905 to grace the corner of South Perry Street and East Montgomery Avenue,was one of the most handsome. Other buildings had multiple facades applied through the years by merchants attempting to appear modern. Photos taken in April 1963.

The nature of businesses changed as office demand increased and archaic stores folded. Attorneys, title companies, bondsmen, and even the town offices moved out of aged structures on the main street into more modern quarters with better parking a few blocks away. At the end of the decade, attorneys David Betts, Robert Bullard, and R. Edwin Brown each constructed office buildings a block from the courthouse. After "Doc" Vinson retired in 1958, his old drugstore across from the courthouse was razed by Ida Goodman, a local landowner, and replaced with the streamlined Abby Building. The new buildings filled with lawyers moving into the county seat, and old-timers were displaced due to fire or poor conditions. IBM moved into modern offices on East Montgomery Avenue.

In the two decades preceding the 1960s, successive mayors and councils attempted to cope with the deteriorating business district. Many elected officials worked there. They listened to merchants' complaints and ideas, installed parking meters, enforced health and building codes, required adequate parking for new developments, sponsored cleanup days, purchased land for parking lots, supported special events and activities, and added police to smooth traffic flow and inhibit loitering. However, through these times, the public policy and practice of both old guard and reform officials contributed as much as economic circumstance to favor outlying development over revitalization of the Central Business District (CBD).

During Mayor Greene's first term in office, 1958–60, the reform council turned to the task of planning for future growth. Consultants produced the series of studies that led to the 1960 *Master Plan*, emphasizing the weakness of the center of town. *Master Plan Report No. 1*, published in August 1959, concluded that "Redevelopment of commercial enterprise in the CBD, with well-planned adequate parking, is justified due to present and future attraction to the center of the city of potential patrons who will combine business and/or employment with shopping trips."[57] Another expert, recognizing that new developments would include neighborhood shopping centers, proposed that the CBD function as a regional shopping center. "Since Rockville is the county seat of a highly favored sector of the Metropolitan fringe, rapid and prolonged county growth will bring unusual demands for increased space to accommodate governmental functions and numerous other public or quasi-public activities which tend to locate at the seat of government. . . ." The consultant also suggested that in the CBD, the city facilitate the grouping of related land uses into such categories as office, government, industrial, regional shopping, and several smaller commercial areas.[58]

Adoption of the city's first master plan in September 1960, based on the consultants' studies, set the stage for redeveloping Rockville's business district. In a spring 1959 survey, residents and merchants opined that Rockville needed more and better parking facilities, a large department store, and a higher class of restaurants serving dinner meals. People also wanted a modern pharmacy and supermarket. "The feeling was, that we had to do something to try to renovate the town, and renovation, gradually, the more you looked at it, the more you realized meant, rebuilding more. After all, this was a county seat of a very thriving county . . ." recalled Frank A. Ecker, elected to the city council in 1956.[59]

The phrase "urban renewal" entered Rockville's vocabulary in 1959. City officials in this period fully understood the newest ideas circulating in the field of municipal management. From the elected Mayor and Council to the staff, they were knowledgeable, youthful, worldly, and intent on bringing professionalism to their tasks at City Hall. Walter A. Scheiber, Rockville's first professional city manager, brought in other trained officials to direct the departments of Planning, Public Works, Finance, and Recreation. When Mayor Greene brought up the matter of an urban renewal committee in September 1959, the rest of the council requested further investigation and put the idea in line behind other pending projects.[60]

Courtesy of City of Rockville

Courtesy of City of Rockville

Urban renewal as a form of redevelopment was not a new concept. Baron Haussmann wiped out whole neighborhoods to remake Paris in the 1870s. World War II damage occasioned reconstruction of major sections of London, Warsaw, and other war-torn cities. The late 1950s saw redevelopment at the St. Louis waterfront, Baltimore's Charles Center, and in southwest Washington. Despite the protests of critic Jane Jacobs[61] and sociologist Herbert Gans that displacement of people and businesses and destruction of urban fabric would accomplish irrevocable harm, some eight hundred American cities opted for urban renewal. Between 1958 and 1963, with federal programs paying many of the bills, cities tackled aging waterfronts, slum housing, dirty industry, and outmoded commercial areas. They replaced them with new office buildings, hotels, luxury apartments, and swaths of highways.[62]

Initially, the Mayor and Council proposed redevelopment simply to solve the most egregious problem—lack of parking. Opening the Rockville Bypass (Hungerford Drive) in 1951 had lessened the volume of traffic through the business district, but parking downtown remained dreadful. The council looked at consolidating the back lots of stores into a parking area, but was frustrated by numerous parcels of land, most of which were under absentee ownership.[63] Further, in 1959 municipalities in Maryland only had power to condemn land for public use, not for a public purpose such as assembling land. It took three years to amend the Maryland constitution and obtain voter ratification and for the General Assembly to enact legislation giving Rockville and other cities the authority to enter into an urban renewal program.[64] The Maryland Municipal League, which met in Rockville in 1960, published an article suggesting how this new tool when accompanied by federal funds might be used to renew blighted areas.[65]

Power and knowledge in hand, in August 1961, Rockville took first steps toward dealing with the ramshackle commercial area. The Mayor and Council adopted a resolution that a blighted condition existed in Rockville and that some form of rehabilitation or redevelopment was necessary. It designated itself the responsible local public agency and requested a federal grant to develop a plan for a thirty-five-acre mid-city urban renewal project. By the end of the year, the city was awarded initial funds for survey and planning, had reorganized the Planning Department into the Department of Planning and Urban Renewal, had hired Peter L. Cheney as urban renewal coordinator, and had created a thirty-member Urban Renewal Advisory Council (as required by federal law).[66]

A new Mayor and Council took office in April 1962, prepared to follow in the path of its predecessors. The All-America City flag above City Hall reinforced the achievements of the Hovsepian and Greene administrations. Two newcomers, Edward J. Mack and L. Ross Roberts, joined the three incumbents, Frank A. Ecker, Achilles M. Tuchtan, and Ralph E. Williams. Ecker, the new mayor, had arrived in Twinbrook only nine years before, the year the wells went dry. Enlisted by his car pool as they drove to federal government jobs, he got his feet wet on the Citizens' Water Committee and helped

URBAN RENEWAL AT A GLANCE: 1960–1984

Project initiated: 1961, with City of Rockville application to federal government
Funded by: Urban Renewal Administration, U.S. Department of Housing & Urban Development; State of Maryland; Montgomery County government; Mayor and Council of Rockville; private sector developers
Acreage of project: 46.84 acres
Parcels of land bought by city: 96
Cost to purchase parcels: $8,955,683.50
Number of buildings demolished: 111
Conservation buildings: Red Brick Courthouse, Gray Courthouse, Farmers Bank, 50 Monroe Street, Brown building, 30 Court House Square, Woolworth building, Fire House, Kelly-Smith building, Oxley building (the last four were later razed)
Number of retail and office businesses relocated: 165
Number of families relocated: 52
Number of individuals relocated: 53
Net number of parking spaces added: 1,560 in Town Center garage
Architects involved: Donald M. Coupard, Robert L. Geddes, Arthur Cotton Moore, HOK
Total City of Rockville cash contribution: $12 million, to build parking garage 1969–71.[67]

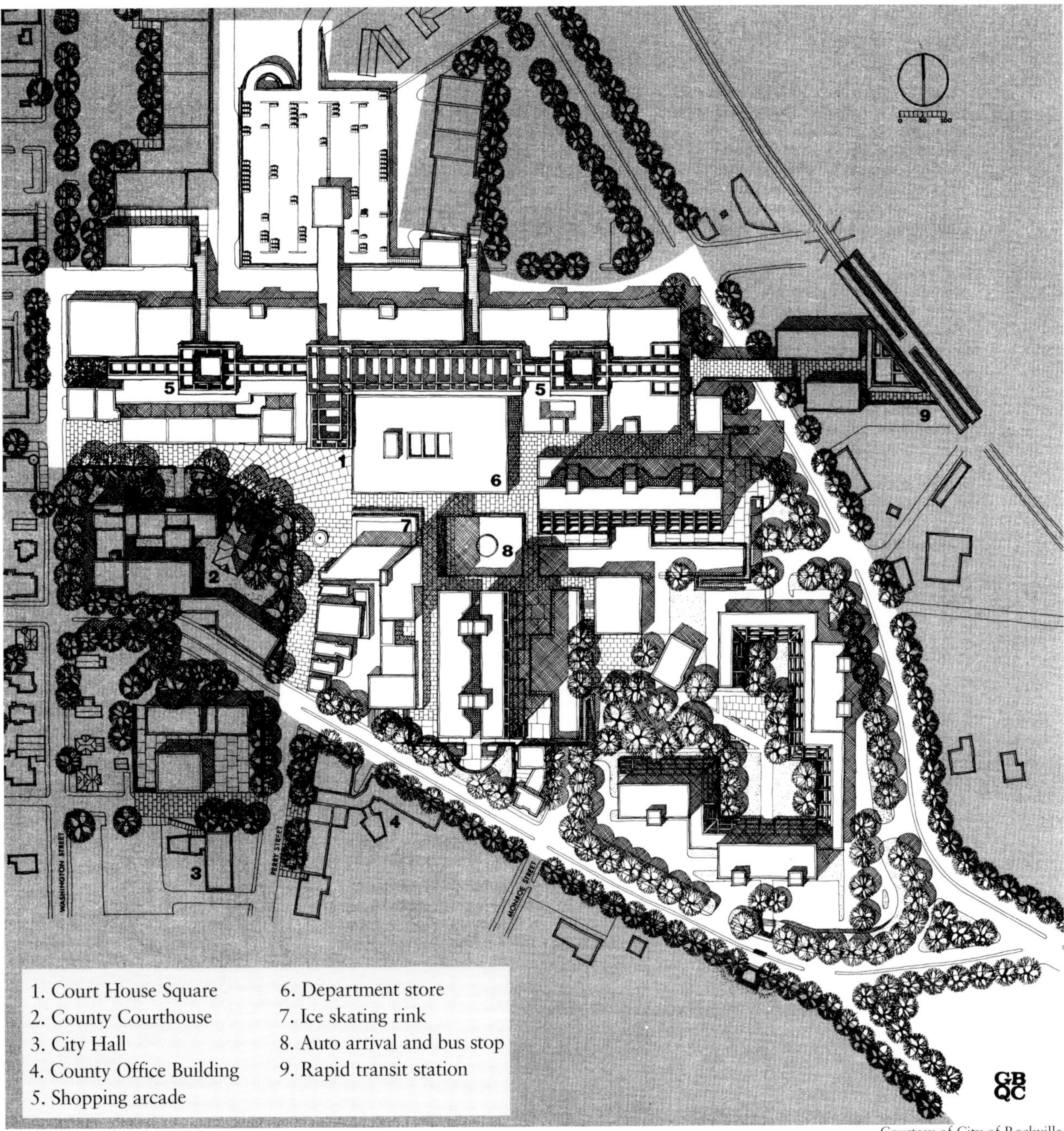

Courtesy of City of Rockville

Robert L. Geddes' design unified plans for retail, office, residential, government, and entertainment uses into a core area which he named the "Town Center." The federal government approved the Geddes plan, a revision of Rockville's original urban renewal submission, in 1968.

form both Rockville Citizens' Action Committee and its successor, Citizens for Good Government. Elected to the city council in 1956, Ecker served three terms before running for mayor. The new council elected in April of 1962 was ready to revitalize the old business district.

How best to accomplish revitalization was the challenge. The Urban Renewal Advisory Council, according to chairman Alex Greene, favored mixed

Roy Perry collection, courtesy of Peerless Rockville

Robert C. Braunberg photo, courtesy of Peerless Rockville

TOP: By 1967, roughly half of the old business district had been razed. This view shows buildings on the south side of East Montgomery Avenue still standing. BOTTOM: One of the last buildings to meet the wrecking ball was Steinberg's Department Store at 241 East Montgomery Avenue. By 1972, the Americana Apartments (in the background) neared completion.

use compatible with Rockville's continuing role as county seat. Drawing on what seemed important to Rockville, the group insisted on a resident population, aesthetic appeal, green space, entertainment and cultural uses, but shunned industry.[68] The city's role was limited to assembling parcels, then selling them to a private developer who would carry out approved plans. The city would retain control through design and use standards. The public investment would be returned through sale of the land and through future increase of the tax base. The picture sharpened later in 1962 when a land utilization and marketability study suggested two alternatives. Both included a mix of apartment, office, and retail uses; one featured retail development centered about a department store and fewer apartments. [69]

City officials unveiled preliminary plans at a public information meeting on November 27, 1962. A model showed the new street pattern, conservation buildings, and location of proposed new uses such as department stores, parking garage, retail shops, high-rise apartments, a theater, and fire station. Beyond a few conservation buildings, little suggestion of the concept of rejuvenating the old buildings or retaining the traditional commercial center remained. The plan proposed a "city of the future that would wipe out the tired heart of Rockville and transform it into a pulsing commercial and high rise apartment center, peopled daily by thousands of bustling shoppers and workers," wrote a *Sentinel* reporter, adding "the plan of the long-awaited urban renewal proposal would, if carried out, literally destroy most of the present downtown area over a five-year period."[70]

If elections measured public opinion, these actions were generally acceptable in Rockville. A light turnout of voters handily reelected Mayor Greene and a combination of incumbents and new candidates in 1960. "CGG can justifiably interpret the election outcome as a voter compliment and take a bow," the *Sentinel* editorialized.[71] The only issue raised during the campaign was whether Rockville needed more apartments. Presidents of the Chamber of Commerce voiced support for urban renewal numerous times, and the Rockville Jaycees endorsed the project.[72] Two years later, the Jaycees conducted a survey of citizen views on the benefits and needs of the city. Most of the 634 respondents knew about the urban renewal program, but had not thought much about it. They wished to see stores, public institutions, office buildings, and public parking in the old commercial area. Additional comments ranged from "Downtown Urban Renewal—The sooner the better" to "If Rockville needs improvement It should be done by local people and by Local Law not by Uncle Sam."[73]

A few voices emerged in the mid-1960s in opposition. Most vocal were a businessman, Richard R. Haight, and a reporter, Lila Thomson. Haight worked at Watkins Appliance, a company that sold and serviced appliances and televisions. A. G. Watkins, who began the business in 1921, built a two-story brick store at 400 East Montgomery Avenue, on the corner of Bridge Street. Accompanied by M. Thomas Lawrey, a federal employee who lived in Twinbrook, Haight protested what he perceived as destruction of the heart and soul of Rockville. The city council appointed both men to the Urban Renewal Advisory Council, but they, and other members, complained that city officials convened them infrequently and told them little.[74]

"Under the grandiose scheme for turning this historic town into an unrecognizable satellite of Metropolitan Washington . . . the old business community with its once-pleasant streets and small stores is neither revitalized nor renewed. It disappears and 'urban renewal' becomes urban replacement. . . ." Lila Thomson, writing for the *Maryland Monitor* from her desk in the Abby Building, described how A. G. Watkins's widow didn't want to sell but was too tired to fight any longer. Thomson, who had run unsuccessfully for city council, attempted to represent "all the fine, good [business] people who've been prospering through hard work long before those who start the bulldozers were even born."[75]

The Pizza Oven, a popular local eatery in the business district, engaged a local cartoonist to draw a mural jabbing at urban renewal. In the drawing, Mayors Ecker, Greene, and Tuchtan drove bulldozers, the theater marquee showed "This Property is Condemned," and the Confederate statue observed, "I told General Lee we could destroy Rockville."[76]

Just as Rockville's downtown business district had formed in layers through generations of use, so too did the revitalization planning effort peel back in layers. Assembling land for parking led to purchase of parcels, enabling the city to clear dilapidated structures and to plan on a larger scale. Deciding to feature department stores precluded basic rehabilitation of traditional main street shops. Enlarging the vision permitted projection of future needs, such as county government expansion and auxiliary office uses, and reconfiguration of retail and residential buildings. Through discussions, meetings, negotiations, and planning

TOP: Court House Square pedestrian entrance to Rockville Mall, with fountain in foreground.
BOTTOM: The Confederate soldier stood guard over construction of the Rockville Mall in the early 1970s. The city relocated the statue—still facing south—in 1971 to the lawn of the Red Brick Courthouse.

Roy Perry photo, courtesy of Peerless Rockville

Roy Perry photo, courtesy of Peerless Rockville

Courtesy of City of Rockville

Looking east on Jefferson Street, circa 1978. In the distance are 51 Monroe Street and the Americana Apartments.

sessions, public officials and private citizens perceived a once-in-a-lifetime opportunity to recast the center of Rockville. As more store windows became vacant, Rockvillians increasingly believed that nothing less than complete revitalization would work.

At each turn, the project became more complicated. To improve access to the CBD, the snarled intersection of Hungerford Drive, Rockville Pike, and Veirs Mill Road had to be revamped. In place of East Montgomery Avenue, East Jefferson Street would be extended. The state had to approve the changes, then plan and fund them. The largest public user in the urban renewal area—Montgomery County—had to endorse concepts and locations. The mix of office, commercial, and residential uses had to be refined. A new street system had to be developed to correlate with the proposed land use pattern. The federal government, although supportive from the start, choked the project with paper requirements and approval procedures. Each time the city revised plans or boundaries, the process returned almost to the beginning.

Through 1963 and 1964, Rockville staff inspected every building in the designated area and interviewed all property owners and tenants. Real estate appraisers valued every parcel except those designated for conservation, and the first property in the urban renewal area was placed under contract. Road crews realigned Jefferson Street from behind the courthouses to the Pike. At the public hearing on March 17, 1964, merchants requested priority in purchasing land in the urban renewal area. In July, the federal Urban Renewal Administration approved the plans and authorized Rockville to proceed, drawing on federal funds for 75 percent of the total cost. In September, the city bought the first parcel of land and issued the first tax-exempt bond for the project. Before long Rockville found itself managing properties it had purchased and trying to relocate businesses, families, and offices from the area.

Mayor Ecker hurled the first stone on May 13, 1965, to ceremoniously start demolition. Ace Wrecking finished off Bogley's Real Estate building at 332 East Montgomery Avenue, then went on to bulldoze four others on Commerce Lane, East Jefferson, Bridge, and Fayette Streets. Public reaction ran the gamut from elation to apathy to sadness, but the destruction brought home the reality of the future. Months later, the Washington-based Lansburgh's Department Store agreed to locate in the mall, the company's first foray into suburbia. Purchases, relocations, boarding up, and demolitions continued. Two dozen stores went out of business. The city began to condemn properties whose owners refused to sell. While most cases settled out of court, a few dragged on for years.

In 1965, Robert L. Geddes, a Philadelphia architect and dean of architecture at Princeton, fixed his imprint on the Mid-City Urban Renewal Project. Rockville hired him as the design consultant to shape the basic functional concepts worked out by city staff into an integrated plan. So dramatic were the revisions that they had to go to public hearing and then to the Urban Renewal Administration for approval, which came in 1968. Geddes introduced to Rockville the term "Town Center"—a core area having a unified design for government, shopping, entertainment, employment, and living. In the plan, Geddes compacted the retail area into an enclosed shopping mall. East Montgomery Avenue was eliminated. Cars and people were separated at different levels, and a three-level parking facility served the

Painting by Connie Ward Woolard

commercial and office area. Town houses or garden apartments nestled among the high-rise towers. Court House Square was the focal point of the plan, kept familiar only by the Red Brick Courthouse, after the Montgomery County Council reversed its decision to raze it. Optimism abounded for, as one architectural critic declared, "you will never quite know where the old ends and the renewed area begins."[77]

On Valentine's Day 1972, a crowd gathered to dedicate Rockville Mall, hear music and speeches, and then wander through ten acres of new retail space built by Taylor Woodrow Blitman, also known as Rockville Redevelopment Associates, of New York. The shopping mall had become the highest priority when developers balked at building apartments. Only the city-owned 1,560-space parking garage and three stores were open—Lansburgh's, Tie Bar, and General Nutrition Health Foods. It had been eight years since the Mayor and Council had contracted to sell the property, five and a half years since the Geddes plan was unveiled. Money had been tight and mortgage rates high. The city had been praised by architecture critics and berated by developers for insisting on high design standards. The mall had cost Rockville Redevelopment Associates eight million dollars. Meanwhile,

Courtesy of Roald Schrack

TOP: Arthur Cotton Moore hoped to bring a sense of place to the Town Center with frequent events around the Red Brick Courthouse, pedestrian-friendly street architecture such as the arcade and gazebo shown here, and other design strategies. BOTTOM: View of Court House Square in 1980, looking east where construction had begun on the Judicial Center and Executive Office Building.

Washington Metropolitan Area Transit Authority photo by Paul Myatt, November 30, 1983

TOP: Aerial of east end of Town Center, a year before Metrorail service began.

Montgomery Mall had opened, White Flint was under construction, and Lake Forest was being planned, with popular department store tenants such as Woodward and Lothrop and Garfinkles. Several Rockville merchants had built freestanding stores on Hungerford Drive. The City of Rockville had begun a second urban renewal project near Montgomery Junior College on Route 355. The reworked intersection at the east end of the Mid-City Urban Renewal Project, where Veirs Mill Road, the Pike, Jefferson Street, and Hungerford Drive came together, had promptly been dubbed "the mixing bowl" and "malfunction junction" when it opened in 1969.

With the mall in place, the planned Town Center began to take shape. That spring, Roy's Place and Steinberg's store fell to the wrecking ball. Soon the first high-rise apartment building of Americana Center opened. Built by Carl M. Freeman Associates, monthly rentals started at $185. Town Center Associates bought land east of the mall and in 1976 opened 51 Monroe Street. The 210,000 square foot high-rise known as the Unibank (later GBS) building at 210 feet was the tallest in the Town Center. In keeping with Geddes design standards, a plaza pedestrian level separated people from the cars below. To celebrate the American bicentennial, the city carved a minipark from Court House Square, complete with the town clock, landscaping, and benches. The Confederate statue found a new home on the courthouse grounds when the public triangle vanished. In 1978, elderly and handicapped senior citizens moved into the federally subsidized Town Center Apartments on Monroe Street.

The mall had a life of its own. More stores opened, and two years later thirty-three were in business.

METRO COMES TO TOWN

On December 15, 1984, hundreds of people gathered at the Rockville Metro Station to attend the ceremonial opening of the Red Line extension between Grosvenor and Shady Grove. Before gleefully stepping into a subway car in Rockville for the first time, they noticed that the architecture of Rockville's station differed from others on the line. Its straight lines echoed the Gothic style of the 1873 B&O Railroad Station nearby. Michael B. Patterson, an architect and member of the Historic District Commission, had insisted that the new construction reflect a place special to Rockville.

Rockville, the fiercely independent municipality, had carefully monitored Metro plans for two decades. City officials and staff had gone head-to-head with WMATA (Washington Metropolitan Area Transit Authority) on a variety of issues such as the location of stations within Rockville boundaries, removal of the terminal station and service and inspection yards north of the city, linkage to the Town Center, impacts on adjacent properties and neighborhoods, closure of Frederick Avenue into Lincoln Park, and parking.

Rescue of the historic B&O Railroad Station caught the imagination of Rockville and the county. Originally slated for demolition because it was too small for Metro use and too large for continued B&O operations, the station found a champion in the city's new historic preservation movement. Rockville's Historic District Commission, created in 1966 when Saint Mary's chapel was almost lost, convinced the Mayor and Council to designate three historic districts in 1974. Sensing the need for additional protection for both West Montgomery Avenue and the B&O Station area, it also wrote nominations for the National Register of Historic Places. Peerless Rockville, a historic preservation nonprofit group formed in 1974 in reaction to the city's disappearing history, jumped in with more spunk than resources. Peerless and the city convinced WMATA to relocate the station out of harm's way and sell it to a sympathetic owner just before the first subway train arrived.

Photo by John Spano won children's color category in a contest sponsored by Peerless Rockville

Courtesy of City of Rockville

TOP: In March 1981, building mover William Patram hoisted all four hundred tons of the B&O Railroad Station on a scaffold atop airplane wheels and moved it from harm's way.
BOTTOM: Metrorail's opening in 1984 provided yet another connection for Rockville with Washington, D.C.

Courtesy of Helen Heneghan

The Raise the Flag project entailed installation of an eighty-foot-tall pole to fly the United States flag in Rockville twenty-four hours a day. City Clerk Helen Heneghan and American Legion Post 86 raised funds to beautify a major entrance to the city. On July 4, 1984, the champion color guard unit ceremoniously unfurled the huge flag in F. Scott Fitzgerald Park (now Veterans Park).

Unfortunately, in the spring of 1973 Lansburgh's declared bankruptcy. Lit Brothers of Philadelphia took over the department store, then was replaced by Sloane's Furniture Store. Rockville Redevelopment Associates, the mall owners, repeatedly took merchants to court for unpaid rent. Disgruntled tenants filed suit in return. RRA was chronically late or in default of rent or mortgage payments to the city.

Having so much invested in urban renewal, the public sector attempted to help it succeed. From the beginning, patrons complained that the garage was too dark, leading the city to counter that the facility had over twenty-five hundred lights and was one of the best-lit garages in the country. Still, the mall appeared unfriendly, and no one felt safe. The city added a fountain sculpture to the courtyard in 1974, at a cost of forty-five thousand dollars. It tried, unsuccessfully, to help RRA to locate tenants and particularly the proposed second department store to anchor the west end of the mall. The county and the city leased office space, as did the Social Security Administration, to assist the owners and also to ease crowding at the County Office Building and City Hall. A special ramp from Route 355 to usher cars directly into the garage was built to aid access. The city commissioned study after study that indicated a bright economic future for the Town Center, and published special newsletters to maintain interest in the project.[78]

The late 1970s and early 1980s brought even tougher times to Rockville Mall. An attempt by Robert Gring, the new manager, to change the mall's image by changing its name to the Commons at Court House Square brought little notice. An indoor tennis facility appeared where the second department store had not. Rockville Redevelopment Associates, after twice amending its agreement with the city, defaulted in 1979. As a result, the city closed access to the mall from the garage. Meanwhile, new buildings had arisen around the Town Center. Some were in the triangle formed by Hungerford Drive, Washington Street, and Middle Lane, and others were on the Rockville Pike and Jefferson Street.

Hope bloomed for the Town Center when the Mayor and Council brought in Arthur Cotton Moore. A Washington architect nationally recognized for urban revitalization projects, Moore set up an office in Rockville from which to create an urban design plan that the city hoped would jump-start the sagging project. From late 1978 through 1979 citizen committees, merchants, city staff, and officials sprang into action, meeting and producing ideas and papers. Moore presented his initial findings with a slide of North Washington Street and a dare: "Find a single blade of grass in this picture!" Out of this came the *Town Center Urban Design Plan,* adopted by the Mayor and Council in December 1979. Rockville emerged from the brief association with imaginative ideas to bring activity downtown—a farmers market, an arts center, a hotel and conference center in place of the second department store, a dinner theatre in the Red Brick Courthouse, and a rubber-wheeled trolley for workers and shoppers.[79] By 1982, Moore's hand was evident in Court House Square, with historic-style street lights, a gazebo and covered arcade, ornamental trees, and benches. But no trolley.

Rockville officials continually revised plans to match those of other jurisdictions. Montgomery County's original grandiose ideas in the Town Center pared down to a new county office building and a new circuit court, with 475 parking spaces, all opening in 1982. As at times since 1776, Rockville officials harbored concerns about the impact of additional county facilities but welcomed people who would eat and shop downtown. Of equal impact was the Metrorail system, which originally planned for Rockville to be the terminus of the line from D.C. into central Montgomery County. It took years for the city to convince WMATA to extend the line from Rockville to Shady Grove and to locate the service and inspection yards there. Rockville was concerned about traffic congestion, parking, and additional industrial use so close to the Town Center.[80]

New hope arrived in 1983. Eisinger/Kilbane, a local developer, agreed to put millions into converting the failed mall to Rockville Metro Center. Eisinger planned to turn the east end into office space, a fitness center, and specialty retail space. Then he would demolish the interior of the mall and redesign the space for restaurants and movies, expand the parking, and develop additional office and retail space. Cutting the mall into visually manageable sections was a key feature. Construction work began in June 1984.

By 1984, the Mid-City Urban Renewal Project had evolved considerably from the original concept. Starting in 1959, the city had developed and revised plans, assembled land and sold parcels off for specific developments, established design and use standards, demolished hundreds of buildings, and completely altered the street system. After twenty-five years, in place of a ramshackle business district, Rockville had a half-empty shopping mall, a new Judicial Center and Executive Office Building, an ice-skating rink, a link to the Metro rapid-rail system, and a newly redesigned brick pedestrian central square. By default rather than choice, it owned a leaking parking garage and land to sell to a willing and, ideally, a qualified developer. Dreams of a major department store were long forgotten. Urban renewal had served as a catalyst for private construction in and near the Town Center—on Hungerford Drive, Rockville Pike, and Southlawn Drive—but no one ventured to whisper "success" for Rockville's central business district.[81]

Photo by Dean Evangelista

Chapter Nine
ROCKVILLE AS A STATE OF MIND
1985–2000

"What does the All-America town do when it grows up? Rockville, . . . hasn't found all the answers yet, . . . since the post–World War II housing boom transformed a sleepy, rural, essentially southern town into Maryland's second-largest city, Rockville has been on an odyssey in search of its new identity. Ask residents whether they live in a small town or a large one, and most will say emphatically that Rockville is both."[1]

A Maine resident, returning to Rockville in 1995 for a class reunion, retraced his steps of nearly fifty years before. Ambling from Rock Creek to his childhood Rockcrest home, to the high school and elementary school, to the old courthouse where his mother was a clerk, to the railroad station by way of Saint Mary's Cemetery, he appreciated how Rip Van Winkle must have felt. His landmark buildings were gone, and the streets were confusing. His, and many of his classmates', estrangement from the *new* Rockville could not lessen his emotional attachment to the small town that resided in his memory.[2]

It wasn't difficult for former residents to become confused about Rockville in the 1980s. Youngsters who knew all the shortcuts to the candy counters at Seen Beane's and Vinson's lost their way amidst new street patterns. Their play fields had been transformed into neat subdivisions. New tall buildings lacked distinction. Downtown, the faltering mall looked forlorn, especially in contrast to the vibrant congestion of the Rockville Pike. Yet, the old neighborhoods had aged well, recent communities were settling in, and the courthouse tower and church steeples still pierced the skyline.

Each wave of newcomers—whether participants in the big changes of the 1950s, 1960s, and 1970s or not—ultimately found themselves charmed by Rockville. The increasing urbanity of one of America's richest counties never totally overwhelmed the sleepy town. Despite the expansive urban visions and detailed master plans, to its residents and boosters Rockville remained a town small enough to meet friends and to walk from end to end on a sunny day. Still, in the final decades of the twentieth century, maintaining Rockville's identity required considerable vigilance.

TOWN CENTER, 1985–2000

It did not take long for official Rockville and the general public to question their exuberance in wiping out the old center of town. By the 1980s commercial development on the Rockville Pike, exceeding expectations, preempted many of the plans for Town Center. Most citizens found it easier to avoid downtown's woes and turn instead to neighborhood improvement. Others became involved in citywide organizations that reflected their interests. Some reacted to the physical loss by putting their energies into protecting the city's remaining historic resources. Elected officials had no choice but to wrestle with the same issues of land use, viable development, county government accommodation, and downtown parking as their predecessors. Every two years elected

Photo by Charles Carroccio

Photo by Dean Evangelista

TOP: Construction of the block next to the Judicial Center, 1997. The new block included thirteen theaters beneath a reconstructed Montgomery Avenue, with a two-story row of retail and restaurant space. BOTTOM: Developer Eisinger/Kilbane planned to rework the mall in two phases. Phase one, which physically opened the mall with a street and brought in popular attractions, gave rise to optimism in the mid-1980s.

officials took office promising, and fully expecting, to make something happen.

In 1983, Eisinger/Kilbane (E/K), the third developer in whom Rockville placed its hopes for rejuvenating the mall, promised a solution to the continued misfires. Following in the optimistic aftermath of Arthur Cotton Moore's vision (codified in 1979 as the *Town Center Urban Design Plan*)—tempered with failure of interim developers (New Rockville Town Center Partners and Hadid Investment Group) to build a hotel—E/K signed agreements with the city and financial backers. Renaming the project Rockville Metro Center, the company split the mall structure in half, opened a through street, and reworked the old parking garage. Tenants moved into new offices surrounding a spacious atrium, convenient to all public functions in the county seat and a block from Metro. Rockville residents joined the new health and fitness center, ate at the popular Hagan's Four Courts restaurant, enjoyed the Potomac polo mural (featuring local faces), and flocked to the ten-screen United Artists theater complex. They awaited E/K's Phase Two, which would bring more eateries, a regional art center, and retail and office uses into the former mall space.

Unfortunately, by the late 1980s the economy faltered, and Eisinger/Kilbane ran out of resources. In 1990, Marine Midland Bank (from whom the developer had borrowed funds) and the City of Rockville notified E/K of default and initiated foreclosure proceedings. After E/K went bankrupt, the city again found itself saddled with a deteriorating garage beneath an enormous commercial development with a reputation for failure. During the lengthy court proceedings, city officials led Town Center roundtable discussions and emphasized the few positive statements that an outside public relations study could muster.

Rockville Center Incorporated (RCI) entered the scene in the early 1990s. It was a subsidiary of Marine Midland, the bank which had purchased Rockville Metro Center for fifteen million dollars at the foreclosure auction. Signing interim agreements in 1991 and 1992, the Mayor and Council acknowledged the reality of three decades of good intentions, grandiose planning, and disappointing results. Flexible goals, driven by the market, became the new rule. A new street grid, suggestive of Rockville's past configuration, would return a welcoming environment with wide sidewalks, on-street parking, and street-level retail. RCI was to pay for more than half of the infrastructure construction and provide one thousand additional parking spaces as development proceeded. RCI planned one and a half million square feet of dense mixed-use development, spread over five city blocks. Schematics showed three office towers, retail shops, theaters, restaurants, and a complex of high-rise apartments or condominiums. Construction schedule and timing would be governed by the market, but RCI projected completion in about ten years.

The Mayor and Council took the city-RCI plan to the people in early 1993, then began to distribute "Rockville Mall—Tear it Down" buttons. The city voted to donate the garage and six million dollars to build new streets, install sidewalks and on-street parking, and build a new, beautiful Courthouse Square Park. In July, after the county and state each had pledged six million dollars to match Rockville's contribution, RCI and Rockville signed a final agreement. RCI would redevelop eight critical acres in the center of Rockville.[3]

No one took greater glee in striking the first sledgehammer blow at Rockville Mall on October 25, 1993, than Mayor Douglas M. Duncan. As city councilman and then mayor 1985–93, he believed the mall had become the major roadblock to restoring economic vitality to downtown. "It was bad karma," he said, ". . . a symbol of failure."[4] Growing up in Twinbrook in the

TOP: Courthouse Square Park is a pleasant, usable public space in the center of Rockville. Brick sidewalks, fieldstone walls, landscaping, and a fountain harmonize with historic and modern backdrops.
BOTTOM: Montgomery County Register of Wills Patricia Dauenhauer posed in front of the judge's bench in the restored grand courtroom of the Red Brick Courthouse, 1996.

Photo by Dean Evangelista

Photo by Dean Evangelista, courtesy of Peerless Rockville

1960s, he recalled Saturday movies at the Villa Theatre and the friendliness of the old downtown with its small shops. Duncan had pushed hard for city, state, and county funding to support RCI's bold redevelopment plan. Now, as he was leaving the mayor's office, his efforts appeared to be paying off.

A flurry of action followed. Using public funds, RCI moved quickly to construct East Montgomery Avenue, Monroe Street, and Maryland Avenue, Courthouse Square Park, and a pedestrian bridge connecting 255 Rockville Pike (Metro Center) to 51 Monroe Street. Reopening the street grid returned a sense of familiarity to the old downtown and visually connected sections of the business district formerly separated by the mall structure.[5] RCI, taken over by Essex Capital Partners of New York, celebrated the long-awaited opening of Regal Cinemas' thirteen-screen theater complex in November of 1998. A few local eateries located nearby, showing promise for a goal repeatedly set for the Town Center—life after 5:00 P.M.

In July of 1997, the Mayor and Council dedicated the Spirit of Rockville fountain in Courthouse Square Park at the front of the Red Brick Courthouse. The Cultural Arts Commission had conducted a nationwide search and selected the artist, Dan Davidson, for a major piece of art in the Town Center. Inside the historic courthouse, in a public-private restoration effort, Peerless Rockville put finishing touches on the grand courtroom. No longer a three-acre void, Court House Square once again bustled with pedestrian and vehicular traffic.

The millennium year—when Rockville's Town Center appeared less desolate than it had for some time—provided an opportunity to reflect on the failure of urban revitalization that had consumed the city for four decades. For many years, urban renewal appeared to be the solution, but in retrospect few

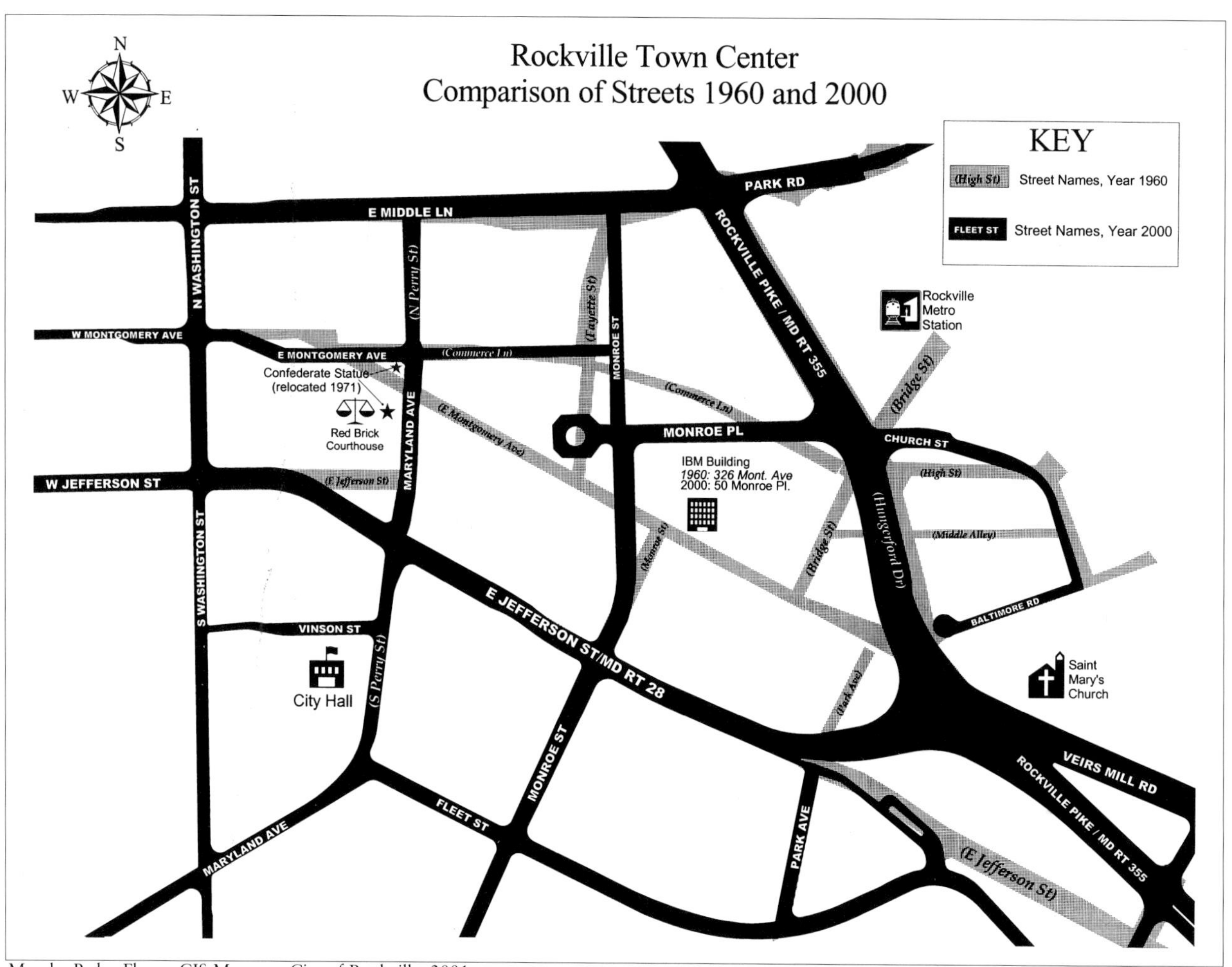

Map by Pedro Flores, GIS Manager, City of Rockville, 2001

Courtesy of City of Rockville

Aerial indicates landmarks in downtown Rockville, 1990. "SITE" refers to future location of the Victoria condominium complex.

said they would again select that route for Rockville. Each of the past and present mayors who gathered in City Hall to unveil an exhibit in 1988, Mayor Duncan recalled, expressed his or her frustration with the revitalization effort. From Alexander J. Greene (mayor 1958–62) to Rose G. Krasnow (mayor 1995–2001), a succession of city leaders, pressed by biennial elections, had attended to specific problems at hand but never succeeded in returning heart and soul to the downtown area.

Frank A. Ecker (mayor 1962–68) observed that "one is always smarter in retrospect."[6] Hindsight permits an attempt to understand what happened and to learn from the past. On paper, the early concept of a regional mall seemed sound, but federal requirements stretched out the process of assembling land. Arthur Cotton Moore in the 1970s strengthened Robert Geddes' design with refinements that better melded old and new. Thirty years of mall failure, partly due to the city's selection of developers, perpetuated a downward spiral for the entire urban renewal project. One city staffer involved in the Town Center for thirty-five years viewed it as a combination of bad luck and poor timing.[7] William E. Hanna Jr. (mayor 1974–82) declared that Rockville had survived and prospered in spite of, and without benefit of, its central business district. The community was healthfully balanced in terms of housing, income levels, and employment opportunities, and had developed into a center for research and technology, Hanna said.[8]

The original concept of a regional mall was obsolete by the time Rockville was ready to implement urban renewal. The Mid-City Urban Renewal Project became more complicated and took much longer than initially envisioned. Dependence upon federal funds tied the city in red tape. Assembling ninety-six parcels of land required almost a decade. All purchases had to be negotiated, some properties had to be condemned, and for each parcel the federal government required two

Courtesy of City of Rockville

Courtesy of City of Rockville

Photo by Dean Evangelista, courtesy of Peerless Rockville

TOP: Runners gather in Court House Square to compare times in the Rockville Rotary Twilight Runfest. The annual run and street festival raises funds to benefit local charities. BOTTOM: Cambridge Heights townhouses were built 1989–91 on a hillside above Watts Branch.

appraisals. In an era when thousands of new shopping centers opened in the United States each year, developers wouldn't wait for the city to package downtown Rockville. As central cities declined, suburban shopping malls took their place as *new downtowns* with commercial, social, and leisure space in weather-protected, safe, clean environments.[9] Between 1961 and 2000, fourteen regional shopping centers opened in outlying Washington, D.C., suburbs. Residential developers built small neighborhood commercial strips. At the same time, through market trends and public policies that competed with Town Center plans, the Rockville Pike became the "Golden Mile."[9]

Public perception also played a major role in the failure of Rockville Mall, which in turn dogged the entire project, including its residential and office components, for two decades. While city officials viewed it as the centerpiece of urban renewal, the mall was uninviting for shoppers who were unwilling to pay for the dark, confusing parking accommodations. People avoided it for the open spaces of the Rockville Pike. The mall's Brutalist style of architecture repelled shoppers. Wags joked about "Fortress Rockville," a mausoleum "where businesses go to die." Developers may have failed because of underfunding or inexperience, but none solved the basic weaknesses of the concept, nor did the city convince them to provide more than "band-aid" solutions. City officials spurned office space in favor of a hotel and conference center to bolster the project. John R. Freeland (mayor, 1982–84) believed the concept failed because chains and developers were not interested in building major hotels next to failing malls. However, even as the mall became the symbol of failure in the 1980s, a succession of developers and city officials insisted on working with the existing structure. Urban renewal from 1960 to 2000 consumed the attention of eleven mayors, five developers, fourteen directors of planning, and managers of almost two dozen city political campaigns. Mayor Duncan called it "The Mall that Ate Rockville."[10]

Urban renewal did produce some positive outcomes. It served as a catalyst for private construction in and near the Town Center, for commercial areas on North Washington Street and the Rockville Pike, residential areas such as Courthouse Walk, and cultural attractions such as Rockville Arts Place. In 1991, when Rockville developers C. M. and James Whalen constructed the Victoria, a mixed-use brick complex fronting on Court House Square, the condominiums brought the first influx of residents into the Town Center since the 1970s. Project architect Barry Dunn, formerly with Arthur Cotton Moore, designed the commercial lower stories of the Victoria to reflect the streetscape lost to urban renewal and to complement the Red Brick Courthouse, employing strong urban design standards developed by the city.

Other benefits accrued. For some merchants urban renewal provided an excuse to close a lingering business or an opportunity to move to a better location. Automobile dealers relocated farther upcounty, into more visible and spacious locations. Downtown residents moved out of a substandard environment into better housing elsewhere. Montgomery County government and the courts constructed needed working space in their traditional central location, bringing more people into town. Demolition of so many old buildings caused nostalgic Rockvillians to unite with newcomers to form Peerless Rockville to preserve local historic places.

By the mid-1990s, Rockville enjoyed some positive publicity and optimism, with headlines such as "A Town Center Revival" and "Rockville's Steep Climb Back Up the Pike."[11] By that time, both the farmers' market and Rockville Arts Place had made their mark on Middle Lane. The seasonal market, sponsored by the city, attracted an average of fifteen hundred people per week, local residents on Saturdays and office workers on Wednesdays. Rockville Arts Place brought artistic talent and metropolitan area art interest into downtown Rockville. Originally in free space in Rockville Mall, the nonprofit organization moved into more lively gallery and studio space in the basement of a 1950s strip shopping center.

The major issue that initially led the Mayor and Council to redevelop the center of Rockville has never been resolved. Parking in the downtown area had been scarce since the 1940s. The scramble for spaces among county and courthouse workers, visitors to public and private offices, and commercial patrons only exacerbated the problem, with no one

Roy Perry photo, courtesy of Peerless Rockville

Courtesy of Gary Funkhouser

TOP: Timeless scene in Rockville.
BOTTOM: In August 2000, current and former neighbors gathered at the home of Charlene and David Janes in Rockcrest for Clagett Drive's fiftieth anniversary picnic.

Roy Perry photo, courtesy of Peerless Rockville

West Montgomery Avenue Historic District, looking east from Wall Street, 1970s. Enhancing the historic district today are period street lamps and brick sidewalks laid in a herringbone pattern specified by the Mayor and Council in 1888.

providing realistic solutions other than a confusing underground garage. Metrorail proved almost counterproductive in relieving parking problems. In 1997 the city, attempting to attract development within Metro proximity and to promote mass transit use, permitted builders to request a reduction of up to 40 percent in the parking requirement. But, as construction continued in areas used for temporary surface parking, spaces became more restricted, and demand grew.

For more than forty years, Rockville has been forced to rethink the role of its Town Center. Just as the regional shopping center concept of the suburban-thinking 1960s lost its appropriateness, so too other needs changed. Certainly, the county underestimated its needs for court, office, and parking space. Perhaps, as the *Gazette* editorialized in 1990, "the Town Center will never be the throbbing heart of the city that city fathers have so long wanted it to be. . . . It cannot be all things to all people, but no other city can, either."[12]

As with previous councils, the highest priority of the 1999–2001 Mayor and Council's policy agenda was the Town Center. In 2000, the city hired consultants to conduct market and parking surveys and to develop a master plan for the Town Center. Greater Rockville Partnership, formed in 1997 to recruit new companies and retain current businesses, now turned full attention to downtown. The city sponsored seventy special events that brought more than 122,000 visitors to the heart of Rockville. At the turn of the twenty-first century, the brightest hopes for downtown revitalization lay in continued vibrancy of the theaters and restaurants and in the planned construction of a new Rockville Regional Library on Middle Lane.

Part of the problem was the lack of consensus among the parties about what constituted success in downtown revitalization. City leadership clung to a vision of what might be accomplished and a hope to receive a good return on its land purchases. Developers desired higher density use, primarily office space. The county demanded adequate provision for its court, office, and parking needs. Residents of Rockville, realizing what was lost in the 1960s, pressed for a downtown of mixed commercial, office, government, and residential uses and public spaces in a user-friendly streetscape. Conflicting visions of the Town Center proved difficult to resolve.

ROCKVILLE IN 2000

A small city, a large town, a state of mind, a suburban environment, yet part of a metropolitan area. Rockville at the end of the twentieth century was all of these. Citizens participating in Imagine Rockville, a grassroots *visioning* process initiated by the Mayor and Council in 1996–97, considered the present and the possibilities. In large and small groups, they analyzed what made the community work and how it might be improved. Some groups, such as the Town Center Action Team, continued meeting afterward to develop ways to meet their goals.

The U.S. Census Bureau reported 47,388 people living in Rockville in 2000. Once Maryland's second largest city, Rockville grew more slowly than other small cities after 1970 and slipped to fifth place behind Baltimore, Frederick, Gaithersburg, and Bowie. Rockville's citizenry had diversified from a historical black-white population into an international panoply. Fifteen percent of Rockville's population described themselves as Asian, 9 percent as black, 68 percent as white, and 8 percent as another race or two or more races. In addition, 12 percent reported their cultural classification as Hispanic or Latino. Nearly half of Rockville residents held managerial and professional positions. Another third worked as technicians, salespeople, or administrative support personnel. Service occupations, operators, manufacturers, and laborers composed the remainder.[13]

Rockville in 2000 was known for its diversity of housing: single-family homes, garden and high-rise apartments, condominiums, cooperatives, town houses, elderly housing, and subsidized housing. Two thirds of Rockville residents owned their own dwellings. Single-family home prices ranged from $130,000 to more than $500,000, and no gated communities existed. Apartments and low-cost housing continued to be in demand.[14] New communities, regardless of price range, were required by law to include moderately priced units as part of the mix. This diversity has always attracted people to Rockville, where they could upgrade their housing and still remain within the corporate limits.

TOP: Residential street in King Farm.
BOTTOM: Tower Oaks is a comprehensive planned development that includes office, residential, and commercial components. This office building, a project of Boston Properties, contains 185,000 square feet of space.

Photo by Dean Evangelista, 2000

Photo by Dean Evangelista, 2001

Since World War II, Rockville had been a city of neighborhoods. The official map identified sixty geographic areas commonly considered to be distinct neighborhoods by city residents and staff. Most (such as Rose Hill Falls and Rockshire) were associated with subdivisions and were named by developers. Others kept historical names such as Haiti and Halpine. Civic associations hosted the Mayor and Council at Walking Town Meetings, where they voiced current concerns during the course of neighborhood tours. Residents identified with their neighborhoods, taking time to guide public policy and private programs there. Reflecting the city's commitment to neighborhoods, three neighborhood resources coordinators acted as liaisons and administered programs such as Rockville University and matching grants for special local projects. The city's theme was "You don't have to move to live in a better neighborhood."[15]

In every section of the city, blends of old and new Rockville could be observed. Historic buildings and scenes of historic Rockville events have been encircled by twentieth-century structures, interpretations, and modifications. To protect these special places and keep them for future generations, the Mayor and Council designated eleven historic districts, five of which were also listed in the National Register of Historic Places. Altogether they showcased historic places representing the community from the 1790s to the present. Property owners took advantage of tax incentives available for rehabilitation of historic buildings.

Barnard T. Welsh's characterization of Rockville as a churchy town in the 1920s still held, but it was also

Map of Rockville's boundaries, 1803–2000.

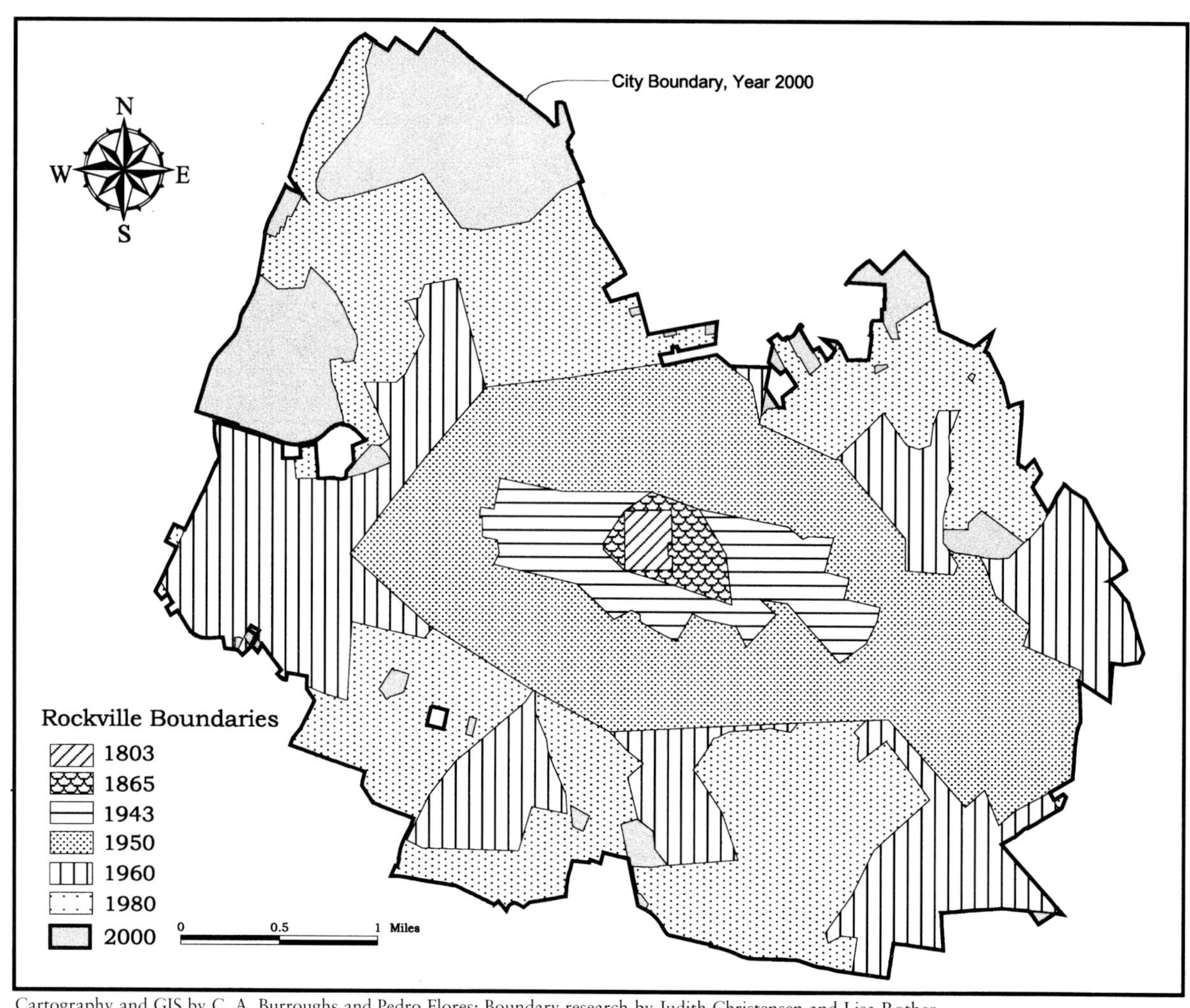

Cartography and GIS by C. A. Burroughs and Pedro Flores; Boundary research by Judith Christensen and Lisa Rother

FROM FARM TO NEIGHBORHOOD

A recurring theme of American history is the transformation of agricultural land into urban usage. The story has played out in Rockville for more than two centuries. In 1784, William Prather Williams hired surveyor Archibald Orme to plat a small portion of his tobacco lands and woodlots into eighty-five urban lots divided by six streets. It was Williams's good fortune to own property along established roads that met in a tiny hamlet known as Hungerford's Tavern, and his good business sense to appreciate the favorable position of the recently selected seat of the new Montgomery County. Thus, Williamsburgh became our first neighborhood.

Agriculture remained the primary industry through the nineteenth century, but more farmland turned to other use. Through the Civil War, Rockville—as Williamburgh was renamed in 1801—clustered around Court House Square. With the coming of the B&O Railroad in 1873, land within half a mile of the tracks sparked suburban visions in the minds of local farmers as well as real estate entrepreneurs. Through subdivision of land to his descendants, Samuel Martin's small farm evolved into a sizeable portion of the neighborhood of Haiti on Martin's Lane. In 1890, developer Henry Copp divided Julius West's large farm into West End Park. The location of both original dwellings is visible now only on outdated maps.

Movement from farm to neighborhood sped up in the twentieth century, particularly after the Second World War. Much of Glenview, the farm of Judge Bowie (and, later, Irene Lyon) was carved into Burgundy Estates, Burgundy Hills, and Burgundy Knolls. While the Hurley-Carter farmhouse still stands on Feather Rock Drive to recall its agricultural past, it is surrounded by tract homes. Agricultural acreage owned by the Woottons eventually became Rockshire. North Farm was the back farm of the Lyddanes and Bradleys, who gave their residential address as the Rockville Pike. The old farmstead is now part of Woodmont Country Club. The Shaw farm became RedGate.

The Dawsons owned one of the last farms in Rockville. Two historic farmhouses may still be seen on the north edge of Hungerford-Stoneridge, subdivisions for which the family sold off acreage in the 1950s and 1960s. Other Dawsons farmed Rose Hill, as later did the Bullards; now the area is Rose Hill Falls. Members of the Anderson family, Rockville farmers since the eighteenth century, waited patiently for developer interest. Eventually the land which produced tobacco, sugar cane, wheat, corn, and other crops sold to newcomers in the developments of Plymouth Woods and College Gardens.

The progression from farm to neighborhood—settlement, agricultural use, construction of access routes and commuter connections, decline of farming, sale of land for future development, annexation into the city, approval of subdivision plans, construction of the new development, then occupancy—continues in Rockville. The agricultural history of King Farm, a 440-acre planned community in northern Rockville, can be traced to the early nineteenth century. Fallsgrove, the 254-acre newest comprehensive planned development, was known as the Thomas farm for six decades.

Developers and architects turn agricultural land into a subdivision reflecting a particular time. After construction crews depart, the residents are responsible for creating a community. Despite the mobility of Americans, every Rockville neighborhood contains original or longtime residents who would not live anywhere else.

a caring community. Nearly forty congregations met in Rockville churches, synagogues, and assembly places. They ranged from the oldest congregation, Christ Episcopal Church, to the Chinese Bible and Korean Baptist Churches organized in the 1990s. Private groups partnered with the city for resources neither could provide alone. Rockville organizations in 1983 created Manna Food Center, to collect and distribute food to the needy. Four shelters took in the homeless, and local residents helped construct three Habitat for Humanity homes in town. Numerous publicly supported and private programs assisted persons with daily living, special problems, financial or health needs, home improvements, and other concerns, many of them sponsored or coordinated by Community Ministries of Rockville.

At the end of the century, managing growth of the municipality through planning remained a local preoccupation. Rockville's third *Master Plan*, adopted in 1993 along guidelines proposed by a

1962 photo from the *Washington Star*, copyright the *Washington Post*, reprinted by permission of the D.C. Public Library

Courtesy of Peerless Rockville

TOP: Rockville's two-sided town clock replaced the earlier four-sided timepiece demolished by an errant car in 1957. Restored as a bicentennial project, the clock appeared in front of Regal Cinemas in 1998.
BOTTOM: Looking east on Route 28 toward Rockville, Roy Perry photographed this scene in the early 1940s. Today, this view would include parts of Research Boulevard and Rockshire.

citizen committee, was in the process of being updated. Three major private developments—all "comprehensive planned developments" in city parlance—stood out. Most of the thirty-two hundred residences projected for King Farm had been approved, with nearly a thousand already occupied and three million square feet of office space ready or in process. The city gained ninety-two acres of parkland. Fallsgrove, formerly known as the Thomas farm, was planned to hold fifteen hundred residences (single-family attached and detached homes, townhouses, and apartments), a community center, research and development, office and retail space, a school, and eighty-four acres of parkland. Three huge modern office buildings were under construction at Tower Oaks, Wootton Parkway, and Preserve Parkway, on the former county Poor Farm property. When completed, these projects would take Rockville to the boundaries of its Urban Growth Area (a refinement of the 1960s Maximum Expansion Limits) and to its anticipated maximum population of sixty-thousand. The goal remained, in the simple words of the 1970 *Master Plan*, "to have a city large enough to provide efficient municipal services, and small enough to maintain a close identification between the city and its citizens."[16]

The historic Rockville Pike transformed in the 1980s from a thoroughfare into a destination. From an Indian path carved through the forest, to Montgomery County's first turnpike (in 1805), to a two-lane paved road (1925), to a four-lane thoroughfare dotted with signs and groupings of stores (1957), to a six-lane economic engine with a prestigious address, the old Pike saw a lot of history. Development of the Rockville Pike corridor, controlled haphazardly for years, became the subject of closer scrutiny and planning in the 1980s. The Pike—in effect the community's new main street—filled with traffic and suburban blight. High-design glass office buildings sat alongside nondescript commercial strips. In addition to traffic congestion, how to channel the considerable private investment into a cohesive streetscape was an issue in the 1985 three-way mayoral campaign, won by Steven Van Grack. The

Rockville Pike Corridor Neighborhood Plan, adopted in 1989, incorporated landscaping recommendations first displayed at Wintergreen Shopping Center in the early 1980s and promoted mixed-use development along the Pike. The use of service drives and of berms to separate parked and moving cars also proved to be welcome additions.[17]

Through the 1990s, the Pike continued to offer mixed blessings to Rockville and Montgomery County. Economic benefits were unquestionable; the Golden Mile came in second only to Rodeo Drive in Los Angeles in gross sales per square foot of leasable retail space. However, the gridlock of cars and buses along the already dense roadway, coupled with county plans for further development near White Flint, heightened tensions. A confrontation came with the issue of *big box* retail stores. Developed under options permitted by the *Master Plan* and the zoning code, individual superstores began to locate on the Pike. The first was Marlo Furniture, whose massive appearance and purple stripe triggered umbrage in 1995. Four years later, after Best Buy opened and others were proposed, the Mayor and Council voted a moratorium to study the impact of big box stores on traffic, surrounding areas, and the character of the Pike. Rockville gained national attention in 2000 when it decided to enact a limitation on the size of individual retail stores.

Research and development continued to grow, as did trade and industry. At the end of the twentieth century, approximately fifty thousand people worked within the city limits. Shopping centers were located in the Rockville Pike corridor, in the Town Center, and in neighborhood retail strips. Industry in Rockville included high tech (centered along the Interstate 270 corridor), light industry in the Southlawn-Gude Drive area, and small shops near the railroad tracks. Many businesses were members of the Rockville Chamber of Commerce.

Sixty percent of the bioscience industries in the state of Maryland were located in the city or had Rockville addresses. Rockville-based Celera Genomics, Inc., a Plera corporation, gained national attention for

TOP: Four generations of the Ross-Powell-Prather-Crutchfield family posed in July 1988 in front of the home their enslaved ancestors built in Haiti, on Martin's Lane. BOTTOM: Concept plan for Fallsgrove. Located on the former Thomas farm, the 254-acre site is bounded by Shady Grove Road, Darnestown Road, West Montgomery Avenue, and Research Boulevard.

Photo by Judith Christensen, courtesy of Peerless Rockville

Courtesy of City of Rockville

genetic databases and detailed analyses of the human genome. To encourage growth in this sector, the Mayor and Council required that space be set aside for research and development firms when it approved plans for Fallsgrove.

Mayor Rose G. Krasnow led the 1999–2001 Mayor and Council. A councilmember since 1989 and Rockville's first elected woman mayor in 1995, she had a graduate degree in urban and regional planning. She was the first mayor to hail from New Mark Commons, where she was administrator of the homeowners association. Serving on the council were Robert E. Dorsey, a computer executive from Twinbrook, Glennon J. Harrison, an international economist from West End, engineer Robert J. Wright from Rockshire, and Anne M. Robbins, an educator from Rockshire. An educated and civic-minded group, the Mayor and Council devoted considerable hours to their part-time duties.

Rockville government grew along with the economy and the population to become almost a full-service city. City Manager W. Mark Pentz supervised day-to-day business with a staff of 492 employees.[18] Like his predecessors Bruce Romer and Rick Kuckkahn, Pentz had been selected by a citizens' committee from a nationwide search. Bursting out of its quarters, the city considered expanding City Hall. Rockville's total budget in fiscal year 2000 amounted to $61,440,321. Public services extended from infrastructure maintenance to leisure time. Public works crews collected refuse, leaves, and recyclable materials, and plowed the streets. They maintained 138 miles of paved streets and 217 miles of sidewalks. The city was responsible for 145 miles of water mains, 188 miles of storm and sanitary sewers, and one-third of the city's 4,723 street lights.[19]

The city created opportunities to connect with its citizens. Community policing and neighborhood outreach marked the professionalism of Rockville's modern forty-eight-officer police department. Although historically the Maryland General Assembly assigned a constable for the village as early as 1801, not until the 1970s did the Mayor and Council hire a large force. A federal grant enabled Rockville to obtain a professional chief and greater numbers of sworn officers to augment county and state protection. Rockville maintained contact with citizens through its own cable television station, a website, and a newsletter, *Rockville Reports*, mailed to approximately twenty-five thousand households and businesses each month.

In large part due to Celera, Rockville is known as the Home of the Genome. Here Nobel Laureate Hamilton O. Smith and gene sequencing expert Mark D. Adams confer in the sequencing lab at Celera Genomics.

Photo by Walter Smalling, courtesy of Celera Genomics

Rockville is greener than most cities in America. About 20 percent of its total land area is parkland. Located throughout the city are fifty-three parks and thirteen special recreation facilities on a total of 961.8 acres. Most Rockville homes are less than one-quarter mile from a city park. The city continues to add trails and green space; a small landscaped park (site of a water tower, 1947–1999) on Grandin Avenue and an athletic park at Mark Twain school opened in 2000. To maintain public parks, grounds, and street trees, the city employs an arborist and a horticulturist. Civic Center Park, with 153 acres of landscaped grounds and woodlands, is Rockville's largest. In 2000, nearly 120,000 people attended social events, classes, performances, or conferences at Glenview Mansion and the F. Scott Fitzgerald Theatre. A total of 1,142 events was scheduled on the property that year. In 2000, the city designed the Croydon Creek Nature Center near the mansion and prepared a master plan for Glenview.

A child who attended Rockville's first summer playground in 1947 would be overwhelmed by the programs of 2000. The city offers more than six hundred different programs to residents of all ages. The Municipal Swim Center extends a complete aquatics program with indoor and outdoor pools and exercise areas. RedGate Golf Course, one of the best-maintained municipal courses in the metropolitan area, hosts tournaments and special golf events in addition to recreational golf. Rockville also supports thirty-four public tennis courts and recently worked with local youngsters to design a skate park at Welsh Park.[20]

Cultural seeds sown in the nineteenth century matured in the twentieth. The white male Cornet Band and the black male 30 Club of prior times gave way to the volunteer Rockville Concert Band and the professional National Chamber Orchestra. The F. Scott Fitzgerald Theatre grew to house resident companies including the Rockville Civic Ballet, Rockville Community Chorus, Rockville Little Theatre, Rockville Musical Theatre, and Victorian Lyric Opera Company. As we begin the twenty-first century, city government also supports the arts and humanities through partnerships with local groups and with professional staff in the Department of Recreation and Parks.

Rockville celebrated the centennial of F. Scott Fitzgerald's birth and his associations with Rockville in a year-long series of events in 1996. A legacy of the centennial is the F. Scott Fitzgerald Literary Conference, held annually in September, with panels of speakers and workshops for budding writers. The F. Scott Fitzgerald Literary Award honored major contemporary American writers William Styron, John Barth, Joyce Carol Oates, E. L. Doctorow, and Norman Mailer.

Photo courtesy of Joyce Staub, Rockville Senior Center

Courtesy of Brenda Bean

TOP: Rockville's Senior Center grew in popularity and services as the city's senior population enlarged. Thousands participate in programs, meals, health services, classes, trips, and special events. Each October, seniors walk from the center to deliver teddy bears to children at Shady Grove Hospital. BOTTOM: Rockville residents of all ages enjoy organized sports. The owners of Taste of Saigon, a popular local restaurant, sponsor a Friday night corec team. Photo taken summer of 1992 after a game at Broome field.

In 2000, traffic and transportation remained sources of vexation. Traffic problems on Interstate 270, now twelve lanes, worsened. As the county and

Photo by Dean Evangelista

Photo by Irene Young

TOP: Norman Mailer signed a book for Virginia Moser at the F. Scott Fitzgerald Literary Conference in 2000. BOTTOM: Rockville resident Sue Richards is four-time champion of the Scottish Harp Society of America.

state planned improvements known as the Montrose Parkway and the Route 355 corridor—roads that border and lead into Rockville—the city faced years of monitoring their effect on Rockville. The large developments planned at King and Thomas farms involved multiple road issues, and pedestrian access and safety required attention by city staff and citizens. Attempting to provide alternative means of transportation as well as recreational facilities, Rockville continued to construct a system of bike paths through the city.

Rockville reinforced its autonomy as a jurisdiction through community identification. Although incorporated in 1860, the shadow of the nation's capital and the rapid growth of Montgomery County kept Rockville in constant need of protecting its independence. Newcomers to Rockville in the second half of the twentieth century planted new roots in the city, established new traditions, developed community symbols, and provided showcases for local pride. Traditions such as the Memorial Day parade, Hometown Holidays, Spirit of Rockville, Antique and Classic Car Show, Veterans and Flag Day ceremonies, Independence Day concert and fireworks, and other celebrations reinforced Rockville's sense of civic pride and place. By 2000, the Mayor and Council could point to an official city flag, seal, coat of arms, logo, motto, and march.

The White House designated Rockville an official Millennium Community in 2000. Beginning on July 4, 1999, Rockville's Millennium Committee sponsored special programs and gave traditional events a unique twist. Local student groups painted fire hydrants in the Town Center with nature, animal, and patriotic themes. Community garden clubs and Julius West middle schoolers helped the city to design and plant a garden of indigenous plants, rocks, and trees at a prominent corner on Falls Road. Quilters submitted hand-crafted blocks depicting Rockville themes for an official Millennium Quilt. Peerless Rockville organized discovery tours of Rockville historic places through the year. A millennium multiuse trail was designed as a circle connecting all areas of the city. In October, the annual Antique and Classic Car Show featured a special display of 104 vehicles, each car representing one year from 1898 to 2001. In a final millennial act, on January 1, 2001, the Mayor and Council buried a time capsule in Court House Square, containing mementoes and symbols of Rockville at the beginning of the twenty-first century.

Citizen Boards and Commissions

Citizen participation in Rockville government evolved as a twentieth-century practice. Special interest groups such as the Volunteer Fire Department and the Woman's Club never shrank from offering advice, but before World War I town problems usually were solved by the volunteer Mayor and Council and its tiny staff. By the 1920s, mayors periodically appointed representative citizens to meet with the State Roads Commission or to suggest locations for street lights or the town clock. In December 1929, the Mayor and Council appointed three men to a new Zoning Commission. Three years later, the council adopted a Zoning Ordinance and appointed a Board of Zoning Appeals. The precedent for citizen advisors thus set, residents began to volunteer. Next came a Recreational Committee, which suggested youth programs such as an experimental Teen Age Canteen.

Events before, during, and after the revolution of 1954 solidified the experience of citizen participation. Overthrowing the old order and completely revising local government operations required delegation of tasks. In their first year in office, the new Mayor and Council appointed ten volunteer committees and commissions to help shape policies and programs. Taking advantage of local talent, the city formed partnerships with its citizens. The new organizational structure and civic involvement were soon reinforced by the first All-America City Award. Even as the reform leaders brought in professional staff to modernize city government, they continued to augment employees with citizen volunteers through boards and commissions.

Courtesy of City of Rockville

Planning Commission in 1965.

Over the years, the scope of citizen advisory boards kept pace with Rockville's enlarging size and complexity. The groups served as nurseries for future elected officials, and mayors occasionally convened commission chairs as a cabinet of advisors. Past and current boards and commissions include: Advisory Commission on Public Education, Animal Control Board, Board of Appeals, Board of Supervisors of Elections, Civic Center Commission, Civic Improvement Advisory Commission, Cultural Arts Commission, Economic Development Council, Energy Commission, Financial Advisory Committee, Historic District Commission, Housing Authority, Human Relations (Rights) Commission, Humanities Commission, Landlord-Tenant Commission, Mayor's Council on Youth Opportunity, Neighborhood Advisory Board, Personnel Appeals Board, Planning Commission, Recreation and Park Advisory Board, Retirement Board, Science Technology and Environment Committee, Senior Citizens Com-mission, Sign Advisory Committee, Traffic and Transportation Commission, and the Urban Renewal Advisory Council. Ad hoc committees have been appointed for special tasks, such as Cable TV Advisory Committee, Goals Committee, Committee to Study Council Compensation, Housing Policy Task Force, and the Centenary, Bicentennial, and Millennium committees.

An American Tradition: The Memorial Day Parade

Rockville's best-known tradition is the annual Memorial Day parade. In 1868, Gen. John Logan, commander-in-chief of the Grand Army of the Republic, proclaimed May 30 the day to honor fallen soldiers by decorating their graves.[21] For years thereafter, the *Sentinel* notified citizens of Memorial Day (the southern name) and Decoration Day (the northern name). Black residents of Rockville in the early twentieth century began the tradition of a regional May 30 homecoming picnic and parade on Washington Street. Montgomery County musician Charlie Ross marched with local bands in the parades.[22] By the 1930s, white American Legion posts in Montgomery County took over the annual parade and program, to which the town made a contribution. Each Memorial Day, members of Henderson-Smith-Edmonds Post 86, of Rockville, placed flags on the graves of veterans in Rockville Cemetery. The *Sentinel* reported on May 28, 1936:

> Practically all town business will suspend Saturday afternoon when the annual Memorial Day parade and program is staged at Rockville. Fully five thousand persons are expected to gather in honoring the living and deceased veterans of wars in which this country has participated. These warriors of the past will include two men who fought in the War between the States. . . . The line of parade will form at the old Fair Grounds and . . . march up Montgomery Avenue. . . . Services will be conducted from the Courthouse portico.

Following a hiatus in the late 1930s and into World War II, William E. Wood (1897–1980) revived the custom. A third-generation resident of Haiti, the Martin's Lane resident organized a parade for Memorial Day of 1944. Wood said he recalled the parades of his youth and was tired of traveling to Washington to play his bugle in a marching band. Around the same time, he helped to found Johnson-Hood-Graham Post 151 of the American Legion, a post for black veterans until it merged with Post 86 in 1998. Wood served as grand marshal of the Rockville parade until 1972. After his death, his wife Rosie and other family members rode in the lead convertible.

Rockville's Memorial Day parade is the oldest and the largest in the metropolitan Washington area. Ceremonies begin the morning as representatives of veterans' groups lay wreaths, followed by brief speeches and musical pieces. Then, one hundred marching units—bands, floats, performers, clowns, scout troops, majorettes, and local elected officials—wend their way down Washington Street past the reviewing stand and twenty thousand spectators into Court House Square. In 1989, the weekend became known as Hometown Holidays, an extravaganza of crafts, music, games, and nationally known entertainment (such as Martha Reeves and the Vandellas, Three Dog Night, and The Commodores) in the center of town. These events attract an average of one hundred thousand people to Rockville each year.

TOP: William E. Wood.
BOTTOM: 1989 parade.

Rosalie Campbell photo, courtesy of Peerless Rockville

Courtesy of City of Rockville

Courtesy of City of Rockville

ROCKVILLE IS A STATE OF MIND

Helen Heneghan, city resident since 1958 and city clerk 1974–88, declared that "Rockville is a state of mind."[23] She referred to the same attraction felt by the man who returned from Maine—identification with a strong community, neatly organized by neighborhood units, and highlighted by special places and activities that created a superior quality of life in a comfortable small-town atmosphere. Shrugging off characterizations of an "Edge City"(a term coined in the 1990s by journalist Joel Garreau to describe nondescript megasuburbia) and a sprawling postal address, a city booster could Imagine Rockville succeeding equally well as a small city, large town, or suburban environment within an energetic metropolitan region.

Photo by Dean Evangelista

TOP: In 1976, while serving on the city council, Richard Haight wrote the "Rockville March." Other Rockvillians arranged the composition and added lyrics, and the city copyrighted the march.
BOTTOM: Many historical figures lie at rest in Rockville Cemetery, located on Baltimore Road. Gravestones for Pumphreys, Englands, and Bealls show in this photograph. In 2000, community organizations made plans to restore Rockville's oldest burial ground.

Four dynamics that created Rockville in the eighteenth and nineteenth centuries continued to shape its development for two hundred years—a favorable location, the presence of county government, proximity to the nation's capital, and status as an independent municipality.

Rockville's location never has lost its appeal. The relatively high, healthy altitude touted in promotions from West End Park in the 1890s to Montrose in the 1960s brought urbanites to the countryside. The "fertile land that produced the richest tobacco crop of a young, growing America" (according to College Gardens literature)[24] soon sprouted suburban homes on large lots. Expansion of the federal government following major wars increased jobs in the nation's capital within commuting distance of Rockville by train, trolley, or automobile. The road network in place by 1794 continued to serve Rockville two centuries later. However, the community's location at the confluence of roads proved both an allurement and a misfortune. Problems of automobile traffic and parking have inundated Rockville since the middle of the twentieth century.

Selection of Rockville as the seat of the newly formed Montgomery County in 1776 also became a mixed blessing. Presence of a courthouse, jail, and county offices assured a busy and productive town from the start, perhaps more sophisticated than in settlements of less political importance. County officials built impressive homes and often engaged in activities to benefit the community. Related to the size and vitality of county government in a given period was its physical and fiscal impact on Rockville. In 1931, the county owned about 10 percent of the taxable basis of the town "from which the town receives no revenue," noted the Mayor and Council.[25] Seventy years later, county and court uses rendered almost 50 percent of the assessed property value in the center of town nontaxable.[26]

Rockville became an independent municipality when it incorporated in 1860. This action, viewed by few as consequential at the time, has defined Rockville's history ever since. As the Montgomery countryside transformed to suburbia in the twentieth century, Rockville grew more passionate about its autonomy. Local government mirrored the national trend of the second half of the twentieth century, of stepping in to fill voids through funding, developing public-private partnerships, or assuming direct responsibilities for needed programs. The city's prerogative to manage its affairs became more precious as time went on. Confident of its identity, Rockville often led the way.

Rockville had its share of innovations. After Baltimore, it was the second Maryland city to adopt a master plan and to hire a full-time planner. Rockville was the first city in Maryland to enfranchise eighteen-year-old voters and to create a Citizens' Forum for residents to speak at regular Mayor and Council meetings. In Montgomery County, Rockville was first to provide public housing, first to have a public high school, first to build a public swimming pool, first to establish historic districts, first to hire black police officers, first to appoint citizen commissions for the arts and the humanities, and first to initiate an Art in Public Places program. Rockville pioneered in youth counseling and in door-to-door voter registration.

The Millennium Committee asked Rockville organizations and individuals to submit quilt squares on the theme of "What Rockville means to you." Rainie Broad designed the quilt and crafted a beautiful keepsake for the community.

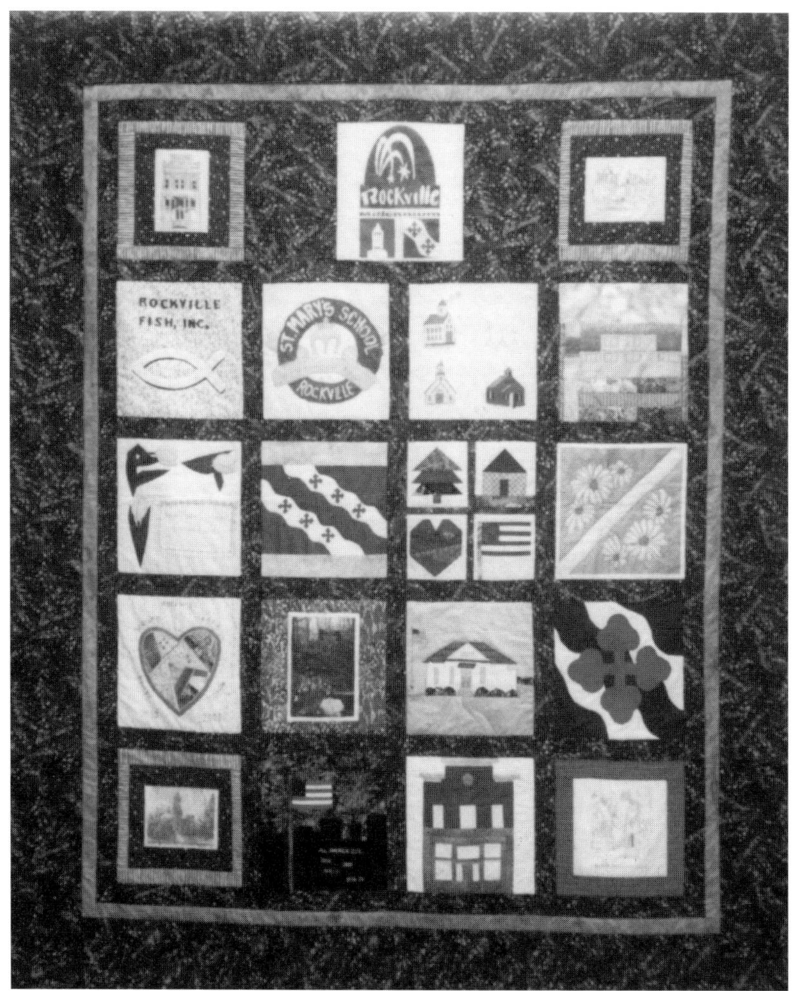

Courtesy of Charlene D'Albora

Photo by Dean Evangelista

Looking northwest from the Metro tracks, new and historic buildings in Rockville's Town Center yield a collage.

The city's progressive attitude provided an incubator for planning and management professionals who made their mark in Montgomery County and elsewhere. Rockville was Maryland's first city to win the All-America award twice, then thrice, then four times. And, the city's SmoothSeal street-paving program (a method of applying asphalt over paved streets invented by Director of Public Works John Gray in 1959) was a national innovation.[27]

The spring of 2001 marked two hundred years since the Maryland General Assembly directed a survey of "lots, streets and lanes" to be "erected into a town, to be called and known by the name of Rockville." Whether crossroads village of the eighteenth century, courthouse town of the nineteenth, small city of the early twentieth, or biotechnology mecca of the Washington metropolitan area of the twenty-first century, Rockville has matured gracefully. Through partnerships between citizens and government, the city continues to meet the challenge of accommodating growth and change while maintaining the flavor that originally proved so attractive.

Rockville is more than streets and buildings. It is the sum of the ideal that residents believe it was in the past and that they want it to be in the present and the future. They imagine Rockville to be a community with a tradition of citizen participation, ample green space, and the positive aspects of the "cozy and personalized" environment ascribed to the town in 1950. In the last decades of the twentieth century, attempting to recapture what Rockville was before the physical changes of rapid growth and urban renewal, the city recreated the street framework of the old downtown and selected the last three city managers of the century for their small city values as much as for their expertise. Rockville has grown to be a bustling city, but in many ways it still behaves like a small town. To appreciate Rockville as a state of mind is to recognize the shared excellence and hometown values of what a small city should be.

Chronology of Rockville History

8000 B.C. Archaic period of prehistory. After thousands of years of following big game herds, hunters settled into seminomadic lives in area which became Montgomery County.

1000 B.C. Indian groups established year-round agricultural villages.

1200 A.D. Indians competed for river and forest resources, resulting in a succession of population displacements.

1717–35 Arthur Nelson surveyed and patented four tracts of land totaling 3,162 acres in the Rockville area.

1739 Chapel of Ease was built to accommodate westernmost settlers in Prince George's (Anglican) Parish. It later became Christ Episcopal Church.

1740s Rolling road in use by tobacco planters and north-south travelers.

1748 Frederick County created, including Rockville area. Frederick Town selected county seat.

1755 British Gen. Edward Braddock camped at Owen's Ordinary en route to his defeat at Fort Duquesne at the start of the French and Indian War.

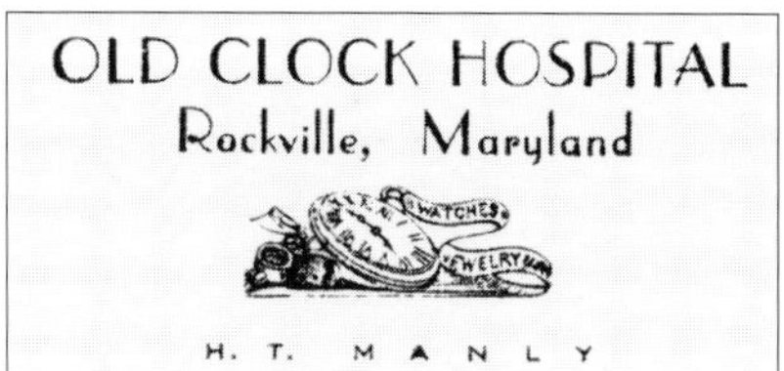

1760s Joseph Elgar built sawmills and gristmills on Rock Creek, later known as Muncaster Mill. William Dent and William Williams also constructed a grist and sawmill, later Horner Mill.

1774 Patriots met at Charles Hungerford's tavern to issue resolves supporting Boston protestors against British taxation.

1776 Frederick County was divided, and the lower section was named Montgomery County. Crossroads settlement at Hungerford's tavern was selected as the new county seat.

1777 First court session in Leonard Davis's tavern.

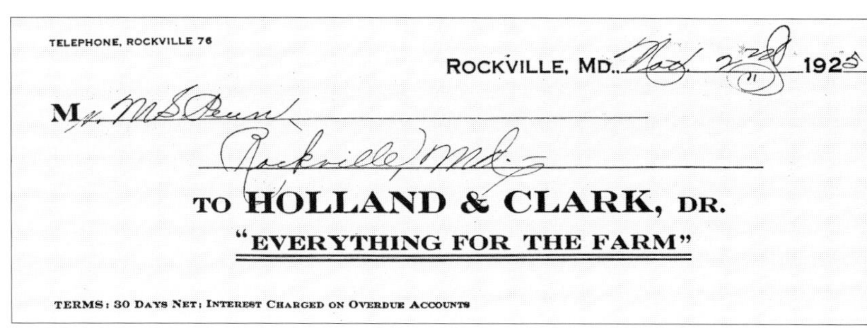
TELEPHONE, ROCKVILLE 76

ROCKVILLE, MD. Nov 22 1925

M

TO HOLLAND & CLARK, DR.

"EVERYTHING FOR THE FARM"

TERMS: 30 DAYS NET: INTEREST CHARGED ON OVERDUE ACCOUNTS

Village was known as Montgomery Court House.

1784 William Prather Williams divided part of Exchange and New Exchange Enlarged into eighty-five "lotts with streets fit, convenient and suitable for a town" which he named Williamsburgh.

1787 Court House Square was surveyed and laid out for a courthouse and jail.

1794 Post office established at Montgomery Court House.

1801 The new county jail was erected.

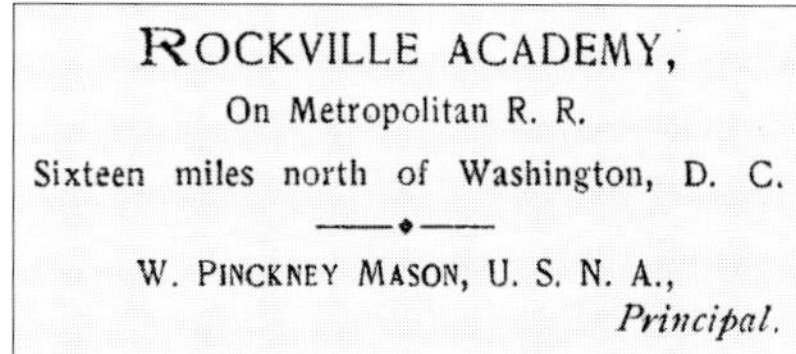

1801–03 The Maryland Assembly passed acts to resurvey lots and erect a town to be called Rockville. The work was completed and the Plan of Rockville, dated May 9, 1803, was recorded in the Land Records of Montgomery County.

1805 Washington Turnpike Company chartered to build a road from George Town to Rockville.

1812 Rockville Academy opened with thirty students.

1813 Henry Shouse and Otho Williams opened a saw and gristmill operation on Watts Branch which was later called Wootton's Mill.

1814 President James Madison, Gen. William Henry Winder, and troops came through Montgomery Court House after the British burned Washington, D.C.

1817 Saint Mary's Catholic Church was constructed.

1822 Christ Episcopal Church moved into town from the old chapel of ease building.

1820s The town was enlarged by the first two additions to Rockville.

1833 Meteor shower dazzled Rockville residents.

1835 Samuel Clark Veirs opened a saw and gristmill on Rock Creek.

1838 Richard Johns and Catharine Bowie purchased tracts of land east of town and built a farmhouse. They named their farm Glenview.

1840 The new Montgomery County Courthouse was constructed.

1846 The Montgomery County Agricultural Society organized. The county fair began in Rockville. The fairgrounds opened on the Pike in 1848.

1860 The town of Rockville was incorporated by act of the Maryland General Assembly. Voters elected three commissioners and a bailiff.

OFFICE OF
W. J. HOYLE,
DEALER IN
GENERAL MERCHANDISE,
AND PRODUCER OF PURE HONEY.
"AVERY APIARY."

1861 First public school opened for white students in Rockville.

1862–64 Rockville slaves were freed.

1863 Confederate Gen. Jeb Stuart captured prisoners, horses, and wagons in Rockville and headed north toward Pennsylvania.

1864 Confederate troops under Gen. Jubal Early skirmished with Union troops and seized town records en route to the battle of Fort Stevens in Washington.

1865 Freedmen's Bureau office opened in Rockville to assist former slaves.

1869 Rockville Library Association and Masonic Lodge formed.

1873 The Metropolitan Branch of B&O Railroad opened through Montgomery County. The town of Rockville enlarged corporate limits and extended the boardwalk to the new depot.

1876 First public school opened for black students in Rockville.

1880 Rockville Cemetery Association incorporated as nondenominational community burial ground.

1884 The first commercial bank in the county, Montgomery County National Bank, opened in Rockville.

1888 The new town charter changed governing body from town commissioners to Mayor and Council of Rockville.

JOS. W. HOWES
HORSESHOEING, BLACKSMITHING,
WHEELWRITING AND PAINTING
OXY-ACETYLENE WELDING

1889 The first telephone was installed at Fearon's drug store on Montgomery Avenue.

1890 The Mayor and Council issued the first building permit to Thomas Dawson. New Rockville Academy building was constructed.

1891 Montgomery County built a new courthouse (Red Brick Courthouse). Lincoln Park subdivision recorded in Land Records.

1892 Montgomery County's first high school (later called Rockville, then Richard Montgomery) opened on Monroe Street for grades eight through eleven.

MEAD'S

EXPRESS

"A Chip Off The Old Block"

Moving by Experience Men

1894 Coxey's Army marched through Rockville on the way to Washington, D.C., to protest unemployment.

1897 Town constructed water pumping station and electric light plant. Electric service available but all areas were not covered until around 1920.

1899 Rockville Base Ball Club organized.

1900 Woman's Club of Rockville was founded. First trolley traveled the Rockville & Tennallytown Electric Railroad up the Pike to the fairgrounds.

c. 1905 Rockville Pike was taken over by the State Roads Commission.

1910 Dr. Dexter Bullard opened the doors of Chestnut Lodge Sanitarium in the former Woodlawn Hotel.

1912 Chautauqua came to Rockville. Order of Galilean Fishermen organized in Rockville as a sick and burial society for black residents. SECO, Rockville's first movie theatre, opened for silent films and vaudeville shows.

1913 Typhoid epidemic occurred in Rockville, resulting in a town sewerage system.

1918–19 Influenza epidemic struck hundreds in Rockville.

1921 Rockville Volunteer Fire Department organized. Rockville Library moved into Dr. Stonestreet's office.

1924 Croydon Park subdivision platted at the courthouse.

Look Who's Here! The Jolly Bunch of Rockville

WILL GIVE

AN OLD FOLK'S CONCERT

at FISHERMEN'S HALL, Rockville, Md.

Thursday Night, April 17th, 1924

For the benefit of A. M. E. Zion Church

1925 Rockville Chamber of Commerce organized. Veirs and Muncaster water-powered mills closed. Hickerson Brothers set up a steam-powered mill at the railroad tracks.

1926 Rockville free delivery postal service began. Dr. and Mrs. James A. Lyon enlarged and renovated Glenview Mansion. Welsh Field opened for athletic events near Jefferson Street.

1927 The first high school for Montgomery County black students was built on North Washington Street. The first traffic signal, a stop-and-go light, was installed at the corner of Washington Street and Montgomery Avenue.

1928 Congressional Airport and School of Aeronautics opened on the Rockville Pike.

1931 Montgomery County opened a new courthouse and jail in Rockville. Author F. Scott Fitzgerald attended his father's funeral at Saint Mary's Church.

1932 Mayor and Council adopted the first zoning ordinance.

1935 Montgomery Hotel on Commerce Lane was razed and replaced by Milo

Theater. Schoolbus and train accident resulted in the closing of Baltimore Road track crossing and in the construction of a new bridge over Veirs Mill Road.

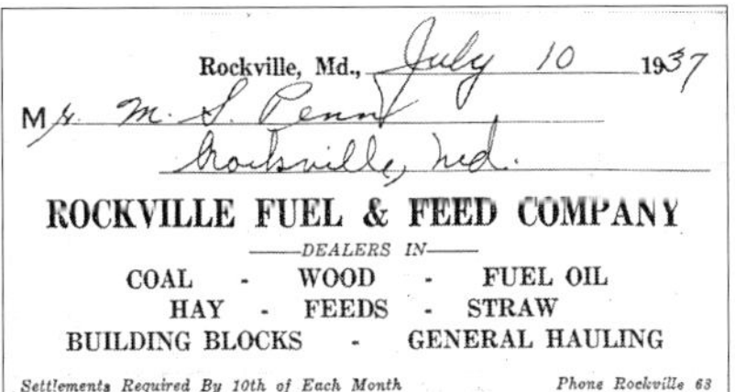
Rockville, Md., July 10 1937
M r. M. S. Penn
Rockville, Md.
ROCKVILLE FUEL & FEED COMPANY
DEALERS IN
COAL - WOOD - FUEL OIL
HAY - FEEDS - STRAW
BUILDING BLOCKS - GENERAL HAULING
Settlements Required By 10th of Each Month
Phone Rockville 63

1936 William B. Gibbs, principal of Rockville Colored Elementary School, filed suit for equal pay.

1939 Rockville's first permanent post office was dedicated at the corner of Washington Street and Montgomery Avenue. Cabin John Creek sewage disposal plant was built.

1940 F. Scott Fitzgerald was buried in Rockville Cemetery. First sections of Rockcrest and Roxboro were developed.

1944 Memorial Day parade tradition was revived in Rockville.

1945 V-J Day was celebrated in Court House Square with parade and speeches.

1946 Parking meters were installed in the business district.

1947 The first large apartment complex was built in Rockville. Rockville Little Theatre was organized. Rockville Citizens Association was formed.

1948 The position of city manager was created. The first summer recreation program started.

1949 Mass annexation into Rockville of 2,210 acres occurred.

1950 Rockville Kiwanis Club was organized.

1951 Rockville Bypass (Hungerford Drive) opened. George Washington Carver High School and Junior College opened. Rockville created a civil defense program.

1951–57 Hill & Kimmel purchased properties on Washington Street and Middle Lane to develop three strip shopping centers.

1953 The new County Office Building replaced Welsh athletic field. Large land area along the Pike near Halpine was annexed into the City of Rockville.

1954 National Municipal League and *Look Magazine* honored Rockville with the All-America City Award. Rockville Boys Baseball Association organized.

1955 The General Assembly granted home rule to Maryland municipalities, giving Rockville annexation and other powers. Rockville Jaycees organized. Rockville Chamber of Commerce was chartered. WINX operated a radio station on Baltimore Road.

1956 The Mayor and Council appointed the first planning commission. Clinton A. M. E. Zion Church relocated in Lincoln Park. Rockville Civitan Club organized.

1957 Rockville joined the Montgomery County library system. The city purchased the Lyon estate (Glenview) and twenty-eight acres for cultural, recreational, and social uses. Rockville Pike widened to four lanes. U.S. Route 240 (now I-270) was completed through Rockville, connecting Washington, D.C. with Frederick County. Pinneberg, Germany established sister city relationship with Rockville. Rockville Art League and Rockville Concert Band were founded.

1958 Unitarian Church of Rockville organized as a fellowship. A new sewer system was installed for Cabin John Creek drainage area. Rockville installed a new water system, supplied by the Potomac River.

1959 The first public housing project in Montgomery

MONTGOMERY COUNTY BRANCH
NATIONAL ASSOCIATION FOR THE ADVANCEMENT OF COLORED PEOPLE
208 FREDERICK AVE., BOX 302
ROCKVILLE, MARYLAND
TELEPHONE: 762-0811

EDITH M. THROCKMORTON
President

REV. THOMAS H. BROOKS
Vice President

County, sixty-five units known as Lincoln Terrace, was built in Rockville. Congressional Plaza shopping center opened on the site of former Congressional Airport. Elwood Smith teen center opened. John Gray, director of public works, developed a formula for SmoothSeal method of asphalting.

1960 Rockville celebrated the centennial of its incorporation. The first *Master Plan* was adopted. An agreement between Rockville and Montgomery County established maximum expansion limits. An auditorium was built at Rockville Civic Center Park. The first Antique and Classic Car Show was held. A modern zoning ordinance was adopted, with a first comprehensive map amendment. Sit-in demonstrations were held at HiBoy Restaurant.

1960s Richard Montgomery High School dominated high school football in Maryland.

1961 Montgomery County Detention Center opened on the Poor Farm property. Rockville Industrial Park opened as the city's first research and development center. City of Rockville initiated an urban renewal project, and the second All-America Award was received. Julius West Junior High School opened.

1962 The new City Hall was built on the site of the former Peter home. Rockville enacted the Public Accommodations Law.

1963 The first comprehensive residential developments—Meadow Hall and Woodley Gardens—began. *Lilith* was filmed in Rockville.

1964 The City of Rockville split Parks and Recreation Department from Public Works. The city continued to add park land as new subdivisions opened. Capital Beltway was completed. The first Citizens' Forum was held.

1965 Demolition in the central business district began. Montgomery Junior College opened a Rockville campus. The solid waste landfill and incinerator opened on Southlawn Lane. The city purchased Beall-Dawson House. The Rockville Football League and Rockville Arts Council were formed. Rockville surpassed Cumberland and Hagerstown to become the second largest city in Maryland. Municipal refuse collection began. First synagogue, Beth Tikva, was built on Baltimore Road.

1966 New Saint Mary's Church was constructed. The near demise of old Saint Mary's Chapel led to a historic district ordinance for Rockville. The first Spring Arts Festival occurred. The first computer was introduced at City Hall, an NCR 500.

1967 The Fair Housing Law passed. Community Ministries of Rockville formed to coordinate welfare services of churches and the community. The first resident moved into New Mark Commons.

1968 The Municipal Swim Center opened.

1969 Wootton High School opened.

1970 Rockville High School opened. Street 70 was created. Lincoln Park Community Center was built. Senior Citizens Commission and Economic Development Council were established. Rockville purchased RedGate Farm.

1971 The new Rockville Library opened on Maryland Avenue.

1972 Rockville Mall was dedicated. The Rockville Community Chorus formed. At a telephone booth in Rockville, James McCord received orders to carry out the plans of the Committee to Reelect the President to bug Watergate office.

C. L. HICKERSON STATEMENT L. R. HICKERSON

Rockville, Md., April 14 1937

Mr. S. Penn

HICKERSON BROTHERS

MANUFACTURERS OF FLOUR, MEAL, FEED OF ALL KINDS

Interest charged on accounts after 30 days.

1974 The Mayor and Council designated the first three historic districts in Montgomery County. Peerless Rockville, Rockville Musical Theatre, and Rockville Civic Ballet were chartered. RedGate Golf Course opened. Maryland Court of Appeals retained the entire city in the new Seventeenth Legislative District.

1975 Remains of F. Scott and Zelda Fitzgerald were moved from Rockville Cemetery to Saint Mary's Cemetery. Twinbrook Library opened on Meadow Hall Road. The Zoning Ordinance was recodified.

1976 The third All-America Award was received.

1978 Art in Public Places was created. The Cultural Arts Commission and Victorian Lyric Opera Company formed.

1978 The fourth All-America City Award was received. Rockville created the Humanities Commission, one of the first jurisdictions in the nation to do so.

1981 The County began operating Ride-On buses in Rockville.

1982 The Rockville Senior Center opened. The Montgomery County Judicial Center and Executive Office Building were constructed. The first neighborhood plans—Croydon Park and Twinbrook—were adopted.

1984 The Metro Red Line extended to Rockville and Shady Grove.

1985 Rockville Cable TV began operations.

1988 The National Chamber Orchestra took up residency at F. Scott Fitzgerald Theatre.

1989 The first Hometown Holidays was sponsored by the recreation department. Rockville Arts Place was organized. Rockville farmers' market opened.

1991 The new highway around Rockville comprised of Gude Drive, Wootton Parkway, and First Street was completed.

1993 Rockville Mall was demolished. Thomas farm was annexed into the City of Rockville. A new comprehensive *Master Plan* was adopted.

1995 King Farm was annexed into the City of Rockville. Marlo Furniture store, the first of the big box retail stores, opened on the Rockville Pike.

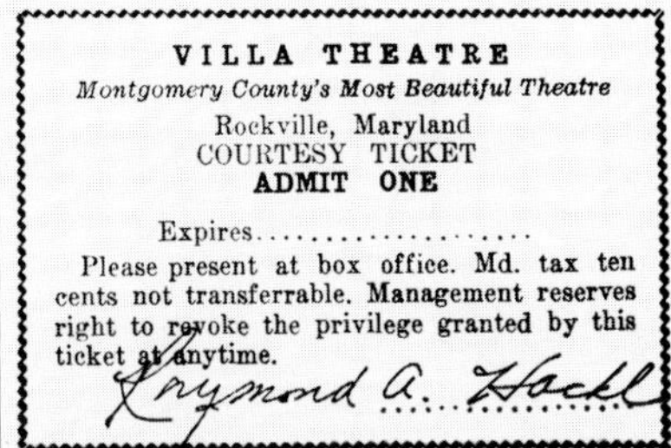

VILLA THEATRE
Montgomery County's Most Beautiful Theatre
Rockville, Maryland
COURTESY TICKET
ADMIT ONE

Expires....................
Please present at box office. Md. tax ten cents not transferrable. Management reserves right to revoke the privilege granted by this ticket at anytime.
Raymond A. Hackl

1996 Restoration of the grand courtroom in the Red Brick Courthouse completed.

1997 Imagine Rockville visioning process began. Courthouse Square Park was created, with the Spirit of Rockville fountain. The street grid returned to Town Center.

1998 Regal Cinemas opened in Town Center.

2000 The City of Rockville celebrated the millennium year with events, contests, and the commissioning of the city's history. Rockville slipped to the fifth largest city in Maryland.

THE SENTINEL **POplar 2-2144**

"Nearly A Century Of Service To Montgomery County"

POST OFFICE BOX 272 ★ ROCKVILLE MARYLAND

EDITORIAL & BUSINESS OFFICE
COURT HOUSE SQUARE

PUBLICATION & PRINTING
213 E. MONTGOMERY AVE.

Governing Bodies of Rockville 1860–2000

The first minutes of any governing body for Rockville bear the date of April 1, 1865, although the town was incorporated in 1860. From 1860–69, voters elected three commissioners for one-year terms. From 1870–79, the Montgomery County Commissioners appointed Rockville's commissioners to one-year terms. From 1880–88, Rockville voters selected three men for two-year terms. When the new charter was adopted in 1888, the Mayor and Council became Rockville's governing body.

COMMISSIONERS FOR ROCKVILLE

One-Year Terms, Elected in May

(The first name listed received the highest number of votes and was the president of commissioners.)

1860–61 James W. Campbell, William Veirs Bouic Sr., John H. Higgins
1861–62 William Veirs Bouic Sr., John H. Higgins, Matthew Fields
1862–63 William Veirs Bouic Sr., John H. Higgins, Melchisdec Green
1863–64 William Veirs Bouic Sr., John H. Higgins, Melchisdec Green
1864–65 William Veirs Bouic Sr., John H. Higgins, Melchisdec Green
1865–66 William Veirs Bouic Sr., James W. Campbell, George Peter
1866–67 Melchisdec Green, David H. Bouic, John H. Higgins (Green resigned in May 1866 and was replaced by Bouic as president), John R. Miller (per special election, May 1866)
1867–68 William V. Bouic Sr. (resigned November 1867 to become judge), Richard M. Williams (president November 1867), George Peter (resigned May 1867), Otho Z. Muncaster (per special election June 1867), John H. Higgins (per special election January 1868)
1868–69 John H. Higgins, John R. Miller, Richard M. Williams
1869–70 E. Barrett Prettyman, Matthew Fields, Melchisdec Green

COMMISSIONERS FOR ROCKVILLE

One-Year Terms, Appointed in May

1870–71 E. Barrett Prettyman, Matthew Fields, Melchisdec Green
1871–72 E. Barrett Prettyman, Matthew Fields, Melchisdec Green (Fields died October 1871; vacancy not filled until following term)
1872–73 William Veirs Bouic Jr., E. Barrett Prettyman, Melchisdec Green
1873–74 William Veirs Bouic Jr., Melchisdec Green, Reuben A. Bogley
1874–75 William Veirs Bouic Jr., Melchisdec Green, Reuben A. Bogley
1875–76 William Veirs Bouic Jr., Melchisdec Green, Reuben A. Bogley
1876–77 William Veirs Bouic Jr., Melchisdec Green, Spencer C. Jones
1877–78 William Veirs Bouic Jr., Melchisdec Green, Spencer C. Jones
1878–79 William Veirs Bouic Jr., Melchisdec Green, James P. Biays
1879–80 William Veirs Bouic Jr., Melchisdec Green, James P. Biays

COMMISSIONERS FOR ROCKVILLE

Two-Year Terms, Elected in May

(The first name listed received the highest number of votes and was the president of commissioners.)

1880–82 William Veirs Bouic Jr., Melchisdec Green, Charles E. Sommers (Bouic resigned in November 1880 and was replaced by Green), Nicholas D. Offutt (special election December 1880)

1882–84 Hattersly W. Talbott, Dr. Edward E. Stonestreet, William Veirs Bouic Jr.
1884–86 Hattersly W. Talbott, Dr. Edward E. Stonestreet, William Veirs Bouic Jr.
1886–88 William Veirs Bouic Jr., Dr. Edward E. Stonestreet, Hattersly W. Talbott

MAYOR AND COUNCIL OF ROCKVILLE

Body Begun 1888, Elected in May For Two-Year Terms

(The first person listed was elected as mayor.)

1888–90 William Veirs Bouic Jr., Reuben A. Bogley, Hattersly W. Talbott, John Kelchner, Dr. Edward E. Stonestreet
1890–92 Daniel F. Owens, Philip D. Laird, William Veirs Bouic Jr., Charles B. Jones, John M. Heagy, John W. Warner, C. W. Baggerley, Samuel B. Haney, Lee Offutt (Owens, Laird, and Bouic resigned in succession 1890–91; Heagy and Warner resigned 1890.)
1892–94 Hattersly W. Talbott, Jacob Poss, Albert S. Dalby, Albert King, Edwin M. West (Talbott resigned November 1893 and was replaced by Poss.)
1894–96 John G. England, Jacob Poss, Albert S. Dalby, Albert King, Edwin M. West
1896–98 Joseph Reading, James F. Allen, Samuel P. Hege, Lee Offutt, William R. Pumphrey
1898–1900 Spencer C. Jones, Hattersly W. Talbott, John T. Vinson, William W. Welsh, John G. England
1900–02 Spencer C. Jones, Hattersly W. Talbott, John T. Vinson, William W. Welsh, John G. England (Jones resigned November 1901 and was replaced by Talbott.)
1902–04 Hattersly W. Talbott, Robert C. Warfield, Lee Offutt, Benjamin C. Riggs, Albert S. Dalby
1904–06 Hattersly W. Talbott, Willis B. Burdette, Lee Offutt, Robert C. Warfield, David J. Bready
1906–08 Lee Offutt, Robert C. Warfield, Willis B. Burdette, David J. Bready, John L. Dawson
1908–10 Lee Offutt, John Brewer, Willis B. Burdette, Samuel Matlock, George Edmonds
1910–12 Lee Offutt, John Brewer, Thomas C. Groomes, Jacob Poss, William R. Pumphrey
1912–14 Lee Offutt, Thomas C. Groomes, Jacob Poss, Joseph Clagett, Clifford H. Robertson
1914–16 Lee Offutt, Jacob Poss, Joseph Clagett, Edward Hege, Willis B. Burdette
1916–18 Willis B. Burdette, Dr. O. M. Linthicum, Joseph Clagett, Martin Heim, H. Worthington Talbott
1918–20 Lee Offutt, Dr. O. M. Linthicum, Joseph Clagett, Martin Heim, H. Worthington Talbott
1920–22 Dr. O. M. Linthicum, Joseph Clagett, Charles G. Holland, Clifford H. Robertson, Washington Hicks
1922–24 Dr. O. M. Linthicum, Joseph Clagett, Charles G. Holland, Clifford H. Robertson, Washington Hicks
1924–26 Charles G. Holland, Joseph Clagett, Frank H. Higgins, H. Worthington Talbott, B. P. Wilson
1926–28 J. Roger Spates, J. Paul Brunett, Joseph Clagett, E. Stedman Prescott, H. Worthington Talbott
1928–30 J. Roger Spates, J. Paul Brunett, Joseph Clagett, E. Stedman Prescott, H. Worthington Talbott
1930–32 J. Roger Spates, J. Paul Brunett, Joseph Clagett, E. Stedman Prescott, H. Worthington Talbott
1932–34 Douglas M. Blandford, Thomas M. Anderson, Curtis L. Ward, Edgar Reed, Cooke A. Robertson
1934–36 Douglas M. Blandford, Thomas M. Anderson, Edgar Reed, Curtis L. Ward, G. LaMar Kelly
1936–38 Douglas M. Blandford, Thomas M. Anderson, G. LaMar Kelly, Oliver H. Perry, Edgar Reed
1938–40 Douglas M. Blandford, Edgar Reed, Oliver H. Perry, G. LaMar Kelly, Dr. William A. Linthicum
1940–42 Douglas M. Blandford, G. LaMar Kelly, Dr. William A. Linthicum, Oliver H. Perry, Edgar Reed
1942–44 Douglas M. Blandford, G. LaMar Kelly, Dr. William A. Linthicum, Oliver H. Perry, Frank E. Williams
1944–46 Douglas M. Blandford, Dr. William A. Linthicum, Oliver H. Perry, Frank E. Williams, Louis J. Ryan
1946–48 G. LaMar Kelly, Oliver H. Perry, Frank E. Williams, F. Bache Abert, Louis J. Ryan
1948–50 G. LaMar Kelly, Murray Bradshaw, Samuel Hersperger, Frank Higgins, Daniel Weddle
1950–52 G. LaMar Kelly, Murray Bradshaw, Samuel Hersperger, Frank Higgins, Daniel Weddle
1952–54 Daniel Weddle, Frank Higgins, Murray Bradshaw, J. Warren Milor, Frank E. Williams
1954–56 Dickran Y. Hovsepian, James Robertson Jr., Alexander J. Greene, John E. Oxley, Wendell Turner
1956–58 Dickran Y. Hovsepian, Alexander J. Greene, Frank A. Ecker, John E. Oxley, Wendell Turner (Turner resigned November 1957 and was replaced by John M. Rausch.)

1958–60 Alexander J. Greene, John M. Rausch, Joseph C. Rodgers, Charles W. Prettyman, Frank A. Ecker (Prettyman resigned October 1959 and was replaced by A. Tuchtan.)
1960–62 Alexander J. Greene, Achilles M. Tuchtan, Frank A. Ecker, Ralph E. Williams, Glen J. Koepenick
1962–64 Frank A. Ecker, Edward J. Mack, Achilles M. Tuchtan, Ralph E. Williams, L. Ross Roberts
1964–66 Frank A. Ecker, Robert S. Bryan, Achilles M. Tuchtan, Matthew J. McCartin, Edward J. Mack
1966–68 Frank A. Ecker, Robert S. Bryan, Matthew J. McCartin, Robert G. Prestemon, Achilles M. Tuchtan
1968–70 Achilles M. Tuchtan, Robert S. Bryan, Rupert G. Curry, William E. Hanna Jr., Matthew J. McCartin
1970–72 Achilles M. Tuchtan, Rupert G. Curry, William E. Hanna Jr., Matthew J. McCartin, David R. Alexander
1972–74 Matthew J. McCartin, Robert S. Bryan, William E. Hanna Jr., Jean R. Horneck, George F. Northway
1974–76 William E. Hanna Jr., Robert E. Buchanan, John R. Freeland, Richard R. Haight, David R. Porter
1976–78 William E. Hanna Jr., Robert E. Buchanan, Phyllis B. Fordham, John R. Freeland, Richard R. Haight
1978–80 William E. Hanna Jr., John R. Freeland, Phyllis B. Fordham, John Tyner II, Kenneth Sullivan
1980–82 William E. Hanna Jr., John R. Freeland, Phyllis B. Fordham, John Tyner II, Stephen N. Abrams
1982–84 John R. Freeland, Stephen N. Abrams, Douglas M. Duncan, Viola D. Hovsepian, John Tyner II
(eighteen month term due to change of election from April to November)
1984–85 John R. Freeland, Stephen N. Abrams, James F. Coyle, Douglas M. Duncan, Viola D. Hovesepian, John Tyner II, Peter R. Hartogensis (Freeland resigned November 1984 and was replaced by Hovsepian. Hartogensis was appointed November 1984.)
1985–87 Steven Van Grack, Stephen N. Abrams, James F. Coyle, Douglas M. Duncan, Peter R. Hartogensis
1987–89 Douglas M. Duncan, Stephen N. Abrams, James F. Coyle, Viola D. Hovsepian, David Robbins
1989–91 Douglas M. Duncan, James F. Coyle, Rose G. Krasnow, James T. Marrinan, David Robbins
1991–93 Douglas M. Duncan, James F. Coyle, Rose G. Krasnow, James T. Marrinan, David Robbins
1993–95 James F. Coyle, Robert E. Dorsey, Rose G. Krasnow, James T. Marrinan, Nina A. Weisbroth
1995–97 Rose G. Krasnow, Robert E. Dorsey, Glennon J. Harrison, James T. Marrinan, Robert J. Wright
1997–99 Rose G. Krasnow, Robert E. Dorsey, Glennon J. Harrison, James T. Marrinan, Robert J. Wright
1999–2001 Rose G. Krasnow, Robert E. Dorsey, Glennon J. Harrison, Anne M. Robbins, Robert J. Wright

POPULATION AND LAND AREA OF ROCKVILLE

Year	Population	Population Increase/ Decrease from Previous Period	Land Area in Acres
1860	365	N/A	134
1870	660	81.0%	134
1880	688	4.2%	139
1890	1,568	127.9%	228
1900	1,110	–19.2%	354
1910	1,181	4.5%	354
1920	1,145	–3.0%	354
1930	1,422	24.2%	354
1940	2,047	44.0%	466
1950	6,934	238.7%	2,753
1960	26,090	276.3%	4,473
1970	42,739	63.8%	7,047
1980	43,811	2.5%	7,416
1990	44,835	2.3%	7,583
2000	47,388	5.7%	8,640

⟜ Origins of Names in Rockville ⊸

By no means an exhaustive list, this appendix associates Rockville place names with people, places, events, common usage, and intentions of those who named them.

Anderson Avenue–early Rockville family of doctors, farmers, attorneys

Ashley Avenue–land patents to Anna Orme in 1786 and 1801; Crabb family home

Baltimore Road–route to port of Baltimore appeared on 1794 map

Beall Avenue–early Rockville family, including clerk of court Upton Beall

Bickford Avenue–Nathan Bickford of Washington, D.C., carved twenty-five lots in 1892.

Blandford Street–Douglas Blandford, mayor 1932–46, developed property in the area.

Bouic Avenue–nineteenth century Rockville family of attorneys, public officials

Broome Athletic Park–Edwin W. Broome, superintendent of schools, 1917–53

Bullard's Park–The Bullard family owned Chestnut Lodge Sanitarium and Rose Hill Farm.

Burgundy Lane, Court–1770 land patent to Ignatius Diggs, 1950s subdivisions

Cabin John Parkway– (tradition) a derivation of Captain John; one of three creeks flowing from Rockville to the Potomac River

Carr Avenue–The Carr family operated the Corcoran Hotel on East Montgomery Avenue.

Chapman Avenue–Leonard and Velinda Chapman of Washington subdivided Halpin along the Rockville Pike.

Clagett Drive–family in Montgomery County since the eighteenth century

College Gardens, Square, Parkway–names of American institutions of higher learning

Congressional Lane–The Congressional airfield was located on Rockville Pike from 1929–1958.

Courthouse Square–location of Montgomery County courthouses since 1788

Crabb Avenue, Crabbs Branch Way–Henry Wright Crabb, early settler

Darnestown Road–route on 1794 map led west to the next large settlement

Dawson Avenue–In the nineteenth century, the Dawsons owned land northwest of town center.

DeBeck Drive–Thomas O. DeBeck, developer of Rockcrest, 1940s

Dorothy Lane–wife and younger daughter of Twinbrook developer Joseph Geeraert

Douglass Avenue–Frederick Douglass was a former slave, an abolitionist, an orator, and an editor.

Duncan Branch Court–family owned Double D farm in Fallsmead

Edmonston Drive–family lived east of Rockville Pike, early 1900s–1940s

Elizabeth Avenue–daughter of Harrison England, who developed Croydon Park in 1924

England Terrace–early family in Rockville; Harrison England developed land near railroad tracks

Evans Street–1937 subdivision by Waring and Kate Evans west of town

Fayette Street–named for General Lafayette, hero of American Revolution; hotel in Rockville 1820s; street removed for urban renewal

Fields Road–Rebecca Fields of the *Sentinel* newspaper farmed along Frederick Road from 1884–1942.

Fleet Street–Fur trader Henry Fleet sailed up the Potomac River and described future Montgomery County in 1624.

Forest Avenue–Lucy Smith's name for the view from her home at 108 Forest Avenue

Fortune Terrace–Wheel of Fortune was the 1747 land patent to William O'Neal.

Frederick Road–main road from Georgetown, through Rockville, to Frederick

Gaither Road–early family in area north of Rockville

Grandin Avenue–name of William Reading's maternal grandfather, see *Reading*

Gude Drive–family horticultural farm, Gude Nursery operated 1920s–1981

Halpine Road–originally Halpin, subdivided by L. S. Chapman in 1889, near Rockville Pike; see *Rollins* and *Chapman*

Horizon Hill–name of mansion on Falls Road that was demolished in 1973

Horners Lane–John and Frank Horner operated a mill on Rock Creek in the nineteenth and twentieth centuries.

Howard Avenue–name in family of Harrison England, who developed Croydon Park

Hungerford Drive–Charles Hungerford operated a tavern in colonial Rockville.

Hurley Drive–farming family west of Watts Branch, nineteenth and twentieth centuries

Janeta–Catherine Jane Harding Maddox and husband Charles J. Maddox sold building lots around First Street and Veirs Mill Road in the 1880s.

Joseph Street–A son of William Reading, Washington merchant and developer, druggist Joseph Reading was mayor of Rockville 1896–1898. See also *Reading.*

Julius West Middle School–nineteenth century farmer west of Rockville, left land to trustees of the Rockville Academy

Laird Street–Philip D. Laird was an attorney, a founder of County Bar Association, and a member of the Maryland House of Delegates.

Lincoln Avenue–Many post-Civil War developments for blacks honored the president who emancipated slaves.

Longhorn Crescent–Irvington Farms featured registered Longhorn cattle.

Luckett Street–Cooke D. Luckett was a Confederate veteran, educator, and realtor.

Lyon Place–adjacent to Glenview, home of Irene and James Lyon for thirty years

Madison Street–once in town center, removed during urban renewal, now in Woodley Gardens

Mannakee Street–F. H. Mannakee was a Rockville dentist in the 1870s.

Marcia Lane–second wife of Twinbrook developer Joseph Geeraert

Martin's Lane–farm of Samuel Martin Jr., a free black man, 1830s–1873

Meadow Hall Drive–Samuel C. Veirs's home above Rock Creek, razed 1960s

Montgomery Avenue–Richard Montgomery was a Revolutionary War hero who never saw Maryland.

Montrose Road–old community on the Rockville Pike, only the schoolhouse remains

New Mark Commons–planned towns and garden cities throughout the world

North Farm Lane–refers to north of Old Farm (earlier Kettler Brothers development) and back farm of Lydannes and Bradleys, owners of land now known as Woodmont Country Club

Orchard Ridge, Way–area was the Rockville Fruit Farm (1920s–1950s), known for apples and peaches

Owens Street, Court–Daniel F. Owens was a Rockville druggist 1872–1901.

Park Avenue, Park Street School–in the Park, an 1888 subdivision with streets named for trees

Pinneberg Avenue–Rockville's sister city in Germany

Pipestem Place, Court–Maude W. Betts, resident of Hectic Hill, described its shape

Potomac Springs–for nearby springhouse where people obtained water, also the Potomac zip code

Randolph Road–James L. Randolph was the chief engineer of B&O who planned route of the Metropolitan Branch tracks through Montgomery County in the late 1860s–1870s.

Reading Avenue–William Reading, a Washington, D.C., coal and lumber merchant, developed Rockville Park east of railroad tracks in 1888. See also *Joseph.*

RedGate–name of the Nagle Farm, now municipal golf course

Research Boulevard–first light industrial park in Rockville, 1960

Richard Montgomery Drive–see *Montgomery*

Rockville Pike–road chartered by Maryland General Assembly in 1805; toll turnpike

Rollins Avenue–Isaac Rollins owned land in area once known as Halpine. See also *Halpine.*

Rosanne Lane–elder daugher of Twinbrook developer Joseph Geeraert

Rose Hill–farm on Falls Road that dates back to early 1800s

Rothgeb Drive–long-time director of Department of Public Works who died suddenly in 1979

Scott Drive–family lived at Horizon Hill mansion on Falls Road

Stonestreet Avenue–family owned land near railroad tracks and in town

Thomas Street–in Rebecca Thomas Veirs's subdivision of 1887

Thompson Dairy Way–King Farm operation sold milk to Thompson's Dairy.

Town Center/West End–streets named for seven of the first eight U.S. presidents (minus Jackson)

Trail House Court–The Trail family lived in Fallsmead area in the nineteenth and twentieth centuries.

Twinbrook Parkway–two streams on property; streets named for military heroes and battles

Upton Street–Upton Beall was second clerk of the circuit court.

Veirs Mill Road–Samuel C. Veirs operated a sawmill and a gristmill on Rock Creek.

Vinson Street–Vinson family home was razed for the Rockville library.

Virginia Avenue–daughter of Harrison England, who developed Croydon Park in 1924

Watts Branch Parkway–one of three major streams flowing through Rockville to the Potomac River

Welsh Park–family donated land for athletic field 1920s–1952; successor park 1967

Williams Street–Richard Williams divided land along stable lane behind his house into lots for sale, 1914.

Windy Knoll Court–across Darnestown Road from Windy Knoll, the Thomas farm

Woodley Gardens–flowers and bushes

Wootton Parkway, Thomas S. Wootton High School–doctor in early Rockville; made motion to create Montgomery County in 1776

ROCKVILLE NEIGHBORHOODS

The following locations and names represent those geographic areas commonly considered to be distinct neighborhoods by city residents and staff.

Brown's Addition
Burgundy Estates
Burgundy Hills
Burgundy Knolls
Burgundy Village
Cambridge Heights
Cambridge Walk
Carter Hills
Chadsberry
Charles Walk
College Gardens
College Square
Courthouse Walk
Croydon Park
East Rockville
England's Second Addition
Fallsbend
Fallsmead
Falls Ridge
Fallswood
Fireside
Flint Ledge
Glen Hills Club
Glenora Hill
Great Pines
Griffith Oaks
Haiti
Halpine
Harriet Park
Heritage Park
Horizon Hill
Hungerford-Stoneridge
Janeta
Jefferson Square
King Farm
Lincoln Park
Lynfield
Markwood
Maryvale
Montrose
Monument Park
New Mark Commons
North Farm
Orchard Ridge
Plymouth Woods
Potomac Springs
Potomac Woods
Redgate Farms
Rock Falls
Rockcrest
Rockdale
Rockshire
Rockville Heights
Rockville Park
Rose Hill Falls
Roxboro
Saddlebrook
Silver Rock
Town Center
Twinbrook
Twinbrook Forest
Village Green
Villages at Tower Oaks
Waddington Park
Watts Branch Meadows
West End
Woodley Gardens
Woodley Gardens East-West
Woodmont Overlook
Woodmont Park
Woodmont Spring

Notes

CHAPTER 1

1. Andrew J. Wahll, *Braddock Road Chronicles* (Bowie, Md.: Heritage Books, 1999), 1–7, 134.
2. Samuel Eliot Morison, *The Oxford History of the American People* (New York: Oxford University Press, 1965), 161–3.
3. In July 1913, the Janet Montgomery Chapter of the Daughters of the American Revolution commemorated General Braddock's stay with a bronze memorial which still stands on the courthouse grounds.
4. Archeology in Montgomery County has been conducted by professionals from the Maryland Geological Survey, Maryland Historical Trust, the Smithsonian Institution, National Park Service, and Maryland-National Capital Park and Planning Commission (M-NCPPC), the volunteer Archeological Society of Maryland, organized student groups, and knowledgeable individuals.
5. James D. Sorensen, "The Piedmont and Coastal Plain Provinces of Maryland: A Culture History" (The Catholic University of America, Department of Archaeology, 1982), 3–4, 8.
6. Mark Walston, "Pre-Contact Indians of Montgomery County," *The Montgomery County Story* 29, no. 1 (February 1986).
7. Files of the Department of Parks, M-NCPPC Archaeology office, Derwood, Maryland.
8. James D. Sorensen, M-NCPPC archeologist, conversation with author, March 2000.
9. John Baines, M-NCPPC naturalist, conversation with author, Black Hill Regional Park, Boyds, Maryland, March 2000.
10. *Maryland Historical Magazine* 15 (May 1920): 388.
11. Eleanor M. V. Cook, "The Land Divided and Mapped," *The Montgomery County Story* 40, no. 4 (November 1997).
12. Robert J. Brugger, *Maryland: A Middle Temperament 1634–1980* (Baltimore: Johns Hopkins University Press, 1988), 4–16.
13. Richard K. MacMaster and Ray Eldon Hiebert, *A Grateful Remembrance: The Story of Montgomery County, Maryland* (Rockville: Montgomery County Government and Montgomery County Historical Society, 1976), 8–9.
14. Florence Howard, Sheila Cochran, and Mary Charlotte Crook, "Montgomery County Land Patents" (Montgomery County Historical Society, Rockville, Md., 1977).
15. Cook, *Story*, 6–10.
16. Donna Valley Russell, "1733 Taxables," *Western Maryland Genealogy* 3, no. 3 (July 1987): 99–101.
17. Brugger, *Maryland*, 42–63.
18. Ibid., 59–70.
19. Ibid., 16–17.
20. MacMaster and Hiebert, *Remembrance*, 13–14.
21. T. H. S. Boyd, *The History of Montgomery County, Maryland, from its Earliest Settlement in 1650 to 1879* (Clarksburg, 1879; Baltimore: Regional Publishing Company, 1968), 50, 75.
22. Brugger, *Maryland*, 52–56.
23. Maude Wilson Betts, *Piscataway to Prince George's Parish* (Rockville, Maryland: n.p., 1976), 2–3, 7–10.

CHAPTER 2

1. Brugger, *Maryland*, 97.
2. Anne W. Cissel, "Public Houses of Entertainment and Their Proprietors 1750–1828," *The Montgomery County Story* 30, no. 3 (August 1987).
3. Brugger, *Maryland*, 102–8. Morison, *Oxford History*, 181–2.
4. *Maryland Gazette* (Annapolis, Md.), 17 June 1774.
5. MacMaster and Hiebert, *Remembrance*, 30–1.
6. J. Thomas Scharf, *History of Western Maryland* (Philadelphia: 1882; Baltimore: Regional Publishing, 1968), 1: 127.
7. MacMaster and Hiebert, *Remembrance*, 37–8.
8. For more information on Montgomery County's participation in the war, see Neal Fitzsimons, "The Maryland Line" *The Montgomery County Story* 19, no. 1 (February 1976). MacMaster and Hiebert, "Montgomery County—1776," *The Montgomery County Story* 19, no. 3 (August 1976).
9. Helen W. Ridgely, *Historic Graves of Maryland and the District of Columbia* (Baltimore: Genealogical Publishing, 1967), 174.
10. Higgins family file, Peerless Rockville collections, Rockville, Md.
11. MacMaster and Hiebert, *Remembrance*, 52–55.
12. Ibid., 55.
13. Martha Sprigg Poole, "The Maryland Constitutional Convention of 1776," *The Montgomery County Story* 10, no. 4 (August 1967), 10–13.
14. Montgomery County Court Minute Book, Maryland State Archives, March 1783.
15. Montgomery County Assessment Records, Maryland State Archives, 1783. Thomas Owen Williams, Elisha Owen Williams, and Edward Williams conveyed their interests to their brother William Prather Williams in August of 1784. Montgomery County Land Records, C67 (1784).
16. Montgomery County Land Records, Judicial Center, Rockville, Md., C67 (1784).
17. Ibid., K442 (1803).
18. Montgomery County Assessment Records, 1798.
19. John C. Fitzpatrick, ed., *Diaries of George Washington, 1748–1799*, (New York: Houghton Mifflin, 1925), 4:201.
20. *Maryland Journal & Baltimore Advertiser*, 23 January 1784.
21. Land Records, C339 (1786).
22. Ibid., JGH6/70 (recorded 1857).
23. *The National Genealogical Society Quarterly* 1, no. 2 (July 1912), 34.
24. Charles Dawson, archeological files, 1973, Archeological Society of Maryland and Montgomery County High School Archeology Club, Peerless Rockville collections, Rockville, Md. (1987).
25. Frederick Gutheim, *The Potomac* (New York: Grosset & Dunlap, 1949), 34.
26. *The George-Town Weekly Ledger*, 23 July 1791.
27. U.S. Bureau of the Census, *Federal Population Census 1800*, National

Archives and Records Administration (Washington, D.C.,1800).

28. Brugger, *Maryland*, 167–172.
29. Maryland Historical Trust Inventory Form 26/10/16, Peerless Rockville collections, Rockville, Md.
30. Mayvis Fitzsimons, "Women in the History of Montgomery County," *The Montgomery County Story* 16, no. 4 (November 1973): 6, 11.
31. Eleanor Cook, "Apprentice and Master in Montgomery County," *The Montgomery County Story* 37, no. 2, (May 1994): 303–5.
32. *Laws of Maryland* (1801), 76.
33. Ibid.
34. *Laws*, Supplemental Act (1802), 28.
35. Land Records, recorded certificate, L183 (1803).
36. William Smith, *Plan of Rockville, Montgomery County* (16 July 1803), City Hall, Rockville, Md.
37. Thomas Anderson, address, *Centennial Celebration of the Erection of Montgomery County, Md. into a Separate Municipality. Held at Rockville, September 6th, 1876* (Baltimore: C.C. Saffell, 1877), 14–15.
38. Maryland Historical Trust Inventory Form 26/11/6.

CHAPTER 3

1. Joseph Scott, *A Geographical Description of the States of Maryland and Delaware* (Philadelphia, 1807), 145.
2. MacMaster and Hiebert, *Remembrance*, 78–9, 397, 402–3.
3. MacMaster and Hiebert, *Remembrance*, 83–7. Anthony S. Pitch, *The Burning of Washington: The British Invasion of 1814* (Annapolis: Naval Institute Press, 1998), 1–12.
4. Pitch, *Burning*, 30–152.
5. Contemporary names are often used throughout this book. In 1814, although the plan read "Rockville," the village was most often called "Montgomery Court House." Also, George Town and Tenally Town were the spellings in the time period.
6. Maureen Altobello, *A House Through Time* (Rockville: Montgomery County Historical Society, 2000), 3–16.
7. Scharf, *Western Maryland*, 1: 683–5. According to unpublished research by Judith Christensen and Gail Littlefield (1998), Scharf mistakenly described Nugent as a Revolutionary War survivor.
8. John H. McGarry III, "The War of 1812 and its Effect on Montgomery County," *The Montgomery County Story* 26, no. 1 (February 1983).
9. MacMaster and Hiebert, *Remembrance*, 93–105.
10. Gutheim, *The Potomac* (New York: Grosset & Dunlap, 1949), 207–8.
11. Brugger, Maryland, 153.
12. "Cumberland Road map of the country through which it is proposed to extend the National Road to the Tidewaters within the District of Columbia" (1826) and "Map of the country embracing the several routes examined with a view to a National Road from Washington to Buffalo" (1827), RG77, National Archives.
13. MacMaster and Hiebert, *Remembrance*, 106–7, 141–3.
14. Eileen McGuckian, *Historic and Architectural Guide to the Rockville Pike* (Rockville: Peerless Rockville, 1997), 2–4.
15. MacMaster and Hiebert, *Remembrance*, 107–8.
16. Scharf, *Western Maryland*, 1:698.
17. Jane C. Sween and William Offutt, *Montgomery County: Centuries of Change* (Sun Valley, Ca.: American Historical Press, 1999), 56.
18. Mary Charlotte Crook, "The Rockville Academy," *The Montgomery County Story* 31, no. 3 (August 1988): 1–4.
19. Mayvis Fitzsimons, "Women's Schools in Rockville," *The Peer*, no. 5 (Spring 1977).
20. Saint Mary's Parish, *Historic Saint Mary's, Montgomery County, Maryland* (Rockville: The Parish, 1963), 14.
21. Moncure D. Conway, *Autobiography* (1904; reprint, Boston: Houghton Mifflin, 1970), described in Eileen McGuckian, "Maryland Methodism and the Jerusalem United Methodist Church, Rockville, Maryland," *The Montgomery County Story* 15, no. 5 (November 1972): 4–5.
22. Saint Mary's Parish, *Historic Saint Mary's*, 1–11.
23. Research by Eileen McGuckian, in Methodist Church file, Peerless Rockville collections, Rockville, Md.
24. Maryland Historical Trust Inventory Form 26/10/72.
25. Maryland Historical Trust Inventory Form 26/10/22.
26. Scharf, *Western Maryland*, 674–5. Boyd, *History of Montgomery County*, 63–66.
27. U. S. Bureau of the Census, *Population Schedules, 1800–1860*. No separate statistics were kept for Rockville prior to 1860, but in most years the enumerator indicated Rockville residents.
28. Martin family files, Peerless Rockville collections, Rockville, Md.
29. Samuel Martin, Inventory of Personal Estate, V193–4 (1837), Maryland State Archives, Annapolis, Md.
30. Hellen Martin, unprobated will (17 June 1837), in personal files of Sharyn R. Duffin, Rockville, Md.
31. MacMaster and Hiebert, *Remembrance*, 114, 124–5.
32. Ibid., 133–148.
33. Barbara Jeanne Fields, *Slavery and Freedom on the Middle Ground: Maryland During the Nineteenth Century* (New Haven: Yale University Press, 1985), 1–22.
34. *Sentinel*, 15 September 1855.
35. MacMaster and Hiebert, *Remembrance*, 152.
36. Ross-Powell family files, research by Eileen McGuckian, Peerless Rockville collections, Rockville, Md.
37. Mayvis Fitzsimons, "Uncle Tom in Montgomery County," *The Montgomery County Story* 18, no. 1–2 (February and May 1975).
38. MacMaster and Hiebert, *Remembrance*, 157–8.
39. Anthony Cohen, *The Underground Railroad in Montgomery County, Maryland* (Rockville: Montgomery County Historical Society, 1995), 13–14, 17–18.
40. Ibid., 11–17.
41. Ibid., 15–17.
42. Anderson, *Centennial*, 27.
43. Mark Walston, "Montgomery County Inventors and Inventions 1803–1873," *The Montgomery County Story* 29, no. 4 (November 1986): 239. U.S. Patent #72370.
44. George M. Anderson, S.J., "The Montgomery County Agricultural Society: The Beginning Years,

1846–1850," *Maryland Historical Magazine* 81, no. 4 (Winter 1986): 305–315.

45. Mary Charlotte Crook, "The Rockville Fair," *The Montgomery County Story* 18, no. 3 (August 1975).
46. Bureau of the Census, *Agricultural Census of Montgomery County 1860*, Glenview file, Peerless Rockville collections, Rockville, Md.
47. Eleanor Cook, "Winemaking in Montgomery County," (Montgomery County Historical Society). Scharf, *Western Maryland*, 722.
48. James W. and Mary Anderson, correspondence, Peerless Rockville collections, Rockville, Md.
49. Jean Russo, "The Early Towns of Montgomery County," *The Montgomery County Story* 34, no. 2 (May 1991): 156–9.
50. *Sentinel*, 27 August 1858.
51. William Thomson, *Thomson's Mercantile and Professional Directory for the States of Delaware, Maryland, Virginia, North Carolina and the District of Columbia*, in Eleanor M. V. Cook, *Guide to the Records of Montgomery County*, 2nd ed. (Westminster, Md.: Family Line Publications, 1997), 10.
52. *Laws of Maryland*, (1817) 79. *Laws of Maryland*, (1825) 25.
53. Scharf, *Western Maryland*, 667.
54. Minutes of the Montgomery County Commissioners, Montgomery County Council Archives, Rockville, Md., 1844–1899, 22 November 1864.
55. Emily Correll, "Crimes in Montgomery County," *The Montgomery County Story* 41, no. 3 (August 1998): 37–38. MacMaster files, Crime folder, Montgomery County Historical Society, Rockville, Md.
56. Patricia Andersen, "The Almshouse, later called the County Home, 1789–1948," *The Montgomery County Story* 41, no. 2 (May 1998): 27.
57. *Laws of Maryland Act*, (1806) 47. Montgomery County Land Records, Y521–523 (1826).
58. Montgomery County Equity Records, Judicial Center, Rockville, Md., 27 October 1828.
59. *Sentinel*, 3 February 1860.
60. "An Act to Incorporate the town of Rockville in Montgomery County," *Laws of Maryland* (1860) 373.
61. Mary Anderson to James W. Anderson, 19 March 1860, Peerless Rockville collections, Rockville, Md.
62. *Laws*, "Act to Incorporate," (1860).

CHAPTER 4

1. Diary of Charles Abert, 20 May 1861–68 July 1863, entry 20 July 1861, Montgomery County Historical Society Collections, Rockville, Md.
2. *Sentinel*, 26 December 1862.
3. Wartime memories passed down through the Anderson, Dawson, and Higgins families enrich this account. F. Scott Fitzgerald wrote in his foreword to Don Swann Jr., *Colonial and Historic Homes of Maryland: One Hundred Etchings* (Baltimore: Johns Hopkins University Press, 1939) that he thrived on stories of Confederate soldiers and spies told to him by his father, Edward. Edward Fitzgerald was born in 1853 on Locust Grove farm in the northwest portion of the Rockville election district.
4. *Sentinel*, 4 January 1861. Jane C. Sween and William Offutt, *Montgomery County: Centuries of Change* (Sun Valley, California: American Historical Press, 1999), 68–70.
5. Brugger, *Maryland*, 269–283.
6. Sween and Offutt, *Centuries*, 69–74. Charles T. Jacobs, *Civil War Guide to Montgomery County, Maryland* (Rockville: Montgomery County Historical Society, 1983), 1–2, 45–46.
7. Excerpts from regimental histories, in the personal files of Charles T. Jacobs, Washington Grove, Maryland.
8. *Philadelphia Inquirer*, 17 December 1861.
9. *New York Times*, 13 September 1861.
10. *New York Times*, 12 September 1861.
11. *Sentinel*, 14 November 1862.
12. Sween and Offutt, *Centuries*, 70.
13. Scharf, *Western Maryland*, 1: 754–56. Leslie Abbe, "The Story of Judge Richard Johns Bowie," *The Montgomery County Story* 15, no. 2 (February 1972). *Biographical Directory of the U.S. Congress, 1774–1961*, 580.
14. F. Terry Hambricht, "Dr. Edward Elisha Stonestreet: A Nineteenth-Century Country Doctor", *The Montgomery County Story* 30, no. 4 (November 1987), 3–7.
15. Slave Military Record of Montgomery County, Maryland, microfilm transcription by Nina H. Clarke, Montgomery County Historical Society, Rockville, Md. Charles B. Clark, "Recruitment of Union Troops in Maryland, 1861–1865," *Maryland Historical Magazine* 53, no. 2 (June 1958).
16. Jacobs, *Guide*, 2.
17. George M. Anderson, S.J., "A Captured Confederate Officer," *Maryland Historical Magazine* 76, no. 1 (Spring 1981): 62–9.
18. Mary Dawson Gray, Mollie's grandniece, conversation with author, July 2000.
19. U.S. War Department, *The War of the Rebellion: A Compilation of the Official Records of the Union and Confederate Armies*, (Washington, D.C.: U.S. Government Printing Office, 1880–1901, reprint, Historical Times, 1985). 3d ser., vol. 3: 363.
20. *Sentinel*, 18 January 1861.
21. Charles and Marian Waters Jacobs, "Matthew Fields and the *Montgomery County Sentinel*," *The Montgomery County Story* 36, no. 2 (May 1993): 253–8.
22. Jacobs, *Guide*, 46. Abert, Diary, 11 September 1862.
23. Charles C. Keeney, U.S. Army surgeon, to Charles S. Tripler, Army of the Potomac medical director, 18 November 1861.
24. John A. Cole, *Personal Reminiscences*, in collection of Charles Jacobs, handwritten, 15–16.
25. Betts, *Piscataway*, 13.
26. Sophia Dorothy Barnard Higgins to Mrs. Robert Barton Barnard, 29 June 1863, Betts, *Piscataway*, 25–28.
27. Richard J. Bowie, John G. England, and James G. Henning to Major General Banks, National Archives, RG393, Part 2, Entry 646, 1862.
28. John Esten Cooke, *Wearing of the Gray: Being Personal Portraits, Scenes and Adventures of the War* (New York: E. B. Treat, 1867).
29. *New York Tribune*, 1 July 1863. Eugene Curtis, personal collections, Frederick, Md.
30. Sophia Dorothy Barnard Higgins to Mrs. Robert Barton Barnard, 29 June 1863, Betts, *Piscataway*, 25–28.

31. (Baltimore) *Sun*, 19 July 1864 (dateline Rockville, 16 July).
32. Michael F. Fitzpatrick, "Jubal Early and the Californians," *Civil War Times* (May 1998): 54.
33. Ibid., 57.
34. Jacobs, *Guide*, 48–9. Fitzpatrick, "Jubal Early," 51–61. Richard Arkin, "Rockville at War in 1864," *Rockville Gazette*, 24 June 1987.
35. Acts of the Maryland General Assembly (1867) 169.
36. Barbara Jeanne Fields, *Slavery and Freedom on the Middle Ground: Maryland During the Nineteenth Century* (New Haven: Yale University Press, 1985), 121–149.
37. Mrs. R. J. Bowie to Captain R. G. Rutherford, 5 March 1867. Freedmen's Bureau Records, RG105, Maryland, Box 12, National Archives.
38. Freedmen's Bureau Records, RG105, Maryland, Box 12, National Archives. Fields, *Slavery and Freedom*, 145.
39. "A Rockville Journal," Part II, *The Montgomery County Story* 28, no. 3 (July/August 1985): 13. Charles Jacobs, personal collections, Washington Grove, Md.
40. Ed Steers Jr. and Jayne L. Greene, "Surratt's Rockville Lecture," *The Peer* no. 4, (Fall 1976).
41. Albert M. Bouic, *Country Lawyer-Third Generation* (n.p., 1958), 12.
42. Election results 1860–1880, Town of Rockville, Montgomery County Archives, Rockville, Md. U.S. Census, 1860.
43. Susan C. Soderberg, *Lest We Forget: A Guide to Civil War Monuments in Maryland* (Shippensburg, Penn.: White Mane Publishing, 1995), 56–58.
44. Corporation Ordinances, 12 June 1866, Montgomery County Archives, Rockville, Md.
45. Minutes of the Town Commissioners, 1865–1876, Montgomery County Archives, Rockville, Md.
46. E. Guy Jewell, *From One Room to Open Space*, (Rockville: Montgomery County Public Schools, 1976), 39.
47. Ibid., 21–65.
48. R. G. Rutherford to Brigadier General O. H. Howard, Bureau of Refugees, Freedmen and Abandoned Lands, 7 September 1866, Freedmen's Bureau Records, RG105, Maryland, Box 12, National Archives.
49. Subscription list for support of school at Rockville, Freedmen's Bureau Records.
50. Nina H. Clarke, *History of the Nineteenth Century Black Churches in Maryland and Washington, D.C.* (Silver Spring: Bartleby Press, 1987), 48–52.
51. Minutes of the Town Commissioners, 4 March 1873, Montgomery County Archives, Rockville, Md.
52. Montgomery County Land Records, Judicial Center, Rockville, Md.: EBP9/477 (1871).
53. Haiti file, 1988–1998, Peerless Rockville collections, Rockville, Md.
54. *National Republican*, 15 August 1873.

CHAPTER 5

1. *Montgomery County Sentinel*, 30 May 1873.
2. William E. Hutchinson, "Gaithersburg and the Railroad" in *Gaithersburg—The Heart of Montgomery County* (City of Gaithersburg, Maryland, 1978). Montgomery County Land Records, Judicial Center, Rockville, Maryland, EBP31.
3. *Sentinel*, 6 June 1873.
4. Anne Cissel and Mead Karras, Peerless Rockville collections, Rockville, Md. Maryland Historical Trust Inventory Form 26/12/4.
5. Genevieve B. Wimsatt, interview by author, 1984, transcript, Peerless Rockville collections, Rockville, Md.
6. Susan C. Soderberg, *The Met: A History of the Metropolitan Branch of the B&O Railroad, its Stations and Towns* (Germantown Historical Society, 1998), 7–8.
7. *Centennial Celebration of the Erection of Montgomery County, Md. into a Separate Municipality. Held at Rockville, September 6th, 1876* (Baltimore: C.C. Saffell, 1877), 28.
8. Maryland Historical Trust Inventory Form 26/10/4.
9. Kenneth T. Jackson, *Crabgrass Frontier: The Suburbanization of the United States* (New York: Oxford University Press, 1985), 20–102.
10. Fredric M. Miller and Howard Gillette Jr., *Washington Seen: A Photographic History, 1875–1965* (Baltimore: Johns Hopkins University Press, 1995), 3–29. MacMaster and Hiebert, *Remembrance*, 207–8.
11. *Centennial*, 29.
12. *Sentinel*, 23 October 1885.
13. Mary Gordon Malloy and Stephen Cromwell Jr., great-grandchildren of Rebecca T. Veirs, conversations with author, 2000. Peerless Rockville collections, Rockville, Maryland. *Sentinel*, 18 January 1918.
14. *Sentinel*, 28 April 1899.
15. Sharyn R. Duffin, "Lincoln Park Historic District," written for the Afro-American Bicentennial Corporation, 1978.
16. Henry N. Copp, *How to Get Health, Wealth, Comfort: What It Offers to Homeseekers and Investors*, (Washington, D. C.: Gibson Brothers, 1890), 16.
17. Montgomery County Land Records, TD17/306.
18. Montgomery County Land Records, 1887–1893. *Sentinel*, 25 April 1873.
19. Maryland Historical Trust Inventory Form 26/10/8.
20. Margaret DeLap, Peerless Rockville collections, Rockville, Md.
21. Maryland Historical Trust Inventory Form 26/15/4. Norma Duffin and Sharyn R. Duffin, conversations with author, 2000. *Sentinel*, 3 September 1915.
22. Minutes of the Mayor and Council of Rockville, Montgomery County Archives, Rockville, Maryland, 13 December 1902.
23. Minutes of the Mayor and Council, 1898–1908. *Sentinel*, 1900–1908.
24. Matt Karp, Francis Tosh, and recollections of Rockville residents, Peerless Rockville collections, Rockville, Md.
25. The phrase "walking city" was coined by Sam Bass Warner Jr. in *Streetcar Suburbs* (Cambridge, Mass.: Harvard University Press, 1962), and was further defined by Jackson in *Crabgrass Frontier*, 14–16.
26. U.S. Census, Population Schedules, 1880 and 1900. Unfortunately, records of the 1890 census were destroyed by fire.
27. Ibid., 1900.
28. Catherine Shaw Bride, interview by author, 1984, transcript in Peerless Rockville collections, Rockville, Md.

29. Bouic, *Country Lawyer*, 11–12.
30. Sarah Berthelsen, Peerless Rockville collections, Rockville, Md. Minutes of the Mayor and Council, 10 December 1895.
31. *Sentinel*, 2 February 1900.
32. Martha Royer, interview by Maria Spiridopoulos and Janet Zachary, 1974, transcript in Peerless Rockville collections, Rockville, Md.
33. Bouic, *Country Lawyer*, 209. Bride, interview.
34. Maryland Historical Trust Inventory Form 26/10/4. Dexter M. Bullard, M.D., "History of Chestnut Lodge" (paper presented in Toronto, Canada, 1968), Peerless Rockville collections, Rockville, Md.
35. James P. Collins, "William Wallace Welsh and His Rockville Store," *The Montgomery County Story* 43, no. 1 (February 2000).
36. *Sentinel*, 23 May 1884.
37. Bouic, *Country Lawyer*, 191.
38. Eileen McGuckian, "Once, Getting Married Was Easy," *Rockville Gazette*, 15 July 1987.
39. Tax Ledger #1, Town of Rockville, 1893–1909, Montgomery County Archives, Rockville, Md. Minutes of the Mayor and Council, 1900.
40. *Fire Insurance Map of Rockville, Md.*, Sanborn Insurance maps, (New York: Parris Map, 1897 and 1915). U.S. Bureau of the Census, U.S. Census, *Population Schedules 1880, 1900, 1910, 1920.*
41. Montgomery County Land Records, JA3/59 (1886).
42. *Sentinel*, 28 May 1897.
43. *Sentinel*, 1 June 1900.
44. Eleanor M. V. Cook, "Life in Montgomery Co at the Turn of the Last Century," *The Montgomery County Story* 42, no. 4 (November 1999): 110. William A. Linthicum, "He Never Left Home," 1977, 46–51,Glenview Mansion historical collections, Rockville, Md.
45. Jill Watts, *God, Harlem U.S.A.* (Berkeley, University of California, 1992), 1–14.
46. Mary Dawson Gray, Fannie and Hal Dawson's granddaughter interview by author, 1994, transcript in Peerless Rockville collections, Rockville, Md.
47. Bride, interview.
48. Robert H. Wiebe, *The Search for Order* (New York: Hill and Wang, 1967), 20.
49. *Montgomery Journal*, 25 June 1845.
50. Minutes of the Rockville Library Association, 1869–1876, Montgomery County Archives, Rockville, Md.
51. *Sentinel*, 8 October 1880. Minutes of the Montgomery County Commissioners, 13 December 1881, County Council Office, Rockville, Md.
52. Roll of Members and Minutes, Rockville Literary Society, 1888, Montgomery County Historical Society, Rockville, Md.
53. Montgomery County Land Records, Judicial Center, Rockville, Md., Articles of Incorporation, EBP1/50 (February 1881).
54. *Sentinel*, 11 February 1881. *Sentinel*, 8 July 1881.
55. *Sentinel*, 14 July 1882. *Sentinel*, 21 July 1882.
56. Time Line, the Woman's Club of Rockville. Woman's Club of Rockville, "Excerpts from the Past: Woman's Club of Rockville, 1900 to 1975" (n.d.), Peerless Rockville collections, Rockville, Md.
57. MacMaster and Hiebert, *Remembrance*, 245.
58. Minutes of the County Commissioners, 21 August 1877.
59. *Sentinel*, 3 August 1877.
60. Minutes of the Mayor and Council, 20 December 1916.
61. Clarke, *Black Churches,* 87–91.
62. Maryland Historical Trust Inventory Form 26/18/1.
63. Obituary of R. T. Veirs, *Sentinel*, 18 January 1918.
64. David Charles Sloane, *The Last Great Necessity: Cemeteries in American History* (Baltimore: Johns Hopkins University Press, 1991), 64–156.
65. Seventy-Fifth Anniversary Homecoming booklet, Free Methodist Church, October 1975, Peerless Rockville collections, Rockville, Md.
66. Maryland Historical Trust Inventory Form 26/16/5.
67. *Montgomery Journal*, 7 February 1846.
68. Noma Thompson, *Western Gateway to the National Capital (Rockville, Maryland)* (Washington: Stewart Printing Company, 1950), 34.
69. Bar Association of Montgomery County, *100 Years of Legal Tradition, 1894–1994*, (Bar Association of Montgomery County, Maryland, 1994), 18.
70. Order of Galilean Fisherman, charter document (1912) owned by Helen Welsh, Rockville, Maryland.
71. Duffin, "Lincoln Park Historic District."
72. Barnard T. Welsh, interview by author, 1983, transcript in Peerless Rockville collections, Rockville, Md.
73. Bar Association, *Legal Tradition,* 17–19.
74. Thompson, *Western Gateway*, 67.
75. Mary and Eben Jenkins, *The First Hundred Years: Maryland State Grange 1874–1974* (Maryland State Grange, 1974), 123.
76. Maryland Historical Trust Inventory Form 26/10/36.
77. *Baltimore Sun*, 2 October 1922.
78. *Laws of the State of Maryland*, Chapter 339 (1888), 135.
79. *Sentinel*, 27 January 1888.
80. Bureau of the Census, U.S. Census, *Population Schedule 1880.*
81. Minutes of the Mayor and Council, April–June 1888, Montgomery County Archives, Rockville, Md.
82. Ibid., 26 May 1890.
83. Ibid., 1888–1895.
84. *Portrait and Biographical Record of the Sixth Congressional District, Maryland* (New York: Chapman Publishing, 1898), 158–161.
85. *Portrait and Biographical Record*, 139–140. Linthicum, "Left Home," 94–6.
86. Ibid., 15 May 1896.
87. Minutes of the Mayor and Council, 1896–99.
88. Public Health Bulletin no. 65 (Washington: Government Printing Office, 1914), 4.
89. Ibid., 14.
90. Ibid., 19. Minutes of the Mayor and Council, 1913–16.
91. Washington Suburban Sanitary Commission, *Report on the Advisability of Creating a Sanitary District in Maryland, Contiguous to the District of Columbia, and Providing it with Water and Sewerage Service*, 64, 21 January 1918. Peerless Rockville collections, Rockville, Md.

CHAPTER 6

1. Hulbert Footner, *Maryland Main and the Eastern Shore* (New York: D. Appleton-Century, 1942), 134.
2. *The Evening Star*, 29 September 1917. Gaither P. Warfield, interview by author, 1984, 55–6, transcript in Peerless Rockville collections, Rockville, Md.
3. Thompson, *Western Gateway*, 105–6. Sween and Offutt, *Centuries of Change*, 119–21.
4. *Sentinel*, 25 October and 20 December 1918. Sween and Offutt, *Centuries of Change*, 232–3.
5. Photo from Bonne Prettyman, Peerless Rockville collections, Rockville, Md. Files of American Legion Post #86, Peerless Rockville collections, Rockville, Md.
6. Eileen McGuckian and Lisa Greenhouse, *F. Scott Fitzgerald's Rockville: A Guide to Rockville, Maryland, in the 1920s* (Rockville: Peerless Rockville, 1996), 3–11.
7. Andrea Rebeck, "Automobile-Related Structures of Early Twentieth Century Montgomery County," (Montgomery County Historic Preservation Commission and the Maryland Historical Trust, 1987), 1–7, List of Auto Dealers and Garages, 4–5.
8. Maryland Geological Society, *Report on the Highways of Maryland* (Baltimore: Johns Hopkins University Press, 1899), 242.
9. MacMaster and Hiebert, *Remembrance*, 237–41. Gladys Hogan Campbell, conversation with author, 2000.
10. Elsie White Haines, "Montgomery Sidelights," *Sentinel*, n.d. Mary Gordon Malloy, conversation with author, 2000.
11. McGuckian, *Pike Guide*, 13–15.
12. Gilbert Gude, conversation with author, 2000; A. Gude Sons Co. catalogs, 1930s.
13. *Sentinel*, 27 September 1929.
14. Maryland Historical Trust Inventory Form 26/21/6.
15. "Go Blue Ridge," *Potomac Edison Connection*, 63, no. 4 (April 1987): 6–7. Minutes of the Mayor and Council of Rockville, 2 June 1938.
16. Folger McKinsey, "No Industries in this Town, 16 miles from the White House," (Baltimore) *Sun*, 13 January 1938.
17. Bureau of the Census, U.S. Census, *Population Schedules 1890, 1900, 1910, 1920, 1930, 1940.*
18. Montgomery County Land Records, 374/358–363 (1925).
19. Maryland Historical Trust Inventory Forms 26/10/90 and 26/10/28.
20. Minutes of the Mayor and Council, 14 and 29 June 1938.
21. Montgomery County Land Records, Plat 272 (1924).
22. Ibid., Plats 341 and 342 (1926).
23. Mary Phoebus, "I Remember When," (n.p., 1998).
24. Maryland Historical Trust Inventory Forms 26/15 and 26/15/5. Mabel Mason Hill, interview with Bridget Bolcik, 1976, Peerless Rockville collections, Rockville, Md.
25. Violet Isreal and Willie Mae Carey, interview by author, 1983, Peerless Rockville collections, Rockville, Md.
26. Wire Hardware store records, Peerless Rockville collections, Rockville, Md.
27. Maryland Historical Trust Inventory Forms 30/1 and 30/15.
28. Maryland Historical Trust Inventory Form 26/17. Miriam E. Thompson, research 1984–2000 at Glenview Mansion, Rockville, Md.
29. McGuckian, *1920s Guide*, 44–5 and 56–7. Maryland Historical Trust Inventory Form 26/5.
30. Bouic, *Country Lawyer*, 135.
31. Linthicum, "Left Home," 12–14.
32. Maryland Historical Trust Inventory Form 26/8. Beth Dawson Rodgers, great-granddaughter of James and Rose Dawson, personal collections, Rockville, Md., 2000.
33. Gail Littlefield and Judy Christensen, 1998, City of Rockville collections, Rockville, Md.
34. Clara Penn Shipe, personal collections and conversations with author, 2000, Rockville, Md.
35. Valentine C. Wilson, interview by author, 1983, Peerless Rockville collections, Rockville, Md.
36. *Sentinel*, 13 August 1926.
37. Thompson, *Gateway*, 76.
38. Louis Grossman and Joseph Steinberg, interview by Jeannine Jeffs, 1984, Peerless Rockville collections, Rockville, Md.
39. Shirley Wolfson Ansell, conversation with author, Silver Spring, Md., 2000.
40. *Sentinel*, 26 September 1935.
41. Sharyn R. Duffin, "Gibbs vs. Broome et al: The Pioneer Teachers' Salary Discrepancy Case, Montgomery County, 1936," (unpublished paper, Rockville, Md., 1974), 2.
42. Records of the Rockville Garden Club, 1917–2000, Peerless Rockville collections, Rockville, Md.
43. Rockville Chautauqua programs, 1914, 1916, 1917, Montgomery County Historical Society, Rockville, Md.
44. Genevieve B. Wimsatt, Chautauqua file, Peerless Rockville collections, Rockville, Md.
45. Thompson, *Gateway*, 49–50. *Sentinel*, 4 November 1937.
46. Welsh, *Rockville Lawyer*, 112. Linthicum, "Left Home," 46–51. Thompson, *Gateway*, 74.
47. Minute Book of Rockville Athletic Association, Montgomery County Archives, Rockville, Md.
48. *Washington Times*, 11 May 1922.
49. Thompson, *Gateway*, 66–73.
50. *Fire Insurance* maps, 1892–1923.
51. Marbery F. Gates, a founder of the Rockville Volunteer Fire Department, written recollections, 1976, Peerless Rockville collections, Rockville, Md.
52. Minutes of the Mayor and Council, 1895–1926.
53. H. Porter Welsh and Robert K. Maddox, conversations with author, Rockville, Md., 1996.
54. Thompson, *Gateway*, 89–92, 94–98.
55. C. J. Maddox, surveyor, Plat of Rockville, Maryland, 1930.
56. McKinsey, "No Industries," *Sun*, 13 January 1938.
57. MacMaster and Hiebert, *Remembrance*, 253–289.
58. Maryland Historical Trust Inventory Form 26/16/20.
59. History Associates Incorporated, draft history of Rockville Fuel & Feed Company, 2000.
60. Sween and Offutt, *Centuries*, 232–3.
61. Maryland Historical Trust Inventory Form 26/11.
62. Delos H. Smith, Plat plan of Montgomery County Court House, 1 February 1930, RG66, National Archives.
63. Jewell, *From One Room to Open Space*, 136–7, 174–7, 207–9, 274–9.

64. Maryland Historical Trust Inventory Form 26/26.
65. Minutes of the Mayor and Council, 1 November 1933.
66. Maryland Historical Trust Inventory Form 26/15/3.
67. Nina H. Clarke and Lillian B. Brown, *History of the Black Public Schools of Montgomery County, Maryland* (New York: Vantage Press, 1983), 44–9, 56–9. Duffin, "Gibbs vs. Broome."
68. *Sentinel*, 11 and 25 March 1937.
69. Minutes of the Mayor and Council, 18 September 1934.
70. Ibid., 3 April 1935.
71. The Mayor and Council of Rockville, *Town Ordinance for Zoning* (Rockville, Maryland, 1931), 15.
72. Minutes of the Mayor and Council, 21 May 1926.
73. *Sentinel*, 11 March 1937.
74. Debra Carbaugh Robinson, *The Rockville Tragedy* (n.p., 1995).
75. *Washington Star*, 18 October 1938.
76. Linthicum, "Left Home," 83–85. Bouic, *Country Lawyer*, 235–238.
77. Minutes of the Mayor and Council, 6 July 1932.
78. *Sentinel*, 4 July 1935.
79. Bouic, *Country Lawyer*, 191–201.
80. *Sentinel*, 4 July 1935.
81. Ibid., 15 August 1935.
82. Ibid., 10 October 1935.
83. Maryland Historical Trust Inventory Form 26/11/2.
84. Thompson, *Gateway*, 106–114.
85. Montgomery County Land Records, Plats 1300, 1318, and 1332. Maryland Historical Trust Inventory Form 26/33.
86. F. Scott Fitzgerald files, Peerless Rockville collections Rockville, Md.
87. Richard Buckingham, D.V.M., interview by author, Rockville, Md., 1984.
88. Bouic, *Country Lawyer*, 224–5.
89. Betts, *Piscataway*, 19–20. Stephen Cromwell Jr., talk to Rockville Rotary Club, 8 June 2000.

CHAPTER 7

1. *The Evening Star*, Real Estate Section, 8 March 1952.
2. Originally developed as "Twin-Brook," the community has used the name "Twinbrook" since the 1950s. Twinbrook is used throughout the chapter for simplicity's sake.
3. Jackson, *Crabgrass Frontier*, 190–218, 231–245.
4. Maryland Historical Trust Inventory Form 26/25. Gladys L. Cross, "This is Twinbrook," *Twinbrook Life* (June and July 1963).
5. Dorothy Geeraert Patterson, conversation with author, 2000.
6. Barbara Kalabinski, "Twinbrook: The History," (Goucher College, Frederick, Maryland, 1998).
7. *The Washington Post*, September 1948.
8. Margaret S. Sante, conversation with author, 2000.
9. *Twinbrook Life*, 1955–65, Peerless Rockville collections, Rockville, Md.
10. Rockville Chamber of Commerce, *The Complete 1962 . . . Rockville Locator* (Rockville, Md, 1962).
11. E. Guy Jewell, *From One Room to Open Space* (Rockville: Montgomery County Public Schools, 1976), 349–50.
12. Valentine C. Wilson to Eileen McGuckian, 1986, Peerless Rockville collections, Rockville, Md.
13. Minutes of the Mayor and Council, 7 April 1948.
14. Ibid., 16 March 1949.
15. "Constitution and By-Laws of the Rockville Civic Association," Article II, n.d., Peerless Rockville collections, Rockville, Md.
16. Ibid. Minutes of the Mayor and Council, 6 August 1947.
17. Minutes of the Mayor and Council, 10 January 1950.
18. Christian L. Larsen and Richard D. Andrews, Bureau of Public Administration, University of Maryland, *The Government of Rockville* (Baltimore: The Maurice Leeser Company, 1950), 66.
19. The report was written by the executive secretary of the Maryland Municipal League, of which Rockville was a member. These kinds of studies were not unusual; a 1941 survey by the Brookings Institution led to charter reform in Montgomery County.
20. Larsen and Andrews, *Government*, 2.
21. "Merchants and Business Men of Rockville, MD" (Rockville: Rockville Chamber of Commerce, 1950).
22. History Associates, Rockville Fuel & Feed, 2000.
23. Elizabeth Tennery, "Remembering Rockville . . . ," in *Legal Tradition*, (Bar Association, 1994), 48–9.
24. *Sentinels*, 12 January through 21 December 1950.
25. *Sentinel*, 3 August and 24 August,1950.
26. *Rockville Times*, 12 October 1951.
27. Minutes of the Mayor and Council, 3 October 1951.
28. Ibid., 20 March 1953.
29. Ibid., 2 September and 7 October 1953.
30. Ibid., 16 July 1953.
31. Ibid.
32. *Sentinel*, 16 November 1977. Dora Demma, personal collections, Kensington, Md.
33. Minutes of the Mayor and Council, 27 June 1953.
34. "Water is the Empire Builder," *Sentinel*, 23 July 1953.
35. *Sentinel*, 23 July 1953.
36. *Sentinel*, 30 July 1953.
37. Minutes of the Mayor and Council, 4 December 1953.
38. *Sentinel*, 4 February 1954. D. Y. Hovsepian and J. F. Allen, scrapbooks in Peerless Rockville collections, Rockville, Md.
39. "To Be or Not to Be—A Citizen," *Sentinel*, 29 April 1954.
40. "Election Postmortem," *Sentinel*, 6 May 1954.
41. Alexander J. Greene, interview by author, 1985, transcript in Peerless Rockville collections, Rockville, Md., 8–9.
42. Dickran Y. Hovsepian, interview by author, 1984, Peerless Rockville collections, Rockville, Md. Alexander J. Greene, interview by author, 1985, Peerless Rockville collections, Rockville, Md.
43. *Rockville Times*, 20 January 1955.
44. *Evening Star* (Washington, D.C.), 2 February 1955.
45. Ibid., 5 June 1955. Hovsepian, interview, 1984. Greene, interview, 1985, and conversations with author, 2000.
46. "Hungerford Towne" (L. I. Brochure Service, Long Island, New York, n.d.), Peerless Rockville collection, Rockville, Md.
47. "At Hungerford Towne," Naomi Ellison, brochure in personal collection, Rockville, Md.

48. Ibid.
49. Marjorie Collins, Jeannine and Joseph Jeffs, longtime Hungerford residents, conversations with author, 2000. Mary Dawson Gray, niece of Rose and Walter Dawson, interview by author, 1994, Peerless Rockville collections, Rockville, Md.
50. *Maryland's 157: The Incorporated Cities and Towns* (Annapolis: Maryland Municipal League, 2000), 6–7. David L. Cahoon, interview by author, 2001.
51. Greene, interview, 42–3.
52. Minutes of the Mayor and Council, 29 June 1949.
53. Hovsepian, interview, 39.
54. *A Report on Your City's Recreation Program, Rockville, Maryland*, 1955–56, Peerless Rockville collections, Rockville, Md.
55. *Sentinel*, 23 November 1955.
56. Minutes of the Mayor and Council, 2 October 1956.
57. Ibid., 23 October 1956.
58. "Our Mansion," *Sentinel*, 14 March 1957.
59. Greene, interview, 24.
60. Steve Murfin, 2000, research in Peerless Rockville collections, Rockville, Md..
61. Minutes of the Mayor and Council, 17 July 1956.
62. *Twinbrook Life*, 5, no. 6 (June 1958).
63. Dickran Hovsepian, "History of Pinneberg-Rockville Sister City Relationship," *Sister Cities 40th Anniversary*, (Rockville: Rockville Sister City Corporation, 1997), 16–17. Klaus May, "Forty Years Sister City Relationship Rockville-Pinneberg: A Small Chronicle 1957 to 1997," Peerless Rockville collections, Rockville, Md.
64. Minutes of the Mayor and Council, 1 October 1952.
65. Ibid., 16 July 1952.
66. Hovsepian, interview, 28.
67. Greene, interview, 28.
68. Resolution No. 61–55, "Resolution Declaring the Need for a Housing Authority to Function in the City of Rockville, Maryland," Minutes of the Mayor and Council, 21 November 1955. Mayor and Council of Rockville, *Report to THE PEOPLE on 1955* (Rockville, Md., 1 May 1956), 9.
69. Joan Lutz Kuckkahn, *Housing the Poor in Rockville, Maryland, A History*, (Baltimore: University of Maryland School of Law, 1996), 12–18.
70. Ibid., 17.
71. MacMaster and Hiebert, *Remembrance*, 329–330.
72. Jewell, *One Room to Open Space*, 345–6, 349. Maryland Historical Trust Inventory Forms 26/15/3 and 26/16/13.
73. *Sentinel*, 30 May 1957.
74. Minutes of the Mayor and Council, 9 December 1952 and 1 April 1953.
75. *Montrose: Another Distinctive Subdivision by Merrimack*, (Bethesda, Md.: Merrimack Construction Corporation, n.d.), courtesy of Eva Rechcigl.
76. D. Y. Hovsepian, conversation with author, 1995.
77. Rockville Chamber of Commerce, *Rockville Locator*.
78. Maryland Historical Trust Inventory Form 26/21/6.
79. Kenneth I. Helphand, "McUrbia: The 1950s and the Birth of the Contemporary American Landscape," *Places* 5, no. 2, 41–43.
80. Minutes of the Mayor and Council, 4 January 1950.
81. Cahoon, interview, 2001.
82. "Case History of a Community Plan" (talk presented by Walter A. Scheiber, City Manager, to conference on local planning in College Park, Md., 3 December 1960).
83. Greene, interview, 39–41, and conversations with author, 2000–01.
84. C. Steed Evans, *100 Rockville Centennial* (Rockville: Rockville Centennial, 1960). A. J. Greene collection, materials and artifacts, Peerless Rockville collections, Rockville, Md.
85. "Rockville All-America City Award Ceremony, April 6, 1962," excerpt from *National Civic Review* (National Municipal League, March 1962).
86. *Sentinel*, 19 April 1956.
87. Ibid., 4 March 1948.
88. Greene, interview, 7.
89. Ibid.
90. Scheiber, "Case History," 5–6.

CHAPTER 8

1. *Sentinel*, 29 November 1962.
2. Nina H. Clarke, "Life of Alphonzo Lee," n.d., Peerless Rockville collections, Rockville, Md.
3. NAACP, Montgomery County Branch, "Eating Places Serving Without Discrimination in Montgomery County, Maryland" (May 1958), Peerless Rockville collections, Rockville, Md. Florence Orbach, Social Action Chairman, Montgomery County Branch, NAACP to Stella Werner, President, Montgomery County Council, 17 April 1959, Montgomery County Historical Society, Rockville, Md.
4. *Sentinel*, 7 January 1960.
5. *Evening Star*, 12 July 1960.
6. Sharyn Duffin and Bessie Corbin, conversations with author, Rockville, Md., 2000.
7. Hovsepian, interview, 45–6, and Cahoon, interview, 2001.
8. Human Relations Study Group, "A Report on Human Relations in the City of Rockville" (Rockville: Mayor and Council, June 1964).
9. "Klansmen Strut in Rockville," *Sentinel*, 18 August 1966.
10. Arlene Simons, "City a Pioneer in Fair Housing," *Rockville Gazette*, 7 May 1986.
11. "History of Community Ministries of Rockville," (Community Ministries of Rockville, 1987), Peerless Rockville collections, Rockville, Md..
12. *Organization and Operation Plan, Rockville, Civil Defense, and Montgomery County Division of Civil Defense, Disaster Information* (1971), Henry Rapalus, personal collection, Rockville, Md. *Sentinel*, 1 February 1951.
13. *Master Plan of Highways* (City of Rockville Planning Commission, October 1958) and *Master Plan, City of Rockville, Maryland* (City of Rockville Planning Commission, September 1960).
14. Morton Hoffman, *Master Plan Report No. 2: Analysis, Population & Economic Base* (Maryland State Planning Department and City of Rockville, Rockville, Maryland, September 1959), 10–11, 15–16.
15. *Master Plan*, 1960, 12–13.
16. *Master Plan, Rockville, Maryland* (City of Rockville Planning Commission, July, 1970), 52–7.
17. *Speaking of Rockville: A Monthly Report to Citizens from the Mayor and Council*, (Midwinter Edition, 5, no. 1, 1961).

18. Obituary, *The Washington Post*, 13 September 1999.
19. *Town Center, City of Rockville* (City of Rockville, issue 16, January 1981).
20. Rockville Chamber of Commerce, *Rockville Locator.*
21. Emmy Savage, "Memories of a Home Close to Home: Rockville, Maryland 1947–1957," unpublished article, 1992.
22. *Sentinel*, 25 August 1960, reported that Lofstrand had been awarded a contract to build the France Jet sports car.
23. Montgomery County Land Records, Plats 6678 and 6679 (1962), Plat 8002 (1965).
24. Maryland Department of Economic and Community Development, *Directory, Maryland Manufacturers, 1973–74*, 278–86.
25. City of Rockville, public hearing record, PRU#1, 19 July 1965, Montgomery County Archives, Rockville, Md.
26. City of Rockville, *Annual Report*, 1965, 4–5. Larry Owens, Rockville planner 1967–1995, conversations with author, 2001.
27. Greene, interview, 25–6.
28. Jennie and Bill Forehand, personal collections, Rockville, Md. Monroe Warren Jr., conversation with author, 2001.
29. Minutes of the Mayor and Council, 1962–63.
30. William Hickman, Rockville, Maryland, outline of College Gardens history, 2001.
31. Thomas Dunne and Luna B. Leopold, *Water in Environmental Planning* (New York: W. H. Freeman, 1978), 698–9.
32. *City of Rockville Newsletter*, December 1964. Judy French, personal collection, Rockville, Md.
33. *Sentinel*, 1 no. 3, 15 January 1970, Special Supplement, Annual Progress Edition.
34. *A Community for All Seasons; Winter, Spring, Summer, FALLSMEAD. History and Memoirs, 1968–1993* (Rockville: Fallsmead Homes Corporation, 1994).
35. MacMaster and Hiebert, *Remembrance*, 375–6.
36. Resolution No. 4–73, Mayor and Council of Rockville, 8 January 1973.
37. William E. Hanna Jr., "Mayor sees bright city future," *Sentinel*, 27 April 1977.
38. William E. Hanna Jr., interview by author, 2001.
39. Federation of Independent Voters, *The Rockville Voter: A Non-Partisan Voter's Guide* (April 1964), Peerless Rockville collections, Rockville, Md.
40. In 1980, Anthony C. Koones Associates replaced Rockville Gardens with Heritage Park, a Federal Section 8 subsidized housing project of sixty-five cooperative townhouse units, and Heritage House, a one-hundred-unit midrise apartment building.
41. Helen M. Heneghan, interview by author, 2001.
42. Minutes of the Mayor and Council, 20 December 1976.
43. Citizens for Good Government to Membership, 22 October 1976, papers of Roald Schrack, Peerless Rockville collections, Rockville, Md.
44. Jayne L. Greene, *Recreation Areas in Rockville*, 1964–65, Peerless Rockville collections, Rockville, Md.
45. William E. Hanna Jr., response to a candidates' questionnaire by Rockville Ministerial Alliance, 16 April 1980.
46. Cultural Arts Commission, *Master Plan for the Art in Public Places Program, Fiscal Years 1999–2004* (Rockville: City of Rockville, 1998).
47. City of Rockville, *Annual Reports* (Rockville: 1970–1980).
48. *Master Plan*, 1960, 20.
49. *Annual Reports*, 1962–76.
50. *City of Rockville Newsletter* (Rockville: August 1965).
51. Neil A. Ofsthun, Director of Recreation and Parks, 1960–72, interview by Maureen K. Hinkle, 9 November 1971, Montgomery County Archives, Rockville, Md.
52. *City of Rockville Newsletter*, April 1968.
53. Steve Murfin, personal collections, Olney, Md., 2000.
54. Field hockey was introduced to students at Richard Montgomery High School in 1937.
55. MacMaster and Hiebert, *Remembrance*, 356–7.
56. Frank A. Ecker, interview by author, 1996, Peerless Rockville collections, Rockville, Md. Greene, interview, 1985. Edward J. Duffy, interview by author, 2001, Peerless Rockville collections, Rockville, Md.
57. Ernest E. Blanche and Associates, *Master Plan Report No. 1: Study, Population & Economic Base* (August 1959), 12.
58. Oscar Sutermeister, *Master Plan Report No. 3: Study, Traffic, Parking and Highway* [September 1959] Rockville City Planning Commission in cooperation with Maryland State Planning Department and U.S. Housing and Home Finance Agency, Peerless Rockville collections, Rockville, Md.
59. Ecker, interview, 1996.
60. Minutes of the Mayor and Council, 1 September 1959.
61. Jane Jacobs's *The Death and Life of Great American Cities* (New York: Random House, 1961) is a classic and influential treatise on urban America.
62. Jon C. Teaford, *The Rough Road to Renaissance* (Baltimore: Johns Hopkins University Press, 1990), 44–167.
63. Greene, conversations with author, 2000.
64. Cahoon, interview by author, 2001.
65. Harry B. Cooper, "County Urban Renewal," *Maryland Municipal News* 13, no. 11 (November, 1960): 5, 14.
66. *Town Center Background Report* (Department of Planning, Rockville, Md., March 1977).
67. Duffy, interviews, 2000–01.
68. Alexander J. Greene, chairman, Urban Renewal Advisory Council to Mayor and Council, 24 August 1962, Peerless Rockville collections, Rockville, Md.
69. *Land Utilization and Marketability Study* (Rockville: Real Estate Research Corporation, August 1962), 1–5.
70. Roger B. Farquhar, "Scores of Buildings Doomed Under Plan," *Sentinel*, 29 November 1962.
71. *Sentinel*, 28 April 1960.
72. Minutes of the Mayor and Council, 18 February 1963.
73. Rockville Jaycees, "Preliminary Report—Rockville Jaycee Community Survey," n.d., Peerless Rockville collections, Rockville, Md.
74. Hanson Watkins, conversation with author, 1995, Rockville, Md. M. Thomas Lawrey, conversation with author, 2001, Rockville, Md.
75. Lila Thomson, "Urban Renewal vs Urban Replacement," *Maryland Monitor*, 1 July 1965.
76. *City of Rockville Newsletter*, February 1971.

77. Wolf Von Eckardt, "Rockville Bent on Becoming Pearl in Capital's Necklace," *Washington Post*, 21 November 1965.
78. *City of Rockville Newsletters*, 1973–1984.
79. *Town Center Urban Design Plan* (Rockville, Md., December 1979).
80. *City of Rockville Newsletters*, September 1973 and February 1974.
81. For a good overview of Rockville's downtown see Patricia Chickering, "The Evolution of the Central Business District, Rockville, Md.—1938–1988," (University of Maryland, 1988).

CHAPTER 9

1. *Washington Post*, 14 February 1987.
2. David Campbell, Cape Elizabeth, Maine, to Eileen McGuckian, Rockville, Md., 6 September 2000.
3. Eileen McGuckian, "Chronology of Urban Renewal in Rockville," 2000, Peerless Rockville collections, Rockville, Md. Edward J. Duffy, City of Rockville "Summary of Mall Documents," 1995, Peerless Rockville collections, Rockville, Md. Duffy, interview, 2001.
4. Manju Subramanya, "Officials See End to Decades of Failed Dreams," *Montgomery Gazette*, 13 November 1998.
5. Joseph A. Lynott, interview by author, Rockville, Md., 2001, Peerless Rockville collections, Rockville, Md.
6. Ecker, interview, 1996.
7. Duffy, interview, 2001.
8. Hanna, interview, 2001. William E. Hanna Jr., "Rockville plans a Party," *Sentinel*, 27 April 1977.
9. Witold Rybczynski, "The New Downtowns," *Atlantic Monthly* (May 1993), 98–106.
10. Doug Duncan, "The Mall That Ate Rockville," *Washington Post*, Outlook, 14 February 1994.
11. Manju Subramanya, "A Town Center Revival," *Rockville Gazette*, 18 November 1998. Benjamin Forgey, "Rockville's Steep Climb Back Up the Pike," *Washington Post*, 6 July 1991.
12. "Rethinking Rockville," editorial, (n.d., 1990), *Rockville Gazette*.
13. U.S. Census, *Population Schedule 2000*.
14. City of Rockville, *Community Profile* (www.ci.rockville.md.us, November 2000).
15. Slogan developed by staff of Neighborhood Resources, City Manager's Office, City of Rockville.
16. *Master Plan*, 1970, 18.
17. Lynott, interview, 2001.
18. The number of employees is full time equivalent and does not include temporary employees or consultants.
19. Statistics from City of Rockville Department of Public Works, Rockville, Md., 2001.
20. Ibid.
21. Grand Army of the Republic, General Orders No. 11 (5 May 1868), Peerless Rockville collections, Rockville, Md.
22. Rosalie M. Campbell, William and Rosie Wood, and Helen D. Israel, conversations with author, Rockville, Md.
23. Heneghan, interview.
24. *Plymouth Village: Colonial Homes in Montgomery County* (Kensington, Md: The Artery Organization, 1970).
25. Minutes of the Mayor and Council, 26 January 1931.
26. Rose Krasnow, mayor of Rockville, "2001 State of the City Address," 4 April 2001.
27. *Sentinel*, 27 April 1977.

SELECTED SOURCES

Much of the research for this history was conducted in three locations: the research libraries of Peerless Rockville Historic Preservation, the Montgomery County Historical Society, and the Montgomery County Archives. Resources at Peerless Rockville and the Historical Society include maps and atlases, Maryland Historical Trust Inventory Forms for historic sites, historic photographs, plats, personal papers and scrapbooks, the collections of organizations, vertical files, newspapers, interviews, directories, publications, and artifacts. Of particular note at the Montgomery County Historical Society are an almost-complete collection of the *Montgomery County Sentinel* from 1855 and an excellent array of genealogical books and files. Peerless Rockville's library specializes in files on Rockville places and holds thousands of photographs. Governmental records at the Montgomery County Archives include the pre-1960s records of Rockville, photographs, and personal and public papers of civic leaders such as Edith Throckmorton.

BOOKS AND PUBLICATIONS

Betts, Maude Wilson. *Piscataway to Prince George's Parish*. Rockville, Md.: N.p., n.d.

Bouic, Albert M. *Country Lawyer—Third Generation*. N.p., 1958.

Boyd, T. H. S. *The History of Montgomery County, Maryland from Its Earliest Settlement in 1650 to 1879*. 1879. Reprint, Baltimore: Regional Publishing, 1968.

Brugger, Robert J. *Maryland: A Middle Temperament 1634–1980*. Baltimore: Johns Hopkins University Press in association with the Maryland Historical Society, 1988.

Centennial Celebration of the Erection of Montgomery County, Md. into a Separate Municipality. Held at Rockville, September 6, 1876. Baltimore: C. C. Saffell, 1877.

Clarke, Nina H. *History of the Nineteenth-Century Black Churches in Maryland and Washington, D.C.* New York: Vantage Press, 1983.

Clarke, Nina H., and Lillian B. Brown. *History of the Black Public Schools of Montgomery County, Maryland 1872–1961*. New York: Vantage Press, 1978.

Coleman, Margaret M., and Anne Lewis. *Montgomery County: A Pictorial History*. Norfolk, Va.: Donning Co., 1997.

Copp, Henry N. *Peerless Rockville: What it Offers to Homeseekers and Investors*. Washington, D.C.: Gibson Brothers, 1890.

Dunham, Mary Deegan. *Rockville: Its History and Its People*. Rockville: Kits and Crafts, 1976.

Evans, C. Steed, ed. *100: Rockville Centennial*. Rockville: Rockville Centennial, 1960.

Fallsmead Homes Corporation. *A Community for All Seasons: Winter, Spring, Summer, FALLSMEAD. History and Memoirs, 1968–1993.* Rockville: 1994.

Gutheim, Frederick. *The Potomac,* 2nd ed. New York: Grosset & Dunlap, 1968.

Inventory of the County and Town Archives of Maryland, No. 15, Montgomery County. Baltimore: Historical Records Survey, Works Progress Administration, 1939.

Jackson, Kenneth T. *Crabgrass Frontier: The Suburbanization of the United States.* New York: Oxford University Press, 1985.

Jacobs, Charles T. *Civil War Guide to Montgomery County.* Rockville: Montgomery County Historical Society, 1983.

Jewell, E. Guy. *From One Room to Open Space: A History of Montgomery County Schools From 1732 to 1965.* Rockville: Montgomery County Public Schools, 1976.

Larson, Christian L. and Richard D. Andrews, *The Government of Rockville.* Baltimore: Maurice Leeser in association with the Bureau of Public Administration, University of Maryland., 1950.

Linthicum, William A. *He Never Left Home.* N.p., 1977.

MacMaster, Richard K., and Ray Eldon Hiebert. *A Grateful Remembrance: The Story of Montgomery County, Maryland.* Rockville: Montgomery County Government and Montgomery County Historical Society, 1976.

McGuckian, Eileen S. *Historic and Architectural Guide to the Rockville Pike.* Rockville: Peerless Rockville Historic Preservation Ltd., 1995.

McGuckian, Eileen S., and Lisa A. Greenhouse. *F. Scott Fitzgerald's Rockville: A Guide to Rockville, Maryland, in the 1920s.* Rockville, Md.: Peerless Rockville Historic Preservation Ltd., 1996.

Montgomery County Historical Society. *The Montgomery County Story.* Quarterly publication, indexed, 1957–2001.

Montgomery County Sentinel, 1855–2001.

Phoebus, Mary. *I Remember When.* N.p., 1998.

Pitch, Anthony S. *The Burning of Washington: The British Invasion of 1814.* Annapolis: Naval Institute Press, 1998.

Portrait and Biographical Record of the Sixth Congressional District, Maryland. New York: Chapman Publishing, 1898.

Scharf, J. Thomas. *History of Western Maryland.* Vol. 1. 1882. Reprint, Baltimore: Regional Publishing Company, 1968.

Saint Mary's Parish. *Historic Saint Mary's, Montgomery County, Rockville, Maryland.* N.p., 1963.

Saint Mary's Parish. *175th Anniversary, Saint Mary's Church, Rockville, Maryland.* Tappan, N.Y.: Custombook, 1989.

Sween, Jane C., and William Offutt, *Montgomery County: Centuries of Change.* Sun Valley, Ca.: American Historical Press, 1999.

Thompson, Noma. *Western Gateway to the National Capital.* Washington, D.C.: Stewart Printing, 1950.

Welsh, Barnard T. *Rockville Lawyer.* N.p., n.d.

GOVERNMENT RECORDS AND PUBLICATIONS

Annual Reports, 1955–1999.

Backward Glance: A Brief History of Rockville, 1983 (reprinted 1985, 1987).

Department of Planning, *Historic Resources Management Plan,* 1986.

Land, Orphans Court, Equity, Judgment, and Assessment Records of Montgomery County, Maryland.

Laws of Maryland.

Maryland Dept. of Economic and Community Development. *Directory, Maryland Manufacturers, 1973–4.*

Minutes of the Town Commissioners of Rockville, 1865–1888.

Minutes of the Mayor and Council of Rockville, 1888–2000.

Public Local Laws of Montgomery County.

Reports, Master Plans, Studies, Analyses, Statistical Profiles, Citizen Handbooks, Community Profiles, and Zoning Ordinances.

Rockville election returns, tax ledgers, construction projects, vouchers, Minutes of the Local Public Agency, 1860–1970s.

Speaking of Rockville: A Monthly Report to Citizens from the Mayor and Council, 1957–1962, *City of Rockville Newsletter,* 1963–1981; *Rockville Reports,* 1981–present.

U.S. Census Records, 1790–2000.

U.S. Public Health Service Bulletin #65. "Typhoid Fever in Rockville, MD." Washington: U.S. Government Printing Office, 1914.

PHOTOGRAPH REPOSITORIES

Peerless Rockville, Rockville, Md.

Montgomery County Historical Society, Rockville, Md.

Washington Star collection, Martin Luther King Library, Washingtoniana Division, Washington, D.C.

National Archives of the United States (Archives II), College Park, Md.

Historical Society of Washington, D.C.

Maryland Historical Society, Baltimore, Md.

Library of Congress, Washington, D.C.

INTERVIEWS

Rockville: Identity in Change (RINC) interviews were conducted by Jeannine Jeffs or Eileen McGuckian.

Leslie M. Abbe (interviewed by Anne Elsbree, 1971, League of Women Voters (LWV), transcript in Peerless Rockville collections.

Charles A. Brewer (RINC, 1983), transcript in Peerless Rockville collections.

Catherine Shaw Bride (RINC, 1984), transcript in Peerless Rockville collections.

Richard Buckingham, D.V.M. (RINC, 1984), transcript in Peerless Rockville collections.

David L. Cahoon (Eileen McGuckian, 2001), notes in Peerless Rockville collections.

Rosalie M. Campbell (RINC, 1984), transcript in Peerless Rockville collections.

Lucie E. Conklin (RINC, 1984), notes in Peerless Rockville collections.

Edward J. Duffy, (Eileen McGuckian, 2000), notes in Peerless Rockville collections.

Frank A. Ecker (Eileen McGuckian, 1996), notes in Peerless Rockville collections.

Mary Dawson Gray (Eileen McGuckian, 1994), Montgomery County Historical Society, notes in Peerless Rockville collections.

Alexander J. Greene (RINC, 1985), transcript in Peerless Rockville collections.

Louis L. Grossman (RINC, 1984), transcript in Peerless Rockville collections.

Burt Hall (Steve Murfin, 2000), notes in Peerless Rockville collections.

William E. Hanna Jr. (Eileen McGuckian, 2001), notes in Peerless Rockville collections.

Helen M. Heneghan (Eileen McGuckian, 2001), notes in Peerless Rockville collections.

J. Ralph Hickerson (RINC, 1984), transcript in Peerless Rockville collections.

Mabel Mason Hill (Bridget Bolcik, 1976), transcript in Peerless Rockville collections.

Dickran Y. Hovsepian (RINC, 1984), transcript in Peerless Rockville collections.

Joseph A. Lynott (Eileen McGuckian, 2001), notes in Peerless Rockville collections.

Neil A. Ofsthun (Maureen K. Hinkle, 1971, LWV), transcript at Montgomery County Archives.

Claude N. Prather (RINC, 1984), transcript in Peerless Rockville collections.

Martha E. Royer (Maria Spiridopoulos and Janet Zachary, 1974), transcript in Peerless Rockville collections.

Joseph Steinberg (RINC, 1984), transcript in Peerless Rockville collections.

Gaither P. Warfield (RINC, 1984), transcript in Peerless Rockville collections.

Barnard T. Welsh (RINC, 1983), transcript in Peerless Rockville collections.

H. Porter Welsh (RINC, 1983), transcript in Peerless Rockville collections.

Frank E. Williams (RINC, 1984), transcript in Peerless Rockville collections.

Valentine C. Wilson (RINC, 1983), transcript in Peerless Rockville collections.

Genevieve B. Wimsatt (RINC, 1984), transcript in Peerless Rockville collections.

Violet Isreal and Willie Mae Carey (RINC, 1983), transcript in Peerless Rockville collections.

MAPS

Bower, Robert F. and Thorton L. Mullins. *Bower's Map of Washington and Environs,* Rockville inset, 1934.

Cissel, R. Humphrey. City of Rockville street maps, 1952, 1954, 1956, 1959.

City of Rockville. *Mid-City Urban Renewal Project*, April 1963.

City of Rockville, street maps. 1971, 1981, 1982, 1993, 1996, 1999.

Coast and Geodetic Survey. *Washington and Vicinity,* 1951.

Deets and Maddox. *Real Estate Atlas of Montgomery County, Maryland,* 1916.

Gray, O. W. and Sons. *Gray's New Map of Rockville, Montgomery County, Maryland*, 1877.

Griffith, Dennis. *Map of Maryland*, 1794.

Hopkins, G. M. *Atlas of Fifteen Miles Around Washington Including the County of Montgomery, Maryland.* Philadelphia: The Compiler, 1879 (Inset of Rockville).

Hopkins, G. M. *The Vicinity of Washington.* Philadelphia: The Compiler, 1894.

Klinge, F. H. M. *Real Estate Atlas of Montgomery County, Md.* Lansdale, Pa.,1959.

Maddox, C. J. *Town of Rockville,* 1914.

Maddox, C. J. *Plat of Rockville, Md.*, 1930.

Marine, William. *Map of the Chesapeake Campaign of 1814.* From Kendric J. Babcock, *The Rise of American Nationality* (New York: Harper & Brothers, 1906).

Martinet, Simon J. *Martinet and Bond's Map of Montgomery County, Maryland.* Baltimore, 1865. (Inset of Rockville).

Maryland-National Capital Park and Planning Commission. *Street Map of Montgomery County, Md.*, 1967.

Plats of subdivisions and estate divisions, proposed extension of Rockville corporate limits, Court House lot and Square, house locations, land surveys.

Rockville Chamber of Commerce. *The Complete 1962 . . . Rockville Locator.*

Sanborn Insurance Map Company. *Fire Insurance Maps of Rockville, Maryland.* New York: Parris Map, 1892–1923.

Smith, William. *Plan of Rockville, Montgomery County*. May 9, 1803.

Town of Rockville. *Master Plan of Sewers,* 1914.

Warfield, Gaither P. *Rockville, 1902–1903.* N.p., 1984.

INDEX